# CLOSING THE ENFORCEMENT GAP

## Improving Employment Standards Protections for People in Precarious Jobs

*Leah F. Vosko and the Closing the Enforcement Gap Research Group*

The nature of employment is changing: low-wage jobs are increasingly common, fewer workers belong to unions, and workplaces are being transformed through the growth of contracting-out, franchising, and extended supply chains. *Closing the Enforcement Gap* offers a comprehensive analysis of the enforcement of employment standards in Ontario.

Adopting mixed methods, this work includes qualitative research involving in-depth interviews with workers, community advocates, and enforcement officials; extensive archival research excavating decades of ministerial records; and analysis of a previously untapped source of administrative data collected by Ontario's Ministry of Labour. The authors reveal and trace the roots of a deepening "enforcement gap" that pervades nearly all aspects of the regime, demonstrating that the province's *Employment Standards Act (ESA)* fails too many workers who rely on the minimum conditions it was devised to provide. Arguably, there is nothing inevitable about the enforcement gap in Ontario, or for that matter elsewhere. Through contributions from leading employment standards enforcement scholars in the United States, the United Kingdom, and Australia, as well as Quebec, *Closing the Enforcement Gap* surveys innovative enforcement models that are emerging in a variety of jurisdictions and sets out a bold vision for strengthening employment standards enforcement.

**Studies in Comparative Political Economy and Public Policy**

Editors: MICHAEL HOWLETT, DAVID LAYCOCK (Simon Fraser University), and STEPHEN MCBRIDE (McMaster University)

*Studies in Comparative Political Economy and Public Policy* is designed to showcase innovative approaches to political economy and public policy from a comparative perspective. While originating in Canada, the series will provide attractive offerings to a wide international audience, featuring studies with local, subnational, cross-national, and international empirical bases and theoretical frameworks.



For a list of books published in the series, see page 447.

# Closing the Enforcement Gap

## *Improving Employment Standards Protections for People in Precarious Jobs*

Leah F. Vosko
Guliz Akkaymak
Rebecca Casey
Shelley Condratto
John Grundy
Alan Hall
Alice Hoe
Kiran Mirchandani
Andrea M. Noack
Urvashi Soni-Sinha
Mercedes Steedman
Mark P. Thomas
Eric M. Tucker

*International Contributors*
Nick Clark
Dalia Gesualdi-Fecteau
Tess Hardy
John Howe
Guylaine Vallée
David Weil

UNIVERSITY OF TORONTO PRESS
Toronto Buffalo London

Toronto Buffalo London
utorontopress.com
Printed and bound by CPI Group (UK) Ltd, Croydon, CR0 4YY

ISBN 978-1-4875-0639-1 (cloth)
ISBN 978-1-4875-2431-9 (paper)
ISBN 978-1-4875-3405-9 (EPUB)
ISBN 978-1-4875-3404-2 (PDF)

**Library and Archives Canada Cataloguing in Publication**

Title: Closing the enforcement gap : improving employment standards protections for people in precarious jobs / Leah F. Vosko and the Closing the Enforcement Gap Research Group.
Names: Vosko, Leah F., author.
Series: Studies in comparative political economy and public policy ; 58.
Description: Series statement: Studies in comparative political economy and public policy ; 58 |
Includes bibliographical references and index.
Identifiers: Canadiana 20190199393 | ISBN 9781487506391 (cloth) | ISBN 9781487524319 (paper)
Subjects: LCSH: Labor laws and legislation – Ontario – Cases. |
LCSH: Precarious employment – Ontario – Case studies. |
LCSH: Labor laws and legislation – Cases. |
LCSH: Precarious employment – Case studies.
Classification: LCC KEO629 .V67 2020 | LCC KF3320.ZB3 V67 2020 kfmod |
DDC 344.71301—dc23

This book has been published with the help of a grant from the Federation for the Humanities and Social Sciences, through the Awards to Scholarly Publications Program, using funds provided by the Social Sciences and Humanities Research Council of Canada.

University of Toronto Press acknowledges the financial assistance to its publishing program of the Canada Council for the Arts and the Ontario Arts Council, an agency of the Government of Ontario.

Canada Council for the Arts | Conseil des Arts du Canada

ONTARIO ARTS COUNCIL
CONSEIL DES ARTS DE L'ONTARIO
an Ontario government agency
un organisme du gouvernement de l'Ontario

Funded by the Government of Canada | Financé par le gouvernement du Canada

Canada

*This book is dedicated to all of the staff and members of the Workers' Action Centre of Toronto in recognition of their decades-long struggle to improve the conditions of work and employment for us all, particularly those in precarious jobs.*

# Contents

# Graphs, Tables, and Figures

## Graphs

## Tables



## Figures

# Authorship

Emerging from the collaborative research initiative on employment standards and their enforcement in Ontario described in the acknowledgments to follow, this book is the product of joint authorship. As such, all of the chapters benefited from the input of its many co-authors. Individuals participating in this book's preparation nevertheless took on specific roles and responsibilities as outlined below.

**Part One: Charting the Employment Standards Enforcement Gap in Ontario**

**Guliz Akkaymak:** As a postdoctoral research fellow under the auspices of Closing the Enforcement Gap, Dr Akkaymak participated in the Archives & Policy, Enforcement Practices, and Worker Interviews Working Groups. In this capacity, she co-authored chapters 2, 3, and 7, assisted in the initial design of the book's glossary, and worked on a team of researchers reviewing, cataloguing, and coding archival material pertaining to the enforcement of employment standards in Ontario and cited in this text.

**Rebecca Casey:** First as a postdoctoral research fellow with Closing the Enforcement Gap and subsequently as a co-investigator, Professor Casey served as the lead trainee in the Survey and Statistics Working Group, through which she mentored numerous research assistants, conducted extensive data analysis informing a wide range of activities and outputs of the research partnership, and co-authored chapter 4 of this book.

**Shelley Condratto:** As a doctoral student, Ms Shelley Condratto served as a research assistant with Closing the Enforcement Gap. She was involved extensively in the Worker Interviews Working Group, providing vital support in coding and analysing such interviews as well as interviews conducted by members of the Enforcement Practices Working Group. She co-authored chapter 7 of this book.

**John Grundy:** Initially holding an independently funded SSHRC postdoctoral fellowship and subsequently a project-based SSHRC postdoctoral fellowship, alongside serving as a co-investigator with Closing the Enforcement Gap, Dr Grundy co-led the partnership's Survey and Statistics Working Group and participated in the Archives and Policy, Enforcement Practices, Worker Interviews, and Alternative Models of Enforcement Working Groups. Dr Grundy not only conducted in-depth policy analysis informing numerous activities and outputs of the research partnership throughout its first five years, he also trained many research assistants in policy analysis. Through this extensive contribution, he co-authored chapters 1, 3, and 4 of this book.

**Alan Hall:** A co-investigator participating from the inception of Closing the Enforcement Gap, and co-lead of the Enforcement Practices Working Group, Professor Hall oversaw and participated in devising, conducting, coding, and analysing interviews with staff groups of Ontario's Ministry of Labour. He also participated in the Archives and Policy Working Group and served as a member of Closing the Enforcement Gap's steering committee. In addition to these contributions, he is co-author of chapter 6 of this book.

**Alice Hoe:** As postdoctoral research fellow with Closing the Enforcement Gap, Dr Hoe participated principally in the Survey and Statistics Working Group, through which she conducted data analyses informing multiple activities and outputs of the research partnership and mentored a number of research assistants. She is co-author of chapter 5.

**Kiran Mirchandani:** Serving as both a co-investigator and co-lead of the Worker Interviews Working Group, as well as lead qualitative methodologist, Professor Mirchandani oversaw the development, collection, and analysis of all of the worker interviews conducted under the auspices of Closing the Enforcement Gap and supervised a large team of trainees directed to this end. She also served as a member of the steering committee and is co-author of chapter 7.

**Andrea M. Noack:** As a co-investigator, member of the steering committee, co-lead of the Survey and Statistics Working group, and lead statistical methodologist for the partnership, Professor Noack oversaw the analyses of both administrative data and Statistics Canada data, and trained a large number of research assistants and postdoctoral fellows. Professor Noack contributed to countless activities and outputs of the research partnership, spanning multiple working groups. She is co-author of chapters 2, 4, and 5 of this book.

**Urvashi Soni-Sinha:** Overseeing the Windsor-based arm of Closing the Enforcement Gap's qualitative research, Professor Soni-Sinha participated in the Worker Interviews Working Group and co-authored chapter 7 of this book.

**Mercedes Steedman:** Alongside leading the Sudbury-based component of the research partnership, and participating in the Archives and Policy and Worker Interviews Working Groups, Professor Steedman co-authored chapter 7.

**Mark P. Thomas:** Professor Thomas's involvement with Closing the Enforcement Gap included serving as co-lead of the Archives and Policy Working Group and overseeing a team of researchers reviewing, cataloguing, and coding archival material pertaining to the enforcement of employment standards in Ontario, resulting in a digital archive upon which this book draws. He also participated in the Worker Interviews and Enforcement Practices Working Groups and served on the steering committee. He is co-author of chapter 7.

**Eric M. Tucker:** In his roles as co-investigator, co-lead of the Archives and Policy Working Group, and chief legal expert on the legal aspects of employment standards enforcement, as well as a participant in the Alternative Models of Enforcement Working Group, Professor Tucker oversaw much of the analysis of laws, legislation, and policies governing the enforcement of these social minima in Ontario. He also played a pivotal role in analysing the findings that emerged from the analysis of administrative data. Professor Tucker's research and input thereby contributed to countless activities and outputs of the research partnership. He is co-author of chapter 6 of this book.

**Leah F. Vosko:** Professor Vosko served as principal investigator of Closing the Enforcement Gap. Working closely with the community lead, Mary Gellatly, she contributed to developing the overall structure of the research partnership and forging its multi-method approach, and participated in all of its five Working Groups as well as most of the public outreach activities and outputs of the research partnership. In this capacity, she oversaw all aspects of this book's development from inception to completion, co-authored chapters 1, 2, 3, 4, 5, and 12, edited and commented on all of the remaining chapters, including those devoted to offering views from elsewhere, and contributed to preparing the book's glossary.

**Part Two: Views from Elsewhere**

**Nick Clark:** Nick Clark, a research fellow at the University of Middlesex and head of the Unpaid Britain Project, who has extensive experience in the British trade union movement and has conducted research on trade unions and unpaid labour, authored chapter 8.

**Dalia Gesualdi-Fecteau:** Professor Gesualdi-Fecteau, a faculty member at the Université du Québec à Montréal, who practised law at Quebec's Labour Standards Commission and whose research focuses on effective implementation of labour law, co-authored chapter 10.

**Tess Hardy**: Dr. Hardy, a senior lecturer at the University of Melbourne School of Law and co-director of the Centre for Employment and Labour Relations Law, who has expertise in regulatory theory, contract, and labour law, co-authored chapter 9.

**John Howe:** Professor Howe, a faculty member at the University of Melbourne School of Law and co-director of the Centre for Employment and Labour Relations Law, who has written extensively on the role of the state in regulating employment and labour markets, served as an international advisor to Closing the Enforcement Gap, as well as visiting scholar at a critical early stage in its development, and co-authored chapter 9.

**Guylaine Vallée**: A professor in the School of Industrial Relations at the Université de Montréal, Guylaine Vallée, whose research focuses on atypical labour relations and how the right to work applies to these new workplace realities with extensive experience studying employment standards regulation in Quebec, co-authored chapter 10.

**David Weil:** Serving as dean and professor at the Heller School of Social Policy and Management at Brandeis University, Dr Weil is an internationally recognized expert in employment and labour market policy and the impacts of supply-chain and industry restructuring on employment and work outcomes. Until his appointment, by U.S. President Obama, as the administrator of the Wage and Hour Division of the U.S. Department of Labor (2014–17), Dr Weil participated in the International Advisory Group to the Closing the Enforcement Gap Research Partnership. He is author of chapter 11.

# Acknowledgments

This book emanated from Closing the Enforcement Gap: Improving Employment Standards Protections for People in Precarious Jobs, a collaborative research initiative on employment standards and their enforcement in Ontario directed by Leah F. Vosko, principal investigator, and Mary Gellatly, community lead, and funded by the Social Sciences and Humanities Research Council of Canada under its Partnership Grants Program.

Unfolding over a seven-year period, the initiative involved a large network of partner organizations: York University, University of Toronto, Ryerson University, University of Windsor, Laurentian University, Wilfrid Laurier University, University of Ottawa, Memorial University of Newfoundland, the Ontario Ministry of Labour, Cavalluzzo Hayes Shilton McIntyre & Cornish LLP, Parkdale Community Legal Services, Ontario Public Service Employees Union, the Law Commission of Ontario, Human Rights Legal Support Centre, Sudbury Community Legal Clinic, Workers' Action Centre of Toronto, Workers' Action Centre of Windsor, Legal Assistance of Windsor, Workers' Health and Safety Legal Clinic, and Community Advocacy and Legal Centre.

The research partnership also involved many co-investigators and postdoctoral researchers. Co-investigators included Paul Chislett, Jennifer Chun, Shelley M. Gilbert, John Grundy, Alan Hall, Samantha Hayward, Deena Ladd, Katherine Lippel, Kiran Mirchandani, Delphine Nakache, Andrea Noack, Randy F. Robinson, Consuelo Rubio, Urvashi Soni-Sinha, Mercedes Steedman, Mark Thomas, Eric Tucker, and Linda Yannucchi. Postdoctoral researchers involved in the project included Elliot Siemiatycki (2013–15), Rebecca Casey (2015–17), Guliz Akkaymak (2016–18), Parvinder Hira-Friesen (2016–17), Alice Hoe (2017–18), and Mark Easton (2018–20).

The project also benefited from a group of international advisors, including Annette Bernhardt, Sara Charlesworth, Sean Cooney, Janice Fine, John Howe, Michael Piore, Nik Theodore, Anna Pollert, and David Weil.

All of the authors of Part One are grateful for the research assistance provided by the six undergraduate, six MA, and thirty-two PhD students involved in Closing the Gap from its inception as well as their families and friends for their abiding support and encouragement. In particular, we would like to thank the following individuals who contributed directly to research assistance towards this book: Shelley Condratto, Rebecca Hii, Alix Holtby, Maria Gintova, Danielle Landry, Olena Lyubchenko, Azar Masoumi, Nadia Ruscitti, and Ruby Kapoor. Thanks to individuals would moreover be incomplete without extending our deep gratitude to Heather Steel, for her tremendous support as the research project administrator throughout the period in which we wrote this book, as well as to her predecessors Min-Jung Kwak and Yuko Sorano, for their support as research project administrators.

As a whole the project from which this book emanated benefited from cash and in-kind support from the following institutions and organizations, which served as institutional research partners: Cavalluzzo Hayes Shilton McIntyre & Cornish LLP, Community Advocacy and Legal Centre, Human Rights Legal Support Centre, Laurentian University, Ryerson University, University of Toronto/OISE, University of Windsor, the Law Commission of Ontario, Legal Assistance of Windsor, the Ontario Ministry of Labour, Ontario Public Sector Employees Union, Association of Management, Administrative and Professional Crown Employees of Ontario, Parkdale Community Legal Services, Sudbury Community Legal Clinic, Toronto Workers' Health and Safety Legal Clinic, Workers' Action Centre of Windsor, Workers' Action Centre of Toronto, and York University.

Some of the analyses of Statistics Canada data presented in chapter 1 of this book were conducted at the York University and University of Toronto Research Data Centres, which are part of the Canadian Research Data Centre Network (CRDCN). The services and activities provided by the York University and University of Toronto Research Data Centres are made possible by the financial or in-kind support of the SSHRC, the CIHR, the CFI, Statistics Canada, York University, and the University of Toronto. The views expressed in this book do not necessarily represent the CRDCN's or that of its partners.

We are especially grateful to the Social Sciences and Humanities Research Council of Canada for funding the larger initiative under its Partnership Grants Program and to the Ontario Ministry of Labour for providing data resources, as well as York University, specifically, the Faculty of Liberal Arts and Professional Studies, Osgoode Hall Law School, and the Office of the Vice-President Research and Innovation, the host institution for the partnership.

This book has been published with the help of a grant from the Federation for the Humanities and Social Sciences, through the Awards to Scholarly Publications Program, using funds provided by the Social Sciences and Humanities Research Council of Canada.

# Abbreviations

| | |
|---|---|
| *AMES* | Administrative Manual for Employment Standards |
| *AO* | Archives of Ontario |
| *ESA* | *Employment Standards Act* |
| *ERO* | Early resolution officer |
| *ESIS* | Employment Standards Information System |
| *ESO* | Employment standards officer |
| *FLSA* | *Fair Labor Standards Act* (United States) |
| *FWA* | *Fair Work Act* (2009) (Australia) |
| *FWO* | Fair work ombudsman (Australia) |
| *LSA* | *Act Respecting Labour Standards* (Quebec) |
| *LSC* | Labour Standards Commission (Quebec) |
| *LSEOHSC* | *Labour Standards, Equity, Occupational Health and Safety Commission (Quebec)* |
| *MOL* | Ministry of Labour |
| *NOC* | Notice of Contravention |
| *OBA* | *Open for Business Act* (2010) |
| *OLRB* | Ontario Labour Relations Board |
| *PVWA* | *Fair Work Amendment, Protecting Vulnerable Workers Act* (2017) (Australia) |
| *WEPP* | Wage Earner Protection Program |
| *WHD* | Wage and Hour Division of the Department of Labor (United States) |

# CLOSING THE ENFORCEMENT GAP

## Improving Employment Standards Protections for People in Precarious Jobs

*Chapter One*

# Mapping the Enforcement Gap: Historical and Contemporary Dynamics

Employment standards are legislated minimum terms and conditions of employment. Existing across jurisdictions, they typically cover areas such as wages, working time, vacations and leaves, and termination and severance of employment, among others. In Ontario, the *Employment Standards Act* (*ESA*) legislates such social minima. Together with the province's *Occupational Health and Safety Act*, as well as *Human Rights, Pay Equity*, and *Workplace Safety and Insurance Acts*, the *ESA* is a principal source of workplace protection for a mounting number of employees[1] in Ontario, especially those in precarious jobs. It reflects a collectively established normative judgment about minimally decent working arrangements that must be extended to all employees. Yet not only are current levels of employment standards protection insufficient, the enforcement of existing standards remains a weak link in employment standards regulation in Ontario, as elsewhere (Bernstein et al. 2006; Gellatly et al. 2011; Vosko et al. 2011; Bernier 2006).

This book analyses and evaluates the enforcement of employment standards in Ontario in comparative context. It emanates from a multi-year collaborative study, "Closing the Employment Standards Enforcement Gap: Improving Protections for People in Precarious Jobs," involving participants from numerous cross-sectoral partner organizations, including researchers from seven universities.[2] The book identifies obstacles to effective employment standards, as well as promising strategies of re-regulation, featuring contributions from leading employment standards researchers studying developments in the province as well as in other jurisdictions facing similar regulatory challenges in Canada and beyond (Quebec, Australia, Britain, and the United States).

Ontario is experiencing changes in employment, and associated regulatory challenges, evident in other industrialized contexts. A declining share of the province's private sector labour force is unionized, a share that dipped from 19 per cent in 1998 to just 14 per cent in 2018. Global industrial restructuring explains part of this trend, as the share of Ontario's labour force employed in manufacturing, previously a highly unionized domain in which standard employment relationships were the norm, particularly among native-born citizen men is also declining. Simultaneously, an increasing share of the provincial labour force is employed in service industries, including accommodation and food services, and management, administration, and other services – industries in which employees often face poor working conditions. Reflecting an ongoing global reconfiguration of employment, many workplaces in Ontario are being transformed through greater use of contracting out, franchising, and extended supply chains. These ways of structuring work contribute to driving working conditions downward while also making the establishment of the traditional parties to an employment relationship – employees and employers – more difficult.

Our central claim is that while employment standards are a key source of formal protection for many employees, they are not living up to their founding promise of providing a floor of minimum terms and conditions of employment, advancing the principles of fairness and universality, partly as the result of deficiencies in enforcement. Employment standards enforcement strategies are not keeping pace with workplace practices that fuel precarious employment, which we define as forms of work for remuneration characterized by dimensions of labour market insecurity. For too many employees, employment standards are paper rights not realizable in practice. The enforcement gap pervades nearly all aspects of the regime: the reactive, individualized complaints system, which does little to prevent violations and remains out of reach for many employees; the under-resourcing of workplace inspections; and the limited use of penalties for employers who violate employment standards. Equally important in fuelling the enforcement gap are the structural barriers that prevent employees from exercising their voice. Such barriers are shaped by processes of racialization[3] and feminization[4] as well as divisions based on citizenship and residency status, ableism, and other forms of social differentiation, all of which are exacerbated by power imbalances inherent in the employment relationship.

Despite this bleak picture, a second contention runs through this book: there is nothing inevitable about the enforcement gap. There is no reason why the prevailing state of affairs – leaving many employees poorly protected – is inexorable. Rather, workers' advocates, especially worker centres and other organizations representing workers in precarious employment, are demanding strengthened enforcement of employment standards as a matter of justice, and they are having some success. Indeed, workers' agency is contributing to some innovative policy experimentation by governments, resulting in forward-looking new models of enforcement, and opportunities for policy learning about what works in employment standards enforcement.

To frame this dual overarching argument, this introduction unfolds in the following sections. Section 1 outlines the conceptual orientation of the text, which is rooted in critical and feminist political economy. Looking through the lens of these approaches, section 2 charts the (pre-)history of employment standards in Ontario. It demonstrates that many aspects of the current weaknesses of employment standards enforcement stem from longstanding features of the province's employment standards regime, especially the historically subordinate status of employment standards in relation to regulations governing collective bargaining. It also shows that, dating from the earliest forms of workplace standards, through to the enactment of the *ESA* and its current form, the development of employment standards legislation and enforcement is the outcome of the intersection of conflicting and uneasily reconciled objectives. On the one hand, policymakers have articulated the need for a floor of decent workplace protections. On the other hand, they have demonstrated reluctance, shaped by competitive pressure and political and ideological resistance, to interfere with employers' business/operational decisions. These legacies continue to shape the status of employment standards violations as warranting compliance rather than punishment, as well as the ongoing dearth of strong enforcement mechanisms.

Against this backdrop, section 3 seeks to illuminate challenges to employment standards enforcement that stem from changes in Ontario's labour market. It begins by offering a statistical portrait of precarious employment in Ontario that illustrates the importance of employment standards to a majority of employees in the province, and the expanding regulatory mandate of the Ministry of Labour (MOL). This section then details labour market dynamics that pose serious challenges to the employment standards enforcement system, including declining rates of unionization, especially in the private sector, the growth in the share of the workforce located in small businesses traditionally more difficult to regulate, and the growing recourse to fissured employment arrangements (Weil 2010) that place downward pressure on the working conditions of employees at the bottom of the labour market, particularly among those confronting processes of racialization and feminization, as well as divisions based on citizenship and residency status. These dynamics throw into relief the inadequacies of the regime as a whole – its reactive (or complaints-based) character and extremely limited use of deterrence.

Section 4 sheds light on a central regulatory driver of the enforcement gap contemporaneously – the increasing appeal of compliance and regulatory new governance strategies – and its gradual adoption and partial disavowal in Ontario. There is evidence that the Ontario government has strengthened employment standards for particular groups of vulnerable employees, in partial recognition of persistent precariousness in the labour market. But aspects of this recalibration are flawed in their elevation of compliance and regulatory new governance approaches to enforcement. Regulatory new governance embraces a shift away from "command and control" regulation identified with traditional, bureaucratic forms of regulation, towards "soft" or "light touch" regulation directed at achieving compliance through self-regulation, persuasion, and information-sharing. Yet, in this book, we demonstrate that models of enforcement that emphasize compliance over deterrence are unlikely to prevent or remedy employment standards violations.

Framing the remainder of the book, section 5 discusses the various ways in which employees are deprived of the promised protections of employment standards, given weaknesses in enforcement. These forms of rights deprivation stem not simply from formal violations, but also from more subtle forms of employment standards evasion, erosion, and abandonment (Bernhardt et al. 2008). We then elaborate our methodological commitments to "active mixing" that serve as touchstones in the investigation of the various facets of Ontario's employment standards enforcement regime to follow. Active mixing of methods is necessary to capture the different positioning of actors within and around the employment standards enforcement system. It also fosters a nuanced account of the situated agency of individual and collective actors to challenge the status quo in practices of employment standards regulation and enforcement (see Coe and Jordhus-Lier 2011).

In conclusion, section 6 reviews the chapters that comprise the body of the book.

## 1. Conceptual Framework: A Political Economy of the Enforcement Gap

In this book we approach the study of employment standards through the lens of critical political economy, drawing particular insights from feminist political economy. While there is considerable variation in the critical political economy literature, most approaches examine developments in the economy with attention to the social dynamics of production (broadly conceived), dominant ideologies, and political struggles (Armstrong 1996; Porter 2003). Most also reflect an abiding commitment to seeing contradictions as sources of change, and hence to using productive tensions as a means of understanding continuity through change (e.g., in the analysis of state policies and their effects) (Armstrong and Armstrong 1983; MacDonald 1991; Vosko 2002). From a critical political economy perspective, markets, including labour markets, are thus not self-regulating. They are "socially embedded institutions" (Graefe 2007, 20; see also Peck 1996) sustained through the exercise of political and economic power, shaped fundamentally by social relations of gender, class, race, sexuality, (dis)ability, and citizenship, and the contradictions and tensions they reflect and engender.

Critical political economy provides insights into the interrelation between employment standards and the structure and organization of labour markets. For example, Vosko (2019) demonstrates, in a review of feminist political economists' interventions into the study of employment standards, how scholars adopting this approach have uncovered the bifurcated (and deeply gendered) structure of labour law and policy, and linked the inferior floor of labour protections provided by employment standards (compared to collective bargaining) to the marginalized status of those to whom employment standards were designed to apply – namely, women and children (e.g., Fudge 1988, 1991b; Sangster 1989; Ursel 1992; International Ladies Garment Workers Union and INTERCEDE 1993; Kessler-Harris, Lewis, and Wikander 1995; Fudge and Tucker 2000; Thomas 2009; Vosko 2010). Feminist political economy thus provides a bridge, building on the formative insight about the integral relationship between production for surplus and social reproduction, revealing that a majority of workers for whom employment standards are the principal source of labour protection are women (Fudge 1991b), presumed to be responsible for social reproduction (or the unpaid work required to produce a supply of workers for the labour force) and to be dependent on a male breadwinner (Vosko 2000, 2010). Indeed, this approach opened space for paying greater attention to not only non-unionized workers but also to unpaid work and how it shaped women's patterns of labour force participation and the protective regimes to which they were subject and hence to underlining the significance of their silences or omissions as well as their noises. It also provided a foundation for exploring how the organization and administration of employment standards reproduce labour market inequities on the basis of processes of racialization as well as immigration status.

Additional insights are found in recent critical and feminist political economy scholarship on precarious employment. Over the last few decades, a key focus of a subset of this literature on work and labour has been the rise of "flexible" and insecure forms of employment, and, concomitantly, the increasingly unequal balance of power between employers and employees. Such inequality in power is fostered through new information and communication technologies, progressively more flexible and globally dispersed modes of service and goods production, along with increasingly mobile financial capital. Against this backdrop, critical and feminist political economists trace how governments across many industrialized market economies foster "flexible" work arrangements through neoliberal reforms to labour market policies, including restrictions on collective bargaining (Panitch and Schwartz 2003), the retrenchment of income security programs designed to provide a modicum of protection (McBride 1992; Peck 2001; Porter 2003; Vosko 2011), and reforms to employment standards, occupational health and safety, and anti-discrimination policies (Fudge 1991b; Fudge and McDermott 1992; Fudge and Vosko 2003; Thomas 2009; Tucker 2013a) that heighten workers' exposure to commodification and market regulation both individually and cumulatively, particularly workers belonging to equity-seeking groups. A critical political economy lens helps to reveal how deepening insecurity confronting workers generates politically effective demands from workers' advocates and the broader public for improved workplace protections. The growth of economic inequality and the decline in the purchasing power of workers at the bottom of the labour market has also become a concern for many mainstream economists and policymakers who fear that weak consumer demand is a drag on economic growth (e.g., Stiglitz 2016; Cingano 2014). In this context, employment standards have become a major terrain of struggle in Canada and elsewhere, given the direct role of these social minima in shaping the nature of employment. Employing this analytic lens emphasizes how employment standards are shaped by the outcome of struggle between business interests seeking minimal legislative intrusion into employers' affairs and workers' advocates pursuing improved standards and renewed enforcement (Cranford et al. 2005; Thomas 2009). Building on the insights of feminist and critical political economy, the following sections trace the formation of employment standards in Ontario and key developments in their evolution to prepare the ground for considering contemporary employment standards and their functioning more closely.

## 2. Legislative Precursors of the Late Nineteenth and Early Twentieth Century: The Subordinate Status of Early Employment Standards

Protective labour and employment law did not develop in any significant way until the last decades of the nineteenth century. Indicative of the principles of "liberal voluntarism" (Fudge and Tucker 2001), legislators were largely opposed to interfering with the nascent industrial capitalist economy. Conditions of employment were established primarily in individual employment contracts (Thomas 2004, 55). When minimum standards first began to be legislated in the period of "industrial voluntarism" in response to demands stemming from organized labour and social reformers, they reflected and reproduced the gendered segmentation of the labour force. Collective bargaining laws such as the *Industrial Disputes Investigation Act* (1907) targeted industries such as mining and transportation, where male workers predominated. It was expected that with minimal state support, these workers would be able to protect their own interests through collective action (Fudge and Vosko 2001). For those unable to defend themselves, the government enacted protective employment laws. For example, while the *Factories Act* of 1884 established health and safety standards applicable to all workers employed in factories, it also created standards that applied only to women and children, including a ten-hour-a-day / sixty-hour work week. Similarly, under the *Minimum Wage Act* of 1920, a provincial board was established to set minimum wages for most female employees. While these protective laws were enacted in response to the demands of organized labour and social reformers that the state needed to establish minimum standards to protect workers vulnerable to exploitation, both were designed to limit their potential impact on employer power and business profitability (Thomas 2004, 56–57; Tucker 1990). Indeed, the factory act inspectors and the provincial board responsible for enforcing the *Minimum Wage Act* demonstrated a reluctance to prosecute employers who violated the laws' terms (Thomas 2004, 57; Tucker 1990).

From the outset, and setting a course for the future, protective labour law made provision for exemptions and special rules to accommodate demands from employers that their operations would be unduly harmed if the general rules were applied to them. For example, the *Factories Act* allowed officials to issue overtime permits to employers under particular conditions in light of the "the customs and exigencies of certain trades" (*Factories Act* s. 8, cited in Tucker 1988, 50), while the *Minimum Wage Act* exempted farm labourers and domestic servants and permitted lower minimum wages to be ordered for inexperienced and young female employees (McCallum 1986). A central, albeit implicit, basis for such "exceptions" (i.e., to full coverage) was that the social groups the evolving employment standards regime principally addressed (i.e., women and children) were presumed to have access to resources beyond the wage.[5] The difficulties that such exemptions pose for enforcement were also recognized early on by officials. Indeed, the Royal Commission on Price

Spreads called for the elimination of minimum wage exemptions in early employment law: "To permit them raises problems of insuperable administrative difficulty, may easily divert the attention of officials from enforcement to exemption, and tends ultimately to defeat the whole purpose of the law. An employer who cannot afford to pay the minimum wage is in the long run a liability to the community" (1935, 130).[6]

The Canadian labour and employment law regime shifted to "industrial pluralism" in the period during and after the Second World War. Collective bargaining laws not only protected the freedom of workers to organize and bargain collectively, but also imposed duties on employers not to interfere with organizing and to recognize and bargain with unions that obtained majority support. Private sector unionization rates increased dramatically, but largely remained confined to male-dominated industries. Minimum standards laws, however, moved away from protecting particular social groups of employees, such as women and children, to protecting all employees. Enlarging the scope of coverage, the *Hours of Work and Vacations with Pay Act* (1944) broadened the application of working hours provisions beyond women and children to cover all employees in industrial undertakings, including by imposing an eight-hour day/forty-eight hour week and introducing a right to refuse overtime as well as an annual paid vacation of one week (Thomas 2004, 65–6). However, this Act provided for exemptions for supervisors and confidential employees, made war industries exempt (s. 5), allowed excess hours in the case of accidents or emergencies, permitted regulations to be made creating further exemptions (s. 10), and inaugurated a process for approving other exemptions. As Thomas (2004, 72) notes, "While the postwar state sought to buffer the effects of the market, as before the Second World War, the manner in which minimum standards were regulated ensured that employers had some 'flexibility' to exceed the legally established minimums."

Although the *ESA* applied to both unionized and non-unionized employees, most unionized employees were able to bargain terms and conditions of employment substantially better than the statutory minima. Employment standards laws applied primarily to female and feminized sectors of the labour market. Fudge (1991a) aptly characterized the situation as one in which employment standards were labour law's "little sister." As a result, unions were generally not heavily invested in employment standards, with the consequence that employment standards laws and their enforcement were not a major priority for government.

Another less-appreciated factor that may have contributed indirectly to the weak enforcement of employment standards is their legal status under the constitutional division of powers between the provinces and the federal government. The enactment of employment standards (outside of the federal jurisdiction) was and remains primarily a provincial responsibility, and provinces are limited to enacting regulatory laws in the areas that fall under their jurisdiction. In Canada, only the federal government can enact criminal law, seen to be "reserved for the most serious offences, those that involve grave moral fault" (Department of Justice 2002). This division of powers is important in shaping public perceptions of employment standards violations, because regulatory infractions do not carry the same moral weight as criminal offences.[7] Although from time to time some politicians have successfully argued that endangering workers and intentionally paying less than the minimum wage are crimes, the ensuing *Criminal Code* amendments are indeed weak and almost never enforced (Tucker 1990, 2017; Bittle 2012). Additionally, the main orientation of employment standards historically and to the present has been to provide restitution to employees. Punishment of employment standards violations through deterrence has not been prominent in employment standards enforcement.

## 3. Enacting the ESA, 1968–1995

By the mid-1960s it was becoming increasingly apparent that collective bargaining was not spreading to or was ineffective in the growing service sector. As a result, the labour movement became more interested in employment standards, as did, in particular, women's groups concerned about poor working conditions for women who increasingly were returning to the workforce. In response, Ontario began exploring the development of new employment standards legislation that would combine and update the existing patchwork of standards (Thomas 2004). Enacted in 1969, the province's first *ESA* provided a minimum wage for both men and women and established maximum hours of work at eight per day and forty-eight per week. An overtime rate of time-and-a-half was set for any hours exceeding forty-eight hours a week, and the Act established the right to refuse overtime work. It also provided for time-and-a-half on seven statutory holidays and guaranteed two weeks of paid vacation per year. The legislation was shaped by, and reproduced, a deep historic tension between the intent of providing a floor of workplace standards and minimizing intrusion into employers' affairs.

As archival records suggest, beginning in this era, the pursuit of decent work in Ontario via the *ESA* arguably reflected three principles: social minima, universality, and fairness (Vosko, Noack, and Thomas 2016). Social minima refer to "ensuring that workers benefit from minimum acceptable conditions of employment and ... actively promot[ing] the adoption of socially desirable terms and conditions of employment" (MOL 1978, July 12). The goal of contributing to their realization underpinned the development of Ontario's *ESA*, as during its development, employment standards legislation was viewed as a means of "raising wages, improving working conditions, and opening up employment opportunities" as a step towards addressing conditions stemming from insecure and low-wage work (MOL 1965, 22 November).

In the development of employment standards in Ontario, the principle of universality, in turn, supported the aims of establishing social minima and recognized that few employees have a strong position vis-à-vis their employer. Universality too is an objective recognized by the Supreme Court of Canada. Indeed, it is acknowledged in *Machtinger v. HOJ Industries Ltd.* (1992), both by its reference to the uniform standards above and by their articulation of an interpretive principle to be applied to the *ESA*: "Accordingly, an interpretation of the Act which encourages employers to comply with the minimum requirements of the Act, and so extends its protections to as many employees as possible, is to be favoured over one that does not."

Finally, the record shows that the principle of fairness refers to both "safeguard[ing] workers against exploitation" and "protect[ing] employers against unfair competition based on lower standards" (MOL 1969). Underlying the principle of fairness is the imperative to address the fundamental power imbalance between employers and employees, particularly those who are without union representation and engaged in the most precarious forms of employment (*Machtinger v. HOJ Industries Ltd.* 1992).

In the years shortly after its development, against the backdrop of the articulation of such objectives, Ontario's *ESA* came to be conceived by government administrators as "the collective agreement of the unorganized or as anti-exploitation legislation" for those with little bargaining power (MOL 1974, June). In this regard, the principle of fairness must be understood to support those of social minima and universality, whereby fairness takes a substantive rather than procedural form, insofar as it works in conjunction with these other principles.

Despite this history, a central and longstanding feature of employment standards regulation in Ontario is the tension between the need for a floor of decent workplace protections and policymakers' reluctance to interfere with employers' operational decisions. As a result of this tension, in both their design and operation, employment standards have, in practice, accounted for, and in some instances functioned in, the interests of industry (Thomas 2009). Though the Act was intended to apply to most workers in the province, in particular those with the least bargaining power, historically it has also sought to strike a balance between social protection and business interests (MOL 1968, 31 May). Since its inception, policymakers have acted in accordance with the assumption that the "social and economic implications of minimum standards are inter-related, and must be largely determined by that which is economically practicable" (MOL 1967, September, 567). Efforts to improve social minima through employment standards have been accompanied by efforts to "keep industry and to attract new industries to the province" (MOL 1968, 31 May). To this end, the *ESA* contained numerous exemptions and special rules at its origins, including in the regulation of hours of work and overtime (Thomas 2004). For example, managerial and supervisory employees were excluded from hours of work restrictions, and the daily hours maximum could be exceeded so long as the weekly limit was not. In the event that an employer maintained a "normal" workday longer than eight hours but a workweek of forty-eight hours or less, the right to refuse overtime would not apply. A permit system allowed for overtime hours to an annual maximum of 100, with the director of employment standards holding the capacity to authorize further hours, depending on the "special nature of the work performed," or the "perishable nature of the raw material being processed" (Kinley 1987).

Despite the stated commitment to the principle of universality at the inception of the *ESA*, starting in the 1970s, from the perspective of Ontario's MOL, the "universal application of all the basic standards [was] not seen as possible," as "variations in terms of employment, types of work, and characteristics of certain industries will always require some exceptions" (MOL 1976, 6 April). Exemptions were also meant to both limit the government regulation of employer-employee negotiated working time arrangements and avoid the imposition of "severe hardships" (MOL 1976, 15 December) on employers (Dewees 1987). Indeed, the record shows that exemptions were often developed in response to lobbying from employer associations that emphasized the unique aspects of a particular occupation; for example, in terms of seasonal employment or the potential impact of the *ESA* on the financial viability of a given business (MOL 1967, 16 May; 1969, 8 January; 1974, 22 October; 1975, 20 June). The existence of exemptions thus points to a deeper tension in the overall aims of employment standards legislation, calling into question the underlying principles of employment standards themselves. Accordingly, in the early years after the enactment of the *ESA*, a report from Ontario's MOL (MOL 1976, 15 December) raised this question, indicating a lack of consensus on the overall purpose of the *ESA* itself: "Much of the controversy that exists around the question of exemptions stems from a lack of consensus as to whether particular standards represent socially acceptable minimal conditions or are regarded as conditions which are desirable so long as they can be enforced practically and do not impose severe hardships on employers – that is, whether we regard these conditions as absolutes or as items for which we are willing to make trade-offs with other social values."

In addition to the explicit exemptions from the legislated standards in the original *ESA*, a system of special permits developed to provide another way in which employers could exceed working time standards. Like the exemptions themselves, the special permits were introduced in order to account for occupational and industry variation in work hours, so that universal standards did not constrain particular sectors where long hours were prevalent or where seasonal variation in production required some flexibility in scheduling. In essence, the permits system, which enabled employers to avoid the hours of work limits established by the *ESA*, contributed to the erosion of the floor set by the *ESA*.

The inspectable standards of the *ESA* were altered through minor legislative reforms in the 1970s, 1980s, and early 1990s, most of which added to the scope of protections for workers in areas of termination notice requirements, severance pay, and pregnancy leave.[8] Marking the end of a period of substantive expansion, bankruptcy protection legislation was also introduced in 1991. The Employee Wage Protection Program was designed to provide employees with compensation for unpaid wages, commissions, overtime wages, vacation pay, holiday pay, and termination and severance pay, up to a maximum of $5,000 per employee. The program was administered through the Employment Standards Branch of the MOL, and employment standards officers (ESOs) were given the ability to order payments under the program.[9] The program was funded out of general provincial revenues. Upon payment of a claim, the government attempted to recover funds from the non-compliant employers and businesses. Terminated in the mid-1990s following the election of a new Progressive Conservative government, the program remains the most extensive attempt undertaken by the MOL to ensure employees recover unpaid wages (for further details about this program, see chapter 4).

### 4. The State of Ontario's Labour Force: Precarious Employment, Persistent Inequities, and Deepening Regulatory Challenges

A closer examination of developments in Ontario's labour force, especially the spread of precarious employment and fissured workplaces, is warranted at this juncture to contextualize more recent legislative and regulatory developments and gaps in their scope and enforcement.

The decade-and-a-half between 1980 and the mid-1990s represented a period of substantial change in Ontario's labour force. During this period, the province saw rising rates of part-time and temporary paid employment as well as solo self-employment. The passage of the Canada-U.S. Free Trade Agreement (1989) and the North American Free Trade Agreement (1994), coupled with a severe recession in the early 1990s, accelerated labour market restructuring in the province and an associated decline in the share of its labour force employed in manufacturing – an industrial sector characterized by high rates of unionization and full-time, permanent employment. Reflecting the rise of neoliberal labour market policies, governments in Canada and elsewhere placed more emphasis on fostering competitive and so-called flexible labour markets by measures such as restrictions on the collective bargaining rights of workers; the retrenchment of income security programs such as Employment Insurance and social assistance; and the general weakening of health and safety and anti-discrimination regulations (Vosko 1996; Panitch and Swartz 2003; Thomas 2009; Tucker 2013b). A consistent theme of labour market policies adopted during this period, within and beyond Ontario and Canada more broadly, was an effort to limit workers' access to de-commodifying protections and hasten their entry into less attractive, poor quality jobs. Contextualizing these more recent laws and policies and gaps in their scope and enforcement, the following statistical profile of precarious employment in Ontario highlights the different dimensions of labour market insecurity that affect many employees in the province, and certain groups of labour force participants more acutely than others.

### *A Profile of Precarious Employment in Ontario*

Precarious employment encompasses forms of work for remuneration characterized by labour market insecurities such as degree of certainty of continuing employment, low income, lack of control over the labour process, and limited access to regulatory protection. Imbued with unequal power relations, it is shaped by the relationship between employment status (i.e., self- or paid employment), form of employment (i.e., temporary or permanent, part-time or full-time), social location (or the interaction between social relations, such as gender and race, and legal and political categories, such as citizenship), as well as social context (occupation, industry, and geography) (Vosko 2006).

While precarious employment and "non-standard" forms of employment are not – and need not be – synonymous, there is a relationship between them, because historically labour laws and policies have taken

Graph 1.1. Part-Time Employees, Ontario, 1976–2018*

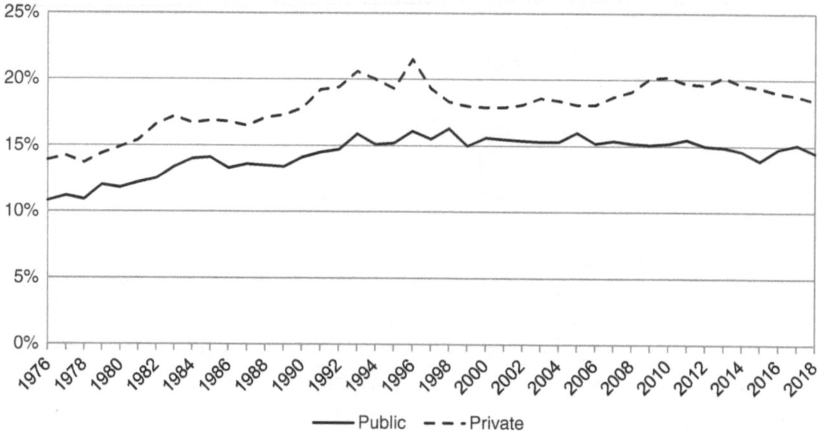


Source: Statistics Canada, Labour Force Survey 1976–2018.
*Annual data weights applied. For the years 1976–86, weights are based on 2001 census data. For the years 1987–2000, weights are based on 2006 census data. Finally, for the years 2001–18, weights are based on 2011 census data.

the standard employment relationship – defined as a full-time permanent employment relationship where the worker has one employer, works on the employer's premises, and has access to statutory entitlements and benefits – to be the norm (Vosko 2010). For this reason, forms of employment differing from this model have come to be linked with greater precariousness. For example, part-time paid employment may not provide workers with income sufficient to maintain themselves and dependents. Temporary paid employment is, by definition, uncertain. And a central characteristic of most employer and solo self-employment is the absence of labour protections.

As graph 1.1 shows, the number of Ontario employees working part-time, a form of employment particularly common among women,[10] increased considerably between 1976 and 1993 and stabilized at high levels thereafter. In addition, as many employers pursued flexibility-enhancing labour strategies in an attempt to reduce their labour costs, especially those associated with termination or severance pay, the share of non-permanent employment, including contract/term, seasonal, casual, agency, and on-call employment more than doubled, from 5 per cent in 1989[11] to 13 per cent in 2018. Between 1997 and 2018, there was also a steady increase in the share of temporary employees, especially in the public sector (graph 1.2).

Trends in forms of employment tell only a partial story of the spread of precarious employment in Ontario. Dimensions of labour market

Graph 1.2. Non-Permanent Employees, Ontario, 1997–2018*

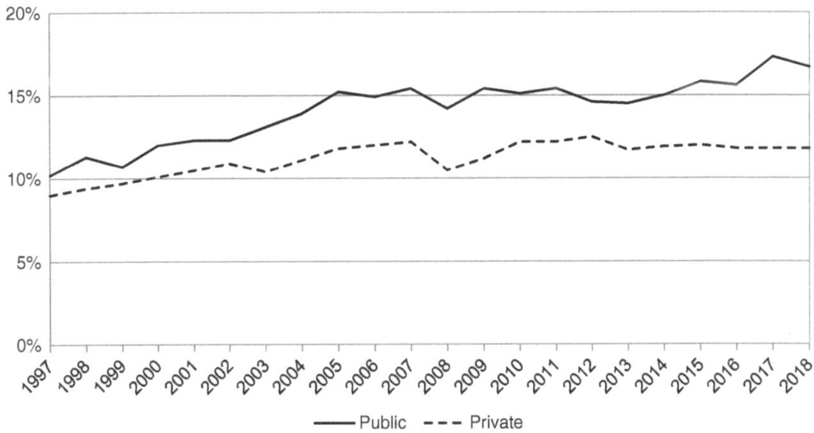


Source: Statistics Canada, Labour Force Survey 1997–2018.
*Annual data weights applied. For the years 1976–86, weights are based on 2001 census data. For the years 1987–2000, weights are based on 2006 census data. Finally, for years 2001–18, weights are based on 2011 census data.

insecurity – such as a lack of control over the labour process, low income, and limited access to regulatory protection – are a central part of the experience of precarious employment, and a number of indicators of such dimensions are particularly relevant to employment standards and their enforcement.

Union status is a critical indicator of degree of control over the labour process. It affects the extent to which employees rely upon minimum employment standards, as those who lack access to a collective agreement regulating workplace conditions and grievance processes (i.e., non-unionized employees) rely exclusively on the *ESA*. Such employees also generally have limited capacity to assert their voices in the workplace and tend to have more limited control over the pace and content of work than do employees covered by a collective agreement. As table 1.1 shows, the share of Ontario's labour force that is non-unionized is increasing, particularly in the private sector, where it stood at 81 per cent in 1998 and fully 86 per cent in 2018.

Low hourly wages are a clear indicator of low income, defined here as less than two thirds of the median hourly wage for full-time employees (e.g., less than $16.67 per hour in 2018).[12] Low-income employees are more likely to rely on minimum employment standards, such as those setting out minimum wages. The share of employees in Ontario's labour force earning low wages is persistently high. Considering both public and private sector employees, it was 29 per cent in 1998 and 27 per cent in 2018. In the private sector, it was 34 per cent in 1998 and 32 per cent in 2018, a slight decline that may be attributable to the rise in the minimum wage from $11.40 per hour to $14.00 per hour on 1 January 2018 (table 1.1).

Job tenure provides a good indicator of both a worker's degree of certainty of continuing employment, as well as protection from job churn. In the *ESA*, access to benefits such as vacation time accrues only after twelve months of employment. In recent decades, the proportion of employees who had worked for an employer for less than a year has remained around 20 per cent. More notable, however, is that the share of private sector employees with short job tenure is almost double that of the public sector, where (in contrast to the private sector) a much higher rate of unionization has helped to ensure that workers have the opportunity to apply for available positions and develop a career.

Finally, small firm size, an indicator of limited access to regulatory protection, is also a predictor of limited employment standards enforcement. Research demonstrates how precarious employment is more prevalent in small firms (Noack and Vosko 2011), as the result of such firms' vulnerability to instabilities generated by rapid fluctuations in demand. Employees in small firms (of fewer than twenty) are less likely to see their rights enforced, because it is difficult for an under-funded labour inspectorate to spread its resources across workplaces. Employment standards complaints received by the MOL are disproportionately filed by employees of small businesses that employ fewer than twenty people. Compared to medium or large firms, small firms are also least likely to engage in voluntary restitution when found to have violated employment standards; in addition, they are least likely to pay what is owed when ordered to do so by the MOL (Vosko et al. 2017, 266). A sizeable share of employees in Ontario works in small firms: fully 21 per cent of employees in the private sector in 2018 (table 1.1).

A multidimensional conception of precarious employment calls for considering indicators of dimensions of labour market insecurity relationally and cumulatively. In pursuit of this objective, we combine four measures (i.e., no union coverage, low income, short job tenure, and small firm size) to create a composite measure of precariousness. This composite measure deems jobs to be precarious if they are characterized either by at least three of these four features or by the presence of low wages and another of the remaining measures. We prioritize low wages, given the growing body of research demonstrating the

Table 1.1. Indicators of Dimensions of Precariousness, 1998, 2008, and 2018*

| | 1998 (%) | 2008 (%) | 2018 (%) |
|---|---|---|---|
| Non-unionized | | | |
| All employees | 71 | 72 | 74 |
| Public sector employees | 31 | 29 | 30 |
| Private sector employees | 81 | 85 | 86 |
| Low wage | | | |
| All employees | 29 | 29 | 27 |
| Public sector employees | 9 | 9 | 8 |
| Private sector employees | 34 | 35 | 32 |
| Job tenure less than one year | | | |
| All employees | 21 | 21 | 20 |
| Public sector employees | 12 | 13 | 12 |
| Private sector employees | 24 | 24 | 22 |
| Small firm | | | |
| All employees | 19 | 17 | 17 |
| Public sector employees | 4 | 4 | 3 |
| Private sector employees | 22 | 21 | 21 |
| Precarious jobs | | | |
| All employees | 29 | 29 | 27 |
| Public sector employees | 8 | 7 | 6 |
| Private sector employees | 34 | 35 | 33 |

Source: Statistics Canada, Labour Force Survey 1998 to 2018.
* Annual data weights used. For the year 1998, weights are based on 2006 census data. For 2008 and 2018, weights are based on 2011 census data.

correlation between low-wage employment and high levels of insecurity (Appelbaum, Bernhardt, and Murnane 2003; Vosko 2006; Bosch 2009; Luce 2014).

The prevalence of precarious employment is shaped both by employment status and form of employment and also by socio-demographic variables such as sex, age, immigration status, and race. In other words, it affects workers belonging to certain social groups more than others. As table 1.2 shows, employees in part-time temporary employment, a form of employment increasing in Ontario and defined by both uncertainty and a paucity of hours, experience extensive precariousness. Eighty-two per cent of these employees are non-unionized, 65 per cent earn low wages, and 48 per cent have worked at the same employer

Table 1.2. The Relationship between Form of Employment and Indicators of Precarious Employment, Ontario, 2018

| | Indicator of Precarious Employment (%) | | | | |
|---|---|---|---|---|---|
| | No union | Small firm | Low wage | Short tenure | Precarious job |
| All employees | 74 | 17 | 27 | 20 | 27 |
| Form of employment | | | | | |
| Full-time permanent | 72 | 16 | 18 | 13 | 18 |
| Full-time temporary | 75 | 18 | 36 | 50 | 38 |
| Part-time permanent | 79 | 24 | 62 | 31 | 59 |
| Part-time temporary | 82 | 22 | 65 | 48 | 65 |

Source: Statistics Canada, Labour Force Survey 2018, annual data weights used.

for less than a year. In contrast, employees in full-time permanent employment are the least likely to experience precariousness. In particular, they are much less likely to earn low wages or to have short job tenure than workers in all other forms of employment. Notably, part-time employees – both permanent and temporary – are more likely to report holding multiple jobs, suggesting that for some of these workers, their part-time status is involuntary and does not provide sufficient income. On this basis, cumulatively, supporting the existence of a continuum of precarious employment by form of employment, part-time temporary jobs are most precarious; indeed, 65 per cent of such jobs were highly precarious by this measure, in contrast to 18 per cent of full-time permanent jobs.

In terms of social location, young people aged fifteen to twenty-four are far more likely to be precariously employed than older workers (see table 1.3). This disparity is attributable in part to young people's tendency to hold part-time and temporary forms of employment. Compared to their older counterparts, young people are more likely to hold non-unionized positions, work in small firms, earn low wages, and have short job tenure. In addition, young people are more likely to report working multiple jobs. Cumulatively, 70 per cent of young employees are in precarious jobs, compared to 19 per cent of employees aged twenty-five to fifty-four, or 21 per cent of those fifty-five years or older.

Gender also shapes Ontario employees' experience of precariousness. Most notably, women are much more likely than men to earn low wages: in 2018 almost a third of women (31 per cent) earned low wages, compared to only 23 per cent of men. Overall, cumulatively, women are also considerably more likely to hold precarious jobs; in 2018 nearly

Table 1.3. The Relationship between Socio-demographic Characteristics and Form of Employment/Indicators of Precarious Employment, Ontario, 2018

| | Indicator of Precarious Employment (%) | | | | |
|---|---|---|---|---|---|
| | No union | Small firm | Low wage | Short tenure | Precarious job |
| All employees | 74 | 17 | 27 | 20 | 27 |
| Age group | | | | | |
| 15–24 | 87 | 23 | 70 | 52 | 70 |
| 25–54 | 72 | 16 | 18 | 16 | 19 |
| 55+ | 69 | 17 | 23 | 8 | 21 |
| Gender | | | | | |
| Men | 76 | 17 | 23 | 21 | 24 |
| Women | 72 | 17 | 31 | 20 | 30 |

Source: Statistics Canada, Labour Force Survey 2018, annual data weights used.

30 per cent of women compared to approximately 24 per cent of men were in this situation.

Recent immigrants to Canada – those who arrived 10 years ago or less also experience high rates of precarious employment in Ontario. They are more likely to be employed in jobs that are non-unionized, that are low waged, and that are in small firms and they are more likely to have a job tenure of less than one year than other employees.[13] Using the cumulative measure of precarious employment, recent immigrants are much more likely to be precariously employed than other employees (37 per cent compared to 26 per cent respectively).

It is worth noting that among immigrants to Canada there are substantial variations in labour market outcomes shaped by migration period (i.e., period of arrival in Canada) and larger patterns of racialization in the labour force. In Canada, and likewise in Ontario, recent immigrants are much more likely to be racialized than those who arrived in the past (see graph 1.3). Prior to 1975, only about one in five immigrants were racialized; in comparison, in 2011, about four in five immigrants were racialized.

The growing proportion of racialized immigrants is notable, since racialized immigrants (and racialized employees more generally) tend to have lower earnings when they enter the labour force (Banerjee 2009; Pendakur and Pendakur 2016). Among recent immigrants in Ontario (i.e., those who arrived between 2006 and 2015), 54 per cent of racialized employees earned low annual wages in 2015, compared to 37 per cent of non-racialized employees (Census of Population 2016). This trend is evident among immigrants who arrived between 1975 and 2006 as

Graph 1.3. Proportion of Non-Racialized and Racialized Immigrant Employees in Ontario by Low to Higher Wages over Time, Year of Arrival in Canada from Pre-1975–2015*

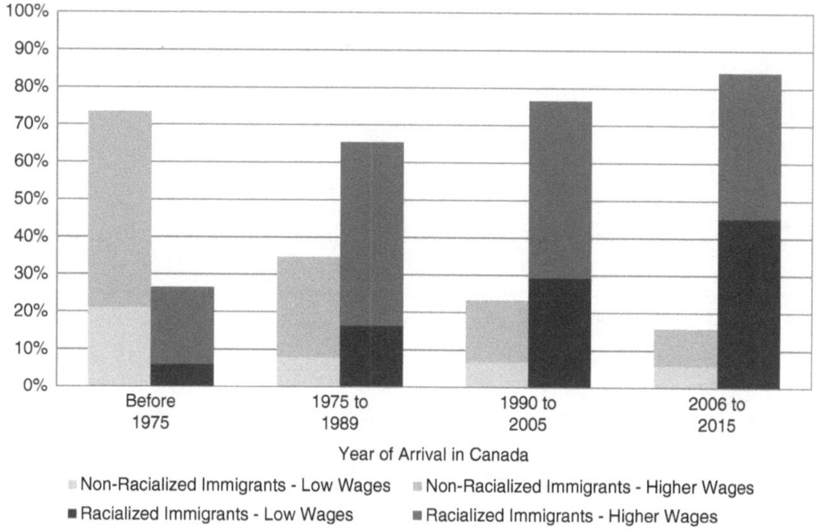


Source: Statistics Canada, Census of Population 2016.
*Annual wage/salary income is used to determine low-wage status (defined as less than two-thirds of the median annual wage/salary among full-time employees).

well. Regardless of their place of birth, racialized people tend to earn less, are more likely to live in low-income and/or in poverty and to be unemployed than those that are non-racialized (Block and Galabuzi 2011; Kazemipur and Halli 2001; Palameta 2004). Despite the importance of racialization in the experiences and outcomes of immigrants, information on race or "visible minority status" is not collected in Canada's Labour Force Survey, inhibiting more detailed analyses of the intersections between dimensions of labour market insecurity, particularly between racialization and firm size, job tenure, and permanent/temporary job status.

The gendered nature of certain facets of precariousness is even more pronounced among recent immigrants than among other employees. For instance, recent immigrant women are more likely than recent immigrant men to be employed in small firms, whereas there is no such gender disparity among other employees. Fully 44 per cent of recent immigrant women earn low wages, compared to only 30 per cent of recent immigrant men. Overall, recent immigrant women are substantially more likely to be in precarious employment, compared to both recent immigrant men and other employed women.

Industry is a valuable entry point into understanding the dynamics of labour market insecurity. It is especially so given the importance of context in shaping whether and to what degree a job is precarious. Indeed, larger economic trends such as industrial restructuring interact with the changing nature and organization of employment to contribute to fissuring, typified by the tendency of lead businesses to avoid having employees through contracting out, franchising, and use of extended supply chains (Weil 2010, 2014).

In Ontario the accommodation and food services industry has the greatest prevalence of employees in precarious jobs, fully 74 per cent (in 2018) (see table 1.4). Unionization rates are extremely low in this industry; 93 per cent of employees are non-unionized, and an overwhelming majority of employees in this industry also earn low wages – fully 75 per cent. These trends are notable, given especially the relatively high proportion of immigrant women employed in this sector (i.e., even though only 3.7 per cent of Ontario employees are recent immigrant women, 6.1 per cent of employees in the accommodation and food services industry are recent immigrant women). Certain occupational groups falling within this industry are also subject to substandard levels of employment standards protection as a matter of course. For example, liquor servers, nearly three quarters of whom are women and fully 43 per cent of whom are twenty-four years of age or younger (in 2016), are subject to a lower minimum wage ($12.20 instead of the general minimum wage of $14.00 as of January 2018) (Vosko et al. 2019, 290). Many liquor servers thus rely on tips, which are a highly uncertain form of income, dependent on a range of factors including the volume of customers, weather, time of day, and customers' perceptions of service quality, among others (Matulewicz 2015). Moreover, research demonstrates that tipping places pressure on workers to tolerate customers' sexist behaviour because it is central to liquor servers' wages. In recommending the phase-out of the liquor servers' minimum wage in their final report, the Special Advisors of the Changing Workplaces Review (2016–17) notes, "One is left uneasy about the demographics of the sector and we question whether this anomalous treatment of liquor servers would have survived this long if most of the servers were male" (Mitchell and Murray 2017, 166).

The retail industry, a highly feminized domain (Coulter 2014), also has a high prevalence of precarious employment. Indeed, 55 per cent of employees in the retail sector hold precarious jobs. The retail

Table 1.4. Relationship between Industry and Form of Employment/Indicators of Precarious Employment, Ontario, 2018

| | Indicator of precarious employment (%) | | | | |
|---|---|---|---|---|---|
| | No union | Small firm | Low wage | Short-tenure | Precarious job |
| All employees | 74 | 17 | 27 | 20 | 27 |
| Industry | | | | | |
| Accommodation/food services | 93 | 22 | 75 | 35 | 74 |
| Retail trade | 88 | 13 | 60 | 26 | 55 |
| Agriculture | 98 | 55 | 51 | 29 | 55 |
| Management/administration/business support services | 87 | 22 | 47 | 29 | 45 |
| Other services | 91 | 54 | 33 | 22 | 37 |
| Information/culture/recreation | 79 | 15 | 35 | 25 | 35 |
| Manufacturing (non-durables) | 83 | 12 | 26 | 16 | 25 |
| Wholesale trade | 94 | 21 | 21 | 16 | 22 |
| Transportation/warehousing | 66 | 11 | 22 | 16 | 21 |
| Construction | 70 | 39 | 13 | 24 | 19 |
| Manufacturing (durables) | 80 | 11 | 16 | 15 | 16 |
| Professional/science/technical services | 95 | 25 | 11 | 24 | 15 |
| Finance/insurance/real estate | 95 | 12 | 13 | 15 | 14 |
| Health care/social assistance | 56 | 16 | 13 | 15 | 14 |
| Forestry & fishing/hunting | 52 | 25 | 11 | 28 | 12 |
| Educational services | 30 | 5 | 13 | 14 | 11 |
| Mining & oil/gas extraction | 79 | 3 | 5 | 21 | 5 |
| Public administration | 28 | 2 | 6 | 12 | 4 |
| Utilities | 35 | 4 | 2 | 10 | 2 |

Source: Statistics Canada, Labour Force Survey 2018, annual data weights used.

industry has very low union density and a high prevalence of low-wage employment.

The agricultural industry has a similarly high concentration of precarious employment; fully 55 per cent of employees in this industry are precariously employed and fully 98 per cent of agricultural employees do not belong to a union.[14] Agricultural workers are also subject to a range of exemptions and special rules established in regulations made pursuant to the *ESA* that further attenuate their (in)access to its social minima (Vosko, Noack, and Thomas 2016). The insecurity facing many agricultural employees subject to employment standards exemptions and special rules is exacerbated by structural inequalities related to race. A sizeable portion of agricultural employees in Ontario comprises racialized workers from Mexico and the Caribbean, as well as increasingly other countries in Latin America such as Guatemala, holding temporary work permits that permit them to participate in temporary migrant work programs exclusively. A large body of literature demonstrates that these agricultural employees experience extreme disadvantage in the labour market as a result of the global system of racialized capitalism within which migration takes place, which structurally embeds the underdevelopment and dependence of the "periphery" or Global South, through what Harvey (2004) labels "accumulation by dispossession," whose forms have varied historically, from direct colonial confiscations to more recent expropriation through debt and discipline (McNally 2011).[15] The existence of this global system, perpetuated by an immigration system through which Canada recruits a racialized workforce from the Global South to participate in its temporary migrant work programs, severely curtails the ability of workers migrating to Ontario to engage in employment to obtain permanent residence (Satzewich 1991; Choudry and Smith 2016; Thomas 2016). Concretely, it means that migrants in agriculture cannot easily exercise the option to leave a job and secure alternative employment as a result of the way in which such programs are organized (Sargeant and Tucker 2009; Thomas 2016). The power of farmers to choose who will be rehired, coupled with the extreme poverty and debt of many migrant agricultural employees, makes the exercise of voice in the face of workplace violations risky and exacerbates problems of employment standards enforcement under a regime that largely fails to make their rights real in the first instance (Vosko 2018; Vosko, Tucker, and Casey 2019).

Almost half (45 per cent) of employees in the management/administrative/business support industry, which includes forms of work such as office administration, security, and building services, are also precariously employed. Low union density and high rates of low-wage work characterize this industry. In addition, both the accommodations and food services industry and the management, administration, and other support service industry have higher levels of temporary employment – another indication of uncertainty – than non-unionized employees in the province overall.

Notably, those industries in which many jobs exemplify precariousness in its fullest sense, such as accommodation and food services, retail, and management/administrative/business support services, are all also characterized by extensive fissuring (Weil 2014). Fissuring refers to a process through which formally integrated employing entities make greater use of subcontracting, franchising, supply chains, temporary help agencies, and other mechanisms, and its growing prevalence contributes to precarious employment in many industries in Ontario.

Through fissuring, lead businesses are able to transfer responsibility for the employees who actually perform the work of concern to smaller intermediary firms. These smaller intermediaries operate in highly competitive environments and are under pressure to reduce labour costs. Indeed, at the lower end of the labour market, in expanding economic sectors such as accommodations and food services, agriculture, and retail and administrative services, the increasing prevalence of fissured workplaces makes employment standards violations a key strategy of labour cost containment (Bernhardt, Spiller, and Polson 2013). As the ensuing chapters will show, the fragmented arrangements characteristic of the fissured workplace (Weil 2010) pose challenges to all aspects of enforcement. Ontario's employment standards regime is not well equipped to extend legal obligations associated with employment standards beyond the intermediaries who are direct employers (narrowly conceived) to lead firms that create and benefit from fissured arrangements.

In sum, changes in Ontario's labour market over the past several decades, including industrial restructuring and fissuring, fuel the spread of precarious employment as well as its concentration in certain industries and among certain segments of the population. Youth, women, and recent immigrants, as well as migrants lacking secure residency status, are most affected by its insecurities. Persistent – and, by certain measures, deepening – labour market insecurities set the context for the most recent discernible phase in employment standards regulation and enforcement in Ontario, which bears the influence of regulatory new governance.

## 4. A New Approach to Managing Precariousness through Employment Standards Enforcement: Regulatory New Governance and Its Limits

From a political economy perspective, the growing precariousness and fissuring of employment can be understood as a strategy by employers to maintain or increase profitability as the long post-war economic boom ran out of steam in the mid-1970s. While employers enjoyed great freedom to restructure their operations and employment practices, they also had to contend with government regulations that limited their flexibility, so they promoted neoliberal reforms to both collective bargaining and employment standards. However, here they encountered considerable resistance from workers and their advocates. Indeed, successive Ontario governments were faced with the problem of managing these contradictory pressures. The Ontario government's recent embrace and subsequent partial disavowal of the regulatory new governance paradigm marks its attempt to do so. We explore these developments here, beginning with a description of regulatory new governance and its internal contradictions, followed by an examination of the development of employment standards since 1995.

Regulatory new governance aims to manage the contradictory demands on government by finding a third way between neoliberal market regulation and traditional regulation, often described as command and control (although, as we have seen, in practice, traditional regulation never lived up to this model, in part because of the extremely limited use of deterrence). Prevalent in the field of employment standards, in Ontario and other jurisdictions of interest in this book, such as the United States, Britain, and Australia, it purports to reconcile the regulatory responsibilities of governments with a greater sensitivity to the competitive market realities confronting regulated parties (Vosko, Grundy, and Thomas 2016).

Approaches to employment standards based on regulatory new governance entail several central features: they envision a smaller role for public regulation and the veritable threat of legal punishment. In their stead, regulatory new governance strategies privilege a compliance orientation to enforcement. That is, they aim to secure compliance through techniques such as persuasion and negotiation, codes of conduct, information-sharing on industry best practices, and non-governmental monitoring. Regulatory new governance's compliance orientation assumes that employment standards violations are the result of employer ignorance and incompetence rather than intentional behaviour. The primary strategy for improving employers' performance of their legal obligations, therefore, is to provide information and compliance assistance on the assumption that most employers will respond by becoming law-abiding corporate citizens. The growing preference among policymakers for the use of "soft-law" enforcement implies various degrees of self-regulation. As Estlund (2005, 325–6) notes, "The locus of enforcement is moving inside the workplace and away from direct public monitoring." For proponents of these measures, soft-law and self-regulation enforcement strategies are more apt to gain the support of the regulated firms. Policymakers also promote regulatory new governance as a solution to the challenges of employment standards enforcement that stem from chronic underfunding of labour inspectorates, especially in light of the growing number of workplaces and workers for whom employment standards are the exclusive source of labour protection (Vosko et al. 2011).

While regulatory new governance prioritizes compliance in the belief that most employers will become law abiding, it also recognizes that some "bad apples" will not respond and that stronger, well-targeted enforcement measures will be needed. These may include a modest program of proactive targeted inspections and the use of increasingly punitive sanctions to bring these outliers into compliance with their legal obligations. This approach is often associated with Ayres and Braithewaite's (1992) responsive regulation approach and its enforcement pyramid, well known for calibrating regulation vis-à-vis differing motives and track records of regulated entities.

Another central feature of regulatory new governance in the field of employment standards enforcement is the promotion of stakeholder participation. One prominent proposal is a greater use of firm-level works councils, envisioned as a mechanism of employee representation, especially in contexts of low union density such as the United States (Estlund 2012, 11). Other proposals that emanate from workers' struggles assign new regulatory roles to professional and industry associations, community groups, and certified monitors (see, especially, Fine and Gordon 2010; Hardy 2011). This pluralization of actors finds theoretical justification in governance theory's repudiation of "the capacity and desirability of state control in a complex society" (Pierre 2012, 190). Proponents of participatory enforcement point to the difficulties labour inspectorates have in keeping up with shifting employer practices and suggest that regulatory efforts suffer unless they draw on the expertise of relevant individuals and groups throughout the regulatory process (Lobel 2012; see also chapter 7 of this book). Overall, supporters of regulatory new governance advocate regulated self-regulation, which they contend avoids the twin pitfalls of neoliberal market or self-regulation and traditional top-down enforcement in favour of a "third way."

While regulatory new governance promises to reconcile employer demands for flexibility with worker demands for protection, numerous studies demonstrate that the paradigm entails serious drawbacks (Davidov 2010; Tucker 2013b; Tombs and Whyte 2013; Vosko, Grundy, and Thomas 2016). Such studies assert that the emphasis on less-adversarial techniques does not sufficiently acknowledge the unequal power relations inherent in the employment relationship and can undermine employees' access to legal redress when faced with violations. In non-unionized environments, employees are often vulnerable to intimidation and are therefore unlikely to exercise voice as workplace protagonists (Tucker 2013b). Moreover, the diminished role for hard-law, deterrence measures in regulatory new governance can inadvertently incentivize non-compliance among employers. Given growing evidence that non-compliance is endemic in sectors with heightened competitive pressures on firms, the potential for regulatory new governance to result in regulatory degradation is even more pronounced (Tombs and Whyte 2013). As a result, workers continue to experience employment standards violations at unacceptable levels, leading to demands for more effective enforcement from worker advocates and social movement actors – demands that are often amplified by sympathetic press coverage. Government commitment to regulatory new governance, therefore, is often partial, as becomes evident in tracing the historical evolution of these conflicting forces in Ontario over recent decades.

*Flexibilization of the* ESA, *1995–2004*

In 1995 a right-leaning Progressive Conservative government was elected in Ontario, and it adopted neoliberal, flexibility-oriented reforms to Ontario's *ESA*, which unfolded in three stages. Marking the first phase of reform, the Employee Wage Protection Program was terminated in 1995 and the minimum wage was frozen at $6.85 – a freeze that would last for nine years. Against this backdrop, in the second phase, in 1996 the *Employment Standards Improvement Act* reduced the time limit for workers to register formal complaints from two years to six months and placed a $10,000 limit on monetary awards for *ESA* violations, regardless of the value of lost wages. The Act also introduced a provision preventing unionized employees from filing employment standards complaints with the MOL. Instead, employment standards complaints by unionized employees were to be pursued through grievance arbitration, placing the cost of administering *ESA* complaints in the hands of unions, rather than the ministry. Finally, in phase three, major legislative changes – amounting to no less than an overhaul – were implemented in the *ESA* (2000). These amendments increased weekly maximum hours of work from 48 to 60 and allowed for the calculation of overtime pay to be based on an averaging of overtime hours across a four-week period: employers could schedule overtime hours without compensation at time-and-a-half, provided the total for the four-week period was less than 167 hours. They also revoked the system of government permits required for excess hours (more than 48 per week), introducing instead a requirement for employee "consent" to the new excess hours and overtime averaging provisions.

However, even a very conservative government did not feel at liberty to ignore all concerns about unfairness in the labour market. For example, the *ESA* (2000) introduced anti-reprisal protections and personal emergency leave. In addition, the provincial government expanded the parental leave provisions of the Act to bring them in line with federal amendments to the *Employment Insurance Act*. It also addressed the issue of enforcement by creating a new deterrence measure, Notices of Contravention (NOC), which could be issued by an ESO for any violation of the *ESA*. NOCs provided for the imposition of escalating administrative monetary penalties for first, second, and third or subsequent contraventions. NOCs were understood to provide ESOs with a lower-level penalty that was much easier to impose than a full-scale Part III prosecution, and thus could be judiciously used to foster compliance. However, as we demonstrate in this book, ESOs rarely used these deterrence measures until the late 2010s (see chapter 6). Overall, from the mid-1990s to the mid-2000s, the protections provided by the *ESA* eroded alongside an increase in precarious employment.

*Growing Recognition of Precariousness by a Strapped Inspectorate, 2004–2010*

The mid-2000s mark the beginning of a shift in the trajectory of employment standards reforms in Ontario towards regulatory new governance. In 2003 a Liberal government was elected, which turned away from efforts to flexibilize Ontario's labour market through neoliberal reforms in favour of modest measures to strengthen employment standards. This change in direction was at least in part a response to increasingly well-organized and media-savvy workers' activist organizations, including the Toronto-based Workers' Action Centre and the Ontario Coalition against Poverty, which worked to build visibility and political pressure around the growth of precarious employment in the province (de Wolff 2000; Gellatly 2007). In early 2004 the provincial government increased the long-stagnant minimum wage and introduced amendments to the *ESA*, placing new restrictions on the capacity of employers to work their employees beyond forty-eight hours per week. In describing these measures, Labour Minister Chris Bentley, stated, "This legislation, if passed, would let vulnerable workers decide, without undue pressure, whether to work extra hours. We will also make sure employees know their rights and employers understand their obligations. Backing this up will be tougher enforcement against those who refuse to operate responsibly, preying on workers and undermining competitors.... Starting today, enforcement is back in style" (MOL 2004, 26 April).

As a part of its stated commitment to more rigorous enforcement, the government also indicated that the MOL would be empowered to publish the names of the individuals and employers convicted of employment standards violations as a deterrent. In 2004 Ontario Regulation

950 was amended to give ESOs the power to issue tickets under the *Provincial Offences Act* (R.S.O. 2000 c. P. 33) for specified *ESA* violations (O. Reg. 162/04). The tickets carry a set fine, $295 at the time of writing in 2019, as well as a victim fine surcharge, which brings the total to about $370. At the time, the government announced that ticketing aimed specifically to benefit vulnerable workers. As the minister put it, "We must ensure the fair treatment of vulnerable employees, and ticketing will help us accomplish that goal" (MOL 2004, 14 July). However, as we shall see, the use of either NOCs and tickets has remained relatively infrequent, and the penalties typically imposed from either are sufficiently low for employers to regard them as a cost of doing business (Vosko, Noack, and Tucker 2016, 54).

At the same time, the limits of a reactive, individualized complaints-based system became increasingly apparent. A 2004 review of the MOL's Employment Practices Branch by the auditor general of Ontario pointed to inadequacies of that system, concluding that the almost exclusive emphasis on investigating complaints from individuals, who nine out of ten times complained only after they left their jobs, failed to protect the rights of employees who remained on the job (auditor general of Ontario 2004b). It indicated, additionally, that while violations were confirmed in 70 per cent of individual complaints, the MOL was not fulfilling its mandate to protect workers by extending investigations to protect the employment rights of currently employed workers who do not file complaints for fear of reprisal, notwithstanding that reprisal is unlawful (auditor general of Ontario 2004b).

The government responded to this report by announcing it would ramp up proactive inspections targeting sectors at higher risk of violations (MOL 2004, 14 July), and it was true to its word. In 2005 the government reported that it had conducted 2,355 inspections, noting that this was an increase from a total of only 151 inspections in 2003 under the previous government (MOL 2005, 27 May). However, the following year, the government's messages stepped back from tougher enforcement and once again emphasized the need for more education and self-regulation (Hall et al. 2019). Concretely, among other measures, it introduced new online tools to assist employees and employers in determining their rights and obligations and an online system for employees to file complaints.

The goal of the online complaint system was to make workers more self-reliant in accessing government assistance and was accompanied by the closure of government intake offices where workers formerly obtained their claim forms and information about how to fill them in. An unanticipated consequence of the online complaint system, however, was an increase in the overall number of complaints received by the MOL (a development also fuelled by the growing number of non-unionized Ontario employees solely reliant on the *ESA*). The changes also generated new difficulties for complainants unable to contact and seek support from frontline government workers, resulting in incomplete or improperly filled-out claim forms requiring further follow up from EROs and ESOs. These developments strained the already limited capacity of the employment standards enforcement system.

Subsequently, the number of unresolved complaints carried from one year to the next increased, while the total annual number of completed complaints remained the same. By 2010 the MOL had a backlog of 14,000 employment standards complaints, and complainants waited, on average, almost a year between submitting their complaint and receiving a decision from an ERO or an ESO (Grundy et al. 2017). Notwithstanding the growth in complaints, the backlog undoubtedly deterred some employees from filing a complaint, as complainants were faced with little hope of a speedy resolution. Such delays were described by one organization as "a key impediment to the creation of a level playing field in this province" (Callan cited in Legislative Assembly of Ontario 2010, 3 August, F-134). Around the same time, a series of high-profile and egregious violations were widely reported in the media, highlighting the lack of strong deterrence. As the auditor general of Ontario's 2004 report noted, prosecutions were virtually non-existent – with 51,000 substantiated complaints in the previous five years, only eighteen prosecutions were initiated (auditor general of Ontario 2004a, 244).

In the face of sustained pressure from workers' advocates (Gellatly 2007), the government of Ontario adopted additional legislative measures that targeted particular groups of "vulnerable workers," such as those employed through temporary help agencies and live-in caregivers. The *Employment Standards Amendment Act* (Temporary Help Agencies) (2009) developed new standards for workers in temporary help agencies. It introduced requirements that temporary agencies must provide information about the agency (name and contact information) and working conditions (including pay, hours, nature of work) to workers. It extended *ESA* coverage for public holiday pay and termination and severance to these workers. Finally, it established prohibitions on charging fees to clients for entering into employment agreements with assignment employees. Specifically, agencies are permitted to charge clients a fee only if an employee is offered a permanent position in the first six months of an assignment with that client (Vosko 2010).

Proceeding along similar bases, in 2010, the *Employment Protection for Foreign Nationals Act* (Live-in Caregivers and Others) introduced a series of legislative protections for those employed as live-in caregivers. Specifically, it banned fees charged by recruiters and employers, allowed live-in caregivers up to three years to make a claim to recover prohibited fees, prohibited reprisals against live-in caregivers for exercising their rights under the legislation, and prohibited an employer or recruiter from taking possession of a live-in caregiver's property (including documents such as passports). The Act also authorized ESOs to proactively enforce the legislation.

Overall, by the end of the first decade of the 2000s, there was growing public recognition of the inadequate protection provided by the *ESA*. Despite reforms modestly augmenting employment standards protections for employees, the *ESA* lacked the provisions needed to regulate the full range of organizational arrangements into which businesses enter, including growing recourse to subcontracting, franchising, supply chains, and use of temporary help agencies, among other mechanisms that lead to uncertainty about who is the employer in a given scenario. Further curtailing the enforcement of the *ESA* were the administrative backlog, the lack of proactive enforcement (e.g., workplace inspections aimed at strategic intervention), and the extremely infrequent use of deterrence. Equally problematic, rather than using mechanisms to achieve systemic change by targeting powerful actors at the top of supply chains (Weil 2008b, 2010), enforcement resources were oriented primarily to responding to individual complaints being voiced at the bottom of supply chains' fissured arrangements.

### *Regulatory New Governance and the* Open for Business Act *(2010)*

In lieu of moving further in the direction of proactive enforcement, in 2010 the Ontario government further embraced numerous tenets of regulatory new governance as part of an effort to "realign resources to improve enforcement and promote compliance" (MOL 2009). It promised to pre-empt future backlogs through an "enhanced compliance strategy ... reaching out to employers through a mix of education, outreach and enforcement to ... stem any problems before they arise" (MOL 2011, 29 July a). Ontario's *Open for Business Act (OBA)* (2010) marked a clear-cut example of the provincial government's adoption of elements of the regulatory new governance paradigm. A key plank of the *OBA* involved streamlining regulation in recognition of the competitive pressures that businesses face. The *OBA* established a requirement for most employees to first seek to resolve their complaints with the employer before gaining access to the complaints system. This provision reflected the tendency of regulatory new governance to approach violations as largely unintentional and stemming from a lack of information or sufficient education, as well as the idea that regulation can be achieved without the heavy hand of state intervention. The requirement for most employees to attempt to resolve their issues directly with their employer aimed to reduce the number of complaints that reach the system. As the minister of labour at the time noted, "In many instances, those claims [i.e., complaints] are because the parties don't have the information beforehand where they can resolve the claim [i.e., complaint] before it has to be dealt with by one of our employment standards officers" (Fonseca cited in Legislative Assembly of Ontario 2010, 2 June, 1899). There were several formal grounds for exemption from this requirement, such as if a complainant was a young worker, a live-in caregiver, or someone who fears retaliation. Nevertheless, complainants were required to detail their efforts to contact their employer, or their reasons why it was not possible, when submitting a complaint. Chapter 2 examines these measures in greater detail.

The *OBA* also introduced a new form of "facilitated" settlement. Prior to the *OBA*, settlements were not facilitated and were reached between employees and employers alone. Such settlements require that a written agreement be provided to the ERO or ESO outlining the agreement, and the complaint is then closed without an admission of wrongdoing and without requiring assessment by an enforcement official. Facilitated settlements involve ESOs as settlement facilitators between the employee and the employer. According to the MOL *Administrative Manual for Employment Standards (AMES)* appendix on facilitated settlements, these enforcement officials are involved in "helping parties understand the strengths and weaknesses of their cases; providing parties with information on how the ESA applies to their cases; [and] helping parties to frame their position and communicate with each other" (MOL 2016a, 3). Under facilitated settlements, the terms of the agreement must be established before an ESO makes a decision following an investigation of the complaint.

### *Regulatory New Governance under Strain*

The move towards reforms inspired by regulatory new governance in the *OBA* met with extensive and persistent contestation by workers' advocates. The government of Ontario, and especially its MOL, has become increasingly aware of regulatory new governance's limits in addressing workplace violations. Indeed, starting in the mid-2010s, there were modest attempts to bolster more traditional enforcement activities. The *Stronger Workplaces for a Stronger Economy Act*, adopted in 2014, made several amendments to the *ESA*'s enforcement provisions.

The Act lifted the $10,000 cap on recoverable wages for employees, extended the time limit on wages that can be recovered through a claim from six months to two years, and established joint and several liability for employees of temporary help agencies for wage and overtime violations. Reflecting widespread trends in employment standards enforcement that emphasize information provision and employer self-regulation (Vosko, Grundy, and Thomas 2016), the Act also introduced new requirements for employers to provide employees with materials produced by the MOL on their entitlements under the *ESA*, and established self-auditing requirements under which employers must conduct self-examinations to ensure their compliance with the law when ordered to do so by an ESO. However, in line with the government's recognition of the limits of regulatory new governance, it also communicated to ESOs the need to make greater use of tickets and NOCs, the low-level deterrence measures available to them.

In 2015 the government of Ontario announced the *Changing Workplaces Review*, the most thorough review of the *ESA* and its enforcement mechanisms in several decades. As the Terms of Reference introduced at the outset asserted, "Far too many workers are experiencing greater precariousness" (MOL 2016b) in employment in Ontario today than in the recent past. Accordingly, with the aim of "creating decent work for Ontarians, particularly for those who have been made vulnerable by changes in our economy and workplaces" (Mitchell and Murray 2016, 13), the government appointed special advisors to investigate the dynamics underlying the magnitude of precariousness in the province's labour force and to pose options for reforming Ontario's *Labour Relations Act* and *ESA*. Subsequently, the *Interim Report on the Changing Workplaces Review* noted, "There is a serious problem with enforcement of ESA provisions ... there are too many people in too many workplaces who do not receive their basic rights" (260). Reflecting the review's impact, the premier's mandate letter of September 2016 to the MOL responded by calling for "strengthening enforcement of ES, through further resources if necessary, ensuring employers who do not respect protections for workers are held to account" on the basis of its findings in this domain.

In May 2017 the government outlined its proposed legislative reforms following the release of the *Final Report of the Changing Workplaces Review*. Despite the government's previous assertion that discussion of a minimum wage rate increase was beyond the purview of the *Changing Workplaces Review*, it was announced that the minimum wage would rise to $15 per hour by 1 January 2019. In addition, the *Fair Workplaces, Better Jobs Act* (2017) included measures addressing unfair scheduling; increased annual paid vacation entitlements from two to three weeks for employees with at least five years job tenure; eliminated a personal emergency leave exemption for small businesses; required, with a few exceptions, temporary help agency employees to be paid the same as employees of the client firm when performing substantially the same kind of work; and required that casual, part-time, temporary, and seasonal employees who are performing substantially the same job as full-time employees be paid the same as full-time employees.

The legislation also included a modest set of measures to improve enforcement of the *ESA*. It made the mis-classification of employees as independent contractors an offence, strengthened the MOL's ability to establish joint liability of related employers, required employers to pay interest on unpaid wages and, for that matter, any amounts owing,[16] and provided the MOL or its authorized collector with the power to place wage liens on the property of employers. The legislation also eliminated the requirement for most employees to attempt to resolve their complaint with their employee before contacting the MOL, committed the government to hiring 175 new EROs and ESOs by 2021 and, accordingly, inspecting one in ten Ontario workplaces annually, starting the same year. However, a central weakness of the *ESA* unaddressed by the *Fair Workplaces, Better Jobs Act* (2017) was the lack of deterrence, a pillar of strategic enforcement. The Act introduced a provision for more flexibility in the use of NOCs, as well as very modest increases to their dollar value, from $250, $500, and $1,000 to $350, $700, and $1,500, respectively. At the same time, as the penalty for Part I tickets fell under the *Provincial Offences Act* (1990), to which the scope of the *Changing Workplaces Review* did not extend, the *Fair Workplaces, Better Jobs Act* (2017) failed to increase the dollar value of Part I Tickets and provided no provision requiring MOL officials to use deterrence measures more frequently and forcefully. The Act's weakness with respect to deterrence measures suggests that regulatory new governance, with its emphasis on soft-law and non-antagonistic compliance, remained influential among the architects of these *ESA* reforms.

Alongside these legislative changes, in 2018 the Ontario government initiated a review, terminated by the successive provincial government later that year, of the complex web of exemptions, partial exemptions, and qualifying conditions, which limit the application of the *ESA*'s protections. These exemptions and special rules provide special treatment for certain industries, occupations, or sectors, and the review began with those applicable to architects, domestic workers, homecare workers, IT professionals, managerial and supervisory employees, pharmacists, residential building superintendents, janitors, and caretakers.

These gestures at improving the substance and enforcement of employment standards in Ontario were largely in response to the sustained campaigns of workers' advocates and community organizers, such as the Fight for $15 and Fairness Campaign, underscoring their importance in fostering new forms of collective agency, especially among groups facing other forms of disadvantage in the labour market, such as migrants, recent immigrants, women, and racialized employees.

But while the Fight for $15 and Fairness remained strong, in late 2018 and early 2019 most legislative changes introduced in the *Fair Workplaces, Better Jobs Act* (2017) were eliminated following the passage of the *Making Ontario Open for Business Act* (2018) by the Conservative government elected in June 2018. Among measures removed from the *ESA* and associated regulations by December 2018 were those set to increase the minimum wage to $15 in January 2019. The 2018 legislation also eliminated recently adopted flexible provisions for ten days of annual personal emergency leave (i.e., which could be used to attend to personal or family illness or other matters), which included two days of paid leave and replaced it with three unpaid sick days, three unpaid family responsibility leave days, and two unpaid bereavement leave days. It repealed a range of scheduling protections that were to come into force in January 2019, the provision of the right to equal pay for part-time, contract, temporary, and temporary agency workers vis-à-vis full-time workers, as well as new public holiday pay calculations introduced under the *Fair Workplaces, Better Jobs Act* (2017). Additionally, the *Making Ontario Open for Business Act* (2018) lowered the monetary penalties issued to employers in contravention of the *ESA* to the previous levels, and it severely weakened the newly added provision against employee mis-classification by eliminating the burden on employers to prove a worker is not an employee. Following on its heels, the government then repealed the longstanding requirement that employers display a poster on *ESA* rights and responsibilities in the workplace and froze workplace inspections. Among other actions, it also eliminated the requirement that the director of employment standards approve work in excess of forty-eight hours a week as well as approve employee-employer agreements to average the weekly hours worked by an employee over a number of weeks for the purpose of determining overtime pay, requiring only that employers and employees agree in writing, so long as the period of averaging is no longer than four weeks. Paradoxically, in contrast to developments in Ontario, in that same year the federal government announced changes to Part III of the Canada Labour Code governing labour standards akin to those adopted in the *Fair Workplaces, Better Jobs Act* (2017).

## 5. A Multi-Method Approach

Thus far, we have suggested that the capacity of employment standards to provide a floor of workplace rights has been undermined by an enforcement gap. This gap is fuelled by the historical weaknesses of employment standards, reflecting policymakers' reticence to interfere too heavily in the private decisions of business. The enforcement gap is also exacerbated by changes in the organization of labour markets and workplaces that fuel the spread of precarious employment – particularly among social groups already marginalized in the labour force – and increasingly confound the terms of employment standards regulation. Moreover, it is worsened by the proliferation of enforcement models bearing the imprint of regulatory new governance in the contemporary period that posit employer non-compliance as largely unintentional and the result of a lack of information, and elevate less adversarial forms of dispute resolution and self-regulation on the part of employers.

Just as the employment standards enforcement gap is driven by many factors, so too are its contours and effects, as well as responses to it. The empirical evidence marshalled for this book demonstrates the variety of ways in which employees are deprived of the protection employment standards that legislation aims to provide. In addition to charting documented violations of the *ESA*, the ensuing chapters thus explore the often more subtle forms of evasion of employment standards, as well as related processes of employment standards erosion and abandonment (Bernhardt et al. 2009). They pursue this undertaking since attempts to redress deficiencies in the enforcement regime will be hampered in the absence of full acknowledgment of the many forms of rights deprivation that have taken shape. Closing the enforcement gap requires giving greater voice to those affected as well as drawing on the knowledge of the broader community of workers' advocates.

Evasion involves employers' adoption of "strategies to evade core workplace laws" by, for example, limiting the law's application by misclassifying employees as self-employed contractors (Bernhardt et al. 2008, 6). Many firms are reorganizing their labour processes so that workers who were once classified as employees are now deemed to be independent contractors. While the extent of the practice has not been formally measured in Canada, misclassification of employees as independent contractors has been identified as a key regulatory problem in Canada (Law Commission of Ontario 2012). Misclassification has been measured in the United States. One prominent study commissioned by the U.S. Department of Labor in 2000 determined that 10–30 per cent of investigated firms across nine states had engaged in employee misclassification (Government Accountability Office 2009). More recent studies estimate that 10–20 per cent of employers misclassify at least one of their employees as an independent contractor, and that misclassification is likely increasing (Carré 2015; Donahue, Lamare, and Kotler 2007; Law Commission of Ontario 2012; Smith and Leberstein 2015). Misclassification imposes costs on workers by depriving them of access to workplace standards. It also makes the playing field uneven, potentially encouraging more employers to abandon standard employment relationships and avoid or evade the *ESA* in order to remain competitive. Yet misclassification is not just a problem under the *ESA*. Misclassified employees are deprived of worker's compensation, employment insurance, and other employment-related benefits. Evasion also entails classifying employees in ways that trigger the application of an exemption, such as classifying an employee as a supervisor in order to evade obligations related to overtime pay and other working time standards.

Erosion weakens normative goals (e.g., social minima, universality, and fairness) and workplace policy objectives (e.g., assuring basic labour standards, protecting against major downside risks of employment, and mitigating against power imbalances and resulting abuses). A standout example of explicit erosion is found in mounting exemptions from and special rules under the *ESA*, especially exemptions for groups of employees documented to experience labour market insecurities. Increasing recourse to settlements as a way to resolve complaints – common where regulatory new governance operates as the regulatory paradigm – may also contribute to the explicit erosion of the normative goals of employment standards, with particular implications for employees in precarious jobs often most compelled to accept some form of compensation, regardless of whether settlement amounts fall below amounts claimed. As the ensuing chapters will show, settlements can reproduce the power imbalances of the employment relationship and result in agreements below the minima established in the *ESA*.

Implicit erosion is, in turn, likely to occur in settings where workers are conditioned to accept working conditions that fall below legally established minima, and on account of this normalization, do not view the legal avenues for redressing violations as relevant or efficacious. Implicit erosion is also an outcome of the MOL's well-documented difficulties in recovering back wages from employers who have been issued Orders to Pay Wages (e.g., see Auditor General of Ontario 2004b). Facing the likelihood of non-recovery, potential complainants may simply opt to avoid the formal complaints processes altogether, while recalcitrant employers derive financial benefits from non-compliance. Implicit forms of erosion are also fostered by the turn to regulatory new governance in employment standards enforcement. A regulatory paradigm that assumes non-compliance to be the result of ignorance rather than intention, and one that emphasizes self-regulation and other non-adversarial mechanisms of redress, regulatory new governance–styled enforcement can exacerbate regulatory degradation and increase the likelihood that non-compliance will go unaddressed (Vosko, Grundy, and Thomas 2016).

If left unchecked, the violation, evasion, and erosion of employment standards may lead to their abandonment, a situation in which growing segments of the labour market diverge "from the legal and normative bounds put into place decades ago" (Bernhardt et al. 2008, 2), and specifically the notion that there is a firm set of enforceable social minima. Widespread workplace violations and evasion of employment standards can lead to their erosion and wholesale abandonment; however, broader political, economic, and social processes can promote erosion and abandonment of norms and objectives, which not only weaken protective laws, but create conditions conducive to evasion and violation. As chapters comprising the body of Part Two of this book show, these linked processes are well documented not only in English Canada, but in the United States, parts of Europe (including Britain), Australia, and Quebec (Tucker 2006; Bernhardt et al. 2008; Sargeant and Tucker 2009; Gautié and Schmitt 2010; Kalleberg 2011; Emmenegger, Häusermann, and Seeleib-Kaiser 2012; Fudge, McCrystal, and Sankaran 2012; Weil 2012).

An approach opting consciously for mixed methods or engaged in "active mixing" (Mirchandani et al. 2016) is necessary to document the multiple drivers of the employment standards enforcement gap, as well as their multidimensional effects upon employment standards violations, evasion, erosion, and abandonment. Whereas many mixed-methods researchers rely on a sequential design, where one data set is used to add on to or extend another (Tashakkori and Teddlie 2006), in conducting research for this book we strove to take a dialectical (or "active") approach that involved negotiating epistemological and methodological differences within and among the multidisciplinary, community–university research team members. As is common in transformative mixed-methods research designs (Sweetman, Badiee, and Creswell 2010), to collect data we opted to use a structured (quantitative) analysis of administrative data, drawn principally from the MOL's Employment Standards Information System (ESIS); analyses of large-scale survey data collected by Statistics Canada; and semi-structured (qualitative) interviews and focus groups with low-income workers, workers' advocates (e.g., community legal clinic personnel and worker centre staff), and members of the employment standards inspectorate as well as policy administrators and policymakers at various levels; and we grounded the inquiries of these groups (as well as of administrative and public use data sets) in historical (i.e., archival) and contemporary policy research. The decision to pursue this multi-pronged, multi-method approach was shaped by an acknowledgment of the power of quantitative results in contributing to meaningful change in a political climate concerned with "evidence-based" research and a simultaneous recognition of deficiencies of administrative and survey data in fully discerning social relations and processes shaping employment standards enforcement, specifically processes of racialization and feminization, and a desire to give our participants, drawn from a range of locations, "voice" and have them "tell their stories" (Maynes, Pierce, and Laslett 2008) while at the same time documenting the history and evolution of employment standards policy and practice in Ontario in comparative context.

The "active mixing" we adopt in this book is operationalized through the pursuit of three distinct research foci and associated methods: statistical analysis, qualitative interviews and focus groups, and archival and policy analysis. The first method entails statistical analysis of employment standards enforcement on a number of fronts. A major focus herein is the analysis of data contained in the ESIS. As the chief administrative data set retained under the provincial *ESA*, to which contributors were granted access by the MOL, the ESIS contains information on all complaints submitted and their outcomes, violations detected, inspections conducted, settlements, the use of enforcement mechanisms, wage recovery, and Ontario Labour Relations Board (OLRB) reviews (also referred to as appeals). Some data are provided by the complainant through the online complaints system, whereas claims processors, employment resolution officers (EROs), ESOs, and other MOL officials enter additional data during the lifecycle of a complaint. A central feature of the ESIS is that it provides a nearly complete census of Ontario's employment standards enforcement activities and their outcomes that is not otherwise readily accessible. To facilitate statistical analyses, data were exported from the ESIS and imported into SPSS for statistical analysis, using a process that maintains the complex relational structure of the data tables (see appendix A.1 for further information). The resulting data files allow for more complex analyses that provide insights into the MOL's enforcement processes, as well as the effects of legislative and procedural changes. In these pages, we make unprecedented use of the ESIS data to document, for the first time, key gaps in the enforcement process, such as declining rates of complaints, despite the growing size of Ontario's non-unionized labour force, scant use of deterrence measures, high rates of settlements for amounts often much lower than was originally claimed, and limits of both the recovery system for complaints that have resulted in an Order to Pay Wages and of the appeals process.

Closer consideration of the ESIS data points to both strengths and limitations – or perhaps more accurately to the noises and silences – of administrative data as a source of information on the enforcement gap, reinforcing the need for the active mixing of methods. At the most fundamental level of data collection, the ESIS has noteworthy silences. Specifically, the MOL neither collects demographic data on the social location of complainants nor the employees in workplaces subject to inspections. This silence poses challenges in apprehending the role of social relations such as race and gender in the enforcement process through analysis of this crucial source of administrative data, directly or exclusively.[17] At the same time, the absence risks contributing to the erasure of employees' gender and race, and thus to what some scholars term "colour-blind" racism and/or "gender-blind" sexism, that is, the passive denial of the salience of race and gender through "pretending" not to notice the social location of, in this instance, complainants or employees in workplaces subject to inspection. As Di Angelo (2011, 106–7) argues, pretending that we do not notice race can have the effect of denying racism and holding it in place; thus, the pursuit of anti-racism in employment standards enforcement or, more specifically, improving employment standards enforcement among racialized employees, does not call for "deny[ing] that race matter[s], but ... actively work[ing] towards creating a society in which it *actually* [doesn't] matter."

With respect to the data that are actually collected, another major limitation of the ESIS is that, as an administrative resource for measuring the efficacy of primarily reactive enforcement practices, with regards to complaints, it can only capture the experiences of complainants who successfully enter the system. It tells us nothing about employees who experience a violation but do not complain and thus are not captured in administrative data (Weil and Pyles 2006; Noack, Vosko, and Grundy 2015). Indeed, in reporting on the magnitude of violations without complaints in the United States, Weil and Pyles (2006) estimate conservatively that for every complaint lodged, there are about 130 employment standards violations, and this ratio fluctuates across industries; many sectors that are characterized by high rates of employment standards violations may also generate few complaints compared to sectors characterized by lower violation rates (Weil and Pyles 2006; see also Bernhardt et al. 2009, 11). The decision of workers to file a complaint hinges on a range of factors. Reprisal, which can entail receiving undesirable assignments and schedules, being subject to harassment from management or co-workers, or being terminated, has been a long-standing factor in discouraging employees from initiating employment standards complaints with the MOL (Fudge 1991a; Employment Standards Working Group 1996). This risk is amplified for workers holding temporary or otherwise tenuous citizenship/residency status (Vosko 2013). For example, employees enrolled in the Temporary Foreign Worker and the Seasonal Agricultural Workers Programs are tied to a single employer and can face non-renewal of their employment or potentially deportation if they seek to access the employment standards complaints system, let alone exercise their rights to organize and bargain collectively (Vosko 2013, 2016; Faraday 2014). Many have financial obligations to households abroad and cannot risk debarment from future employment. Furthermore, in light of histories of colonialism and systemic racism, racialized people in precarious jobs may not be in a position to "choose" to engage state authority. For people of colour, state law enforcement may be inextricably bound up in oppressive racial orderings. For this reason, many racialized and recent immigrant employees may not see employment standards enforcement by government officials as a suitable means of securing labour protection.

Still other individuals remain invisible within administrative data on complaints because they do not experience employment standards violations as such, as a result of the normalization of violations and/or substandard conditions among employees in workplaces and industries, particularly those affected by exemptions and special rules and/or labour market insecurity. As Pollert and Charlwood (2009, 347) point out, the threshold at which workers register employment standards violations as a problem may be quite high, "especially at the lower end of the labour market, where habituation to experiences such as work intensification, insecurity, low pay and coercion lower expectations of working life." Even workers with good knowledge of their employment standards rights may assess whether they have experienced a violation of employment standards by comparing their situation to social norms established by their previous work experience and the experiences of others in their workplace and social milieu.

Our recognition that employment standards enforcement differentially affects workers in different industries and from different social groups, with particular consequences for workers historically marginalized in the labour force, informs our conscious pursuit of a transformative, dialectical, mixed-methods approach. We conducted seventy-seven in-depth interviews with workers in Toronto, Sudbury, and Windsor who were engaged in low-wage work with no access to union representation. To develop an understanding of the diverse ways in which workers respond to workplace problems, roughly half of those interviewed had filed a complaint with the MOL. In recognition of the fact that the social location of employees and the contexts in which they are employed can shape their experiences and scope of action, we interviewed employees in different social locations, paying particular attention to social relations of gender, race, and age, as well as to citizenship/ immigration status and in different industries and occupations.

The interviews sought to capture and give voice to the subjugated knowledge of individuals and groups with limited social power and thereby to help augment our study of the agency of the actors affected (Hesse-Biber 2012). For example, our guides for worker interviews aimed to reveal the nature and extent of explicit or demonstrable violations of the law in the province without requiring respondents to have any knowledge of employment standards provisions, given that many people are not familiar with Ontario's *ESA* and its associated protections. In addition to assessing outright violations of employment standards, worker interviews entailed open-ended questions about problems at work, in order to acknowledge and elicit workers' own definitions of a workplace problem. This process aided considerably in elucidating the multidimensional conception of the enforcement gap described above.

The interviews conducted with workers drew on a combination of purposeful sampling techniques in order to identify information-rich respondents (Patton 1990). We adopted a stratified form of criterion sampling, as potential respondents were included only if they met particular criteria. With the intent of highlighting the experiences of the precariously employed, we focused on recruiting workers receiving low pay in their main job (less than $18 per hour).

Our approach to worker interviews was premised on an understanding of participants' agency as diverse in form and situated in relation to "formations of capital, the state, the community and the labour market in which workers are embedded" (Coe and Jordhus-Lier 2011, 214). We were interested in tracing how workers thought about possible actions they could take and how and why they consulted with other people to navigate and ameliorate the negative conditions at their workplaces, particularly conditions that translated into violations of the *ESA*.[18] Contrary to the noteworthy silences in administrative data, worker interviews – especially workers' descriptions of their experiences – were saturated by perceptions of how social relations of race and gender as well as immigration status and often age operate in employment standards enforcement. In telling the stories elicited in worker interviews, therefore, a central challenge involved documenting social relations shaping employment standards enforcement and disentangling (and also sometimes seeking to entangle) experiences of sexism and racism as well as (albeit less frequently) ageism and ableism and explicit violation, evasion, erosion, and/or abandonment of the normative goals and policy objectives underpinning the *ESA*.

The chapters comprising Part One of this book also draw on a different subset of qualitative interviews, specifically those seeking to document the day-to-day enforcement practices adopted by staff of the MOL. Unlike those conducted with workers, these interviews were structured as a condition of access to this personnel under our research agreement with the MOL. On the basis of this agreement, we conducted interviews with fifty-two EROs and ESOs. We asked them to describe their work process, the principles informing their approach to claims investigation, the challenges that both employees and employers face in the complaints process, what improvements they have seen in enforcement during their tenure as an enforcement official, and finally what reforms they would like to see. For ESOs involved in workplace inspections, we asked how businesses are selected for inspection, the steps involved in inspections, including what ESOs do once violations have been discovered, as well as in what circumstances and, if so, to what extent follow-up is involved. These interviews provided insights into the way front-line staff carry out investigations and the scope of discretion afforded to them in their work with complainants and employers. They also revealed how ESOs negotiate contending requirements for rapid complaint closure and expectations of due process, and how they approach "difficult" cases, that is, complaints in which the circumstances are highly contested by employees and employers. For a higher-level view of the MOL's enforcement system, we also conducted interviews with fifteen employment standards program and district managers covering the five regions of Ontario in which enforcement takes place, and with six regional program coordinators across the province as well as with eight provincial specialists and policy advisors. We asked these groups of MOL staff to share their views of the central challenges facing the enforcement activities of the MOL.

Overall, ERO and ESO interviews revealed, in particular, the importance of enforcement orientation to processes of employment standards enforcement; they highlighted, at once, the significance of generation (particularly when front-line staff joined the Employment Practices Branch) as salient to informants' understanding of enforcement challenges and, in particular, enforcement officials' assumptions about why, how, and when complainants and employers act the way they do. Many of these assumptions, too, were saturated by particular conceptions of social relations of race and gender. For example, although seemingly innocuous on the surface, a noteworthy theme emerging in interview data, echoed in the analysis of the ESIS data, was the problem of small employers. In describing this problem, several EROs and ESOs attributed non-compliance of small employers to employers who are themselves immigrants and the lower workplace standards assumed to characterize employment in the Global South[19] and viewed encouraging such employers to abide by Canadian standards as a central part of their jobs. Such themes emerging in the MOL interview data and their effects are noteworthy in two regards: their perpetuation of stereotypes that contribute to the racialization of the employers concerned, as well as their workforces (James 2012) and, more subtly, to the frequent decision to "tolerate" rather than punish small firms' otherwise objectionable (i.e., non-compliant) behaviours in favour of greater education.[20]

Beyond workers and MOL staff, we conducted individual interviews as well as a focus group with representatives of community organizations including workers' centres, several legal clinics, and an immigrant-serving organization. Across these interviews with workers, and all levels of MOL staff, as well as the focus group, we sought to capture the continuities and gaps between precariously employed workers' understandings of their rights, enforcement officials' understandings of their role and practices, and the roles played by other actors such as worker advocates and legal case workers. While we were interested in stakeholders' perspectives, in conducting these interviews we diverged from conventional approaches to capturing stakeholder perspectives that focus on standardization of instruments and triangulation of results wherein the researcher is expected to draw on the different perspectives of interview groups to attain the "real" or "true" answer or experience (Janesick 1994). To fill out our study of enforcement practices, we also analysed MOL press releases, staff training manuals, and other documents that provide information on the organization and operation of employment standards enforcement.

Extensive historical (i.e., archival) and contemporary policy research also grounded our inquiries. We undertook a detailed survey of archival records related to the development of Ontario's *ESA* and its enforcement, acquired through detailed records requests to the Archives of Ontario. Dating from the 1960s through to the 1990s, these records contain materials from MOL records including ministerial correspondence, background research papers, legislative records, and communications from employers, employer associations, women's organizations, and organized labour, including the Ontario Federation of Labour and

Canadian Labour Congress. We took pictures of the documents and converted the pictures into word-searchable PDFs using ABBYY FineReader software. To facilitate timely documentary analysis, we developed a comprehensive inventory of records. The inventory allowed us to analyse records according to themes such as *ESA* exemptions, *ESA* enforcement, specific *ESA* provisions related to working time, wages, non-wage benefits, termination, and severance, as well as to explore different legislative reviews that have transpired, and industry and sector profiles developed by the MOL. This archival research supported the analysis of the evolution and normative framing of employment standards laws in Ontario and the social processes surrounding the evolution of the substance of employment standards and their enforcement. It helped us better understand how exemptions and special rules limiting coverage of the *ESA* were established, revealing the central role of industry lobbyists in advocating for exemptions and the principled reticence among MOL officials over the adoption of some exemptions. Archival research also illuminated the roots of principles and practices that underpinned workplace inspections. The extensive analysis of contemporary policy documents, such as annual reports, legislative hearing testimony, or internal administrative documents such as administrative directives, made accessible to the research team through research agreements reached with the MOL, supplemented this archival component. In these ways, historical and contemporary policy analysis represents both a starting point and an aid in understanding the roots of aspects of the prevailing employment standards regime.

**6. Chapter Overview**

The chapters that follow explore different dimensions of the enforcement gap in the province in comparative perspective in two parts. Those chapters centring on Ontario, representing a collaborative outcome of the Closing the Enforcement Gap research partnership and comprising the body of Part One, do so by following the enforcement process as it typically unfolds therein. They chronicle its different, yet often overlapping stages or aspects, from educational measures that seek to prevent employment standards violations before they occur, through to the complaints intake system, options for settlement, the organization of workplace inspections, the recovery of entitlements, and finally, deterrence measures. The chapters comprising Part Two offer views from elsewhere. They contextualize and further illuminate the analyses of contours of the employment standards enforcement gap in Ontario and are prepared by internationally recognized experts in the field studying developments outside the province. Each explores parallel challenges that prevail in Australia, Britain, and the United States at various scales (i.e., the national and subnational), as well as the province of Quebec, and canvasses promising practices offering potential lessons for closing the enforcement gap in Ontario.

*Part One: Charting the Employment Standards Enforcement Gap in Ontario*

Initiating Part One's enquiry into the enforcement gap in Ontario, chapter 2, "Responsibilization, Reprisal, and (Non-)Remediation: Interrogating the Role of an Individualized Complaints System," examines the formal employment standards complaints system under the *ESA*. After outlining the complaints process in Ontario, the chapter argues that making individual complaints entails challenges and barriers for many employees who seek redress for workplace violations, as the employment standards enforcement system, reflecting patterns of erosion, is not organized in a way that fosters the exercise of employee voice (Vosko 2013). In particular, the expectation that employees initiate complaints disregards power imbalances in the employment relationship, often shaped by social relations of inequality such as gender, race, and immigration status, which make engagement with the complaints system very risky for many employees – risks that are not offset by confidence in the ability of government officials to recover monetary entitlements and prevent retaliation. The chapter draws on administrative data to demonstrate that only a small minority of employees who initiate complaints attempt to access the legislative protections of employment standards while they are still employed in the job in which they experienced violations, and that claims of retaliation increased in the early 2010s – likely related to the now overturned requirement, formalized under the *OBA*, that employees must attempt to resolve grievances with their employers as a condition of accessing the complaints system. The chapter also draws on qualitative interviews with employees and MOL officials to reflect on employees' experience of challenges and barriers to gaining effective redress in the complaints-handing process. In conclusion, the chapter identifies measures that may make the complaints system more accessible to more employees, including allowing for third party and anonymous complaints, strengthened anti-retaliation provisions, and extending liability for employment standards violations beyond the direct employer.

Chapter 3, "Administering Complaints: Dilemmas of Accountability," moves beyond the accessibility of the complaints system for aggrieved employees to explore its administration in greater detail. The chapter examines how the MOL's reactive and individualized complaints system, designed initially on the assumption that employment standards violations would be less frequent than they are, has become overwhelmed, often resulting in chronic backlogs and delays for employees seeking redress. Drawing on the ESIS data, as well as worker and MOL staff interviews, the chapter then explores the MOL's attempts to manage the deluge of complaints through an emphasis on new public management – an administrative paradigm that aims to remake the bureaucracy by, among other things, introducing rigorous forms of performance measurement that attempt to speed up complaints processing as well as regulatory new governance–inspired reforms that seek to limit the number of complaints that reach the MOL. It argues that while both new public management–oriented measures and regulatory new governance styled reforms, particularly the embrace of regulated self-regulation, can relieve pressure on the complaints system, by overlooking power imbalances in workplaces, they risk eroding its accessibility and integrity and impose undue burdens and costs onto the shoulders of workers. While recognizing recent efforts to re-invest in complaints handling, the chapter argues that the problem of an overburdened complaints system cannot be separated from weaknesses in the overall enforcement system. That is, in a context where there is so little risk to employers for violating employment standards – given the historical dearth of inspections and so few deterrence measures used against employers who are caught – pressure on the individual complaints system will likely continue to grow. The chapter concludes that, while maintaining its commitment to investigate every permissible claim, the MOL must also invest more heavily in strengthened recovery mechanisms, workplace inspections, and deterrence measures that impose a meaningful penalty on violating employers, to ultimately alter employer behaviour in ways that will reduce the rate of violations in the first place.

Chapter 4, "Recovering Employees' Wages?," examines the MOL's ability to collect money from employers demonstrated to have violated monetary employment standards. Drawing on an analysis of data contained in the ESIS, as well as interviews with workers and MOL staff, the chapter identifies features of monetary claims that shape the likelihood that they will result in an Order to Pay Wages rather than be resolved voluntarily. It then examines more closely the recovery rates of Orders to Pay Wages, highlighting both their low overall recovery rate and predictors of non-recovery. Complainants with large entitlement amounts and complainants from small firms (fewer than twenty employees) are less likely to be paid voluntarily, and when Orders to

Pay Wages are issued, the probability of recovery is low. The chapter argues that the MOL's challenges in recovering monetary orders to pay are a fundamental weakness in its enforcement system, which erodes all other aspects of enforcement. Enhancements to the accessibility of the complaints processes, or efforts to increase employees' awareness of their workplace rights, are of limited value if those employees who assume the risk of coming forward wind up with little more than symbolic victories. Low rates of recovery of monetary orders also implicitly suggest to employers that they will not face severe consequences if they ignore the MOL. In conclusion, the chapter suggests that deficiencies in recovery are not intractable, however, and thereby outlines measures that hold potential to strengthen the MOL's collections capacity.

Chapter 5, "The Contradictory Role of Workplace Inspections," begins by outlining growing recognition among provincial legislators of the need to move beyond complaint-based, reactive enforcement and adopt more proactive strategies. Starting in 2004, the MOL directed more resources to workplace inspections, with the goal of ensuring compliance and increasing awareness of employers and employees' rights and responsibilities. The chapter offers an overview of the different types of workplace inspections conducted by the MOL since that time, as well as the types of businesses that tend to be inspected, focusing on the employees and employers most likely to be affected by these inspections. Against the backdrop of this profile, it argues that the shift towards devoting greater resources to workplace inspection occurred alongside moves, emblematic of regulatory new governance, towards regulated self-regulation and a greater compliance orientation emphasizing responsibilization, adhering to the belief that violations occur as a result of employers' lack of knowledge rather than a deliberate cost-cutting strategy. Thus, the convergence of proactive enforcement with a compliance-oriented approach substantially limits the efficacy of workplace inspections and its potential to reduce the number and severity of employment standards violations. In developing this argument, the chapter identifies steps in the inspection process that reflect the underlying assumptions of the regulatory new governance paradigm, such as the emphasis on education, and inspections' limited scope. It also draws on both the ESIS and interview data to demonstrate the impact that adherence to regulatory new governance has on the use of potential deterrence measures.

Chapter 6, "The Deterrence Gap: Towards an Explanation," turns to the question of penalties for employers who violate the *ESA*. It begins by demonstrating the very limited but variable use of meaningful deterrence measures. Using both archival and interview data, it argues that deterrence policy has been mediated through competing political, economic, ideological, and institutional factors, some of which are historical and some of which are emergent. While recognizing the contradictory effects of neoliberal governance and globalization on enforcement politics, economics, ideologies, and practices, the chapter seeks a more grounded, in-depth understanding of the gap between policy and practice through an examination of the enforcement decisions and rationales of front-line inspectors and managers. Along with demonstrating substantial variation in inspectors' willingness to use different deterrence measures, it identifies shared rationales for limiting the use of deterrence grounded in current MOL policy and the longer-standing institutional emphasis on individual complaints and compliance over inspections and deterrence. The chapter also examines time constraints and procedural requirements as important factors in shaping ESO judgments on the use of enforcement. In conclusion, it suggests that these constraining influences can be partially overcome, although it is difficult to sustain a more deterrence-oriented policy and practice.

Chapter 7, "Strengthening Participatory Approaches to Enforcement," starts from the premise that, although the enforcement of employment standards is generally conceptualized as the responsibility of government agencies, in practice, both governmental and non-governmental actors may participate in the process of ensuring compliance with employment standards. The chapter considers the potential for participatory employment standards enforcement involving community organizations – especially workers' centres – to counter the employment standards enforcement gap and to create alternatives to both individualized complaint-based enforcement mechanisms and "top down" enforcement strategies of government agencies that accord workers a passive role in the enforcement process. The chapter begins with a review of scholarly literature on models of "participatory enforcement," focusing attention on models of employment standards enforcement that include the participation of community organizations. Based on an analysis of data drawn from individual interviews, focus groups, and government documents, the chapter then highlights limits to the current enforcement regime and points towards ways in which it may be strengthened through the participation of community organizations. Next, using examples of workers' centres based in Sudbury, Windsor, and Toronto, the chapter addresses the ways in which – through activities that include advocacy, legal assistance, labour rights education, assistance with complaints, and community organizing – these organizations support workers in navigating the enforcement process. While not always engaged in enforcement directly, by contributing to the empowerment of workers in precarious jobs and thereby enhancing worker agency, and by fostering a worker-centred approach to employment standards enforcement, these community organizations counter some of the weaknesses of the current approach to government-centred employment standards enforcement. The chapter concludes by assessing the potential for a model of participatory enforcement that can address the crisis of employment standards enforcement in Ontario.

*Part Two: Views from Elsewhere: Contextualizing the Employment Standards Enforcement Gap in Ontario*

A key premise of the Closing the Gap research partnership through which this book emerged is that the province of Ontario is not alone in confronting the spread of precarious employment and its associated regulatory challenges. Other jurisdictions in Canada and beyond are grappling with the ossification of traditional employment standards enforcement models and experimenting with new ones in attempts to shore up employment standards. To understand developments elsewhere, and to maximize opportunities for policy learning, the partnership incorporated an international reference group composed of leading employment standards scholars in other liberal market economies. From the outset, Ontario-based researchers worked closely with this group, initially in research design, and subsequently throughout the life of the study through regular meetings with individual reference group members, and ultimately through a workshop focused on this book.

Reflecting the cross-jurisdictional scope of the larger research partnership, Part Two of this book places developments in Ontario in a comparative perspective. It encompasses contributions by leading employment standards specialists from beyond Ontario who were invited to reflect on whether or not there is an enforcement gap in their respective jurisdiction and, if so, its similarity to or difference from the one documented in Ontario in chapters 2–7. Contributors were also asked to examine the responses from legislators and workers' advocates to enforcement challenges in their jurisdiction, and to identify pitfalls to avoid and promising policies and practices to consider pursuing in redressing such challenges. And they were encouraged to do so with an emphasis on their own focal areas of research in this domain. The result is a segment of the book devoted to views from elsewhere.

Based on his exploration of the similarly compliance-oriented system of employment standards regulation in Britain, in chapter 8, Nick Clark points to the significant problems of enforcement with an emphasis on the phenomenon of wage theft. The portrait painted in the chapter draws on collaborative research carried out under Clark's leadership of the Unpaid Britain Project at Middlesex University, an initiative identifying the ways in which non-payment of wages occurs by studying the processes and attitudes that surround its incidence and resolution to identify improved means of both restitution and prevention. "Unpaid Britain: Challenges of Enforcement and Wage Recovery" utilizes survey data from the British government's Labour Force and Family Resource Surveys, administrative data from various sources, documentary analysis of judgments, and interviews with workers, employers, and third parties. What emerges is a textured understanding of how parties experience non-payment in Britain and deficiencies in the complex web of laws and policies that comprise the regulatory framework permitting its expansion. Clark shows that while Britain's system of enforcement is quite different from the other jurisdictions covered in the book (e.g., Britons lack a central government agency responsible for enforcement), many of the same enforcement problems, several of which bear the imprint of regulatory new governance, plague the British and Ontario cases. Clark points to striking parallels in employers' rationales and workers' responses to wage theft.

Next, chapter 9, by Tess Hardy and John Howe, explores the emergence of a federal labour inspectorate in 2006 in Australia – a new statutory agency known as the Fair Work Ombudsman (FWO) – with the centralization of employment standards enforcement at the federal level therein. In "Out of the Shadows and into the Spotlight: The Sweeping Evolution of Employment Standards Enforcement in Australia," Hardy and Howe explore the prominent role played by this agency on the workplace relations stage against mounting evidence of a persistent enforcement gap fuelled historically by the longstanding assumption, shared in Ontario, that most Australian employers are law abiding and that non-compliance with employment standards may be explained principally by a lack of knowledge or education and thus corrected by regulated self-regulation. Rather than accept this explanation, however, these authors' point of departure is that structural factors fuel this gap and should thus inform responses to it – a sentiment that, they argue, increasingly informs the FWO's approach. Emphasizing key innovations forged under the FWO, chapter 9 thus charts and evaluates the efficacy of the agency's attempts to move away from an individualized, complaints-driven orientation towards a detection and sanctioning approach drawing on both the theory of responsive regulation and elements of the strategic enforcement paradigm. In the process, the chapter highlights several noteworthy developments in Australia, such as the introduction of accessorial liability under the *Fair Work Act* (the Australian equivalent to the *ESA* at the federal level), which, in instances in which a contravention is found, makes all persons "involved" potentially liable under a civil remedy provision. It also profiles a series of measures, adopted simultaneously under the *Fair Work Amendment, Protecting Vulnerable Workers Act*, directed at making franchisors and parent companies operating under business models premised on wage underpayment more accountable for such practices.

While also highlighting innovations in their jurisdiction, chapter 10, "Enforcing Employment Standards in Quebec: One Step Forward, Two Steps Backward?," by Dalia Gesualdi-Fecteau and Guylaine Vallée, focuses more centrally on the unique features of the province's *Act Respecting Labour Standards (LSA)* and their utility compared to Ontario's *ESA*. While a single branch of the MOL, with recourse to a Labour Relations Board with a wider mandate, oversees the administration of employment standards in Ontario, a new institution, the Labour Standards, Equity, Occupational Health and Safety Commission, operates in Quebec. As Gesualdi-Fecteau and Vallée show, the commission arguably presents opportunities to integrate these areas of law but also some significant risks, particularly the potential loss of the specialized knowledge of the commission. With regard to representation, however, as Gesualdi-Fecteau and Vallée demonstrate, the Quebec model offers greater supports for aggrieved employees than its Ontario counterpart. Indeed, complainants who make claims in areas such as unpaid wages, wrongful dismissal, and psychological harassment receive legal representation. Claims-processing times are also shorter than in Ontario. The regime in Quebec is thus an exemplar in some areas yet lags behind other jurisdictions under study in other areas.

Finally, in chapter 11, "Improving Workplace Conditions through Strategic Enforcement: The U.S. Experience," David Weil reflects on his experience as administrator of the Wage and Hour Division (WHD) of the U.S. Department of Labor under President Obama, placing emphasis on the agency's experimentation with strategic enforcement. Weil's reflections are those of a career academic with a unique opportunity to lead a major agency with responsibilities directly related to his longstanding research interests – a rare opportunity on account of the frequent divide, which this book seeks to transcend, between the worlds of practice and academia. The chapter, then, offers a mix of traditional scholarly analysis and a reflection on a personal journal that provides a fruitful middle ground enquiry into the world of employment standards enforcement in the federal jurisdiction in the United States.

More specifically, although, under Obama, the WHD made significant changes to the scope of labour protection (e.g., by increasing coverage considerably) and, among other things, providing for paid family leave for federal contractors for the first time, the chapter focuses on fundamental changes the agency undertook to adopt a strategic approach to enforcement and the major organizational transformation it underwent in the process. Through this strategic enforcement experiment, Weil explores how the WHD sought to expand the capacity of the agency to ensure that the 130 million workers covered by federal labour standards laws would receive their protection and the trade-offs involved in pursuit of this important aim. One such trade-off was the decision to reduce resources directed to complaints in order to extend greater resources to the agency's proactive investigative functions – a necessary and innovative experiment in this jurisdiction, elements of which offer promise in improving proactive measures in Ontario, but one misfit to the province in other ways, if adopted wholesale (as the findings of chapters 2 and 5 suggest). A related trade-off was to reorganize agency targets, and hence the organization of the agency, to devote greater emphasis to industries and sectors characterized by high levels of violation and practices such as subcontracting, franchising, and the use of supply chains more broadly – an inspiring move in creating greater openings for outreach to communities affected by the enforcement gap and thus to participatory enforcement – and likewise minimize longstanding modes of evaluating success, centring more on individual firms and cases.

Collectively, these views from elsewhere offer a range of insights into closing the enforcement gap in Ontario. After interrogating core aspects of Ontario's employment standards regime in Part One, revealing a gap of substantial depth and magnitude as well as structural barriers that prevent employees from exercising their voice (shaped by racialization and feminization as well as divisions based on citizenship and residency status, age, etc.), and canvassing the state of employment standards enforcement in Britain, Australia, Quebec, and the United States, with attention to the adoption of innovations therein, chapter 12 considers how such policies and practices taking shape can inform changes in Ontario. In conclusion, it suggests that the employment standards enforcement gap is preventable and points the way towards addressing the most serious problems.

# PART ONE

# Charting the Employment Standards Enforcement Gap in Ontario

# Responsibilization, Reprisal, and (Non-) Remediation: Interrogating the Role of an Individualized Complaints System

In Ontario the detection and enforcement of employment standards violations rely primarily on individual employees reporting and pursuing claims via a complaints system. Employees covered by the provisions of the *Employment Standards Act (ESA)* are encouraged to file a complaint with the Ministry of Labour (MOL) if they believe that a current or recent employer has violated their rights under the Act. This complaints-based enforcement system is premised on the assumption that individual employees are the best source of information about employers' practices and that they have the most immediate interest in obtaining a remedy for those that are illegal.

This chapter critically interrogates the role of the complaints system in employment standards enforcement. Drawing on qualitative interviews with employees and MOL officials as well as administrative data collected by the MOL, we illustrate how labour market insecurities and workplace power imbalances can make engagement with the complaints system a risky venture for many employees, especially given the threat of reprisal and the lengthy and uncertain processes surrounding the resolution of individual grievances. These constraints, coupled with the continuing prominence of the individual complaints system in Ontario's employment standards regime, mean that only a small fraction of aggrieved employees is likely to ever see their legal rights under the Act enforced.

The incorporation of a compliance orientation – emanating partly from tenets of regulatory new governance that emphasizes the need for de-bureaucratized and less adversarial forms of intervention – into the employment standards enforcement system further exacerbates the inaccessibility of the complaints process. This influence was most clearly visible in the imposition of a relatively long-lived requirement that most employees attempt to resolve their complaint with their employer before filing a complaint, as well as in the range of accompanying self-help and informational materials encouraging employees to step into the role of "workplace protagonist" (Tucker 2013b) and enforce their own rights. In the analysis that follows, we chart how and to what extent the share of Ontario's labour force that files a complaint has decreased, as well as the increase in the number of complaints that include a claim of reprisal, alongside the implementation of these requirements.

These interrelated arguments unfold in three parts. Section 1 reviews key insights from scholarly literature on the inadequacies of a reactive, individualized, complaints-based employment standards enforcement system. It also defines and critically assesses how principles associated with the compliance orientation of regulatory new governance are incorporated into the employment standards complaints system, focusing particularly on the role of self-regulation (i.e., dispute resolution efforts in which workers themselves engage in efforts to eliminate workplace problems) and responsibilization (i.e., placing greater onus on employees in enforcement). After offering a brief outline of the complaints process in Ontario, section 2 details the challenges and barriers that employees face when attempting to file a complaint – which stem from their labour force position and/or the organization of the complaints system itself. Section 3 then illustrates how reforms influenced by regulatory new governance have exacerbated rather than alleviated many of these barriers to filing a complaint. In conclusion, we identify measures that may make the complaints system more accessible to more employees. While raising employees' awareness of their legal rights is arguably an essential part of any enforcement regime, this emphasis, in and of itself, is inadequate. Rather, it must be teamed with robust measures, such as allowing for third-party and anonymous complaints, strengthened reprisal provisions to reduce the risk associated with making a complaint, and extending liability for employment standards violations beyond the direct employer.

## 1. Growing Precariousness and the Inadequacy of a Reactive Compliance-Oriented Complaints System

Patterns of economic restructuring over the past four decades, which were described and analysed in chapter 1, have prompted growing interest in the adequacy of legally mandated employment standards to provide an enforceable floor of workplace rights (Davidov 2010; Weil 2010; Gellatly et al. 2011; Vosko et al. 2011), particularly among labour researchers and workers' advocates.

Several studies on employment standards enforcement highlight the weaknesses of reactive and individual complaints-based enforcement regimes. A central insight of this literature is that workers are often unable to complain formally for a variety of reasons, with the result that only a small fraction of violations are ever redressed through complaints systems (Grundy et al. 2017). As noted in chapter 1, in the U.S. case, for example, researchers find that only a fraction of violations of the *Fair Labor Standards Act*'s (*FLSA*) overtime provisions are reflected in the number of complaints received by the Wages and Hours Division (WHD) (Weil and Pyles 2006, 76). Some workers may not perceive the employment standards violations that they experience as a problem to be solved, especially when such violations are normalized in the workplace and/or when they do not possess or cannot acquire the documentary evidence required to validate their claims (Grundy et al. 2017; Vosko et al. 2017). Additionally, workers may not fully understand the different legislative frameworks governing the workplace (employment standards, occupational health and safety, human rights) and which is most relevant in particular situations.

Workers' decisions to file complaints hinge partly on their perceptions of the efficacy of the complaint process in achieving remediation, as well as the assistance available to them throughout the complaint process (Weil and Pyles 2006; Grundy et al. 2017). Additionally, the literature on employment standards violations points consistently to reprisals as a core problem disrupting the effectiveness of complaints-based systems of enforcement (Davidov 2010; Vosko et al. 2011; Grundy et al. 2017). This problem has intensified with declining rates of unionization, since collective agreements have long served as a buffer against arbitrary and sudden dismissal and a means of ensuring voice at work. Vulnerability to reprisal is thus a major impediment to the exercise of voice and undermines any regulatory arrangement premised upon it – a risk that is amplified substantially among employees historically disadvantaged in the labour force, such as women and people with temporary or otherwise tenuous citizenship/residency status (Vosko 2013).

In their recognition of the inadequacies of reactive, complaints-based labour enforcement, numerous studies have pointed to the growing popularity of regulatory new governance approaches, albeit levelling different critiques of how various elements of this paradigm are applied in the context of employment standards enforcement (Estlund 2005; Davidov 2010; Vosko, Grundy, and Thomas 2016). As noted in chapter 1, a central tenet of regulatory new governance is that the traditional forms of top-down regulation are "inherently cumbersome, ineffective, and heavily executed" and need to be replaced with "light touch" regulation (Lobel 2004, 308; Lobel 2005; Estlund 2005). This "soft-law" approach envisions a smaller role for public regulation and the threat of legal punishment as a means of achieving compliance, based in part on the view that actors previously assumed to be adversaries actually have shared interests and mutual dependencies, making them suitable partners in the pursuit of a public good (Lobel 2004). In the context of employment standards, to the extent that it reflects these tenets, the compliance orientation of regulatory new governance is built on the assumption that employers principally disobey the law inadvertently, and thus the frequency of employment standards violations can be substantially reduced by mandating workplace practices and procedures that foster learning and mutual engagement (Lobel 2004). As such, compliance with the law can be achieved through techniques premised on the notion that employees and employers can express themselves equally freely, persuade one another to reach a middle ground, and share information (Davidov 2010).

While the move away from hard-law approaches and towards soft-law regulation may appear at first glance to reflect a neoliberal, deregulatory approach to governance, regulatory new governance proponents insist that they "offer a third way vision between unregulated markets and top-down government controls" (Lobel 2012, 3). Reflecting the notion that governments should steer rather than row, they construe governments as actors responsible for developing and monitoring regulatory processes with the goal of fostering a culture of compliance within softly regulated industries (Lobel 2012). Regulated self-regulation, ostensibly promoting increased workers' voice within workplaces, is at the core of this third-way approach. Emblematic of this approach are dispute resolution efforts in which workers are encouraged or required to engage in reflexive efforts to eliminate workplace problems. As such, they are expected to identify problems and to continuously seek possible solutions, starting with their workplace. If internal problem-solving fails, then it is the responsibility of workers to seek government assistance (Lobel 2012). Proponents of regulated self-regulation contend that it introduces flexibility and responsiveness into the regulatory regime and reduces the cost and inefficiency associated with top-down regulation, while promoting the internalization of employment law and its enforcement into the workplace itself (Estlund 2005). Accordingly, by institutionalizing norms and procedures inside the workplace, regulated self-regulation creates "the opportunity to revive employees' voice inside firms" and to promote "democratic self-governance within the workplace" (Estlund 2005, 324–6).

Within the realm of employment standards enforcement, scholarly literature on the rise of soft-law in general, and regulated self-regulation in particular, raises several powerful critiques. A range of scholars argue that advocates of soft-law often fail to adequately recognize how adversarial relations may impede the enforcement of the law (Gray 2006; Davidov 2010; Gunningham 2016; Vosko, Grundy, and Thomas 2016). More specifically, reforms premised on regulated self-regulation overlook power imbalances inherent in the employment relationship, including those shaped by social relations of race, gender, citizenship and immigration status, ability, and age, among others (Vosko, Grundy, and Thomas 2016). Research calls into question the central assumption of the compliance orientation that underpins regulatory new governance: that violations flow from ignorance or incompetence and are therefore not intentional or shaped by industry structures that encourage systemic violations (Bernhardt et al. 2008; Weil 2014; Vosko et al. 2017). Additionally, studies stress that non-compliance with employment standards is a labour cost reduction strategy for a growing number of employers (Davidov 2010; Bernhardt et al. 2013) occurring within the context of a broader shift in the balance of workplace power towards employers, the rollback of trade union freedoms, and deregulation (Burgess and Campbell 1998; Panitch and Swartz 2003; Vosko 2006; Bernhardt et al. 2008; Pollert 2009; Thomas 2009). In this environment, a focus on fostering internal responsibility to achieve compliance at the expense of strong external enforcement creates a major risk of "lowering the standards and legitimizing employment terms below the minimum that society finds acceptable" (Davidov 2010, 2). Indeed, "soft" law and "self" regulation can deepen rather than mitigate the asymmetries of power that fuel regulatory crises in the first place (Vosko, Grundy, and Thomas 2016). Under these conditions, soft and self-enforcement mechanisms undermine the ability of workers to access their rights (Seidman 2009; Davidov 2010; Tombs and Whyte 2010; Tucker 2013a, 2013b) and thereby contribute to the reproduction of power imbalances in the workplace. The case of the employment standards complaints system in Ontario bears out these critiques of reactive, complaints-based enforcement, while demonstrating how compliance-oriented reforms that emphasize regulated self-regulation contribute to making the complaints system less accessible overall.

## 2. Who Accesses the Employment Standards Complaints System? Understanding Labour Force and Social Locations

To access the employment standards complaints system, employees must formally file a complaint with the MOL. This process entails completing a form, ten pages long prior to January 2018 and four pages long thereafter, that requests information about the employee, the employer, the nature and history of the employment relationship, and details of alleged violations, as well as collecting supporting documents (such as pay stubs, records of hours worked, employment contracts, or termination notices), and then submitting the material online or by mail. Employees can file complaints that make claims relating to one or more standards specified in the *ESA* (i.e., complaints can, and typically do, include more than one claim), such as payment of wages, overtime pay, public holiday pay or vacation pay, or eating periods and rest periods. Crucially, the *ESA*'s definition of who constitutes an "employee" establishes whether or not a worker is covered by its provisions and can access the complaints system. Contrary to jurisdictions like Australia, Quebec, and the United States, the *ESA* has a narrow scope of coverage, directed principally to non-unionized employees and their employers[1] and subjecting various groups of employees to a range of exemptions and special rules (on exemptions and special rules, see chapter 1; on scope and coverage elsewhere, see chapters 9, 10, and 11). Workers who are not formally classified as employees, such as unpaid family workers, are therefore not covered by the provisions of the *ESA*. Nor are those who are misclassified as non-employees (i.e., as dependent or independent contractors; on the question of employee misclassification and its effects on coverage, see chapter 1). Similarly, unionized workers cannot file a complaint with the MOL, as they must resort to the grievance systems established by their collective agreements. The *ESA* also does not cover those engaged in a secondary or post-secondary school approved work program; those who hold political, judicial, religious, or elected trade union office; individuals engaged in Ontario Works (workfare) community programs; inmates or young offenders involved in work programs; and those working in federally regulated industries, as their conditions are governed by the Canada Labour Code. As discussed in chapter 1, exemptions and special rules under the *ESA* further limit the application of its protections. Indeed, the majority of Ontario employees work in occupations or industries where their coverage under the *ESA* may be affected by exemptions and special rules.

The vast majority of complaints filed with the MOL relate to outstanding money that employees claim their employer owes them (as opposed to complaints about non-monetary issues, such as those related to working time or record-keeping) (for a parallel profile of complaints in Britain, see chapter 8). Administrative data providing a near-census of employment standards complaints in Ontario show that employees most commonly make claims for unpaid wages, termination pay, and vacation pay/time (see graph 2.1). From the fiscal years 2008/09–2014/15, the median total amount claimed by complainants was approximately $1,250, a substantial sum of money that may cause hardship for low-wage workers and their families. The prevalence of claims for unpaid wages is noteworthy because, among the standards that can be claimed, unpaid wages are unlikely to be simply attributable to incompetence or a lack of information on the part of the employer. The likelihood that unpaid wages are the result of an employer's intentional practice is underscored by their size: the median amount of unpaid wages claimed by employees is $727 (the median entitlement for unpaid wages after assessment by an early resolution officer (ERO)/employment standards officer (ESO) is $793). These unpaid wages can represent a substantial portion of expected earnings for low-wage workers and suggest that wage-related violations are typically more egregious than acknowledged in a compliance framework, which downplays employers' intentional violations of the law.

Notably, employees in some industries are far more likely to file employment standards complaints. As elsewhere, employment standards complainants are concentrated in industrial sectors characterized by multiple dimensions of precariousness and insecurity. For instance, compared to their share in the Ontario labour force, the MOL receives a very high number of employment standards complaints from employees in accommodation and food services (see graph 2.2) – an industry characterized by low wages and low union density in which racialized women are over-represented (Block and Galabuzi 2011). Given especially that a sizeable portion of complainants have left their jobs, the high level of employment standards complaints in the accommodation and food services industry is likely not an indicator that employees in this industry encounter fewer barriers in accessing the complaints system but rather an indicator of high levels of employment standards violations in this industry. Fissuring (Weil 2010) or subcontracting is also prevalent in the three industries with the highest levels of employment standards violations, suggesting that the offloading of labour costs onto smaller firms generates intensive pressures and opportunities for employers to violate employment standards (Estlund 2005; Bernhardt et al. 2013; Fine 2013). The location of many complainants in highly fissured industries suggests that employment standards violations are being driven by broader economic factors, including industrial restructuring and the concomitant rise of precarious employment, rather than simply employers' ignorance or incompetence. Additionally, given that research reveals a causal relationship between fissuring and an increased risk of employment standards violations (Weil 2014), the current configuration of employment standards enforcement benefits franchisors and those who contract out considerably (see also chapter 5). The fissuring of what were formally integrated employing entities

Graph 2.1. Prevalence and Median Amount of Employment Standards Claims Submitted, by Standard, 2008/09–2014/15

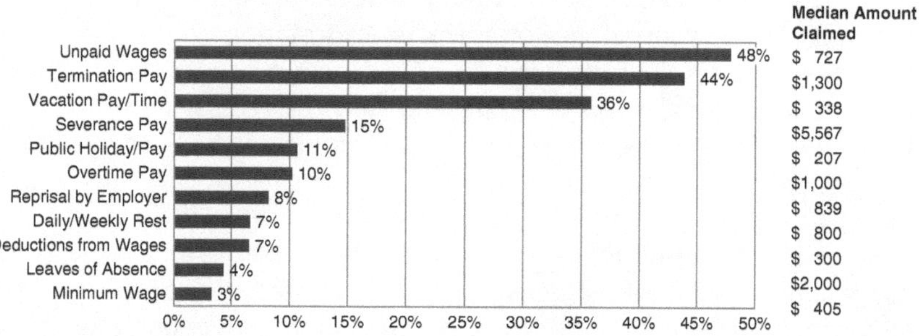


Source: Ontario Ministry of Labour, ESIS data 2008/09–14/15 (pooled).

through such means, among other mechanisms tied to extended supply chains, poses challenges to effective enforcement, raising, in particular, problems with the current definition of the employer under the *ESA* and parallel legislation elsewhere (on the subject of extended liability, see chapter 9 on Australia; see also Vosko et al. 2017).

Employees of small firms are also more likely to file complaints than employees of larger firms (see graph 2.3). For instance, whereas slightly over 20 per cent of non-unionized employees in Ontario work in firms with fewer than twenty employees, more than half of all employment standards complaints are submitted by employees in these small firms – a noteworthy finding, given that recent immigrant women are more likely than other employees to be employed in small firms (see chapter 1), suggesting that they may be disproportionately affected by employment standards non-compliance among small firms. Complaints from employees of small firms are also more likely than those from employees of larger firms to include a claim for unpaid wages, reflecting the financial constraints of small firms and their greater likelihood of having employees in arrears (Vosko et al. 2017). It may be that small firms lack the human resource capacities to ensure full compliance with labour regulations, in support of the compliance orientation narrative. But given previous research demonstrating how precarious employment is more prevalent in small firms (Noack and Vosko 2011), the result, in part, of such firms' vulnerability to economic fluctuations, it is more plausible that small firms are more likely to transgress employment standards as a strategy to reduce labour costs (Davidov 2010; Bernhardt et al. 2013).

Graph 2.2. Employment Standards Complaints Submitted, by Industry, 2014/15 [2]

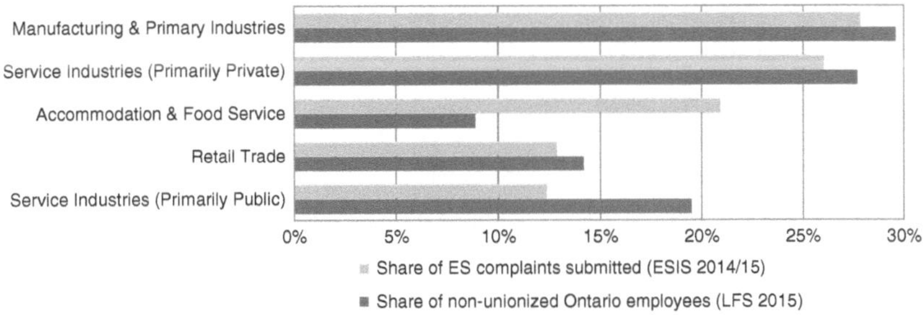


Source: Ontario Ministry of Labour, ESIS data 2014/15, and Statistics Canada, Labour Force Survey 2015, annual data weights used.

The prevalence of employment standards violations may contribute to their normalization, to the extent that employees either do not recognize that their rights are being violated or disregard all but the most egregious violations. As Weil and Pyles (2006) demonstrate in the U.S. case, industries characterized by high rates of violations, thereby, may generate relatively low levels of complaints, and vice versa. For instance, one employee in the construction sector explained processes of normalization in this way: "[Many] employers in Toronto are ripping people off and it's getting to the point that people are accepting it, so when they get up to work, they go, 'Oh well,' you know, 'it's part of life.'" Employees' decisions about whether or not to file a complaint with the MOL relates, in part, to the culture of the firm or the industry they work in, which shapes their perceptions of what constitutes a violation and the potential for remediation. Such normalization is also bound up with their perceptions of the effectiveness of the complaints system as a means through which to seek redress.

*Challenges and Barriers to Pursuing Complaints*

Employees' social location can affect how they respond to an employment standard violation and their decision to file (or not file) a complaint with the MOL. For example, those with precarious citizenship or immigration status, such as migrant workers, recent immigrants, and refugees, may be more hesitant to engage in the formal complaints process. The reflections of one employee, a refugee from Colombia, exemplify this hesitancy: "When you are new in the country, you don't want

Graph 2.3. Employment Standards Complaints Received, by Firm Size, 2014/15

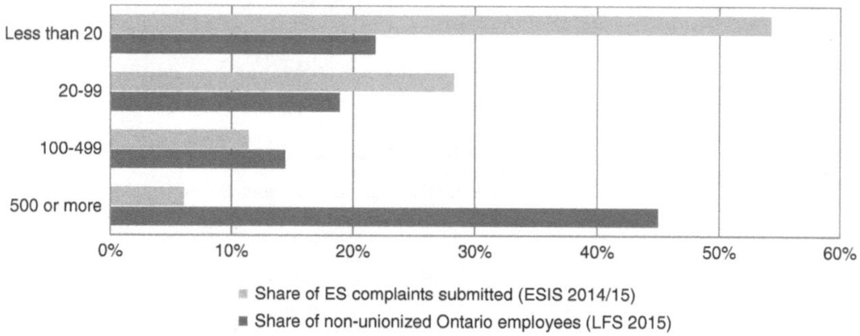


Source: Ontario Ministry of Labour, ESIS data 2014/15, and Statistics Canada, Labour Force Survey 2015, annual data weights used.

to start to make problems or to be a problem." This employee added, "I work and I apply for many jobs and I put [up with] that [work] experience because it's important to have experiences in Canada to take another job." Numerous studies demonstrate that some employers place a high value on Canadian work experience, limiting the employment opportunities of otherwise qualified immigrants and refugees (Vosko 2000, chap. 6; Reitz 2001; Buzdugan and Halli 2009; Akkaymak 2017). The risks associated with complaint-making are compounded for employees who are not confident that they can secure equivalent, alternate employment, thus constituting an additional disincentive to taking action to rectify employment standards violations.

Some immigrant employees who risk entering into the formal employment standards complaints system nevertheless eventually decide not to proceed with their complaint. For example, one Caribbean-born refugee filed a formal complaint with the MOL because she did not get paid for the last week she worked as a babysitter, her first job in Canada. In a conversation with her employer at the time, she realized that her employer was unwilling to make the last payment and decided to file a complaint for the monies owing. Despite initiating the complaint, however, this employee eventually withdrew her complaint on account of her precarious migration status, that is, because she "was working on [getting] my [immigration] papers." Although the employee presumed that employment standards complaint and immigration processes are separate, she "was afraid at the time" and did not want to put her application for permanent residency at risk by lodging a complaint. To serve employees in more uncertain social locations, the employment standards complaints system requires a more explicit recognition of how making a complaint may potentially affect other aspects of employees' lives, and explicitly seek to mitigate these impacts, such as by letting complainants know with whom their complaint information is shared and by adjudicating claims quickly (on the adjudication process, see chapter 3).

In addition, many employees refrain from filing complaints out of an actual, perceived, or potential fear of reprisal, such as receiving undesirable assignments and schedules, being subject to harassment from management or co-employees, or being terminated. This fear appears to be well founded. The proportion of employment standards complaints that include a claim of reprisal grew in the early 2000s: whereas reprisal claims were included in only 6 per cent of all complaints in 2008/09, this proportion increased to 8 per cent in 2010/11 and 10 per cent in 2014/15. Not surprisingly, reprisal claims are more common among complainants who are still working for their employer when they file a complaint. Indicative of the fear of reprisal, one employee in the construction sector noted that he did not even consider complaining to his employer for any violation other than unpaid wages, for fear of job loss: "If I complain, I lose my job.... This is why I didn't complain." Likewise, another employee in construction tried to contact his employer about his working hours and was threatened with being fired: "[You need to] figure out your own hours and when you argue with the boss about your hours ... he tells you, '[If] you don't like it, then quit. Get yourself another job.'" Similarly, an employee in the transportation industry was fired after he told the employer that he was considering filing a complaint with the MOL. He reported, "I knew there was [the] potential I'd be let go.... They never used the word *fired*, but [I was told] 'You're no longer needed.'" Not surprisingly, between 2008/09 and 2014/15, over a quarter of complainants (28 per cent) reported that they had been fired. An additional 15 per cent said that they were laid off, and 25 per cent said that they quit. Another quarter reported some other status in regard to their employment relationship; for instance, some employees had not been formally terminated but had ceased being assigned shifts.

The fear of reprisal and increase in reprisal claims are arguably predictable, given the opportunities for retaliation enabled by the now-overturned *Open for Business Act (OBA)* requirement that employees disclose the nature of their grievance to their employer as a condition of filing a complaint. Employee vulnerability to reprisal, as discussed in detail in the following section, is a major impediment to the exercise of employee voice and undermines any regulatory arrangement premised on such voice.

Crucially, employees' perception of the potential for remediation shapes their willingness to enter into the formal employment standards complaints system. The perceived low benefits of filing a complaint may, in practice, limit employees' access to the complaint system (Weil and Pyles 2006). The idea that filing a complaint would not result in substantial change in employer practices emerged frequently during interviews with employees. As one employee in the telecommunications industry put it, "If I were to pursue this further, what's going to be the gain at the end of all that when all the smoke clears? What's going to be the gain? Other people aren't going to be helped by my decision [of filing a complaint]. I'm not going to be helped." This comment underscores employees' lack of confidence in the MOL's ability to redress violations and improve workplace conditions via the complaints system. Although the primary objective of the complaints system is to provide employees with an avenue for redress, there are serious challenges associated with recovering unpaid wages for complainants when employers do not voluntarily comply with the assessment of an ERO or ESO (on the subject of recovery, see chapter 4 on Ontario; chapter 8 on Britain; chapter 9 on Australia; chapter 10 on Quebec). The fact that few employees receive the money they are owed erodes the efficacy of employment standards legislation and enforcement. In this way, poor recovery rates render efforts to increase employees' awareness of their workplace rights meaningless, given that employees who risk speaking up and engaging the complaints process may wind up with little more than unenforceable paper victories.

### 3. The Rise of Regulated Self-Regulation: Responsibilizing Employees

Although regulated self-regulation has always been a feature of Ontario's employment standards enforcement system, the restructuring of the complaints system in the mid-2000s consolidated the structural emphasis on employee self-regulation and led to the adoption of a more thoroughgoing compliance orientation to labour regulation. Prior to 2005/06, employees who experienced employment standards violations could file a complaint by going in person to one of several intake offices located across Ontario, where an MOL employee would assist them in filing a complaint. In 2005/06 the MOL established a centralized Provincial Claims Centre in Sault Ste Marie, closing regional intake offices and requiring that complaints be submitted by internet, fax, or mail (for discussion of a similar change in Quebec, see chapter 10). A call centre, providing information about employment standards legislation in several languages, replaced the in-person assistance provided at intake offices. In practice, this restructuring of the complaints system embraces regulated self-regulation as a central pillar of employment standards enforcement, shifting more responsibility to employees.

For some employees, these changes created additional obstacles to accessing the employment standards complaints system. For instance, as one employee in the telecommunications industry noted, "Now everything is computerized. You don't even get a live person. So you have to go on the website. I didn't have computer access, so I had to work through the community centres, through the libraries. You get one hour per day at the library and then it kicks you off. So it's more complicated now and less personal."

Nonetheless, the move to an online submission system resulted in a jump in the number of new complaints (Gellatly et al. 2011). As in other jurisdictions, in the absence of a corresponding increase in investigative resources, a complaint backlog grew, reaching approximately 14,000 complaints by 2010 (Vosko et al. 2011, 13). In an effort to reduce the number of formal complaints entering the system, as noted previously, the *OBA* introduced a requirement in 2010 for employees to contact their employer about any violation(s) before a complaint was filed with the MOL. This strategy reflected the MOL's tendency to approach employment standards regulation in a manner that assumes that employees and employers share a joint responsibility for employment standards compliance, on the premise that most employers will comply with the legislation if they are provided the correct information (Thomas 2009), an approach in line with the employment standards enforcement mechanisms employed in other jurisdictions (see the chapters comprising Part Two). Notably, the *OBA* gave the director of employment standards discretion to relieve employees from contacting their employer if they were a young person, were a live-in caregiver, or feared retaliation. These exceptions acknowledged the difficulties that some employees in precarious employment may have in accessing the complaints system (Tucker et al. 2016). Yet, even in such cases, complainants were required to detail their efforts to contact their employer, or their reasons for why it was impossible, when submitting a complaint. Notably, among employees who submitted complaints in the years following the establishment of this requirement, the most commonly cited reason for not contacting or attempting to contact an employer was "being afraid." While this requirement clearly aimed to address the backlog of complaints (by reducing the number of complaints reaching the MOL), it heightened the risk that instead of resolving employment standards concerns directly with their employers, some employees would take no action, at least while they were still on the job. In the period during which this "self-help requirement" was in effect, the Employment Standards Information System (ESIS) data show that the number of employment standards complaints received annually by the MOL declined, despite growing numbers of non-unionized employees in Ontario – a development paralleling the introduction and subsequent withdrawal of fees to complain to an Employment Tribunal in Britain around the same period (see chapter 8). Whereas there was one complaint submitted for every 173 non-unionized employees in 2008/09, there was only one complaint submitted for every 285 non-unionized employees in 2014/15 (Vosko, Noack, and Tucker 2016, 20). Moreover, fewer than one in ten complainants (9 per cent) were still working for the employer about whom they were complaining, a proportion that remained relatively constant. Although this does not establish conclusively that the requirement to contact an employer before filing a complaint with the MOL resulted in employee inaction, the fact that employees rarely initiated complaints against their current employers and that the number of complaints dropped when the requirement was in effect are an indicator of the barriers it created.

The *ESA*, in fact, prohibits employers from penalizing or threatening to penalize employees for exercising or trying to exercise their rights under the law (MOL 2017e). However, reprisal provisions apply only to a finite set of circumstances, despite the wide-ranging forms retaliation may take (Vosko 2013). Additionally, even though the onus is on employers to disprove reprisals, employees still have to prove their case – a requirement that often necessitates extensive documentary evidence and legal arguments, and employers often have extensive opportunities to obscure retaliatory behaviour by invoking other reasons. Importantly, a number of measures that could mitigate the risk of reprisal are missing in Ontario. For example, contrary to some other jurisdictions, there is no provision for anonymous or confidential complaints, or for complaints filed by third parties. Indeed, employees who file an employment standard complaint are required to provide their name, "which is shared with the employer during the claims [investigation] process" (Mitchell and Murray 2016, 273). Under these circumstances, employees who have experienced an employment standards violation would likely be hesitant to seek legal redress.

These requirements to independently assemble documentary evidence and to directly contact an employer in an effort to resolve employment standards violations exemplify the ways in which employees have been "responsibilized" and in turn constructed as independent actors in the employment standards system. They presume that employees are knowledgeable about how they should apply general legal rights to their particular situations, and that they are in a position to advocate (and hence negotiate) with their employers for these rights. The requirements further assume that employers will readily provide the documentary evidence required to launch complaints to their employees. Indeed, the responsibilization of employees requires that they become active participants in a surveillance culture by documenting legal violations as they occur in their workplaces. The compliance approach to enforcement assumes that employers are maintaining employees' rights, unless it can be proven otherwise. Although the *OBA* allowed EROs and ESOs to complete assessments on the basis of the "best available evidence" (see chapter 3), the standard of proof required to establish that a violation has occurred and is in need of redress may be impossible for employees in precarious jobs to achieve, especially without the assistance of a lawyer or legal caseworker. Additionally, the strong emphasis on responsibilization and regulated self-regulation fails to acknowledge the complexity of the law and its exemptions and special rules (Vosko, Noack, and Thomas 2016), as well as the unequal power relations inherent in the employment relationship. Some employees, for example, may not have the numeracy or literacy skills required to fully identify and understand the violations of their workplace rights, or the computer skills or resources to find the necessary information (Law Commission of Ontario 2010; Vosko et al. 2011; Vosko 2013; see also chapter 10).

In recognition of the challenges that employees might encounter in assembling employment standards complaints themselves, the MOL has devoted substantial resources to providing education and self-help tools for employees to use if they want to protect their workplace rights. For instance, in the early 2000s the MOL launched a range of online videos and fact sheets on employment standards – tools to help workers assess whether and how they are covered by the *ESA*, and worksheets to calculate amounts owing. Until early 2019, when the government enacted the *Making Ontario Open for Business Act* (2018), employers were also required to display the most recent copy of the province's *ESA* poster in each workplace and to provide each new employee with a copy of the poster within thirty days of being hired. In recognition of what it terms the "vulnerable" situation of employees who are recent immigrants, the MOL also required employers to provide posters in languages other than English if an employee requests a translation of the poster, and in January 2011 the MOL distributed thousands of posters in multiple languages to more than seventy community organizations that work with immigrants and employees in precarious employment (MOL 2014, 20 August b). In March 2014 the MOL also conducted a month-long advertising campaign, Know Your Workplace Rights, to help employees in precarious employment understand their workplace rights and to raise public awareness about fair treatment of workers on the job, producing advertisements in over twenty-five languages and disseminating them via various media outlets including television, digital media, and ethnic print publications (MOL 2014, 20 August 20 b). As one MOL manager commented, however, this emphasis on self-help and the proliferation of educational materials can have perverse consequences: "We make the filing of the complaint pretty complicated. So we ask them to read through tons of brochures and go through the self-help process and then fill out the forms and ask them all sorts of questions."

The MOL notes that in emphasizing self-help and providing educational materials and tools, they strive to "help employers and employees be more self-reliant in resolving employer-employee issues and be more compliant with the ESA" (MOL 2017d). This approach de-emphasizes the role of government in ensuring that employers uphold minimum working conditions and standards. It also individualizes the problem of non-compliance with employment standards, effectively disavowing a more complex understanding of larger issues shaping non-compliance, including the persistence of precarious employment and fissuring.

## 4. Conclusion

In this chapter we have raised cautions about the utilization of regulated self-regulation in the employment standards complaints system. The transfer of employment standards enforcement to employees through the requirement of seeking resolution with employers before complaining and through self-help tools clearly reflects an emphasis on employee responsibilization, which casts employees as fully engaged, empowered actors in the enforcement process. As such, this regulatory new governance–inspired approach obscures unequal power relations in the employment relationship that are often gendered and racialized and expects employees to be well versed with the requirements of the *ESA* and to monitor and resolve employer wrongdoing in the absence of government intervention. Such expectations operate in conjunction with an assumption that employers principally disobey the law inadvertently, and thus employment standards violations stem largely from ignorance or incompetence. The prevalence of employment standards violations – particularly in small firms and in industries where subcontracting and fissuring are predominant – suggest that many are motivated not by ignorance, but by the potential for a competitive advantage or economic gain.

Regulated self-regulation, which is central to Ontario's employment standards enforcement system, does not adequately reflect the limits to employees' personal control of their working environment (see Walter and Haines 1988; Hall et al. 2006). Despite experiencing employment standards violations, the vast majority of employees do not file formal complaints (Weil and Pyles 2006; Noack, Vosko, and Grundy 2015). In some industries, such violations have become normalized, reducing the odds that employees will identify and report their occurrence. Further, several structural barriers limit some workers' access to the employment standards complaints system. In a context in which many employer violations are strategic rather than inadvertent, for some employees, initiating a complaint may mean facing contradictions between their desire for a violation-free workplace and their need for a job. In such cases, explicit reprisal protections under the *ESA* do not prevent employers from engaging in retaliation against an employee, including dismissal. In addition, many non-unionized employees are deprived of the assistance and support provided to unionized employees when they act against an employer. Although legal clinics and worker centres play a crucial role in assisting workers when they come forward with complaints, their scope of action is limited by structural constraints, such as insufficient funding and lack of direct input into the enforcement process (see chapter 7). As a growing number of studies in Canada and elsewhere show, unions could play a role in countering the barriers that emanate from highly individualized employment standards regulation (Fine and Gordon 2010; Weil 2012; Vosko and Thomas 2014; see also chapter 9). As such, augmenting unions' roles in employment standards enforcement could enhance their regulatory function, especially their role in supporting collective organizing undertaken by non-unionized workers, as well as the ongoing efforts of other workers' organizations, to improve employer compliance with employment standards.

If the promise of a compliance-based approach to enforcement is to be fulfilled, all employees must be able to effectively access the system. As Weil (2015, 21) observes in critiquing the self-help paradigm, "We want workers to understand their rights and *feel able to* exercise them" (emphasis added). This freedom to exercise voice requires addressing asymmetries in the employment relationship that affect employees' decision to enter (or not enter) into the formal complaints system (Vosko 2013). Otherwise, regulatory new governance–styled regulated self-regulation will likely devolve into a regime of neoliberal market or self-regulation in which workers face considerable barriers to enforcing their rights.

Without addressing these power imbalances and structural barriers, a reactive, individualized complaints system is ineffective in resolving employment standards violations: relatively few employees file complaints and even fewer receive adequate remediation. Without adequate recognition of the constraining factors, this system relieves the MOL from the responsibility for enforcing all but the most egregious violations of the law. Effective evidence-based workplace regulation in Ontario thereby requires enforcement models that reduce the challenges and barriers employees face in raising complaints, through allowing anonymous and third-party complaints. The anonymous and third-party complaints processes operating in the province of Saskatchewan, as well as to some extent in Quebec and Australia, offer alternative models to which Ontario could look (see chapters 9 and 10). Administrative protocols in Saskatchewan allow a third party, such as a family member or friend, to submit a written complaint against an employer. Upon receiving an anonymous complaint, the Employment Standards Division of the Ministry of Labour Relations and Workplace Safety "contact[s] and work[s] with the employer to correct the employment standards problem" (Government of Saskatchewan 2017). The anonymous complaint option is also available for employees who "want to remain employed with an employer and want a workplace employment standards issue addressed and corrected" (Government of Saskatchewan 2017). Similarly, the *Fair Work Act* in Australia allows anonymous third-party reporting among those who wish to bring forward alleged violations (Australian Government 2017).[3] And the *Act Respecting Labour Standards* in Quebec provides for anonymous tips (Gesualdi-Fecteau 2015a). Third-party representation also holds the potential to enhance unions' role in the enforcement of employment standards for all workers, regardless of their union status.

Although it could be stronger, this sort of anonymous and third-party representation is crucial, as it maximizes routes to accessing the complaints system and reduces its associated risks to employees (see Vosko 2013 for more discussion on anonymous and third-party complaint procedures available in various common-law jurisdictions). It is equally important that anonymous complaints and third-party reporting not be assigned a lower priority than complaints launched by individual workers, disclosing their identity. Otherwise, as Hardy and Howe show in considering the Australian context, such complaints risk becoming intelligence-gathering mechanisms rather than mechanisms that enable workers to come forward with their grievances (see chapter 9).

Effective regulation further requires the creation of an expansive suite of anti-reprisal measures and greater protection against unjust dismissal. Several jurisdictions in the United States have sought to strengthen the reprisal provisions of their respective labour laws by adopting stronger language relating to the presumption of retaliation. For example, the state of Arizona and the District of Columbia both specify that adverse action against a person within ninety days of asserting a right under the state's labour law "shall raise a presumption that such action was retaliation, which may be rebutted by clear and convincing evidence that such action was taken for other permissible reasons" (District of Columbia 2014 cited in Grundy et al. 2017, 199). Another example is a provision in New York's *Wage Protection Act,* which provides enhanced rules against retaliation by making it illegal for any employer to retaliate and by providing for greater damages (New York State Department of Labor 2011). Ontario could follow these jurisdictions and reduce the costs of exercising employment standards rights through more rigorous enforcement of the anti-reprisal provisions of the law (Grundy et al. 2017; Vosko et al. 2017).

Lastly, to rectify the foregoing situation and realize improved enforcement of employment standards, a more robust proactively oriented complaints system requires improvements in complaints administration (canvassed next in chapter 3) and a strengthened inspectorate characterized by a thoroughly proactive approach (as discussed in chapter 5).

*Chapter Three*

# Administering Complaints: Dilemmas of Accountability

The administration of Ontario's employment standards complaints system has experienced a long-building crisis. The complaints system was designed on the assumption that only a modest number of uncomplicated complaints from a relatively limited population of employees would be filed. Yet, as prevailing scholarship suggests, this assumption has proven false, leaving the complaints system riddled with problems dating from its inception due to a lack of sufficient resources (Lane 1977; Thomas 2009). These problems were magnified in the late twentieth century with the growth of the non-unionized labour force reliant on employment standards as an exclusive source of labour protection and, more broadly, the spread of precarious employment and concomitant expansion in the volume of complaints. In the face of these challenges, the Ministry of Labour (MOL) has sought to minimize the administrative burden inherent in complaints handling by drawing increasingly on compliance-oriented soft-law and self-regulation strategies to achieve rapid claims closure. At the same time, a historical review of the complaints system from the enactment of the *Employment Standards Act (ESA)* to the present reveals continuities in the MOL's efforts to minimize its administrative burden at the expense of other principles of employment standards enforcement such as investigative integrity and due process.

In developing these contentions, this chapter unfolds in four parts. In section 1 we begin with a brief overview of the complaints administration process, sketching the challenges that have long plagued this individualized, reactively oriented, employment standards enforcement system (also evident in other jurisdictions). In section 2 we offer a historical overview of complaints administration, highlighting persistent challenges to it and revealing the longstanding use of soft-law and self-regulatory measures in efforts to expedite the closure of complaints and reduce their receipt. Section 3 then examines three primary strategies used to manage the complaints system, each of which seeks to streamline and limit complaints in ways that erode effective enforcement: the reconfiguration of intake; the extension of greater support for various types of settlements; and the institutionalization of new mechanisms for evaluating early resolution officers (EROs) and employment standards officers (ESOs) preoccupied with performance measurement characteristic of new public management. Section 4 proceeds to explore the persistence of the backlog of complaints, despite regulatory new governance and especially new public management–styled interventions. In conclusion, the chapter suggests that the complaints system will continue to be overburdened unless serious weaknesses in other aspects of the enforcement regime, such as the lack of deterrence and the dearth of workplace inspections, are addressed to reduce the rate of employment standards violations that generate complaints in the first place.

## 1. Managing Dilemmas Inherent to the Complaints-Oriented Enforcement System

Since the inception of the *ESA*, the policy of the MOL has been to accept every complaint filed by a complainant falling under the jurisdiction of the *ESA*. This policy stems from section 96(1) of the *ESA*, which states that "a person alleging that this Act has been or is being contravened may file a complaint with the Ministry in a written or electronic form approved by the Director" (*ESA* 2000, c. 41, s. 96 (1)). To fulfil this commitment, the MOL devised an elaborate multi-staged process to investigate complaints, partly in an attempt to secure entitlements for employees. Once a complaint is submitted, a claims processor verifies that the necessary information has been provided and that the complaint falls under the jurisdiction of the *ESA*. Complaints that fall under *ESA* and include the requisite information are then forwarded to an ERO for an initial investigation. In this first investigative stage, EROs examine the documents forwarded by the claims processor, along with direct communication with the complainant and the employer to gather additional information and to give both the opportunity to present evidence in support of their case. When EROs investigate complaints, they assess whether they are substantiated in whole or in part, and, if applicable, they determine the amount of money owed to complainants. EROs may also assess entitlements that exceed claims made in the original complaint. Following the initial investigation, they may close the complaint by processing complaint withdrawals, securing voluntary compliance or voluntary settlement, or issuing a denial (MOL 2017a, 7). EROs also determine whether there are grounds for further investigation by an ESO. There are specific cases outlined in the MOL's *Administrative Manual for Employment Standards* that require EROs to forward the complaint directly to an ESO: those involving reprisals, retail business establishments, temporary agency provisions, and equal pay for equal work.

Investigation by ESOs involves processes parallel to those of the EROs, although it is more extensive, as they are responsible for making a final decision. ESOs may visit the employer's premises and/or call a "fact-finding meeting" between the complainant and the employer. The parties can settle the complaint at any time during the investigation by agreeing to terms that will resolve the complaint, either between themselves or with the facilitation of an ESO. The pursuance of visits, meetings, and facilitated settlements are means of further investigation and/or achieving voluntary compliance undertaken exclusively by ESOs (for further discussion of ESO discretion and judgment in employment standards enforcement, see Tucker et al. 2016). If monies are found to be owed, ESOs, similar to EROs, can seek voluntary compliance by the employer, although as of fall 2018 the program policy was that voluntary compliance was to be used rarely. This process involves an employer adhering to an ESO's decision and rectifying the infraction by paying money or modifying other workplace practices (MOL 2015). If voluntary compliance is not achieved, and even when it is achieved, an ESO can use enforcement tools. Orders to Pay can be issued when unpaid wages or other entitlements are found to be owed to an employee. Other options available to ESOs include a Compliance Order, an Order to Compensate and/or Reinstate, a Notice of Contravention (NOC), a "ticket," which imposes a set fine under Part I of the *Provincial Offences Act*, or the much more infrequently used option of initiating a prosecution (for a review of such tools, see chapter 6 on deterrence; see also Vosko, Noack, and Tucker 2016; for an overview of the claims investigation processes in Australia and Quebec, see chapters 9 and 10).

Notably, the Ontario Labour Relation Board's (OLRB's) power to overrule puts a check on bureaucratic discretion. Employees, directors, and employers may apply to have a decision by an ESO reviewed by the OLRB, a quasi-judicial administrative tribunal that makes decisions entirely independent of the MOL. The OLRB reviews three types of applications: (1) ESO Orders to Pay Wages, Fees, Reinstate and/or Comply; (2) Refusals of ESOs to make an Order; and (3) NOCs. The right to a review is extended under the *ESA*, which also establishes the parameters for the review. For example, in reviews of ESO orders, the Act stipulates that applications for reviews must be made within thirty days of the order being served.[1]

At an administrative level, the individual complaints system has never been resourced adequately for the magnitude of responsibilities assigned to EROs and ESOs and their limited numbers – a common problem in many jurisdictions (see the chapters comprising Part Two). Historically and to the present, this abiding feature of the system has prompted MOL officials to find ways to both minimize the administrative burden inherent in complaints handling and expedite complaints processing. Since the earliest years of the *ESA*, officials have drawn on many strategies that reflect a compliance orientation to achieve complaints closure. On account of the limited resources available for resolving complaints, these strategies have been directed at minimizing the use of hard-law measures and seeking self-regulation and voluntary compliance by employers (Estlund 2005; Lobel 2005; Vosko, Grundy, and Thomas 2016; see also chapters 9 and 10 in this book). In this way, the tenets of regulatory new governance are ingrained in the complaints processing system.

From the 1990s onward, the administrative paradigm of new public management provided another vehicle or set of overlapping strategies that complement and indeed sustain a compliance orientation. A product of Thatcher-era Britain, drawing intellectual inspiration from neoclassical economic theory, new public management is premised on a critical view of public sector bureaucracy. It seeks to remake this bureaucracy through the introduction of more rigorous forms of performance benchmarking protocols applicable to public sector employees, by restructuring labour processes in search of measurable efficiencies (Clarke and Newman 1997; Diefenbach 2009; Klijn 2012; Griffith and Smith 2014). In regulatory agencies, such as the MOL, new public management has fuelled the rise of performance-based regulation whereby more rigorous performance targets play a larger role in administrative and budgeting decisions (Gellatly et al. 2011).

The historical overview to which we now turn reveals the longstanding adoption of soft-law and self-regulatory approaches – associated most recently with regulated self-regulation – in the administration of the complaints system, and the recent rise of new public management in officials' efforts to streamline administration with an emphasis on cost-containment. It suggests that historically and contemporaneously expedited complaint processing has often been achieved at the expense of the accessibility of the larger system, adequate enforcement, and due process. More broadly, it becomes clear that administrative choices hold important consequences for employees' ability to access employment standards enforcement in practice, and particularly for those in precarious jobs.

## 2. Troubled History of Complaints Administration

Since the enactment of the *ESA* in 1968, MOL officials have drawn on many strategies that reflect a compliance orientation to address persistent and deepening challenges of employment standards enforcement in general, and the complaints system in particular. More specifically, an interrogation of the strategies introduced in the first three decades of the Act demonstrates that the MOL's efforts to alleviate administrative burdens have entailed bids to speed up complaint closure and reduce employees' access to the complaints system.

The establishment of the *ESA* and its complaints system was widely publicized in the late 1960s and 1970s, whereby the MOL initially envisioned a robust command-and-control system of enforcement (MOL 1970). Complaints were to function as triggers for full audits by ESOs, who were to assess employer compliance with the new legislation and issue Orders to Pay when necessary. Under certain circumstances, co-operative employers were allowed to pay employees directly without the issuance of a formal order (Lane 1977). Moreover, whereas pre-1968 legislation enforced only minimum standards, the MOL was also empowered to enforce unpaid wages (MOL 1971). Put differently, the MOL's new power to enforce the terms of an individual employment contract "marked a sharp departure from the capacity to enforce minimum standards which had characterized the activities of the [Employment Standards] Branch under previous legislation" (Lane 1977, n.p.).

Pressure on the Employment Standards Branch of the MOL quickly became evident as ESOs were drawn more deeply into the investigation of complaints. Simultaneously, the *ESA*'s legislative protections were augmented, adding to enforcement officials' responsibilities. In 1970 the government extended the time limitation for initiating prosecutions from six months to two years and increased the maximum collectable from employers for a single employee from $1,000 to $2,000 (MOL 1970, 21 October). In 1971 termination notice or pay in lieu was enacted (MOL 1985). In 1974 four paid public holidays (with complicated eligibility criteria) were added to the holiday pay provisions, and vacation time/pay standards were increased to two weeks or 4 per cent (MOL 1982b). Maternity leave, initially enforced by the Women's Bureau of the ministry, also came under the enforcement of the MOL's Employment Standards Branch (MOL 1977, March; for more discussion on amendments of employment standards coverage, see Thomas 2009). With such an increase in the statutory protections for workers covered by the Act, the number of complaints continued to grow from 9,742 in the fiscal year of 1971/72 (MOL 1972, 21) to over 14,000 in 1977/78 (MOL 1978, 42). Additionally, telephone inquiries at the Toronto office grew from 55,000 between July–December 1970 to fully 251,000 in 1975 (Employment Standards Branch cited in Lane 1977, n.p.).

While the enforcement responsibilities of the MOL grew, funding and staff levels remained nearly stagnant. The Employment Standards Branch had a staff complement of 103 in 1968/69; 119 in 1969/70, and only 115 in 1976/77. Appropriations to the branch were $1.5 million in 1972/73 and $2.6 million in 1976/77 (Lane 1977, n.p.). By contrast, the Construction and Industrial Safety Branch of the MOL had 255 staff in 1976/77 and $5.3 million in funding (Lane 1977, n.p.). Indeed, the Employment Standards Branch itself identified insufficient staffing and inadequate funding as factors inhibiting a more comprehensive enforcement effort and contributing to reduced servicing capacity (MOL 1982a, 1983).

The insufficient staffing levels, coupled with the increase in employment standards protections and the expansion of Ontario's labour force, led to increased workload for enforcement officials. Within the first decade of the *ESA*'s enactment, the average workload per officer increased over 40 per cent while the branch experienced an average yearly increase of only 2.4 per cent in its staffing complement (Thomas 2003, 324). Notably, all of these factors resulted in an increased backlog of employment standards complaints (Thomas 2003, 2009). Faced with growing enforcement responsibilities amid inadequate resources, the MOL adopted numerous measures to limit its jurisdiction and to streamline complaints processing. The system of formal enforcement initially envisioned for the *ESA* gave way to soft-law, compliance orientation techniques aimed at minimizing administrative burden on the complaints system.

In 1971 the MOL began promoting telephone resolution of complaints without the use of more formal enforcement measures available under the legislation (MOL 1978, 40). Many complaints were streamed into telephone resolution and closed upon confirmation from an employer that an employee had been paid wages owed, typically without further confirmation with the employee that the money had been received (Lane 1977). Additional streamlining measures were adopted for complaints where a field investigation by an ESO was needed. In 1974 the MOL adopted a partial/self-audit and direct pay system that involved the ESO in a limited investigation of employer records to assess compliance. When violations were found in the investigation, employers were required to complete a full audit themselves and pay any back wages owed to employees directly. This system was accompanied by a 1976 directive to narrow the complaints process to the substance of the complaint only, that is, to investigate only the records relevant to the complaint, and to consider only the standards included in the complaint (Lane 1977, n.p.). The implementation of the partial/self-audit and direct payment protocol was associated with reduced findings of violations and reduced use of Orders to Pay. In 1971, 54 per cent of the 11,575 employers found in violation were issued an Order to Pay Wages; but in 1976, 4 per cent of the 7,495 employers in violation were issued Orders to Pay (Lane 1977, n.p.). At this juncture, MOL officials discouraged the use of Orders to Pay, as their use entailed the risk of an employer request for a review, which would absorb further staff resources. The number of employees who received payments as a result of enforcement dropped from 52,263 in 1971 to 19,038 in 1976 (Lane 1977, n.p.). These figures are particularly striking, given the sizeable increase in complaints received between 1971 and 1978. Furthermore, despite provisions that enabled the MOL to prosecute employers who violated the Act, these provisions were rarely used (Fudge 1991a, 1991b, cited in Thomas 2003, 352). To illustrate, only ninety-eight employers were prosecuted under the Act between May 1973 and January 1977 (Lane 1977, n.p.).

In 1976, in turn, the MOL adopted a policy that it would no longer accept claims for unpaid wages, then the second most frequent claim received by the MOL and the standard that resulted in the largest amount of money collected (Lane 1977). Complainants with claims of unpaid wages were to be encouraged to seek civil remedies through the court system (Thomas 2009). The policy was passed by the branch director, unbeknownst to the senior executives of the MOL, including the deputy minister, and was revoked the following year. Nevertheless, its brief existence highlights MOL efforts to contain the administrative burden on the complaints system, a noteworthy antecedent to contemporary developments (Lane 1977).

In short, in the first decade following the enactment of the *ESA*, in order to deal with severe resource constraints alongside an increasing demand for its enforcement, the MOL retreated from the robust vision it initially espoused. Sowing the seeds for a compliance-oriented approach to complaints handling, bearing the early imprint of tenets of regulatory new governance, government officials established a cursory complaints-handling process that relied on employer self-reporting, whose scope was exceedingly limited, and sought to limit use of formal enforcement measures such as Orders to Pay. As a management strategy for an impending crisis in the administration of the complaints system, this expedited complaints-handling process stemmed from political pressure to reduce the complaints backlog and increase processing times.[2]

Many of the deficiencies characterizing the complaints handling system in the 1970s, and its emphasis on soft-law and a compliance orientation, persisted and deepened in the next decade, in which the MOL also introduced more self-regulation initiatives. A 1991 report by the auditor general of Ontario indicated that the backlog of complaints persisted, rising from 2,453 in 1987/88 to 4,760 in 1990/91 (Auditor General of Ontario 1991, 143). There was a correspondingly long delay in complaints processing: the days to complete a complaint grew consistently from seventy in 1988/89 to seventy-seven in 1989/90 and eighty-five in 1990/91, with 38 per cent of complaints taking more than ninety days to complete in 1990/91 (147).[3]

Indicative of the persistence of investigative practices adopted in the 1970s to expedite complaint closure, the auditor general was also critical of the limited scope of complaints investigations. The report of the auditor general noted that, in the context of complaint-triggered audits, enforcement staff were not looking beyond individual complaints, even when they uncovered other possible violations. Following the review of 360 complaint files, the auditor general found that only eighteen files had evidence that a test audit had been done, even though thirteen of the eighteen test audits resulted in $31,000 in recovered wages for 137 more employees (Auditor General of Ontario 1991, 146). The auditor general viewed the reliance on early telephone resolution, a strong manifestation of the increasingly compliance-oriented approach also emblematic in the growing resort to settlements at the time, as inappropriate, given the incentives of employers to underreport their own violations. Accordingly, the auditor general's report (1991, 146) cited the following case as an illustration of under-reporting in telephone settlements: "An officer investigating an overtime violation could have quickly resolved the file over the telephone by accepting the employer's offer to pay 30 employees a total of $9,000 for overtime owing. However, the officer visited the employer and conducted a full audit resulting in payments to 102 employees totalling $75,000." Throughout the 1990s, under-resourcing of the employment standards complaints system, exacerbated partly by decisions to prioritize other areas for spending (e.g., the establishment of a wage recovery fund), continued to drive the bulk of resources into compliance activities. The termination of approximately one-quarter of the enforcement workforce in the mid-1990s intensified this emphasis (Thomas 2009). In 1996, in an attempt to reduce administrative burden on the complaints system, several amendments were made to the *ESA* that limited the conditions under which complaints were accepted. The *Employment Standards Improvement Act* of 1996 reduced the time limit for employees to submit a complaint from two years to six months. It also capped the maximum payouts so that they could not exceed $10,000 in most cases, regardless of the value of unpaid wages (Bill 49 c. 23, S.O. 1996, cited in Thomas 2003, 250). Both measures constrained employees' abilities to access the complaints system and secure protection from violations of their workplace rights.

### 3. Strategies to Manage a Growing Backlog: The Pursuit of Compliance Orientation through New Public Management and Its Contribution to a Deepening Crisis, 2000–Mid-2018

The complaints system continues to be under strain. The absolute size of Ontario's labour force grew from nearly 5.9 million in 1998 to almost 7.7 million in 2018.[4] Simultaneously, the share of Ontario's non-unionized labour force increased, particularly in the private sector, where it stood at 81 per cent in 1998 and fully 86 per cent in 2018. In large part, this growth is shaped by the expansion of employees in service industries as a share of the labour force, fissuring, and the declining share of jobs in manufacturing, traditionally a domain of secure and indeed unionized employment (see chapter 1). In the face of these dynamics, the MOL adopted three primary strategies to manage the complaints system, each of which contributes to streamlining or reducing complaints at the cost of quality enforcement: reconfiguring intake; promoting settlements; and instituting performance measurement in the evaluation of EROs and ESOs. Overall, these interrelated strategies reflect continuity in the MOL's efforts to expedite complaints processing, most recently through the augmentation of regulatory new governance–inspired soft-law and compliance-oriented measures, as well as new public management–inspired managerialism.

#### *Relieving Administrative Burden by Reconfiguring Intake*

In 2005/06 the MOL shifted from receiving complaints by mail or fax to electronic online filing of complaints and closed down intake offices where workers formerly obtained their Claim Form and information about how to fill in these forms. The MOL posted a self-help kit, exclusively in English, to assist workers in filing complaints online (on the

Graph 3.1. Median Length of Processing Time for Assessed Complaints, 2006/07–2014/15

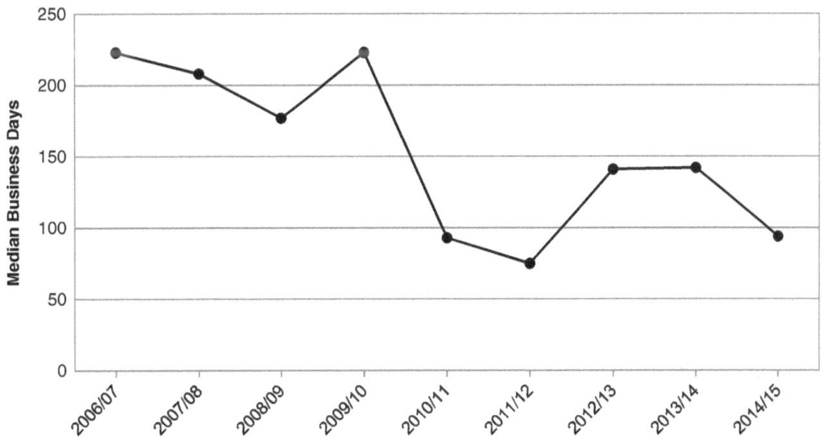


Source: Ontario Ministry of Labour, ESIS data 2006/07–2014/15.

subject of self-help, see chapter 2 on Ontario, chapter 9 on Australia, and chapter 10 on Quebec). The number of new complaints nevertheless increased, as did the number of complaints carried from one year to the next, while the total annual number of completed complaint investigations remained the same. The consequence was a growing backlog in complaints: as an indicator of this backlog, the median processing times for assessed[5] complaints between 2006/07 and 2009/10 was over 200 business days on average – a period of nearly a year (see graph 3.1).

Passage of the *Open for Business Act (OBA)* in 2010 saw further soft-law reforms to the MOL's complaints processing system in an effort to reduce the intake of complaints. As discussed in chapter 2, the *OBA* introduced a mandatory self-resolution step whereby most employees were required to demonstrate an attempt to resolve their complaint with their employer before filing a complaint with the MOL (for parallel developments in Australia and Quebec, see chapters 9 and 10). Workers' advocates immediately contested this measure on the basis that it imposed substantial barriers for workers, many of whom are not in a position to approach their employer as the result of workplace power imbalances. They contended further that the requirement presumably afforded employers an opportunity to convince their employee not to come forward, or an opportunity to retaliate. While it is impossible to discern the dynamics behind this trend, after the introduction of the

*OBA* the MOL received more reprisal claims, not surprisingly, given the retaliatory opportunities afforded by the requirement (see chapter 2), which can be complicated to adjudicate, as the automatic elevation of such complaints to ESOs suggests.[6]

Against this backdrop, in the face of growing recognition of the limits of regulatory new governance–inspired reforms and that more support was needed for complainants, the government retreated from its course somewhat by adopting two measures to improve accessibility of the complaints system. Amounting to a modest recalibration, the *Stronger Workplaces for a Stronger Economy Act* of 2014 expanded the time period in which employees can file complaints from six months to two years and lifted the $10,000 cap on restitution, while retaining the requirement that most complainants contact their employer as a first step alongside a continuing emphasis on self-help and a greater emphasis on complaint closure through settlements.

*Hastening Claims Closure through Settlements*

As the MOL reconfigured intake, between 2006/07 and 2008/09 the number of complaints received far outpaced the number of complaints completed by the MOL, resulting in a backlog of over 14,000 complaints. Against this backdrop, the MOL struck an Employment Standards Task Force in 2010 with a two-year mandate to advance the goal of increasing the speed of complaint processing by streamlining investigations (MOL 2011, 19 January b). Simultaneously, the *OBA* enabled the MOL to require that certain information be provided in writing along with the Claim Form before an employee's complaint would proceed. The intent of this provision, which was rescinded in January 2018, was to reduce the amount of time EROs and ESOs spent compiling documents for an investigation. Overall, in this period, there was a substantial increase in the number of complaints completed. Enforcement officials were able to complete 10,000 more complaints than they received (i.e., completing 27,637 complaints, with 17,094 complaints received) in 2010/11, and the number of complaints completed continued to outpace the number of complaints received in 2011/12 (table 3.1). This increase in complaints completed reflected "additional temporary resources" devoted to the Employment Standards Task Force to eliminate the complaints backlog (MOL 2017d).

The *OBA*, in line with employment standards enforcement practices in other jurisdictions, also supported the expanded use of settlements, prompting a spike in this mode of resolving complaints (as chapter 4 will show), partly by assigning ESOs a new role as facilitators. Prior to

Table 3.1. Complaints Received and Completed by the MOL, 2006/07–2016/17

| Fiscal year | Complaints received | Complaints completed | Carry forward (difference) |
|---|---|---|---|
| 2006/07 | 22,620 | 15,995 | 6,625 |
| 2007/08 | 20,789 | 18,533 | 2,256 |
| 2008/09 | 23,286 | 21,304 | 1,982 |
| 2009/10 | 20,381 | 20,764 | (-383) |
| 2010/11 | 17,094 | 27,637 | (-10,543) |
| 2011/12 | 16,140 | 19,032 | (-2,892) |
| 2012/13* | 15,016 | 12,344 | 2,672 |
| 2013/14 | 15,485 | 14,656 | 829 |
| 2014/15 | 14,872 | 17,453 | (-2,581) |
| 2015/16 | 16,398 | 15,553 | 845 |
| 2016/17 | 16,813 | 15,493 | 1,320 |

Source: MOL Published Plan and Annual Report 2016/17 and 2017/18 (MOL 2017d; 2018b).
* For 2012/13, completed complaints reflect reduced number of staff working on complaints as modernization strategy focuses on a more proactive approach to enforcing the *ESA* and the timing of recruitment and training of new enforcement officers to replace retiring staff.

the *OBA*, ESOs did not formally facilitate settlements; settlements were reached between employees and employers alone. Such non-facilitated settlements require the parties to submit a written agreement to the ERO or ESO outlining the terms. With this paperwork complete, the complaint is closed without an admission of wrongdoing and without an assessment by an ERO or ESO. Facilitated settlements, in contrast, involve an ESO in facilitating an agreement between the employee and the employer. Neither type of settlement involves a formal investigation or a determination that money is owed to the complainant(s) concerned. Whereas 4 per cent of complaints were settled in 2008/09, this rose steadily each year to 15 per cent in 2014/15. Although non-facilitated settlements still represent the majority of settlements, facilitated settlements showed a slight increase in the proportion of total settlements in 2013/14 and 2014/15, compared to previous years (see chapter 4). While assisting in the rapid closure of complaints, a central goal consistent with easing the backlog, settlements achieve this end by placing greater onus on employees and employers in dispute resolution. Unfortunately, settlements may result in the negotiation of minimum standards instead of their enforcement, which in turn may lead employees to accept less than their legal entitlement (for more discussion on settlements and recovery in Ontario, see chapter 4; on settlements elsewhere, see chapters 9 and 10).

*Altering the Approach to Evaluating ERO and ESO Performance: The Balanced Scorecard*

Starting in mid-2003 the MOL mandated quality assurance reviews of ERO or ESO investigation reports for each regional or district office. The new initiative required that 5 per cent of all investigation reports completed by each ERO or ESO be reviewed by the program coordinator of the region or district each year (Auditor General of Ontario 2004b, 249). However, as the 2004 report of the auditor general revealed, the principles engaged to evaluate enforcement staff performance and effectiveness were inadequate. As the report noted, in introducing performance evaluation, "the Ministry had not defined the critical aspects of performance nor had it explained the Program's key risk and capacity considerations" (251). Furthermore, at the time of its audit, the auditor general observed the adoption of "only one measure – the percentage of cases [i.e., complaints] closed within 60 days ... and [emphasized that] in doing so, the Ministry focused on reducing processing time as a priority in order to enhance client service" (251). It thereby concluded that, while processing times are a valid measure, on their own they are "insufficient to inform the Legislature and the public of the Program's success in contributing to the protection of employment rights for workers" (251). In response, the MOL advised the auditor general that its 2004/05 results-based plan involved implementation of other measures of effectiveness. However, according to the auditor general, the plan itself included only two further measures – the percentage of non-compliant workplaces found and employee complainants' satisfaction rate regarding the resolution of their complaints – neither of which met the need for more comprehensive and appropriate performance indicators to inform the general public as well as the legislature about the success of the program (Auditor General of Ontario 2004b). In response to the measures recommended by the provincial auditor, the MOL initially introduced new program measures to track the success of officers in rendering decisions on 80 per cent of complaints within ninety days, although it failed to respond to the critiques comprehensively (Auditor General of Ontario 2004b).

In the face of such persistent concerns about performance evaluation, the MOL implemented a new measurement system, the Balanced Scorecard, in 2013, which was designed to induce EROs and ESOs to process complaints more efficiently. Superseding the simple quota-based system, which was based solely on a certain number of complaints closed per year, the Balanced Scorecard is a points-based performance measurement system that assigns a score to tasks in which EROs and ESOs must engage – e.g., closing files within a certain time frame (forty days for EROs and seventy-five days for ESOs), escalating complaints to ESOs, serving tickets, preparing prosecutions, conducting approved committee work, etc. – and introduces a yearly cumulative closure target that EROs and ESOs are expected to meet. The intent of the Balanced Scorecard is to encourage rapid complaints processing, while recognizing the need for greater flexibility than was possible under the performance measurement system, which only measured complaints closed (on the subject of performance measurement in Australia, see chapter 9).

Informed by the conception of accountability underlying new public management that emphasizes administrative performance, the Balanced Scorecard can nevertheless reshape complaints processing in ways that are in tension with more traditional notions of accountability, related to administrative integrity and due process, as well as the overarching accountability of government for enforcing the *ESA*. For example, the Balanced Scorecard allots a certain standardized number of points for closing a complaint within a given time period, even though certain complaints may be more difficult and time-consuming to process, potentially providing incentive for enforcement staff to limit their efforts in complicated or multifaceted complaints. Accordingly, some ESOs comment on the pressure to close complaints quickly, even in complicated cases:

> I have gotten an exceedingly complicated reprisal "sale of a business" multiple employer or related employer [complaint]. It is going to take me weeks to get through this. I have got a foot of documentation in the lawyer submissions. I'm getting ten points for that and, if it takes me over seventy-five days, I'm getting nine points – as opposed to "Oh, my God, you have seventy-five claims" [i.e., complaints] against this one company. And you are going to get fewer points, despite the fact that it is a more complicated file and you have more work to do.

The failure to acknowledge varying levels of complexity among complaints discourages ESOs from spending the time and resources required to adequately address complex cases. The false equivalence assumed by the Balanced Scorecard can contribute systematically to inhibiting adequate responses to complaints in which employment standards violations are part of larger workplace inequities and discriminatory practices on the basis of race, gender, ability, and citizenship that are prohibited under human rights legislation. According to ESOs, a deep dive into claims investigation requires extra effort, given the pressure to close complaints:

> I constantly have to remind myself, "Slow down, slow down, make sure that you've seen it all before you make a decision." It's so tempting to just make your decision because you've got your points, you move onto the next file and ... because if you don't reach your points then you have to answer to your manager and then ... there are consequences if you don't meet your performance metrics. So the temptation is very great to try and achieve your points however you can. That doesn't necessarily serve the program or the people that we're trying to serve.

Other ESOs also explain the extent to which the points system can shape the administration of the complaints system:

> If there are entitlements to be paid, you have to try to get those paid voluntarily. If the evidence is not clear, then I can try and mediate the settlements. And, if all else fails, I issue an order. There are compliance tools besides an order that I can issue, but we just don't have time, really, to be honest. We have the opportunity to issue tickets, which is a big deal because of the set-up [required]. The processes are difficult.... There are very few people doing it because there just is no time. The main focus is for us to ... obtain our points.

Further reinforcing a compliance-oriented soft-law approach, the false neutrality of the Balanced Scorecard also contributes to the limited capacity of, and impetus for, ESOs to use deterrence as a result of the nature of performance-based measures applied to them.

### 4. The State of Processing Times: Persistent Problems

The adoption of reforms influenced by regulatory new governance and new public management to speed up complaints processing have not eliminated lengthy wait times for complainants. Processing times remain substantial: indeed, in 2014/15 the median was still nearly five months (i.e., ninety-four business days) (see graph 3.1). In reflecting on persistent problems with backlogs in the 2010s, MOL officials suggest that a key problem is that complainants do not provide properly filled out forms, requiring greater effort on the part of EROs and ESOs to investigate and resolve complaints, thereby reinforcing the logjam (MOL 2010b). However, data on processing times indicate that gathering evidence and/or dealing with incomplete evidence is not the central source of delays, an assumption that underpinned efforts to streamline evidence requirements under the *OBA*. Whether or not complainants submit documents with their complaint appears unrelated to processing times. An analysis of the 2014/15 Employment Standards Information System (ESIS) data shows that the median duration in business days of assessed cases where the complainant did not submit any documents compared to those cases where they did differed only by one business day, on average.[7] The median length of time to close both types of cases was over ninety business days. Furthermore, when comparing complaints with no documents submitted to those that have all nine possible document types submitted, the median length of time needed to close complaints without documents was only five business days longer (ninety-two compared to ninety-seven) than needed to close complaints submitted with documents. One explanation for this pattern can be that EROs and ESOs normally make decisions based on the best available evidence. As one ESO notes, "What also happens, quite often, is the employee does not have any records, and it is just based on their recollection. Sometimes the employer's records are not that great either. And sometimes you don't really have everything you need to make a factual analysis or assessment. Sometimes you do have to base it [a decision] on the best available evidence."

Complaints tend to encounter substantial delays waiting for assignment to an ERO or ESO, a factor that reflects the capacity of the MOL to handle the volume of complaints it receives (see table 3.2). For example, in 2014/15 the median waiting time for assignment to an ERO was thirty business days and around twenty-two business days for an ESO. While evidence gathering and fact-finding took some time, the total wait time for ERO or ESO assignment far exceeds the amount of time officers take to gather evidence. Furthermore, data show that the long waiting time prior to complaint assignment may contribute to complainants withdrawing their complaints: approximately 70 per cent of complainants with non-assessed[8] complaints telephoned the MOL to check in on their status, compared to 50 per cent of assessed complaints, and withdrawn complaints showed a particularly high number of status calls. This trend may reflect complainants' frustration with the slow progress and contribute to their decision to withdraw or settle a complaint (see also chapter 10).

Table 3.2. Duration (Median Business Days) of Complaints Adjudication in Assessed Cases, 2014/15

| | Waiting to be assigned to an ERO | Waiting to be assigned to an ESO | Assigned to ERO or ESO, waiting for active assessment | ERO evidence gathering | ESO evidence gathering | ERO and ESO non-evidence processing** |
|---|---|---|---|---|---|---|
| Complaint assessed by both ERO and ESO | | | | | | |
| Evidence gathered by both ERO and ESO | 30 | 21 | 6 | 10 | 28 | – |
| Evidence gathered by ERO only | 29 | 22 | 2 | 9 | – | 40 |
| Evidence gathered by ESO only | 30 | 23 | 5* | – | 32* | 1 |
| Complaint assessed by ERO only | 31 | – | 2 | 14 | – | – |

Source: Ontario Ministry of Labour, ESIS data 2014/15.

* *N* differs for these steps, as fourteen complaints had evidence processed only after a final decision was made.

** This captures the time that a complaint rests with an ERO or ESO who did not collect evidence for that complaint (e.g., they did not engage in any of the following tasks: contacting or attempting to contact the complainant and/or the employer via letters or telephone calls, conducting decision-making and fact-finding meetings, and adding supporting documents). It thereby represents an alternative path to evidence gathering by an ERO/ESO.

Fact-finding is, moreover, rarely extensive, and contact efforts are quite limited. In the majority of assessed cases (58 per cent), EROs and ESOs attempted to contact the complainant or employer only by letter, and another 3 per cent did not attempt contact through either letter or phone. These limited efforts at fact-finding and contacting the parties can be considered manifestations of the pressure placed on officers by the Balanced Scorecard.

Under mounting pressure to manage complaints, alongside the introduction of the *Fair Workplaces and Better Jobs Act* (2017), the MOL promised to hire up to 175 more enforcement officials (MOL 2017d), in order to devote greater resources to both complaint resolution and workplace inspections; however, only 75 new officers were hired before the new provincial government issued a province-wide hiring freeze in the summer of 2018 (Mojtehedzadeh 2018, 29 June). At this time, reminiscent of efforts to address the complaints backlog in the early 2010s under the *OBA* and indicative, more broadly, of continuity through change, as a way to reduce current wait times for complaint resolution, an internal memo of the MOL leaked to the media indicated that workplace inspections were being put on hold so that greater resources could be devoted to complaints (Mojtehedzadeh 2018, 28 October). Yet the evidence suggests that, on its own, an increase in the number of officials is insufficient to the task of improving the efficiency of the complaints system and its administration. Rather, changes to other aspects of the enforcement regime aimed at addressing and reducing the factors that lead to complaints being generated in the first place are required.

## 5. Conclusion

Long-term solutions to the problem of complaint volume are found in neither administrative reforms nor in the hiring of additional enforcement officers on its own (despite this necessary measure). Pressure on the complaints system is likely to continue to mount, given the growth of Ontario's non-unionized labour force, the spread of precarious employment, and new ways of organizing work that fuel employment standards violations, such as fissuring and subcontracting. Ultimately, the problem of an overburdened complaints system is inseparable from weaknesses in the overall enforcement regime.

In a context where there is so little risk to employers of being caught, and of facing a meaningful penalty if they are caught, engaging in employment standards violations will continue to "pay" for many employers. As a result, the complaints administration system will still struggle, even if only a small fraction of aggrieved workers come forward. Greater parallel investment is thereby required in the form of more proactive, strategic enforcement, and especially deterrence measures that raise a reasonable threat to violators of getting caught and facing a meaningful penalty (see chapter 6; see also Casey et al. 2018). Ultimately, it is measures such as these, together with changes to managerial and organizational structures, including those that encourage cooperation among MOL officials at various levels, that have the potential to change employers' behaviour in ways that reduce the rate of violations in the first place (Weil 2010, 2014; on the U.S. case, see chapter 11). There must be recognition that "good performance" and "success" are not simply matters of maximizing efficiencies in claims processing. Complex, multifaceted violations of employment standards – which are frequently shaped by power asymmetries inherent in the employment relationship, including those shaped by social relations of race, gender, and immigration status, among others – often warrant in-depth rather than expedited treatment. Greater recognition of this imperative is necessary to address false neutralities in the administration of the complaints system.

*Chapter Four*

# Recovering Employees' Wages?

There is growing scholarly interest in the development of new models of enforcement aimed at preventing violations in the first instance. Yet remarkably little research examines the ability of labour inspectorates to recover monies employers owe to employees. The dearth of research, however, should not be taken as an indicator that recovery is unproblematic. To the contrary, some research points to persistent difficulties that employees face in collecting monies they are owed as well as to the detrimental effects of being awarded "hollow victories" that result, in practice, in no restitution (Cho, Knoose, and Mischel 2013). Greater attentiveness to recovery is therefore necessary, since ineffective recovery of employees' monetary entitlements fundamentally erodes all other aspects of employment standards enforcement.

Responding to this lacuna, this chapter examines the two main avenues available for wage recovery[1] under Ontario's employment standards enforcement system.[2] Most commonly, an early resolution officer (ERO) or employment standards officer (ESO) investigates claims and determines whether or not wages are owed. In this case, recovery can occur through voluntary payment by the employer, or the employer can incur an Order to Pay Wages, issued to an employer or, in some circumstances, to corporate directors or a related employer. Another way in which wages are recovered is via settlements reached between employee and employer. Settlements do not involve an investigation by an ERO or ESO, and hence there is no determination that a violation occurred or of the amount of monies owing to a complainant. Finally, beyond the *Employment Standards Act (ESA)* enforcement system, in cases of employer bankruptcy or insolvency, an employee may seek to recover wages by filing a proof of claim with the trustee to be entitled to payment under the provisions of the *Bankruptcy and Insolvency Act* (1985).

Across the different avenues for recovery, complainants often face barriers to restitution that hinder recovery and undermine the fundamental legal and normative underpinnings of employment standards. The frequent inability of the Ministry of Labour (MOL) to recover monies owed to employees exacerbates the erosion and abandonment of the floor of social minima that employment standards are established to provide. It deters employees from assuming the risk of filing a complaint with the MOL, while also conveying the message to employers that they can violate the *ESA* with little risk of being caught, and effectively ignore the MOL in the unlikely event they are caught. There is, however, nothing inevitable about ineffective recovery. A wide range of options for strengthening recovery are available and used in other jurisdictions, including measures that secure wages in advance, such as a wage protection fund or a wage bond, and measures that make non-payment potentially very costly for employers, such as wage liens and licence debarment. Provisions of the *Fair Workplaces, Better Jobs Act* (2017) that establish the MOL's capacity to impose wage liens, strengthen related employer liability for Orders to Pay Wages, and authorize ESOs to award interest on unpaid wages are important first steps in addressing ineffective recovery of back wages.

In developing these arguments, our analysis proceeds in three sections. Section 1 briefly surveys the central insights emerging from the few studies that examine wage recovery specifically. Section 2 considers the recovery of wages in historical perspective, demonstrating that officials have long struggled to develop mechanisms that can recover employee entitlements from abandoned or formally bankrupt businesses. Section 3 then turns to the current period. Here, we examine the distinct challenges faced frequently by complainants whose employer has been issued an Order to Pay Wages; by the growing share of complainants who agree to settlements, a key means of embedding the soft-law emphasis of regulatory new governance in the recovery process; and by complainants who seek restitution from an insolvent or bankrupt employer. The fourth section outlines measures that have the potential to strengthen the capacity of Ontario's MOL to recover monies owed by employers.

The analyses below examine the recovery of monies related to employment standards complaints initiated between 2012/13 and 2014/15, drawing on administrative data collected by the MOL and interviews with MOL officials, as well as interviews with low-wage workers. They do not address the recovery of monies stemming from workplace inspections carried out by ESOs. In developing the analysis of complaint outcomes in section 2, logistic regression models are used to generate predicted probabilities of incurring an Order to Pay Wages (as opposed to a complaint being resolved through voluntary compliance) and not recovering an Order to Pay Wages (as opposed to recovering it). Both logistic regression models include the following variables: complainant employment status, employer firm size, industry, entitlement size (quintiles), and fiscal year. In the in-depth interviews with EROs and ESOs and managers, we draw on aspects in which these officials discuss the challenges they encounter in recovering wages, how they address these challenges, and their approach to the use of settlements. In parallel, we analyse interviews with workers, in which they reflect on wage recovery.

## 1. Situating the Problem of Wage Recovery

Amid concerns about declining job quality in many industries, and growing economic inequality, the question of whether and, if so, to what degree, employment standards provide a basic floor of workplace conditions is increasingly salient. The prominence of anti-wage-theft campaigns across jurisdictions, coupled with government experimentation with new models of enforcement, is fuelling scholarly interest in employment standards enforcement. Indeed, as indicated in chapter 1, an extensive body of literature on employment standards enforcement is taking shape around a number of themes. Surprisingly muted in studies of employment standards violations and enforcement, however, are discussions of the basic capacity of labour inspectorates to recover back wages for employees. The dearth of scholarly attention to recovery is surprising, given its primacy in employment standards enforcement. The few studies that take wage recovery as their focus point to poor recovery rates among enforcement agencies. For example, in a study of wage recovery in California, Cho, Koonse, and Mischel (2013, 2) found that, between 2008 and 2011, only 17 per cent of employees who received a judgment in their favour received any payment (see also Colodny et al. 2015; for a discussion of recovery challenges in Britain, see Clark and Herman 2017, November). A key lesson to be drawn from studies of wage recovery is that the limited capacity of inspectorates to collect back wages for employees erodes all other aspects of employment standards legislation and enforcement. Enhancements to the accessibility of the complaints processes, or efforts to increase employees' awareness of their workplace rights, are rendered meaningless if employees who speak up and engage the complaints process wind up with little more than unenforceable entitlements. In this way, poor recovery rates call into question the very existence of an enforceable floor of workplace rights for employees. As the following analysis demonstrates, deficiencies in Ontario's wage recovery process have the potential to undermine the effectiveness of employment standards in the province.

## 2. The Challenge of Wage Recovery in Ontario in Historical Perspective

Recovering wages owed to employees has been a central purpose of employment standards and their legislative precursors. Mechanisms for recovering wages were set out in early British master and servant statutes (Hay and Craven 2004). A review of the *ESA* produced for the MOL notes the existence of early legislation in Ontario, dating to the nineteenth century, that allowed employers to be summoned before a court if employees' wages were not paid, as well as legislation governing public works projects that authorized the provincial government to withhold full payment to contracted employers to ensure that employees engaged on public work projects received their pay (MOL 1970, 21 October). However, given the lax enforcement of successive *Minimum Wage Acts* in force in Ontario from 1920 to 1968 (McCallum 1986; Thomas 2004), it is fair to assume that many workers had difficulty recovering unpaid wages.

Consolidating standards enumerated under several different statutes, the *Employment Standards Act* (1968) established requirements for employees to receive a statement describing their earnings over a given pay period, as well as deductions, if any. The 1968 Act also authorized the director to require payment of back wages, initially capped at $1,000 but raised to $2,000 through an amendment in 1970 (MOL 1970, 21 October). Yet weaknesses in the *ESA* recovery system were recognized from its outset. MOL records indicate officials' recognition that the $2,000 cap on back wages was insufficient in a number of cases, especially those involving a claim for termination pay in lieu of notice (MOL 1973, 2 October a). Moreover, while the director could issue an order, non-payment of wages (beyond minimum wages) was not a direct offence under the *ESA*. As one official put it, "To collect unpaid wages, we must charge him [the employer] with failure to comply with an order of the Director. This means there can be no offence until the Director investigates and issues an order. This is a time consuming and a 'back door type of enforcement'" (MOL 1973, 2 October b).

Two scenarios posed particular challenges for the MOL's recovery mechanism. One was from what MOL officials called "fly by night operations" (MOL 1979, 29 November; MOL 1982, 5 March). As one report notes, "There have been many cases where employers simply lock the door and leave the premises, and leave Ontario" (MOL 1972, 12 October). The second recovery challenge involved cases of formal bankruptcy, a scenario in which the federal government came into play, given its jurisdiction over bankruptcy under the *Bankruptcy Act* (1949). The *Bankruptcy Act* allowed employees to claim a maximum of $500 in unpaid wages. However, wage claims were unsecured and thus fell below secured creditors on the list of those entitled to assets from bankruptcy proceedings. In light of these difficulties, one document noted, "Current protection ... is inadequate. Workers frequently receive only a small proportion of what is owed them and even that small proportion is not received until six months to two years after it was earned" (MOL 1979, 29 November). The challenges in recovering unpaid wages in these situations were confirmed in a study by Adams (1987, 61), who concluded that the collections system "does not work very well against insolvent employers and those determined to flaunt [*sic*] the law."

From the mid-seventies, the government of Ontario and the federal government considered the development of a wage protection system for employees of bankrupt businesses (Thomas 2003). In 1975 the federal government proposed an amendment to the *Bankruptcy Act* to grant priority to wages among other creditors, capped at $2,000. This proposal was dropped in the face of resistance from the banking sector (Thomas 2003, 339).

The need to improve wage recovery for employees continued to be considered by the government of Ontario. Facing growing pressure from workers' advocates to better protect employees from the severe recession of the early 1980s (Thomas 2003), the provincial government struck a Wage Protection and Insolvency Task Force in 1983 to consider ways to improve recovery. The 1985 report of the task force recommended that, in the event of federal inaction, the province should establish a wage protection fund. Discussions among officials focused on the thorny question of how it could be financed. Officials from other branches of the provincial government, including the Treasury and Management Board, did not see the use of general government revenue as a viable funding source, given the open-ended liability posed by the fund. The Treasury and Management Board also considered financing the fund through a payroll tax as an option. Concern was also expressed that the establishment of such a fund at the provincial level would prevent measures being taken at the federal level. The minister of labour also proposed a private insurance option, whereby employers would be responsible for acquiring insurance against the non-payment of wages. Officials from the Ministry of Financial Institutions pointed out that insurance companies would only underwrite firms at very low risk of non-payment, and the wage insurance that would be available to companies at risk of non-payment would be very expensive. They also claimed that insurance companies would likely stop providing coverage during a recession (MOL 1989, 13 March).

In 1991, building on recommendations of the Wage Protection and Insolvency Task Force report, the newly elected centre-left NDP government established the Employee Wage Protection Program. Under this program, which was administered by the Employment Standards Branch of the MOL, if the employer did not pay an Order to Pay Wages, the employee was entitled to receive a maximum of $5,000 from the government, and the government would then attempt to recover money from the employer (*Employment Standards Amendment Act* (Employee Wage Protection Program), 1991 S.O. 1991, c. 16). Given that the fund used general revenue, it was heavily criticized as a public subsidy for failing or unscrupulous businesses (Fudge 1991a, 92; Thomas 2003) and was terminated in 1995.

With the passage of *An Act to Improve the Employment Standards Act* in 1996, reforms to the *ESA*, including its recovery provisions, took a more neoliberal form. The 1996 amendments placed a time limit of six months on making complaints and capped the maximum payouts in most cases to $10,000. It also allowed the MOL to contract out its collections function to private collections agencies. In a submission regarding the amendments, the Canadian Federation of Independent Business applauded the move to privatized collections, noting that "specialists in that field will undoubtedly have better success than busy Employment Standards Officers" (1996). Yet the privatized collection system did not result in dramatically improved recovery rates. In its 2004 annual report, the Office of the Auditor General of Ontario criticized the collections process, noting that the collection rates achieved by the private collection agencies between 2000 and 2002 hovered between 15 and 20 per cent (Auditor General of Ontario 2004b, 246). According to its report, there was a "general lack of strong, timely enforcement measures by both the collection agency and the Ministry when employers did not pay. For example, employers were not reported to a credit bureau; liens and writs were either not registered against them or not acted on to seize assets; and legal action was seldom taken against the employer. Also, there were no management reports on the types of enforcement measures used or which measures were more successful" (Auditor General of Ontario 2004b, 247). In an effort to improve recovery rates, the collections system was transferred back to the public sector, when, in 2014, the Ministry of Finance took over its operation. In addition, since 2008, there have been some improvements in the protection of employees of formally insolvent or bankrupt businesses. Legislative reforms adopted by the federal government in that year strengthened the ability of employees of bankrupt or insolvent business to recover wages, in part through the establishment of the Wage Earner Protection Program (WEPP). Under this program, employees who worked for a bankrupt or insolvent employer are eligible to receive up to $7,148.05[3] in unpaid wages, vacation pay, termination pay, and severance pay earned six months prior to the date of the employer bankruptcy or receivership. Through the WEPP, the government pays the employees certain eligible wages prior to the conclusion of insolvency or bankruptcy proceedings. The government then assumes the place of the employee (and the risk) as a creditor. To facilitate recovery of funds from a bankrupt entity, amendments to the *Bankruptcy and Insolvency Act* accompanying the establishment of the WEPP gave super priority status to eligible unpaid wages, up to a maximum of $2,000 per employee.

This brief history suggests that the MOL has long struggled with implementing an effective wage recovery system, especially when dealing with recalcitrant or informally shuttered businesses as well as situations of formal bankruptcy. The following analysis of recovery mechanisms in the current period demonstrates that these problems continue to undermine *ESA* enforcement efforts.

### 3. An Absence of Meaningful Redress

At the outset of our assessment of current recovery challenges, it is helpful to determine the average size of complainants' monetary entitlements. The severity of wage recovery challenges in Ontario is underscored by the large sums of money at stake. From 2012/13 to 2014/15, the median total entitlement for complaints with monetary entitlements was $936, a sum that represents over eighty-five hours of unpaid labour at minimum wage ($10.25 per hour from 2012 to June 2014, then rising to $11.00 per hour). The median entitlement amount for complaints where employers required a formal recovery order was almost twice the amount for complaints where employers paid voluntarily. These entitlements represent a substantial portion of weekly or monthly earnings for many complainants, particularly among low-wage employees (Vosko et al. 2017).

In the following analysis, the difficulties in recovering wages faced by complainants are explored in three different scenarios: those in which the complaint has resulted in either voluntary payment from the employer or the issuance of an Order to Pay Wages; those where complaints are settled during the complaints process, at the collections phase or in the context of an Ontario Labour Relations Board (OLRB) review; and, finally, those where restitution from bankrupt employers is sought. The analysis begins with complaints resulting in either voluntary payment by the employer or an Order to Pay Wages because, of the three different avenues of recovery under consideration, these cases are the most prevalent and are also most directly subject to the formal policies and processes established by the MOL. In contrast, settlements and bankruptcy both reflect alternative processes of complaint resolution.

*Recovering Wages through Voluntary Compliance or Orders to Pay Wages*[4]

When employers are found to owe wages to complainants, the MOL attempts recovery either through voluntary compliance or by issuing a formal Order to Pay Wages when voluntary compliance seems unlikely or is impossible. According to the MOL's *Administrative Manual for Employment Standards (AMES)*, in the case of employers with no history of violations, or with previous violations of different standards, ESOs are generally encouraged to seek voluntary compliance first, and resort to Orders to Pay Wages only if voluntary compliance is not possible. As one ESO explains, "If monies are owed, I almost always provide the employer with an opportunity to voluntarily comply with that decision. If they communicate that they won't comply or they ignore it or they refuse to accept the package, for example, or the delivery, then the next step is to issue an Order to Pay Wages."

A monetary order can take the form of an Order to Pay Wages (s. 103), Director's Order to Pay Wages (s. 81), Related Employer Order to Pay Wages (s. 4), Order for Compensation (ss 104, 74.16, 74.17), and/or an Order to Pay Fees (s. 74.14). Orders to Pay Wages, Directors' Orders to Pay Wages, and Related Employers Orders to Pay Wages are the focus in this analysis.[5] If Orders to Pay Wages remain unpaid, they are usually turned over to collections (*ESA* Part XXIV). As noted above, until 1998, the MOL performed the collections function; at that time, collections were outsourced to private agencies. In 2014 the Ministry of Finance began to undertake collections. The MOL can also file an unpaid order with a court, at which point it assumes the same status as a court order (s. 126). When the MOL exercises this option, remedies available to creditors, such as writs of seizure and sale and garnishments, become available to the MOL (Mitchell and Murray 2016). Among all complaints with monetary claims received by the MOL between 2012/13 and 2014/15, 23 per cent were resolved through voluntary compliance and 22 per cent required an Order to Pay Wages directed at the employer.

Thus, more than half of complaints (55 per cent) were resolved using one of these two mechanisms, whereas only 13 per cent of complaints were settled and 4 per cent involved bankruptcy proceedings.[6]

An ESO's assessment of whether or not an Order to Pay Wages is warranted, based on employer actions, is a critical juncture in the recovery process. The ESIS data indicate that when voluntary compliance is possible, and orders are not issued, entitlements are almost always fully recovered. Several factors shape whether or not an entitlement is likely to be resolved through voluntary compliance or an Order to Pay Wages. After controlling for employment status, industry, entitlement size, and year, small firms are much more likely to be issued an Order to Pay Wages than to comply voluntarily (see graph 4.1). Among firms with fewer than 20 employees, there is a 65 per cent probability of receiving an Order to Pay Wages, whereas among medium-sized companies with 20–99 employees, there is a 54 per cent probability of receiving an Order to Pay Wages. Large firms of 100 or more employees tend to voluntarily comply with entitlements much more often. Among firms of this size, the probability of receiving an Order to Pay Wages is only 34 per cent. The high frequency at which small firms are issued Orders to Pay Wages is consistent with other findings related to small firms. For example, research demonstrates that precarious employment is more prevalent in small workplaces (Vosko 2006; Noack and Vosko 2011), partly as a result of their vulnerability to economic fluctuations,[7] and because small firms are more likely to transgress workplace standards in order to reduce labour costs. Complaints related to small firms are also more likely to include claims for unpaid wages than complaints related to larger firms, reflecting the financial constraints of small firms and their greater likelihood of having employees in arrears (Vosko, Noack, and Tucker 2016).

One of the most important factors predicting whether a complaint will be resolved through voluntary payment or require an Order to Pay Wages is the size of the entitlement. In this analysis, complaints' entitlements are divided into five equal-sized quintiles (graph 4.2). Not surprisingly, larger entitlements are much less likely than smaller entitlements to be paid voluntarily. Among complaints with an entitlement amount in the top 20 per cent, the probability of requiring an Order to Pay Wages is 85 per cent. In comparison, among complaints with an entitlement amount in the lowest 20 per cent, the probability of requiring an Order to Pay Wages is only 33 per cent. Therefore, the greater the monetary entitlement, the less likely the employer will voluntarily comply at the recovery stage. Complaints resolved through voluntary compliance had a median total entitlement of $611, compared to $1,600 for complaints requiring the use of an Order to Pay Wages.

Graph 4.1. Predicted Probability of Receiving an Order to Pay Wages (Compared to Voluntary Compliance), by Firm Size*,**

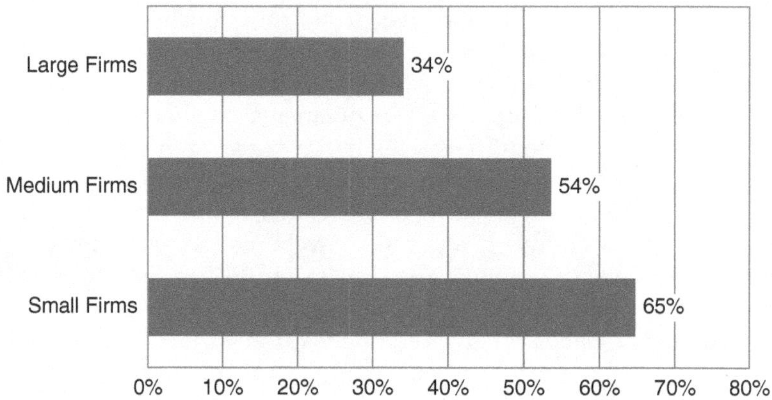


Source: Ontario Ministry of Labour, ESIS data 2012/13–2014/15 (pooled).
* Models control for complainant employment status, industry, entitlement size (quintiles), and fiscal year.
** These predicted probabilities are calculated for complaints initiated in 2014/15 by complainants who quit a job in the accommodation and food services industry, and who have an entitlement amount in the third (or middle) quintile. Employment standards complaints are most commonly received from complainants in small firms, and from firms in the accommodation and food services industry. Complaints are also most commonly received from respondents who quit or were fired; the situation of an employee who quit is highlighted here because it is less likely to be complicated by a termination/severance entitlement. An entitlement in the middle quintile provides a median point of reference.

Recovery rates for Orders to Pay Wages are disturbingly low. Only a minority of employers comply with Orders to Pay Wages (graph 4.3). The rate of full payment of such Orders was 40 per cent in 2012/13, and 37 per cent in 2014/15.

In the period from 2012/13 to 2014/15, after controlling for complainant employment status, firm size, industry, entitlement size (quintiles), and fiscal year, data show that small firms were less likely to pay Orders to Pay Wages. Among firms with fewer than 20 employees that were issued Orders to Pay Wages, the probability of non-recovery was 71 per cent, compared to only a 53 per cent probability of non-recovery for Orders to Pay Wages issued to large employers with 100 or more employees (graph 4.4). The lower rate of recovery among smaller firms is especially problematic for several reasons. Workplace fissuring, whereby larger firms off-load responsibility for employment to smaller firms, is increasingly prevalent in Ontario. Should this trend continue,

Graph 4.2. Predicted Probability of Receiving an Order to Pay Wages (Compared to Voluntary Compliance), by Entitlement Size Quintile*,**

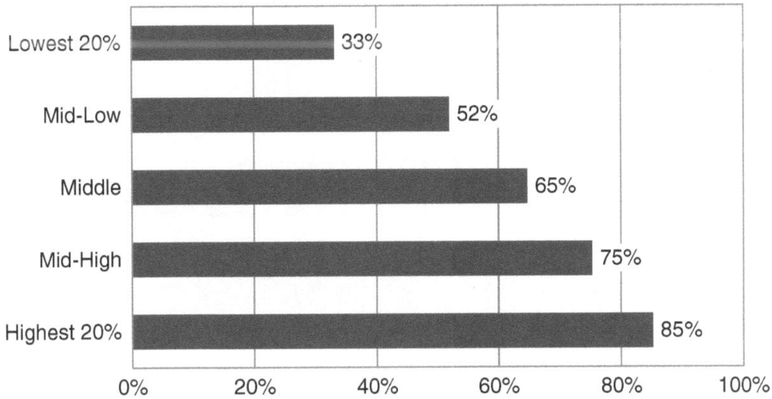


Source: Ontario Ministry of Labour, ESIS data 2012/13–2014/15 (pooled).
* Models control for complainant employment status, firm size, industry, and fiscal year.
** These predicted probabilities are calculated for complaints initiated in 2014/15 by complainants who quit a position in a small firm in the accommodation and food services industry (see ** under graph 4.1).

Graph 4.3. Recovery of Orders to Pay Wages, 2012/13–2014/15

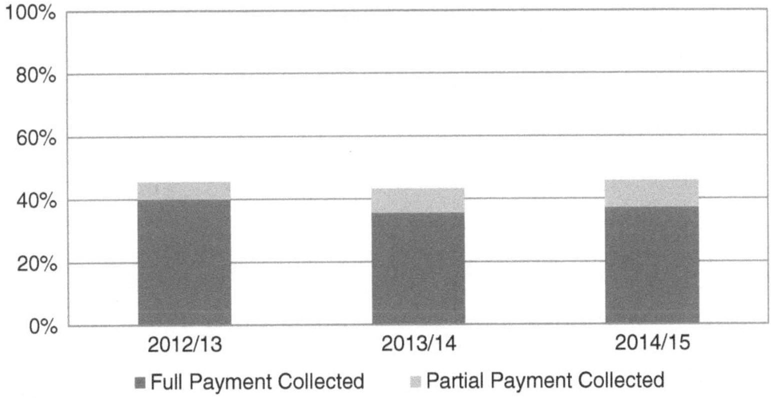


Source: Ontario Ministry of Labour, ESIS data 2012/13–2014/15.

a growing share of Ontario employees may be employed in small firms less likely to pay wages in arrears when ordered to do so. Moreover, the lower recovery rates confronting employees in small firms exacerbate labour market disadvantage of certain groups; for example, as chapter

Graph 4.4. Predicted Probability of Not Recovering an Order to Pay Wages (Compared to Voluntary Compliance), by Firm Size*,**

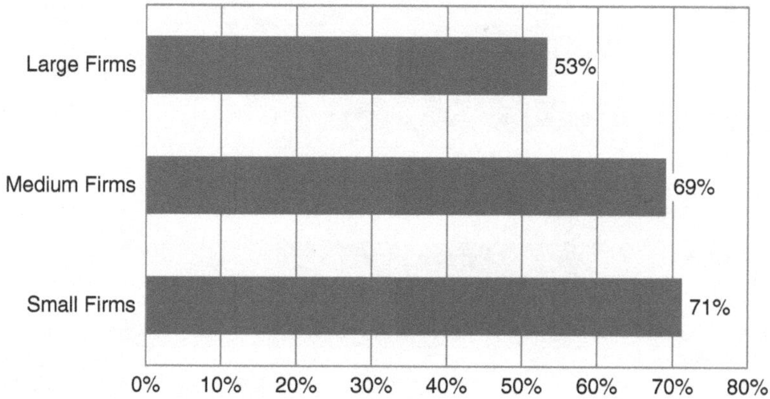


Source: Ontario Ministry of Labour, ESIS data 2012/13–2014/15 (pooled).
* Models control for complainant employment status, industry, entitlement size (quintiles), and fiscal year.
** These predicted probabilities are calculated for complaints initiated in 2014/15 by complainants who quit a position in the accommodation and food services industry, and who have an entitlement amount in the third (or middle) quintile (see ** under graph 4.1).

1 shows, young employees are more likely than older employees to be working in small firms. As well, a larger percentage of recent immigrant women are employed in small firms, compared to other employees in Ontario.

Orders that are not paid within forty days of being issued are sent to the Ministry of Finance, the MOL's designated collections agency. Many MOL officials interviewed acknowledge that private collection agencies contracted beginning in the mid-1990s were ineffective, and "a lot of money went uncollected" during their tenure. One manager expressed the view that private collections agencies prioritized larger Orders to Pay Wages for collection over smaller ones: "The collections people weren't as diligent about getting the smaller [wage] claims. Like, they'd go after the large ones, because they get more money versus the one that's a $150, or so, you know ... there's this always ongoing equitable or balancing piece.... I know it's $150, but $150 to this person means a lot more than $400 to that other person or $2000 to that other."

Broadly, MOL officials considered the shift of responsibility for collection from the private collection agencies to the Ministry of Finance as an important move. One manager, for example, said, "Now it is with the Ministry of Finance, they will collect on the $40 and they will collect on the $100 and they will – they will collect on the $10,000, so – so from the administrative point of view, it was – it was an extremely good move... there are some services that always need to remain with the public service even if it costs us more.... [A]t the end of the day, there's some services that need to be managed within the public service, regardless of the cost."

Another manager expressed the view that the Ministry of Finance had enhanced the credibility of the collections: "The collection piece having gone to the Ministry of Finance has certainly, certainly changed the credibility of – of that piece of it. There's a higher retrieval rate, people get their money, you know, that kind of stuff.... [Y]ou've not very many opportunities to escape (*laughs*) from the Ministry of Finance. That it certainly helps hold people accountable and it ensures a greater level of retrieval of funds, money going to people that it needs to, so I think that has been – that's big a really big shift."

But while sources at the MOL suggest that the Ministry of Finance's recovery rate improved between 2017 and 2018, at the time of publication, robust data were not available to substantiate officials' perceptions that the move to the Ministry of Finance has improved the recovery of Orders to Pay Wages.

Collectively, these results point to several troubling features of the MOL's capacity to recover wages. The median size of employee entitlements is relatively large ($936) and thus may amount to a substantial share of low wage earners' weekly or monthly earnings. The larger the entitlement amount, however, the less likely the employer is willing to pay voluntarily. Many employers whom the MOL identifies as being in violation of employment standards and owing wages to employees appear to simply ignore Orders to Pay Wages.[8] In interviews with non-unionized, low-wage workers, those who filed a complaint that resulted in an unpaid Order to Pay Wages expressed their dissatisfaction with the enforcement of the *ESA*. "They [the Ministry of Labour] had issued an order to pay ... [but] the problem is that there is no enforcement, there's no real cost to employers breaking the law.... [Y]ou can do this [issue an order to pay], but then nothing comes of it, and that is basically where you feel that your case is stuck."

Many often felt "cheated" and articulated frustration with the ineffective recovery system, as well as their employers' disregard for the order:

> I haven't been paid ... and I'm very upset about that part. There has been no penalty.... She [the employer] hasn't responded and she's just letting it go. And I'm out of that money.

> Yeah, it's like a waste of time, you know. I'm never gonna get my money from it anyways, you know.... [H]e [the employer] doesn't care about the Ministry of Labour.

The lack of free legal representation for complainants, which is available in Quebec for employees seeking recovery of back wages from recalcitrant employers (see chapter 10), means that unpaid Orders to Pay Wages receive little follow-up. However, there is reason to believe that the MOL's ability to recover Orders to Pay Wages may improve, at least partly, in the future. Before many of its provisions were replaced, the *Fair Workplaces, Better Jobs Act* (2017) set out provisions to bolster recovery. Specifically, it improved the MOL's ability to establish the joint liability of related employers and provides the MOL (or its authorized collector) with the power to place wage liens on the property of employers, thus making creditors' remedies immediately available upon the issuing of an Order to Pay Wages rather than requiring the MOL to file the order with the court. Additionally, the Act allowed employers to be assessed interest on unpaid wages.

## The Use of Settlements

Settlements offer another avenue for complainants to receive monies under Ontario's employment standards enforcement system. Settlements can occur at various points in the complaints handling and appeals process. The focus here is on settlements that are achieved during the complaints process. As noted in chapter 3, the MOL has supported the expanded use of such settlements as a means to close complaints quickly. The use of settlements in this way in Ontario, as well as other jurisdictions under study in this book (see chapter 9 on Australia), reflects longstanding efforts to minimize the administrative burden on the MOL through regulatory new governance–styled arrangements that eschew more formal enforcement mechanisms such as Orders to Pay Wages. Broadly, through settlements, a complainant and their employer agree to certain terms, and the complaint is subsequently closed.

Two types of settlements can occur during the complaint process: non-facilitated and facilitated settlements. Non-facilitated settlements, outlined in section 112 of the *ESA*, may be reached at any point after a complaint is filed and require that a written agreement between the employee and the employer be provided to the ERO or ESO. After a settlement is reached and recorded, and the parties do what they agreed to do in the terms of the settlement, the complaint is considered withdrawn. Facilitated settlements (s. 101) were introduced under the *Open for Business Act (OBA)* in 2010 and involve the ESO as an agreement facilitator between the employee and the employer. According to the MOL's *AMES*, facilitated settlements may be appropriate where there are credibility issues, the facts are unclear, the application of the law is uncertain, or each party's evidence has equal strengths and weaknesses. Reflecting on their experience with settlements, an ESO noted, "Usually I only employ them if there is quite an element of doubt. I will tell them, 'Look, here is what you got.' This is the situation and I explain to them, 'Everything in the settlement applies including [a loss of the right to] appeal.'"

Some MOL officials criticize settlements, arguing that they allow employers to "buy off their [employees'] rights under the Act" by encouraging employees to settle for less. The following comments from a manager and an ESO are representative of such criticism:

> I don't think settlements should be conducted unless there are specific cases.... I don't want to settle for minimum wage, I don't want to settle for overtime, I don't want to settle for vacation pay. I can settle for termination pay or severance pay, because sometimes that part of the business is grey. People get terminated and it's just between two people in a room and it's a coin toss. Those situations I can see get settled.... But for the minimum core standards, I have never believed that that should be something that we should be doing, settling on.

> The employment standards act says if you work more than forty-four hours you are entitled to overtime pay. If the records show they are entitled to overtime pay and if that works out to $1,000, they should not have to settle for $600.

The use of settlements has increased since 2010/11: they accounted for less than 7 per cent of complaint outcomes in 2010/11 and 15 per cent in 2014/15 (see graph 4.5).

The use of settlements in minimum standards enforcement regimes can be problematic for several reasons. Some scholars have raised concerns about their use because settlements potentially involve the negotiation of minimum standards instead of their enforcement, which may lead employees to accept less than their legal entitlement (Fairey 2005). The use of settlements potentially allows for the contracting out of employment standards and can turn questions of law enforcement into matters of dispute resolution (Vosko, Noack, and Tucker 2016, 35). Furthermore, research investigating developments in employment standards in other

Graph 4.5. Proportion of Complaints Closed via Settlements, 2010/11–2014/15

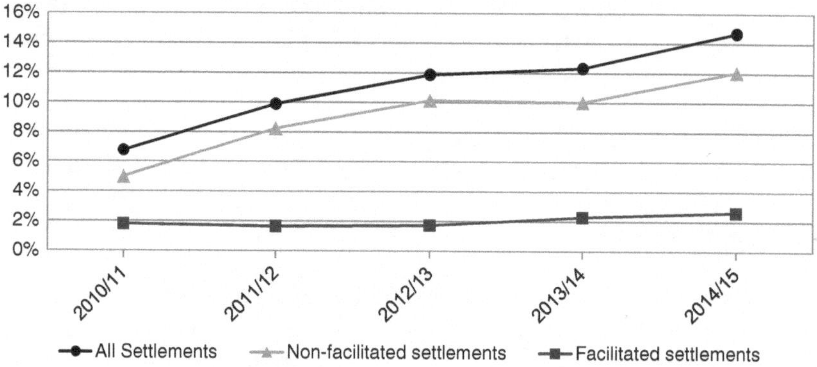


Source: Ontario Ministry of Labour, ESIS data 2010/11–2014/15.

Canadian jurisdictions shows that settlements can reproduce the power imbalances of the employment relationship, with employees subject to pressure to "agree" to substandard terms from employers who often have legal and human resources representation throughout the settlement process (Fairey 2005; Fairey and McCallum 2007).

One way to measure the effectiveness of the settlement process is to examine how settlement amounts compare to the total amount claimed in complaints that were submitted. Because settlements do not involve assessments by an ERO or ESO, it is not possible to compare how settlement amounts compare to the actual entitlements that might have been awarded by an ESO. Interviews with workers who engaged in the settlement process suggest that settlement for less than the claimed amount is a common problem. For example, one worker in the retail industry filed a complaint for unpaid wages, and the original amount calculated by the ESO was $6,800. Through the facilitated settlement process in which the complainant and the employer engaged in extensive bargaining, both parties ultimately had "come to a compromise settlement of $5,000." The ESIS data indicate that both facilitated and non-facilitated settlements tend to be made for less than the original claimed amount. Indeed, the system of facilitated settlements formalized under the *OBA* appears to result in outcomes less favourable for complainants than non-facilitated settlements. For all years under consideration, a higher percentage of facilitated settlements than non-facilitated settlements were settled for less than half of the original total claimed amount in the complaints. Additionally, since 2011/12, more than 30 per cent of non-facilitated settlements were settled for all or more than 100 per cent of the original claimed amount, compared to just slightly more than 20 per cent among those with facilitated settlements (Grundy et al. 2017, 198). One explanation for this surprising result is that facilitated settlements tend to be used for higher-value claims, which may be more rigorously contested by employers.

Settlements can also occur after an Order to Pay Wages has gone to the Ministry of Finance's collections branch. Section 129 of the *ESA* authorizes the collector (currently the Ministry of Finance) to engage in a settlement with the person who owes money, but only with the written agreement of the employee, or the director in the case of Notices of Contravention (NOCs). If the settlement amount is less than 75 per cent of the employees' entitlement, the director's written approval must also be obtained by the collector. While we do not have empirical data on settlements made in the context of collections, anecdotal evidence suggests that such settlements are common. Moreover, as with the facilitated and non-facilitated settlements described above, employees may feel pressure to settle at this point, given the likelihood of receiving nothing in the absence of a settlement.

Finally, settlements can be reached in the context of reviews (appeals) at the OLRB. As noted in chapter 3, the *ESA* provides that applications for review may be made in three situations: (1) ESO Orders to Pay Wages, Fees, Reinstate and/or Comply; (2) ESO refuses to issue an order; and (3) NOCs. Applications for review may be initiated by a complainant, an employer, or a director. Section 120 of the *ESA* empowers the OLRB to authorize a labour relations officer to attempt to affect a settlement of a disputed order. According to the *OLRB Information Bulletin No. 24* (2018), labour relations officers do not decide cases or act as advisors to any of the parties; their role is to help the parties reach a settlement. In so doing, they will often explain the case law, but they do not offer legal advice (OLRB 2018). Settlements are final and binding unless the employee can demonstrate to the board that it was entered into as a result of fraud or coercion (*ESA*, s. 120(5)). As with other adjudicative bodies, settlements are an important dispute resolution mechanism to manage caseload. Indeed, between 2011/12 to 2014/15, 56 per cent of applications for review were settled. However, the settlement process must be designed to limit the opportunity for strategic behaviour that allows one party to gain unfair leverage over the other.

The ESIS data show that, in settlements of employer-initiated reviews, employees typically receive less money than was originally ordered by the ESO; in these instances, between 2011/12 to 2014/15, fully 52 per cent of employees received less than half of the amount of the original Order to Pay Wages. Settlement outcomes are even worse when the review is initiated by a director; almost 80 per cent of employees received less than half of the value of the original Order to Pay Wages. While it can be expected that employees would not receive their full entitlement amount when reviews are settled, as settlements often involve a compromise, employees often appear to be giving up a substantial part of their ESO-assessed entitlement. Moreover, unless it can be assumed that employees are substantially more likely to agree to settlements only when the likelihood of employer success is strong, the fact that 57 per cent of adjudications result in the employee receiving all of their entitlement suggests that employees are better off not settling employer-initiated reviews at the OLRB (Tucker et al. 2016).

Lengthy delays at the review stage might also generate pressure for employees to settle. Although the timeline for applying for review is rather short (30 days), the time to disposition after an application for review has been made is not. As Vosko, Noack, and Tucker (2016, 67) found, in 2014/15, 36 per cent of *ESA* review cases were not disposed of by the OLRB within 168 days. Data on the average time it takes after an application for review has been filed until an *ESA* case is adjudicated are not available, but it would be safe to assume that almost all adjudicated cases are resolved after, perhaps well after, the 168-day mark. The overwhelming majority of *ESA* complaints are made after the employment relationship has been severed, so it can be assumed that many complainants lack resources that enable them to hold out for final adjudication and so again may be tempted to settle for less than their entitlement.

In sum, it is reasonable to conclude that the stages at which a complainant can settle – before assessment by an ERO/ESO, during the collections process, or during an OLRB review – represent points at which complainants may receive less than their legal entitlement. Further research on settlements is warranted to better understand this process.

*Recovering Wages through Bankruptcy Proceedings*

Insolvency or bankruptcy presents another set of challenges for complainants seeking compensation, because there is often a lack of funds to pay employees' earnings. The need for better protections for employees whose employers become insolvent or bankrupt has long been acknowledged by provincial and federal governments (Smith 2002; Thomas 2003). However, the development of robust protections for employees in these situations has been hampered by the complex jurisdictional issues that are raised at the intersection of provincial employment standards and federal bankruptcy legislation.

Of all complaints with monetary entitlements received between 2012/13 and 2014/15, 83 per cent were related to employers who were still in business, 9 per cent were related to employers who were out of business (not bankrupt/insolvent), and nearly 8 per cent were related to employers who were bankrupt or insolvent. Research in other jurisdictions demonstrates that recovery rates in bankruptcy are much worse than when the employer is solvent and still in business (Cho, Koonse, and Mischel 2013, 2). Until 2016, in the event of a formal bankruptcy, ESOs had the option of assisting the complainant in filing a Proof of Claim with the trustee in bankruptcy or monitor. However, from 2009/10 to 2014/15, among complaints where the business appeared to be bankrupt or insolvent and where monetary entitlements were still owing, the ESIS data suggest that only 7 per cent had a Proof of Claim filed by the MOL (Vosko, Noack, and Tucker 2016, 76). Proof of Claims filed with the trustee or monitor are not under the jurisdiction of the Ontario *ESA*. Instead, they fall squarely under the jurisdiction of the federal *Bankruptcy and Insolvency Act*, which, among other things, establishes the priority among different kinds of creditors (s. 136(1)).

Under the federal Wage Earner Protection Program (WEPP), which compensates employees prior to the conclusion of insolvency or bankruptcy proceedings, 90 per cent of applicants receive a payment, and the average amount recovered is 64 per cent of the amount they had earned during the proscribed period (Employment and Social Development Canada 2015, 15). Moreover, the average date of payment is fifty-four days from the time the WEPP application was submitted (15). This is a substantial improvement on the situation confronting employees prior to WEPP. Before WEPP, employees typically waited from one to three years to see any money, the average amount recovered was thirteen cents on the dollar, and only 5 per cent of employees who filed claims with trustees recovered this amount (11).

While the WEPP addresses a pressing need for protecting employees in situations of bankruptcy, a number of serious challenges remain. Many employers enter informal insolvency or bankruptcy, that is, they default on their creditors and abandon their business without formally filing for bankruptcy. The vast majority of Orders to Pay Wages are issued to businesses that are still in business or informally insolvent or bankrupt.[9] Former employees of such businesses are ineligible for WEPP funds. Additionally, the six-month time limit on WEPP claims can exclude many former employees from receiving compensation if they are owed money that should have been paid during the period preceding the six months before the bankruptcy.[10]

## 4. Options for Improving Wage Recovery in Ontario

Declining rates of unionization and the spread of precarious employment require an enforceable floor of workplace standards below which no employment should fall. Yet the MOL's own data demonstrate that the floor of rights that the *ESA* intends to establish is not available to all, in part as the result of weaknesses in the MOL's ability to consistently recover wages. The low rates of recovery of Orders to Pay Wages facilitate the erosion and abandonment of employment standards more generally. Employees may choose not to file a complaint if they perceive that they will not recover their legal entitlements. Given that employees who come forward with complaints face risks, including employer reprisal, the likelihood of non-recovery may further discourage employees from seeking help when their workplace rights are violated. On the other hand, an ineffective recovery system provides an incentive for non-compliance with the law for recalcitrant employers. As Tucker et al. (2019) demonstrate, employers who violate employment standards already face a very small chance of suffering adverse consequences for doing so. Given the limited resources devoted to workplace inspections in Ontario, and the low rate of complaints filed by employees who experience violations (Weil and Pyles 2005; Grundy et al. 2017), non-compliant employers face little chance of being drawn into the employment standards enforcement system. And even when employers are found to be in violation of employment standards, they face little likelihood of having to do much more than pay the wages that were already owed, and not even necessarily in full. Thus the challenges that the MOL faces in recovering wages inadvertently facilitate further financial advantages for unscrupulous employers and creates incentive for the behaviour of recalcitrant employers who have no intention of complying. While the MOL will prosecute employers who refuse to comply with Orders to Pay Wages, such prosecutions are infrequent. The growing prevalence of workplace fissuring presents additional challenges, as this process contributes to the transfer of more employment from large firms to smaller ones less likely to comply with Orders to Pay Wages. Yet it is important to realize that the MOL's difficulties in recovering unpaid wages are not intractable. A variety of options, many of which are used in other jurisdictions, could be enacted to strengthen this critical stage of the employment standards enforcement system.

*Securing Wages in Advance: Wage Protection Programs and Wage Bonds*

A wage protection fund run by the government of Ontario and covering situations of non-payment excluded from the WEPP is needed. It is critical that such a fund provide protection to employees in situations of informal bankruptcy, given their prevalence, especially among under-capitalized businesses often found at the bottom of supply chains in highly fissured industries (e.g., cleaning, etc.). Such a program should also provide avenues for collecting money that exceeds limits currently in place at the federal level. Any future wage-earner protection program should be funded through a payroll tax. This approach has the potential to shift the burden of wage recovery from the general public to industries where non-compliance is more prominent, many of which encourage fissuring structures that often foster insolvency among businesses at the bottom of subcontracting chains.

The creation of a Wage Protection Fund would relieve employees from having to pursue extraordinary measures in order to secure the payment of what they are owed. However, in order to ensure to the extent possible that the employer or other responsible parties pay what they owe, a wide range of recovery mechanisms should be made available to the administrators of the Wage Protection Fund. The recommendations made in the *Final Report of the Changing Workplaces Review* (Mitchell and Murray 2017, s. 5.8) for creating a statutory charge in favour of the director of employment standards to secure unpaid remuneration and for enhancing director liability should be considered first and foremost as mechanisms to reimburse the Wage Protection Fund, rather than as instruments that employees would have available to secure payment of monetary orders. The same principle applies to the mechanisms proposed below. That is, if a wage fund is to be created, these proposals would be tools available to the administrators of the fund. However, in the absence of such a fund, these mechanisms would be needed to assist employees to secure payment of the monies they are owed.

The requirement that employers post a bond or carry some form of insurance that would guarantee the availability of funds to satisfy complainants' monetary claims, even in the case of a bankruptcy, would also provide some protection for employees of insolvent firms. This measure could be selectively adopted in cases where, based on an employer's history, or because the sector is characterized by high rates of violations, there is a strong likelihood of future monetary violations (Mitchell and Murray 2016). Such measures have a long history in industries such as construction and agriculture, but they are increasingly being proposed as a tool for combatting employment standards violations in other sectors.

### *Making Non-Payment of Orders Risky: Liens and Licence Debarment*

To reduce the non-payment of Orders to Pay Wages, it is necessary for the risks associated with non-payment to become more pronounced. Two measures have proven effective in augmenting the risks of non-payment.

One is wage liens that allow complainants or inspectorates to place a temporary lien on the real and personal property of employers. As mentioned previously, the government of Ontario's *Fair Workplaces, Better Jobs Act* (2017) included provisions to enable the director of employment standards to place liens on real and personal property of an employer and hold security to enforce recovery (s. 125.3; see also MOL 2017, 22 November). The Act also empowered the director to issue warrants to enforce payment of Orders to Pay Wages that have the same effect as a writ of execution ordered by a court (s. 125.2). In adopting these measures, the government in power in Ontario followed developments in several jurisdictions in the United States that allow for post-judgment wage liens to be filed by employees or enforcement agencies.[11] However, studies point to a number of limits of post-judgment liens. In situations where an employer has hidden assets during the investigation, where an employer's assets are not easily identified, or in bankruptcy, post-judgment liens are often ineffective (Cho, Koonse, and Mischel 2013, 8–9).

A pre-judgment wage lien would provide an even more powerful mechanism for reducing the non-payment of Orders to Pay Wages. In the United States, Wisconsin and Maryland allow for pre-judgment wage liens to be filed against employers. If the Wisconsin Department of Workforce Development believes that an employer's assets are at risk of being liquidated while a wage claim is being investigated, it has the ability to file a lien against the employer's property. One study determined that, between 2005 and 2015, seventy-nine of the ninety-eight cases (80 per cent) in which the department brought suit to enforce the lien resulted in full or partial payment (a very high percentage, given that these were all cases in which assets were determined to be at risk) (Cho, Koonse, and Mischel 2013, 8–9). Additionally, the study's authors suggest that the mere possibility of a wage lien serves to deter employment standards violations among employers.

A growing number of American jurisdictions are implementing licence debarment to combat employment standards violations and to improve wage recovery. While they do not directly augment collections capacity, such measures make non-compliance with judgments costly and risky for employers. In Cook County, Illinois, an employer found to have engaged in repeated or wilful violation of state and federal wage laws in the past five years faces a number of penalties. Such employers are ineligible to contract with Cook County, face the revocation of their business licence, are ineligible to receive property tax incentives from the county, and may be required to pay back previous incentives. When applying for business licences or tax incentives, applicants must submit an affidavit indicating that they have not violated federal or state wage-payment laws, including the *Illinois Wage Payment and Collection Act*, the *Illinois Minimum Wage Act*, the *Illinois Worker Adjustment and Retraining Notification Act*, the *Employee Classification Act*, the *Federal Labor Standards Act*, or statutes or regulation of any state that governs the payment of wages. In Jersey City, New Jersey, under the recently passed Wage Theft Ordinance, the city department responsible for issuing a business licence (e.g., the Department of Health and Human Services in the case of a food service establishment) sends a request to the state's Department of Labor and Workforce Development for any wage claim forms filed against a licence applicant. Businesses with outstanding claim forms will have thirty days to prove payment, or that they have appealed the order. Failure to pay will result in business licence suspension. The *Interim Report of the Changing Workplaces Review* set out the option of granting the MOL the power to suspend "operating licences, liquor licences, permits and driver's licences of those who do not comply with orders to pay" (Mitchell and Murray 2016). However, licence debarment was not included in the *Fair Workplaces, Better Jobs Act* (2017). Taken together, both wage liens and the revocation of business licences are desirable options because they dramatically raise the potential costs and risks of disregarding Orders to Pay Wages.

*Expanding Liability: Related Employer and Joint and Several Liability*

Any set of measures that aims to improve wage recovery must include expanding the scope of employer liability for Orders to Pay Wages. The scope of employer liability established under the *ESA* is increasingly outmoded. Traditionally, the direct employer was the entity liable for complying with employment standards. In light of the growth of fissuring, whereby a range of entities can carry out employer-like functions, it is inadequate to impose liabilities only on direct employers narrowly conceived. A large body of literature suggests that the expansion of liabilities across the supply chain leads to better outcomes for complainants (Rawling 2006; Weil 2010; Hyde 2012; Hardy and Howe 2015).

The *Fair Workplaces, Better Jobs Act* (2017) modestly strengthened employer liability. It repealed what was known as the "intent or effect" requirement for establishing related employer liability found in the *ESA*. In other provincial jurisdictions' employment standards legislation, related employer provisions simply require that the businesses are associated or related. Ontario was unique in further requiring, following an amendment to the *ESA* in 1987, that the "intent or effect" of the arrangement directly or indirectly defeats the purpose of the *ESA*. Moreover, the OLRB adopted a narrow interpretation of the "intent or effect" requirement that imposed a stringent causation test in order to establish related employer liability. Implementation of this interpretation long inhibited employees who have suffered considerable monetary losses from collecting what they are owed, even when the parent corporation or one of its subsidiaries continued to operate. Thus the removal of this requirement could improve recovery of workers' entitlements. Still, even the strengthened related employer liability is limited in that it does not cover many arm's-length relationships that typically exist in supply chains. For this reason, making joint and several liability apply to supply chain and contracting-out arrangements, and/or expanding the scope of employment standards entitlements for which directors might be liable would strengthen recovery. Employers who enter into contracts with subcontractors and other intermediaries, either directly or indirectly, must be liable both separately and together for money owed and statutory entitlements under the *ESA* and its regulations. If more than one entity directs, controls, or supervises the work and is in control of the employment conditions, whether or not that control is exercised, the pertinent entities should be held jointly and severally liable for complying with the *ESA*. Such measures foster compliance at the bottom of supply chains. As a means of ensuring compliance with the *ESA*, joint and several liability should also be applied to franchisors. Franchisors have extensive power over franchisees. Franchise agreements impose detailed requirements on franchisees and control how they conduct their businesses, to ensure that customers will have the same experience in every franchised location and to protect the brand. In this context, it would be relatively straightforward for franchisors to include requirements regarding *ESA* compliance in franchise agreements as well as to provide franchisors with remedies against the franchisees in the event of *ESA* violations for which they are jointly liable.

Finally, the *ESA* should allow for the recognition of accessorial liability, as provided by Australia's *Fair Work Act*. Under section 550 of the Act, liability for violations can be extended to persons who "have aided, abetted, counselled or procured the contravention; or have induced the contravention, whether by threats or promises or otherwise; or have been in any way, by act or omission, directly or indirectly, knowingly concerned in or party to the contravention; or have conspired with others to effect the contravention." Under this provision, in 2017, the fair work ombudsman (FWO) obtained court-ordered penalties against an accounting firm that knowingly aided one of its clients in committing wage violations. The central importance of accessorial liability lies in its recognition of the full network of actors that can be involved in employment standards violations.

*Making Non-Payment Costly: Liquidated Damages and Interest on Orders to Pay Wages*

Liquidated damages should be introduced in recognition of how employment standards violations can impose severe financial hardship on employees, who often must resort to credit cards or loans from friends and family to make ends meet. In the U.S. context, the *Fair Labor Standards Act* allows a court to assess liquidated damages in the amount equal to the unpaid wages or unpaid overtime pay (29 U.S. Code, chap. 9, s. 260). The *New York State Wage Theft Prevention Act*, which took effect in 2011, increased the amount of liquidated damages available to employees who prevail in pursuing a complaint involving monetary violations from 25 per cent of the back wages owed to 100 per cent of the back wages owed, in addition to other civil penalties and interest. Treble damages allowing for three times the amount of actual financial loss to employees are also available to aggrieved employees in a number of U.S. states (National Employment Law Project 2011, 20). Under the District of Columbia's *Wage Theft Prevention Amendment Act* of 2014, employees can be awarded damages that are three times the back wages owed, in addition to the back wages, so that total restitution is essentially quadruple damages (Code of the District of Columbia s. 32-1012). As well, punitive damages are a common feature in wrongful dismissal cases in Ontario's small claims proceedings. Similar measures are necessary in the province's employment standards enforcement system. Falling short of liquidated damages, the *Fair Workplaces, Better Jobs Act* (2017) solely included a provision authorizing ESOs to award interest on employees' unpaid wages, under terms set by the director of employment standards and approved by the minister of labour.

*Exercise Greater Caution When Facilitating Settlements*

As noted above, settlements facilitated by an ESO can be problematic where weaknesses in the formal complaints process, such as long processing times or poor recovery rates, result in pressure on complainants to settle their complaints so that they will receive something rather than nothing. MOL policies should thus require ESOs to exercise even greater caution when facilitating settlements to ensure that complainants are not pressured to accept settlements that are likely to be below what they are owed. ESOs should also exercise caution when facilitating settlements with employers who have a record of previous violations and/or where multiple employees are likely to be affected by the claims included in the complaint being settled.

Settlements effected at the review (or appeals) stage also warrant careful consideration. Specifically, the government of Ontario should modify the OLRB review process to better protect employees. In particular, consideration might be given to creating an independent worker advisor to assist workers whose monetary entitlements are being challenged before the OLRB (Vosko, Noack, and Tucker 2016, 68).

**5. Conclusion**

The idea that employees should benefit from a minimum floor of workplace standards underpins employment standards legislation. The *ESA*'s role in establishing and ensuring the provision of social minima implies the existence of formal legal recourse for employees who experience employment standards violations. It also requires that regulatory agencies be able to recover the legal entitlements of aggrieved employees. However, long-standing deficiencies characterize the *ESA*'s wage recovery regime. First, the median dollar value of employee entitlements is relatively large ($936) and potentially represents a substantial portion of weekly or monthly earnings for complainants, especially those earning low wages. Second, entitlements with higher dollar values are less likely to be resolved voluntarily, and Orders to Pay Wages have a low recovery rate. In short, most employers who do not voluntarily agree to pay entitlements to employees simply do not pay, and the vast majority do not face serious consequences for withholding payment. There are other recovery challenges for complainants seeking back wages from bankrupt employers. The MOL is very constrained in its ability to assist these complainants, and those whose former employer is in default but has not formally filed for bankruptcy or as insolvent are not eligible for assistance under the federal WEPP program. Finally, settlements, which are increasing in use, can introduce another set of challenges. They can reproduce the power imbalances of the employment relationship and lead to the contracting out of employment standards. ESO-facilitated settlements tend to result in outcomes even less favourable for complainants than non-facilitated settlements. Taken together, these deficiencies in recovery facilitate the erosion and abandonment of legislated social minima. Aggrieved employees may assume great risk in coming forward with a complaint and never see any benefit for doing so. Others may simply come to believe that there is no point in filing a complaint, given the questionable likelihood of recovering back wages. Employers may be emboldened in the knowledge that not only can they engage in employment standards violations with little risk of being caught, but, if caught, they can simply ignore

Orders to Pay Wages without facing serious consequences. The cumulative effect is the abandonment of the legal and normative tenets of employment standards.

Weaknesses in the recovery of wages are not intractable, however. The *Fair Workplaces, Better Jobs Act* (2017) included several measures strengthening the MOL's recovery system, including establishing liens, strengthening related employer liability, and allowing for interest to be paid on Orders to Pay Wages. Other jurisdictions are experimenting with policy measures such as business licence debarment and liquidated damages that hold promise in improving the wage recovery for employees. Lessons learned about wage recovery in jurisdictions such as Britain and the United States (on these national cases, see chapters 8 and 11) can guide efforts to improve the enforcement of employment standards in Ontario.

*Chapter Five*

# The Contradictory Role of Workplace Inspections

Employee-initiated complaints are the foundation of most regimes for enforcing employment standards. After all, violations are experienced by workers, and thus they have the most direct and immediate interest in obtaining a remedy. However, there is growing recognition by both the government and public at large that relying on reactive (or complaints-based) enforcement is inadequate with the rise of precarious and/or complex employment relationships and in the face of resource-strapped inspectorates. As illustrated in chapter 2, reactive enforcement often fails to recognize barriers to accessing the complaints system and the workplace power imbalances that impede the exercise of employee voice.

Consensus is emerging among scholars and policymakers on the need for inspectorates to incorporate more proactive enforcement strategies (Vosko 2010; Vosko et al. 2011; Weil 2010; see also chapters 2, 3, and 11 of this book). Proactive enforcement strategies attempt to allocate enforcement resources in accordance with established priorities. This allocation process often involves identifying sectors or employers where enforcement officials have reasonable grounds to believe that employment standards violations are more prevalent and/or that workers are more reluctant to file complaints.

In the early 2000s, in confronting mounting public criticism for having underutilized workplace inspections, the Ontario Ministry of Labour (MOL) sought to reinvest in proactive enforcement by establishing a "dedicated enforcement team" responsible primarily for conducting workplace inspections and initiating blitzes of industries and workplaces in which employment standards violations are endemic, among other measures. As a result, there was an increase in the number of workplace inspections undertaken by the MOL beginning in the mid-2000s. Building on this greater emphasis on inspections, as part of the changes to the *Employment Standards Act (ESA)* initiated under the *Fair Workplaces, Better Jobs Act* (2017), the MOL committed to inspecting 10 per cent of Ontario's workplaces and hiring up to 175 new employment standards officers (ESOs) by 2020. In June 2018, however, the new Ontario government issued a hiring freeze across the province's public sector after only 75 new ESOs were hired, making it uncertain when or if the remaining 100 would be hired. Shortly thereafter, it also issued a halt on workplace inspections until further notice, in favour of a focus, once again, on complains resolution (Mojtehedzadeh 2018, 28 October) and introduced other legislative changes related to inspections.[1]

Against the backdrop of this swinging pendulum of support for workplace inspections, in this chapter we argue that the potential for workplace inspections to reduce the number and severity of employment standards violations is limited in several ways. First, the focus of inspections is on self-regulation and on educating employers. These practices reflect the underlying assumptions of regulatory new governance, which neglect power imbalances inherent in the employment relationship, and its related compliance orientation, which assumes that most violations are unintentional. Second, the narrow scope of inspections, in terms of the range of "inspectable standards," erodes their ability to address non-compliance with the *ESA* (MOL 2017a, chap. 4, s. 4.1).[2] Third, inspections make very little use of deterrence measures, which are a vital component of any legal regime (for further exploration of deterrence, see chapter 6). In revealing these limitations of the inspection regime, our empirical analysis relies primarily on the previously described Employment Standards Information System (ESIS) administrative data (chapter 1) and data collected via interviews with MOL staff, including ESOs and their regional and district managers.

To set the context in which inspections originate, section 1 considers how proactive modes of enforcement can vary in their degree of reactivity/proactivity by introducing the different types of inspections that the MOL conducts and their outcomes. Section 2 provides a brief profile of the types of businesses typically inspected, with particular focus on the types of employees and employers who are most likely to be affected by workplace employment standards inspections in Ontario. Against this backdrop, section 3 identifies and analyses three key limitations on the efficacy of inspections: first, the provision of advance notice to employers and the related emphasis on self-audits, which reflect the regulatory new governance paradigm and a focus on enhancing administrative efficiency; second, the narrow scope of inspections as it relates to exemptions and the limited number of standards evaluated in inspections; and third, the lack of emphasis on deterring employment

Graph 5.1. Number of Proactive Workplace Inspections, 1983/84–2015/16

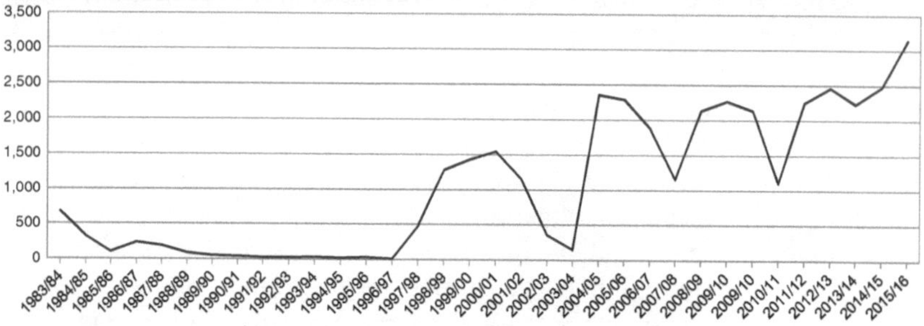


Source: MOL Annual Reports (MOL 2017d; 2018b); fiscal year Reports, MOL Employment Practices/Standards Branch, 1983/84–2015/16 (MOL n.d.).

standards violations through the use of available legal penalties. To conclude, the chapter offers a synthesis yielding recommendations for moving towards a more effective, more deeply proactive, comprehensive model for workplace inspections.

## 1. Inspections: Frequency of Use, Types of Inspections, and Rate of Violations Uncovered

Workplace inspections play a critical role in the employment standards enforcement regime, given that a reactive system based solely on complaints may not accurately reflect the number or types of violations that occur (e.g., Weil and Pyles 2005). As demonstrated in chapter 2, reactive enforcement is limited by the barriers employees who experience employment standards violations encounter when filing complaints. Furthermore, enforcement under a reactive system places responsibility for employment standards regulation onto employees, neglecting power imbalances in workplaces. As such, proactive enforcement strategies are crucial to constructing an effective employment standards enforcement regime.

Although workplace inspections have always played a role (albeit, a relatively small role at certain times, see graph 5.1) in employment standards enforcement, the MOL's efforts to increase proactive enforcement measures re-emerged in 2003/04. Growing pressure from community organizations and worker advocates around precarious employment, as well as a report by Ontario's auditor general (2004b), which found that the exclusive focus on investigating claims made in complaints was failing to protect workers unable to file complaints, spurred this re-emergence. In response to these pressures, the MOL made an operational decision to direct more resources towards proactively inspecting workplaces to improve employer compliance with employment standards, creating the "dedicated enforcement team" to conduct those inspections. Since then, at least twenty ESOs have been assigned to conduct 2,000 to 3,000 workplace inspections each year (Vosko et al. 2011; Auditor General 2004b), with the formal aims of ensuring compliance with employment standards, conveying the requirements of the *ESA* to employers, raising employee and employer awareness of their respective rights and responsibilities, and promoting self-reliance in the workplace (MOL 2017a, chap. 4, s. 4.2). In the most recent year for which data are available (2015/16), fewer than 1 per cent[3] of businesses in Ontario were inspected.

The MOL classifies workplace inspections in five main ways: expanded investigations, inspections of previous violators, targeted inspections, regular inspections, and re-inspections (MOL 2017a, chap. 4, s. 4.7.1A). The analyses below reflect these five groupings, combining re-inspections with inspections of previous violators, and adding two additional groups: inspections that are both expanded (i.e., based on a complaint) and part of a targeted campaign[4] and an "other" category.[5]

Relative to investigating and resolving individual complaints, all workplace inspections emanate from a proactive orientation to employment standards enforcement. They provide a potential opportunity to detect and rectify employment standards violations for a large number of employees. Compared to each other, however, the different types of inspections can also be conceptualized along a continuum that reflects their degrees of reactivity/proactivity (see figure 5.1). As revealed below, inspections yield different outcomes relative to where they fall on this continuum, and thus there is a potential for different types of inspections to produce different deterrent effects.

Expanded investigations are triggered by a complaint (or, in some instances, multiple complaints) formally submitted to the MOL by an employee or employees; they represent the prototypical reactively oriented type of workplace inspection. Workplaces to be inspected are determined by the ESO who is investigating the complaint(s).[6] Generally, a workplace is chosen for an expanded investigation if an ESO detects a violation of one of the eleven MOL-identified "inspectable standards" for inspection and the ESO has reason to believe that more employees are affected (see below for a fuller discussion of the inspectable standards).

On the other end of the spectrum, the most proactively oriented types of workplace inspections are targeted and/or blitz inspections.[7]

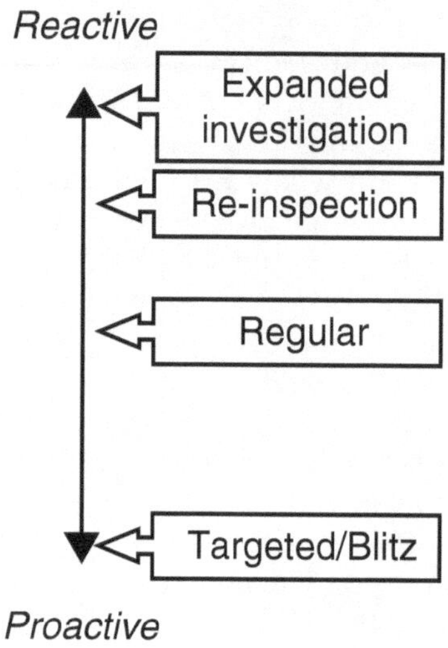


Figure 5.1. Situating Inspection Types on a Continuum of Reactivity/Proactivity

Employers pursued in targeted inspections are drawn from sectors identified by the MOL's Employment Practices Branch through an operational plan or other program initiatives (MOL 2017b, chap. 5, s. 4.7.1A). They differ conceptually from blitz inspections, which result from campaigns directed typically at certain industries, occupations, or forms of employment. For instance, recent province-wide blitzes have often focused on temporary foreign workers and young workers. Local offices may also launch their own blitzes. Blitzes are generally associated with substantial publicity, since they aim to both educate and alert employers in specific sectors about the importance of complying with employment standards. Emphasizing the deterrence effect of this publicity, one ESO noted, "One of the other things is when we are doing the blitzes ... we are going out and blitzing vulnerable workers or we are looking at seasonal employers like we did last year.... [W]e make it known that we are coming out. We are going to be there we are going to look at your business. I think that has been huge.... Even though there is no way we are going to hit every golf course in Ontario, the thought that we might kind of scares them and puts them into compliance."

Situated in the middle of the reactive/proactive spectrum, regular inspections are determined by ESOs or regional/district offices in a process distinct from blitzes. They tend not to be initiated by external sources. Some ESOs note that the selection of sites for inspections is random: "It is completely random.... I will be driving down the road and I think I will inspect that place, I write down the name and go home and open up the file and serve them with a notice of inspection."[8] Other ESOs, in contrast, suggest that inspections are not entirely random; specifically, that ESOs' time and workload constraints shape the ways in which they engage in their tasks and use their discretionary power. Regular inspections may also emerge from "events" that occur when the MOL receives anonymous tips about certain businesses.

Re-inspections may be conducted with previous violators to ensure continuing compliance with the *ESA* and generally occur at least six, but no later than twelve, months following the initial inspection. The purpose of re-inspections is to deter future violations and impose greater sanctions on those who are still in violation (Casey et al. 2018). As such, they are conceptually similar to expanded inspections, in that they seek to inspect an employer who was previously found to be in violation of the *ESA*. The proactive effectiveness of re-inspections is weakened by the limited use of deterrence tools (discussed below). Employers may be re-inspected for adherence to all eleven inspectable standards or only for those standards they were found to have contravened previously. ESOs have discretion in determining which employers to re-inspect; however, in an attempt to ensure immediate and future compliance, employers who are issued Orders to Pay or those with more than one monetary[9] employment standard contravention are strongly recommended for re-inspection. Between 2012/13 and 2015/16, fewer than 8 per cent of inspections each year were classified as re-inspections (in the ESIS). In addition to the main types of inspections described above, the MOL undertakes several other types of inspections, including those prompted by other ESOs, regional and district managers, and/or the staff of the Employment Practices Branch, as well as the Compliance Check program.[10] Since these inspections are less common, the current analysis thereby groups them together as "others."

The ESIS data show that, in the years between 2012/13 and 2015/16, types of workplace inspections undertaken by the MOL have changed (graph 5.2) such that more proactive (i.e., targeted/blitz) inspections are used less often, whereas the use of more reactive (i.e., expanded investigation) inspections is growing. Expanded investigations grew from 10 per cent of all inspections in 2012/13 to 29 per cent in 2015/16, whereas targeted/blitz inspections declined from 63 per cent to 31 per cent in the same period. These changes likely flow from variations in provincial directives (MOL 2013, 14 February) and decisions on provincial blitz campaigns. For instance, the temporary help agencies campaign in 2012 may account, in part, for the higher use of targeted/blitz inspections in the 2012/13 fiscal year. The use of regular inspections

Graph 5.2. Inspection Types by Fiscal Year, 2012/13–2015/16

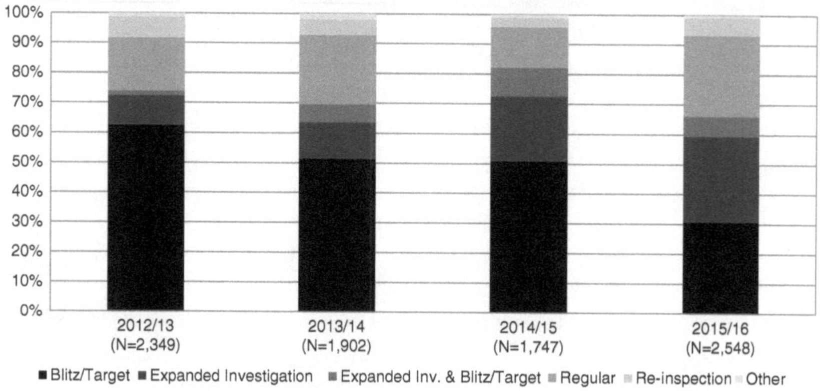


Source: Ontario Ministry of Labour, ESIS data 2012/13–2015/16.

also varies across time, constituting between 14 and 27 per cent of all inspections in each fiscal year.

Consideration of inspections by type is important for another reason: different types of inspections vary in their efficacy in detecting employment standards violations (graph 5.3). Violations are most often detected in the "hybrid" category of inspections that have the features of both expanded investigations and targeted/blitz inspections (80 per cent), followed by expanded investigations (77 per cent). The higher rates of violations among these reactive forms of inspection are not surprising, since they are triggered by an employee complaint, and the employers in question are already identified as non-compliant. In contrast, the employers evaluated in more proactive inspections (regular and targeted/blitz inspections) do not generally have prior records of violation, and somewhat lower rates of violation are detected (75 and 68 per cent respectively). Re-inspections of previous violators are the least likely to detect employment standards violations (40 per cent), suggesting that workplace inspections may have at least some deterrent effects.

## 2. Profiles of Businesses Inspected and Employees Therein: Who Is Most Affected by Inspections?

Since 2014 the MOL has taken the growth of precarious employment into account, in part by focusing on proactive enforcement in industries and sectors in which employees are known to experience greater vulnerability and where non-compliance with the *ESA* is well documented

Graph 5.3. Percentage of Inspections with Violations and Average Number of Violations by Inspection Type, 2012/13–2015/16

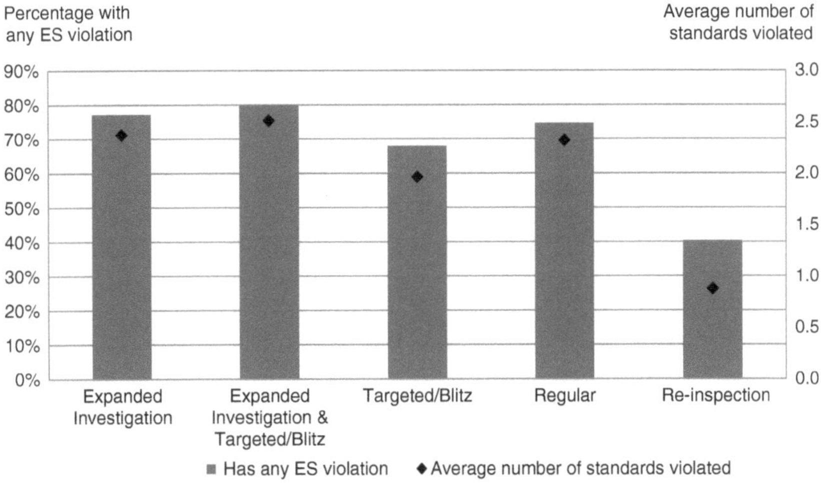


Source: Ontario Ministry of Labour, ESIS data 2012/13–2015/16 (pooled).

(e.g., through blitzes). The accommodation and food services industry, for example, which includes 7 per cent of all employees in Ontario (Statistics Canada 2016d), has both a high incidence of employment standards violations and a high prevalence of precarious jobs. While only 7 per cent of Ontario businesses with employees are in accommodation and food services (Statistics Canada 2016a), fully 26 per cent of employment standards inspections were conducted in accommodation and food services workplaces in 2015/16. Similarly, whereas only 12 per cent of Ontario businesses with employees are in retail trade (Statistics Canada 2016a), in the period under study 20 per cent of employment standards inspections were conducted in retail trade workplaces.

In addition to targeting specific industries or sectors, enforcement carried out by the MOL suggests that greater attention is paid to smaller firms. Although the majority of employees in Ontario work in large firms (52 per cent in 2016), workplace inspections often focus on firms with fewer than twenty employees (69 per cent of all inspections). While the preceding chapters show that smaller firms tend to be at greater risk of non-compliance with the *ESA*, interview data point to other factors that may promote inspections of small firms. One factor is that ESOs experience time and workload constraints that may shape the ways in which they engage with workplace inspections. For example, some officers may actively pursue inspections at smaller workplaces, as explained by one ESO: "Smaller businesses are easier. There is less payroll. Bigger businesses are more difficult because they often have more than one work location. A good example of that would be Sears Canada or Home Depot.... We have to get multiple payrolls from [them]."

Inspecting smaller businesses has the potential to reduce the complexity of an inspection and thus the time spent at each workplace, enabling officers to meet efficiency targets and maximize the number of inspections they conduct. Another ESO highlighted the pressure of meeting targets and how it shapes enforcement practices: "It doesn't matter if the employer has 2 employees if the employer has 500 employees. You have to do a certain number of inspections.... [I]t doesn't matter if you have an employer who is larger or smaller you still have to do ... let's say twenty inspections this month."

ESOs may also focus on smaller firms, given the assumption that larger firms will have human resource departments and thus are presumed to have a better understanding of employer obligations under the *ESA*, whereas smaller firms may lack this infrastructure and consequently are more likely to violate the *ESA* as a result of their lack of knowledge. As one ESO stated, "I think one of the biggest barriers is that the employers themselves, I find, are not really aware of what is required by the *Employment Standards Act* (2000).... [O]ftentimes we'll get claims from smaller employers, and I think those are the ones that don't really have a proper understanding of what their duties and obligations are as an employer and what standards they have to adhere to." Another ESO explained that, because employers in smaller firms lack knowledge about their obligations, "sometimes inadvertently they will cause infractions." As explored below, these assumptions typically reflect a more general compliance orientation and are premised on the notion that employers who fail to comply with the *ESA* do so unintentionally, and often as the result of a lack of knowledge.

The MOL's focus on conducting inspections in specific industries and firms of certain sizes can have an indirect effect on the employees of these businesses, who often belong to social groups that are disadvantaged in the labour force. For instance, blitzes targeting agricultural workplaces may inspect farms where temporary foreign workers, who face multiple layers of vulnerability, making them unlikely to report employment standards violations, are employed (Vosko, Tucker, and Casey 2019). Similarly, inspections targeting industries characterized by high levels of precarious employment, such as accommodation and food services and retail trade, may affect the disproportionate numbers of women employed therein (59 and 56 per cent female in each industry, respectively). Racialized employees are also overrepresented in accommodation and food services, constituting over 10 per cent of employees in the industry in Ontario, compared to around 7 per cent of the province's total labour force (Block and Galabuzi 2011). Finally, in concentrating inspections in small firms, the MOL is also actively engaging in enforcement in workplaces in which recent immigrants to Canada are overrepresented (see also chapter 1).

Since precarious employment and the likelihood of experiencing violations of workplace rights are not experienced equally across social groups, strategic enforcement of the *ESA* plays an important role in ensuring that employees who belong to social groups that have been historically disadvantaged in the labour force, such as recent immigrants and women, receive the legally mandated employment protections.

While targeting firms and industries with a high prevalence of precarious employment is certainly consistent with the tenets of strategic enforcement, fissuring contributes to high levels of uncertainty (financial and otherwise) among the proliferating number of small firms it engenders, including subcontractors and franchisees. Furthermore, as discussed in chapter 1, the central focus on inspecting small firms may, in some instances, be shaped by stereotypes about the social location of employers in such contexts – specifically, their immigration status and/or their cultural backgrounds. Such assumptions were echoed by one ESO: "They're going to try and get away with whatever they can.... [T]here's some employers that have different nationalities, they come from different backgrounds, so maybe they don't have the knowledge of the employment standards."

The degree of precarious employment in particular industries and among smaller firms, as well as the social location of employees employed in these high-risk contexts, should remain a central focus of enforcement strategy. It is, however, important not to lose sight of how fissuring has fundamentally altered working arrangements. Employers at the bottom of extensive subcontracting or franchise chains, many of whom are in tenuous financial positions themselves, can bear the brunt of enforcement, whereas those at the top remain unaffected. Indeed, behind small, seemingly autonomous firms are often extended supply chains, through which pressures from the lead firms are exerted. In highly competitive markets, employers in small firms face pressures to contain labour costs, and evading their responsibilities under the *ESA* represents a potential cost-cutting strategy. As a result, targeting firms at the bottom of the supply chain exclusively can obscure larger structural issues in play.

## 3. Limitations of Inspections

As previously noted, there is widespread recognition that proactive inspections are a critical component of the MOL's enforcement practices. Despite their potential impact on the overall enforcement regime, and more narrowly, to ameliorate employment standards violations likely to affect those who are precariously employed or who have been disadvantaged in the labour force, various practices that characterize the current workplace inspection regime in Ontario reduce its efficacy. Below, we identify three central weaknesses of the inspection process that reflect the adoption of a regulatory new governance–styled approach to regulation: an emphasis on administrative efficiency and self-regulation, the limited scope of workplace inspections, and a dearth of deterrence measures.

*Efforts to Expedite Investigations through Advance Notice and Self-Audit*

Prior to beginning an inspection, ESOs engage in advance planning, where they ensure that a business is still in operation and determine whether there are any open complaints or recent inspections, and if employees are unionized (inspections focus on workplaces composed principally of non-unionized employees). Following these checks, ESOs issue a notice to employers, up to ten business days in advance, to alert them of the upcoming workplace inspection. According to the *Administrative Manual for Employment Standards (AMES)* (MOL 2017a, chap. 4, s. 4.7.2), the *ESA* does not require ESOs to issue advance notice of inspection to employers; however, the *AMES* indicates that they should be given advance notice unless there are specific reasons for not providing them.[11] During our interviews, many ESOs confirmed that they may conduct inspections without notice but emphasize the importance of preparation time in the inspection process. As one ESO said, "Even though we have the ability to do the inspection on the spot, we don't actually do that.... We don't do that unless we believe evidence is going to be destroyed.... In most cases we walk in and say, 'An inspection has been scheduled ... for two weeks from today, gives you lots of time to put your records together and make them available for me.'"

The main function of advance notices is to provide employers time to assemble their records, which the ESO will review to determine whether or not they are in compliance with the *ESA* (a process that is framed as a "test audit"). As noted by the ESO above, advance notice is generally issued "unless there is a specific rationale for not providing notice" (MOL 2017a, chap. 4, s. 4.7.2).[12]

The provision of advance notice to employers may lessen the likelihood that inspections will turn up violations. As another ESO commented, "A lot of employers don't have records on site anymore. Some of them like to create the records in that two-week period – which is hard to prove, unless you're talking to an employee and they tell you that the records are entirely different from what you have been given." ESOs also typically interview a selection of employees during workplace inspections; providing advance notice may thus allow employers to adjust employees' schedules so that only certain individuals believed to be less likely to complain will be present to participate in interviews during an inspection. Since interviews with employees depend on their availability during the inspection, employers can effectively select the employees who will be interviewed by making sure that those employees are present at the time of inspection.[13]

Given the ways that advance notice can create opportunities for obscuring violations, it is not used typically in many other fields of regulation. For instance, inspections conducted by the MOL's Health and Safety Branch are usually unannounced (MOL 2013, 28 January). In the realm of public health, the City of Toronto's food premises inspection system is based on unannounced inspections occurring at intervals mandated by the Ontario Ministry of Health and Long-Term Care (Medical Officer of Health 2014). In the United States, unannounced inspections are a key part of the Wage and Hour Division's proactive enforcement arsenal (Department of Labor 2012). The use of advance notices in employment standards enforcement in Ontario reinforces a longstanding perception that employment standards do not warrant the same the type of stringent enforcement practices required in other fields of regulation. This practice furthermore assumes that non-compliance is generally inadvertent, and that unscrupulous employers can be easily detected or predicted.

Self-audits are another tool upon which the MOL's proactive inspection process relies considerably. Self-audits are usually concerned with employment standards compliance over a minimum of six months, and employers are required to report the results of their self-assessments to the assigned ESO, including the evidentiary records of employment standards violations. Typically, self-audits are sought when the initial assessment (i.e., test audit) by an ESO reveals *ESA* contraventions related to monetary standards and that warrant a more exhaustive review of employment records. The ESIS data show that about one third of all workplace inspections prompt an employer self-audit, and almost all workplace inspections where a self-audit is required detected employment standards violations during the test audit.

Such audits can be considered a form of "monitored self-regulation" (Estlund 2005), in which firms are encouraged to regulate and monitor their own compliance under the supervision a governing body. Self-audits are increasingly used in various industries and sectors and express the shift to a regulatory new governance paradigm and its emphasis on more cost-effective and "light touch" enforcement policies. Many scholars have raised concern about this shift: now firms must not only decide what to do (i.e., whether to comply with regulations) but also what to report that they are doing (Heyes 2000). Audits done by firms themselves have an inherent conflict of interest, given the incentives to report compliance and not report contraventions (Guttman and Roback 1995).[14]

In terms of compliance with the *ESA*, self-audits are intended to reduce the investigatory burden on ESOs; however, they depend entirely on the honesty of firms in reporting any violations they find. When employers do not report the employment standards violations that are being perpetrated in a workplace, any gains in efficacy are thereby lost, and violators are effectively permitted to continue undetected.

In three specific circumstances, ESOs may also complete a full audit of an employer's records: where the employer does not agree to conduct a self-audit or agrees to conduct the self-audit but does not complete it; where the employer has repeated violations; or where the ESO has all the records and prefers to complete a full audit (MOL 2017a, 18). ESOs have the discretion to undertake a full audit if they suspect that an employer may not be honest. As one ESO stated, "Depending on the employer, I might even do a full audit where if I don't think they are going to be honest in their own calculations." Based on the ESIS data, less than 5 per cent of all workplace inspections involve a full audit by an ESO.

Both advance notices and self-audits aim to expedite workplace inspections by making the process more "efficient" or "streamlined." As indicated above, efforts to expedite inspections are also tied to the emphasis on inspecting small firms, which is presumed to be easier and faster. This approach to streamlining allows ESOs to meet the targeted number of inspections they must complete in accordance with the Balanced Scorecard performance measurement system. This approach is also consistent with the assumption, common among some ESOs, that employers of smaller firms lack knowledge about the *ESA* and are consequently more likely to violate employment standards – although ESOs must simultaneously assume that employers' knowledge is comprehensive enough to complete a self-audit. Ultimately, these practices may, however, make it easy to violate the *ESA* without detection. Once

Table 5.1. The Eleven Inspectable Standards Evaluated during Workplace Inspections

| |
|---|
| 1. *ESA* poster requirement |
| 2. Wage statements |
| 3. Unauthorized deductions |
| 4. Record keeping |
| 5. Hours of work |
| 6. Eating periods |
| 7. Overtime pay |
| 8. Minimum wage |
| 9. Public holidays |
| 10. Vacation with pay |
| 11. Temporary help agencies charging employees fees and providing information |

Source: *AMES*, chap. 4, s. 4.1 (MOL 2017a).

again this contradictory outcome indicates governments' struggle to balance the competing interests of protecting workers while minimizing interference with businesses' activities. As a result, prevailing practices emphasizing self-regulation and administrative efficiency may ultimately obscure rather than redress violations.

*The Limited Scope of Workplace Inspections*

The efficacy of inspections in enforcing employment standards is also fundamentally constrained by their narrow scope, circumscribed, first, by the emphasis on assessing compliance with eleven employment standards exclusively, and second, by occupation- and industry-based exemptions and special rules.

ESOs are only directed to evaluate employers' compliance with eleven standards that have been designated as "inspectable" and thereby "core" standards during workplace inspections (table 5.1). Notably, many of the employment standards designated as inspectable standards for inspections are administrative or non-monetary standards, such as record keeping and poster requirements. The substance of these eleven inspectable standards is dissonant with the substance of a majority of complaints. As the analysis in chapter 2 shows, most complaints involve claims for violations of monetary employment standards, most commonly unpaid wages and termination pay (neither of which is included in the inspectable standards). Although the prioritization of these eleven standards for routine inspection may derive from the well-intended assumption that their enforcement is of collective rather than individual concern, there is a disconnect between these inspectable standards and employees' routine, lived experiences of employment standards violations. In this context, even where ESOs conduct inspections, employees who experience employment standards violations may not experience redress if the violations do not relate to one of the eleven inspectable standards. Given the prevalence of complaints containing claims for unpaid wages especially (Vosko et al. 2017), excluding many monetary violations from consideration during workplace inspections both reduces the efficacy of employment standards enforcement for aggrieved employees and dilutes the potentially proactive role of workplace inspections in deterring a wide range of employment standards violations. The standardization of employment standards evaluated during workplace inspections also obscures the potential for understanding how the prevalence and type(s) of employment standards violations may differ by industry and occupation.

The employment standards evaluated during workplace inspections are even more limited for employees who have occupations or work in industries with exemptions or special rules. Described in chapter 1, exemptions and special rules under the *ESA* reflect the underlying tension between establishing acceptable social minima and the need for flexibility in order to avoid imposing undue hardship on employers (MOL 1967, 16 May). In the context of workplace inspections, the complex system of special rules and exemptions affects which employment standards employers are evaluated for and expected to comply with, for various (sub)groups of employees in a workplace. For example, agricultural workers, such as farm employees and harvesters, are exempt from employment standards relating to overtime pay, working time, and public holidays (MOL 2018a). Consequently, during workplace inspections of agricultural sites, compliance with these employment standards is not evaluated, and inspections probe compliance with the *ESA* only minimally, as it pertains to these employees. As one ESO noted, "We looked at temporary foreign workers, and most of them are agricultural workers. They are exempt from everything except record-keeping and deductions from wages. So, really, [we] are only looking for two things. You can be done an inspection in an hour." In such instances, it appears that the question of whether or not employees subject to exemptions or special rules confront working conditions falling below the social minima related to other employment standards is left unaddressed. While investigating adherence to only eleven standards is, on its own terms, already a limited means of evaluating compliance with employment standards, ESOs investigate even fewer standards for employees subject to exemptions and special rules.

Despite the narrow focus of workplace inspections, their outcomes suggest that employment standards violations are widespread; 70 per cent of all inspections conducted between 2012/13 and 2015/16 detected some type of violation. Notably, inspections detect proportionately more non-monetary than monetary employment standards violations (85 per cent compared to 60 per cent, respectively). This outcome is not surprising, given the prominence of non-monetary standards among the eleven inspectable standards. The most common types of monetary employment standards violations detected via workplace inspections relate to public holiday pay and overtime pay (identified in 47 and 20 per cent of inspections with violations, respectively), whereas the most common types of non-monetary employment standards violations detected relate to record-keeping and hours of work (identified in 38 and 37 per cent of inspections, respectively; see graph 5.4). The violations that ESOs identify in workplace inspections stand in sharp contrast to those employment standards violations that prompt individual complaints (compare graph 5.4 with graph 2.1 in chapter 2).

The emphasis on administrative efficiency through advance notice and self-auditing, together with the narrow scope of inspections, limits the efficacy of inspections in achieving redress for employees. By relying on employers' self-regulation, violations may go undetected if employers fail to report existing violations, or, alternatively, hide evidence of non-compliance. Moreover, by restricting the scope of inspections to the eleven inspectable standards, employment standards violations may remain unaddressed if they are not included in the selected list. For instance, many of the industries/sites selected for blitzes are defined typically by their precarious working conditions, which may include violations of employment standards that go beyond the eleven inspectable standards (or the even fewer standards subject to inspection when employees in such industries are affected by exemptions and special rules).

In the inspection process, the role prescribed for ESOs in conducting workplace inspections does not provide for enforcing the full range of standards outlined in the *ESA*. Indeed, this move underscores how the embrace of regulatory new governance, especially its focus on compliance, can contribute to deepening regulatory degradation in subtle ways, even in a context characterized ostensibly by the increased use of proactive enforcement measures.

Graph 5.4. Types of Employment Standards Violations Found in Inspections, 2012/13–2015/16

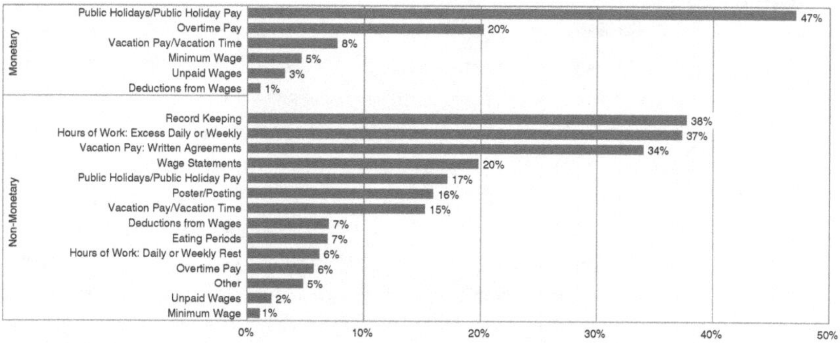


Source: Ontario Ministry of Labour, ESIS data 2012/13–2015/16 (pooled).

### *Limited Use of Deterrence Tools*

Another factor undermining the efficacy of workplace inspections is the scant use of deterrence tools that impose meaningful penalties on employers when violations are discovered. In the context of inspections, an ESO may use enforcement tools (e.g., Orders to Pay, Compliance Orders, Notices of Contravention [NOCs], tickets under Part I of the *Provincial Offences Act*) if contraventions are revealed during inspections. The commitment to "light touch" regulation invoked by regulatory new governance, however, is apparent in a widespread reliance on compliance tools (such as Orders to Pay) and the very infrequent use of deterrence measures such as fines or tickets, which ultimately weakens the deterrence effect of workplace inspections. ESIS data show that, despite the relatively high proportion of workplace inspections that detect employment standards violations, very few employers receive tickets under Part I of the *Provincial Offences Act*. For workplace inspections conducted between 2012/13 and 2015/16, only 19 per cent of employers with violations of at least one ticketable offence[15] were issued a Part I ticket. Of all violations detected, less than 8 per cent had tickets issued.[16] Tickets were more commonly issued for monetary employment standards violations than for non-monetary employment standards violations (14 per cent compared to 5 per cent; see table 5.2), but they were most often used when both monetary and non-monetary employment standards violations were detected (32 per cent). Workplace inspections that detect higher monetary entitlements owing to employees were also more likely to incur tickets.

Table 5.2. Types of Violation and Use of Tickets in Inspections, 2012/13–2015/16

| | No ticket issued | Ticket issued |
|---|---|---|
| Type of Violation | | |
| Monetary only | 86% | 14% |
| Non-monetary only | 95% | 5% |
| Monetary and non-monetary | 68% | 32% |
| Number of ticketable violations (mean) | | |
| Monetary | 1.3 | 1.7 |
| Non-monetary | 2.3 | 3.0 |
| All violations | 2.7 | 4.1 |
| Total entitlement amount | | |
| Median | $591 | $1,576 |
| Mean | $2,602 | $4,773 |

Source: Ontario Ministry of Labour, ESIS data 2012/13–2015/16 (pooled).

The use of deterrence tools also varies on the basis of the inspection type. More reactive types of workplace inspections (i.e., expanded investigations, and expanded and targeted/blitzes) with violations are more likely to result in a ticket than more proactive types of inspections (graph 5.5). For expanded investigations, which are prompted by individual employee complaints, nearly one quarter (24 per cent) of employers with violations of a ticketable offence received at least one ticket, compared to less than 18 per cent among regular and targeted/blitz inspections. This variation may reflect efforts to enhance the deterrent effects of expanded investigations, where employers have presumably already been educated about the appropriate application of employment standards in the context of resolving the individual complaint but have not taken steps to comply with employment standards for the rest of their employees.

In contrast, countering the premise of re-inspections (i.e., to deter repeat violators by escalating penalties if non-compliance continues), fewer tickets are issued to those with ticketable offence in re-inspections than in expanded investigations (only 18 per cent of employers with violations receive at least one ticket in re-inspections). Although the findings suggest that re-inspections detect fewer violations (as noted above), employers who still fail to comply would presumably be expected to receive harsher penalties than first-time violators. Yet it

Graph 5.5. Use of Tickets among Employers with Violations, by Inspection Type, 2012/13–2015/16

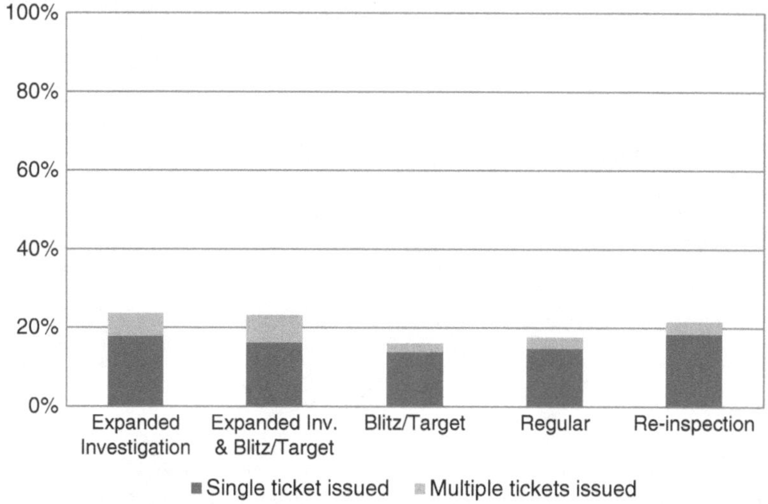


Source: Ontario Ministry of Labour, ESIS data 2012/13–2015/16 (pooled).

appears that re-inspections do not result in greater use of penalties. Indeed, the use of Part I tickets and NOCs in the context of workplace inspections seems to be rather idiosyncratic, suggesting that there is no strong policy impetus to use these formal penalties to enforce employment standards, nor to deter repeat offenders. Even when penalties are imposed, amounts owing typically range between $250 and $360, amounts sufficiently low for employers to regard them as costs of doing business. The low probability of being subject to an inspection, along with the reliance on self-regulation and limited use of deterrence, offers employers little incentive to refrain from employment standards violations (see also Vosko, Noack, and Tucker 2016).

## 4. Conclusion

The government of Ontario sought to improve employment standards enforcement by devoting greater attention to proactive strategies beginning in the early 2000s through to mid-2018. A closer review, however, suggests that the efficacy of workplace inspections in detecting and deterring violations is constrained by an emphasis on administrative efficiency and self-regulation, their limited scope, and the infrequent use of penalties when violations occur.

A key focus of workplace inspections through to 2018 involved ensuring employer compliance through employer education; that is, to remind employers of the content of the *ESA* and communicate its requirements, thereby raising awareness of rights and responsibilities, and promoting self-reliance (MOL 2017a, s. 4.2). As one manager noted, "What you do is not just enforcement, [it] is also education for the employer. You want to make sure the [employer] understand[s] where they went wrong and why they went wrong and how to fix it."

While employer education is critical, the common assumption that employers' non-compliance is rooted in ignorance undermines the efficacy of inspections by neglecting power imbalances inherent in workplaces and the related possibility that non-compliance may be an ongoing strategy for cost reduction. A growing body of research on workplace fissuring and precarious employment suggests that ignorance may not be the driving factor behind employers' non-compliance; rather, industry structures and increased competition generate enormous pressure for employers to reduce costs, creating incentives to violate laws (Weil 2010). "Light touch" regulations presuming employer benevolence neglect inequalities inherent in employment relationships and, together with the limited use of penalties and an emphasis on education, undermine the potentially deterrent effects of workplace inspections.

Recognition of the need for proactive, more strategic enforcement, coupled with a greater overall adherence to the principles of regulatory new governance, which emphasizes a compliance approach to regulation, inevitably creates tensions for government officials as they attempt to balance business interests with the aim of ensuring social minima for workers. These tensions inherent in Ontario's employment standards enforcement system are also observable elsewhere. Similar to Ontario, the enforcement of Quebec's *Act Respecting Labour Standards* leans towards a compliance orientation, limiting the use and effectiveness of penal sanctions in encouraging compliance with existing standards (Gesualdi-Fecteau and Vallée 2016; see also chapter 10 of this book). In the United States, Weil (2010) notes that, even though deterrence has long been recognized as fundamental to enforcement of employment standards, the application of penalties is not central to the inspection process. Clearly, therefore, an increase in deterrence is required, in the forms of greater use of sanctions as well as higher penalties (see chapter 6). Along these lines, greater adherence to the principle of escalating deterrence measures for repeat violators is necessary, not only in the amount of the penalty, but also through other measures.

Fissuring, moreover, poses additional challenges to the enforcement of employment standards, as longstanding approaches to regulation become less relevant to changing workplaces and, therefore, less effective and applicable. As Weil discusses in chapter 11, inspecting individual workplaces without considering the larger structure of companies today, which may include several layers of contracting, subcontracting, or franchising, neglects the context and motivations behind employer practices at the bottom of the supply chain. Similarly, in Australia (see chapter 9), there is increased attention to fissuring (e.g., franchising), such that accessorial liability provisions now offer greater opportunities for holding lead contractors, franchisors, and holding companies accountable. Likewise, strategic enforcement in Ontario also necessitates a renewed emphasis on the firms at the top.

Alongside this meta-level adaptation, workplace inspections must change to reflect the increasing number of businesses operating without a defined physical location to inspect. Employees who perform their work in multiple locations, such as those employed in cleaning services, personal support work, some construction crews, and temporary agencies, for example, often lack a physical "workplace" that can be inspected. New technologies have further facilitated the rise of companies – in industries like software development and customer support – where employees work from home, and where meetings are conducted virtually or in a co-working space. Currently, ESOs serve notices of inspection in person at the location of the workplace; businesses where there is no physical workplace to inspect appear to fall out of range of the employment standards inspectorate. Despite the shortcomings of workplace inspections, they nevertheless remain an essential component of the overall employment standards enforcement regime in Ontario, as well as in other jurisdictions. The growth of precarious employment and forms of employment that are characterized by multiple dimensions of labour market insecurity mean that more employees rely on the *ESA* to protect their rights at work. Effective enforcement is particularly important for workers who belong to social groups that have historically been disadvantaged in the labour force, such as women and recent immigrants, who are disproportionately found in precarious jobs and industries characterized by extensive fissuring, many of whom are also unlikely to file complaints for fear of reprisal (chapter 2).

Although the government of Ontario promised changes to improve the efficacy of workplace inspections in 2017/18 in tabling the *Fair Workplaces, Better Jobs Act* (2017), such as hiring up to 175 more ESOs by 2020/21, many such changes were either never implemented or were implemented and subsequently withdrawn by a successive government. Most significant for the foregoing analysis is the hold put on workplace inspections in the fall of 2018 and the instruction to MOL staff to focus their energies on resolving complaints instead.[17] Rather than proactively targeting workplaces where employees are likely to experience violations, such changes return to relying on individual employees to report violations. They also remove a crucial deterrence measure in employment standards enforcement in Ontario, a topic addressed in chapter 6, such that violations of employment standards can remain undetected so long as employees do not complain.

Once this freeze is lifted, aspects of workplace inspections that undermine their efficacy must be addressed to improve their outcomes. For instance, the expansion of the scope of inspections to encourage ESOs to reach beyond the eleven inspectable standards would ensure that workplace inspections have the potential to ensure that the employees have their full employment standards rights realized. While it may not be necessary to assess compliance with every employment standard in every workplace, a more nuanced understanding of the types of violations likely to occur in particular industries and types of businesses might enable ESOs to conduct inspections efficiently without resorting to a "one-size-fits-all" framework. For instance, the inspection of workplaces where employees are subject to exemptions and special rules might include attention to the potential misclassification of employees for the purpose of evading employment standards (i.e., detecting such practices as the misclassification of employees as managers, even if their duties do not support such a classification, in order to avoid being required to provide overtime pay).

The *Fair Workplaces, Better Jobs Act* (2017) also included a number of changes, since repealed, that moved in the direction of a more strategic approach to enforcement, which, as Weil (2010; see also chapter 11 of this book) envisions, entails promoting inspections that are informed by deep knowledge of industry structures and therefore enhance deterrence. The adoption of a similar approach in Ontario might include a more active effort to address fissuring, and the economic pressures that prompt employers to violate employment standards, by subjecting lead firms to inspection along with their subcontractors. This approach would be strengthened by the ability of ESOs to assign joint liability up the supply chain. One possibility might be to establish another category of inspection, similar to the in-depth "inquiry" used in Australia, that seeks to map out the relationships between networks and industries in order to better understand the systemic drivers of non-compliance.

Another strategy for increasing the deterrent effect of workplace inspections would be to promote the consistent and routine use of tickets under Part I of the *Provincial Offences Act*, for all detected ticketable violations. Although the fines associated with tickets/NOCs and the frequency of imposing these penalties remain low, legislation in Ontario also includes a deterrence measure that mirrors one in Quebec: it gives the director of employment standards the ability to publish names of employers who have been issued penalties, along with the contravention and amount of penalty (Gesualdi-Fecteau and Vallée 2016). This strategy may promote compliance through its influence on firms' reputation, their fear of public disapproval, and the possible repercussions that negative publicity may have on the firms' business opportunities (van Erp 2008, 2011). This "naming and shaming" approach is also being used in several other jurisdictions. For example, California's *Employee Misclassification Act* requires employers found to have misclassified workers to display a notice on the company website, or in another prominent space, which indicates that "the Labor and Workforce Development Agency or a court ... has found that the person or employer has committed a serious violation of the law by engaging in the willful misclassification of employees."[18]

Such changes would represent incremental improvements towards strategic enforcement, with the aim of ensuring that the employment standards rights of all Ontario employees are protected. Yet obstacles prompted by the focus on compliance, administrative efficiency, and the limited scope of inspections remain challenges to highly effective enforcement. Evidence-based enforcement strategies require continuous development and improvement, particularly in evaluating employment standards relevant to employees in different industries and occupations, as well as in emerging and changing business structures.

*Chapter Six*

# The Deterrence Gap: Towards an Explanation

A central claim of this book is that the *Employment Standards Act (ESA)* is failing to live up to its founding promise of providing a floor of minimum protections that advance the principles of fairness and universality. There are a number of reasons for the Act's deficiencies. The foregoing chapters focus on flaws in Ontario's compliance-oriented employment standards enforcement approach. These flaws include barriers facing employees in making complaints against their current employers (chapter 2); the inevitability that the complaints system will remain overburdened as long as the enforcement regime prioritizes reactive over proactive enforcement (chapter 3); the weaknesses of a recovery system that leaves large numbers of employees who have experienced monetary violations without a remedy (chapter 4); and the ways in which the potential benefits of more proactive enforcement are undercut by prevailing forms of workplace inspection (chapter 5).

In this chapter, we turn our attention to another important limitation of employment standards enforcement – the deterrence gap. All rigorous theories of enforcement recognize deterrence as key to effective enforcement, even if they disagree on its precise role. Even in more "light touch" approaches associated with regulatory new governance, such as responsive regulation, which emphasizes starting with education and persuasion to secure compliance, the hammer of deterrence must be available when employers do not respond. This insight is not new. In 1926 E.M. Burns published a treatise on the minimum wage in which she took up the question of enforcement. As she concluded in her discussion, "A well administered system would be supplied with an adequate inspectorate ... and would enforce payment by criminal proceedings. Cases would be conducted by the inspectorate, and fines accompanied by orders for the payment of arrears, except in cases where the offence could clearly be proved due to ignorance, would make non-compliance unprofitable" (179). Yet despite widespread recognition of the importance of using deterrence in employment standards enforcement systems, researchers in many jurisdictions consistently find a significant gap between the deterrence measures available to enforcement officials and their actual use (de Tonnancour and Vallée 2009; Gesualdi and Vallée 2016; Hepple 2013; Thomas 2009).

Section 1 briefly documents a persistent deterrence gap in Ontario, which fluctuates within a limited range. Informed by our critical political economy approach, section 2 is attentive to the ways in which ongoing demands by workers and social activists for protection from exploitative workplace practices conflict with an array of structural and ideological constraints that limit government regulation and sustain the enforcement gap. Grounded in a historical analysis, we show that these tensions are evident in the earliest protective employment legislation and enforcement practices. As chapter 1 suggests, this background is not just a matter of historical interest; the weight of history contributes to the creation of an enforcement culture, a bureaucratically embedded "common sense," that shapes the attitudes and approaches of future generations of officials. Moreover, as the foregoing chapters demonstrate, this deeply rooted compliance culture is sustained by the continuation of conflict over employment standards regulation as manifested in regulatory new governance approaches that shape government policy and practice. Nevertheless, as this chapter demonstrates, the conflict between demands for improved protection and relief from regulation, as well as the weight of an enforcement culture, are dynamic, and therefore the dimensions of the resulting deterrence gap are continually shifting.

To fully appreciate the enforcement culture operating in Ontario, section 3 examines more closely the world of the front-line officials who produce employment standards enforcement daily in the context of contradictory and often shifting pressures around the regulation of business. These contradictory pressures, operating in what Bourdieu (1990) conceptualizes as organized social fields, yield what Snider (2009) and others (Ugwudike 2011) have called a compliance-oriented "regulator habitus," that is, internalized rationales and practices among inspectors and managers, which tend to accept the need to emphasize compliance over deterrence measures on various grounds – albeit with some variability shaped by administrative directives.[1] In revealing this habitus, we draw on interviews with enforcement officials, ranging from early resolution officers (EROs) and employment standards officers (ESOs) to managers and regional program coordinators,[2] which offer insight into the attitudes of these officials and the factors they identify as significant for the use or non-use of deterrence measures, often within the context of varying and, to some extent, conflicting enforcement rationales. Building on these insights about a compliance-oriented habitus, section 4 then considers the role that regulatory new governance plays in sustaining and modifying this habitus. It demonstrates that while the attempt to address inconsistencies in the use of deterrence measures through an "informed judgement matrix" is hampered by the degree of discretion still exercised by ESOs, as well as the challenge of managing complaint loads efficiently, regulators can still shift the boundaries of the enforcement gap. However, we conclude that an increase in the use of deterrence measures is not sustainable if based exclusively upon the short-term policy preferences of a particular political party. Not only do governments change, but the continuing structural contradictions under which the state operates in financial globalized capitalism and the weight of history, which helps produce, and is reproduced by, the regulatory habitus of frontline enforcement officials, lean in the direction of a compliance orientation. Sustained external campaigns for stronger enforcement that promotes a long-term commitment to changing that habitus are needed but are themselves difficult to sustain.

## 1. Establishing the Current Deterrence Gap in Ontario

As discussed in previous chapters, in Ontario employment standards are enforced principally through the investigation of individual complaints, expanded investigations in workplaces where individual complaints have been identified, and other types of workplace inspections. ESOs are responsible for conducting investigations and inspections, including making decisions about whether or not to penalize employers when violations are detected. Three deterrence measures can be applied against employers. The first two, Notices of Contravention (NOCs) and tickets under Part I of the *Provincial Offences Act*, were added to the enforcement repertoire in 2000 and 2004 respectively. NOCs are available for any violation of the *ESA*, whereas tickets may be issued only for prescribed offences. They both constitute low-level penalties for employers: $250 for NOCs where it is a first offence[3] and $295 for a ticket (plus a $75 victim surcharge).

The third deterrence measure is a prosecution under Part III of the *Provincial Offences Act*, available for any violation of the *ESA*. An employer convicted in a Part III prosecution potentially faces far more serious penalties. Individuals can be fined up to $50,000 and face the possibility of incarceration for up to twelve months, while corporations can be fined as much as $100,000 for a first offence and up to $500,000 for offenders with two or more prior convictions. Finally, in principle, a criminal prosecution might also be launched in cases where an employer has defrauded employees of money they are owed by, for example, intentionally misclassifying them as independent contractors. To our knowledge, however, no employer has faced a criminal prosecution for wage theft in the last eighty years.

While the Ministry of Labour (MOL) provides ESOs with guidance in the use of enforcement tools, ESOs exercise broad discretion over the use of NOCs and tickets. However, ESOs can only recommend Part III prosecutions. A manager must approve the ESO's recommendation to prosecute, in which case the ESO will be required to prepare a Crown brief, a lengthy document detailing the evidentiary basis for the recommendation. The final decision to prosecute rests with the Legal Services Branch of the MOL.

As the enforcement data show (see table 6.1), the deterrence gap in Ontario varied considerably in the period from 2012/13 to 2016/17.[4] For the years from 2012/13 to 2014/15, there is strong evidence of a substantial deterrence gap in Ontario (Tucker et al. 2019). First, with respect to the use of low-level deterrence measures, employers caught violating the Act received no penalty over 95 per cent of the time; that is, between 2012/13 and 2014/15, ESOs detected 34,177 violations, either through complaints or workplace inspections, and imposed a low-level deterrence measure 1,493 times, or in 4.4 per cent of all detected violations (see table 6.1).

The gap during this period appears somewhat smaller when we disaggregate violations detected in complaints and violations detected through inspections, which is notable inasmuch as inspections are central to a more proactive enforcement strategy. While ESOs rarely used low-level deterrence measures when they detected violations while investigating complaints, they issued tickets (but not NOCs) more frequently when they detected violations while conducting workplace inspections (9 per cent vs 2 per cent through complaints).[5] Between 2012/13 and 2014/15, ESOs issued tickets on approximately 20 per cent of the inspections where they found at least one ticketable violation. On the other hand, ESOs issued tickets or NOCs for only 9 per cent of all violations detected by inspections, so that even after taking into account the use of NOCs, in the context of inspections, over 90 per cent of detected violations did not attract a deterrence measure.

Part III prosecutions were exceedingly rare between 2012/13 and 2014/15. Over these three years, there were forty prosecutions involving thirty-eight defendants and ninety-two charges. Perhaps more importantly, the large majority of the prosecutions were for employers' failure to comply with an ESO's order (i.e., Order to Pay Wages) or for

Table 6.1. Use of Tickets and Notices of Contravention in Complaints and Workplace Inspections*

| | 2012/13 | 2013/14 | 2014/15 | 2015/16 | 2016/17 | 2017/18 |
|---|---|---|---|---|---|---|
| **Part I tickets** | | | | | | |
| Complaints | | | | | | |
| Ticketable violations | – | 11,732 | 10,298 | 11,721 | 12,369 | – |
| Part I tickets | – | 121 | 185 | 450 | 161 | – |
| % of ticketable violations with tickets | – | 1.0% | 1.8% | 3.8% | 1.3% | – |
| Inspections | | | | | | |
| Ticketable violations | 4,832 | 3,690 | 2,748 | 5,192 | 5,215 | 3,686 |
| Part I tickets | 282 | 337 | 249 | 450 | 451 | 82 |
| % of ticketable violations with tickets | 5.8% | 9.1% | 9.1% | 8.7% | 8.6% | 2.2% |
| **Notices of Contravention** | | | | | | |
| Complaints | | | | | | |
| Total violations | 12,088 | 12,088 | 10,598 | 12,018 | 12,808 | – |
| Notices of Contravention | 65 | 80 | 68 | 157 | 1,701 | – |
| % of violations detected on complaints with Notices of Contravention | 0.5% | 0.7% | 0.6% | 1.3% | 13.3% | – |
| Inspections | | | | | | |
| Total violations | 4,920 | 3,753 | 2,818 | 5,263 | 5,271 | 3,717 |
| Notices of Contravention | 46 | 22 | 38 | 49 | 267 | 507 |
| % of violations detected on inspections with Notices of Contravention | 0.9% | 0.6% | 1.3% | 0.9% | 5.1% | 13.6% |

Source: Ontario Ministry of Labour, ESIS Data 2012/13–2017/18.
* Data for complaints for 2017/18 were not yet available at the time of publication, as it takes longer to determine the outcome of complaints than inspections. For 2012/13, data on tickets for complaints are withheld due to small cell counts.

interfering with the execution of the ESO's powers. In short, in those limited instances when employers were prosecuted, it was mostly for defying the authority of the ESO and the state, not for violating employees' rights (see Gesualdi-Fecteau and Vallée 2016 for a similar finding in Quebec).[6]

The extreme deterrence gap described above closed substantially in the period from 2015/16 to 2017/18. In particular, the use of low-level penalties increased considerably, including a shift from a preference for tickets to NOCs. Looking at tickets and NOCs together for the years 2015/16 and 2016/17, penalties were imposed for 10 per cent of all detected violations, compared to a little less than 5 per cent in the previous three years.[7] This increase in the use of penalties occurred during a period when the number of recorded violations on inspections during this period was substantially higher (about 5,200 per year between 2015/16 and 2016/17, compared to about 3,800 per year between 2012/13 and 2014/15). While there was some increase in the use of tickets during the latter period, the use of NOCs increased dramatically, especially in the context of complaints. Overall, 10 per cent of all violations detected in complaints resulted in a penalty, compared to 2 per cent in the previous period. This change is most evident in 2016/17, when ESOs issued NOCs for 13 per cent of all violations they detected in complaints. The increase in the use of penalties for violations detected on inspections was more modest, 12 per cent compared to 9 per cent.

The use of Part III prosecutions also increased substantially, beginning in 2015/16. Between 2015/16 and 2017/18, an average of nearly 100 Part III prosecutions were initiated each year, compared to an average of about 10 a year between 2012/13 and 2014/15. While the frequency of prosecutions increased, the fines did not; in fact, the opposite occurred. In 2015 employers were convicted on 38 counts and the average fine per conviction was $3,642. In 2016, employers were convicted on 175 counts and the average fine per conviction was $3,243. Along with being quite small in relation to the maximum fines available (which are $50,000 for individuals and $100,000 to $500,000 for corporations), the size of the fines is markedly lower than it was for the 2012/13 to 2013/14 period, when the average size of the fine was around $25,000. Apparently, the regulator's changes to enforcement policy and practice are not being interpreted by the courts as requiring comparable or tougher penalties than in the past, which may indicate that judges and/or prosecutors see the cases as being less serious than those pursued previously.

Despite these changes, nearly 90 per cent of all employers found in violation of employment standards received no penalty, and Part III prosecutions were still being launched primarily for failure to comply with an ESO's order, rather than for the underlying employment standards violation for which the order was issued. While the most recent enforcement activities signal a significant shift in enforcement policy and practice, the MOL is still falling short of what is needed to meet the requirements of responsive regulation or strategic enforcement models.

Responsive regulation theory and its enforcement pyramid, as developed by Ayres and Braithwaite (1992), envision the consistent use of progressive deterrence measures for repeat offenders. As we will show, while the MOL uses an explicit policy and training model grounded in responsive regulation theory, we found no consistent escalation of enforcement for repeat offenders. An enforcement blitz conducted from 1 September to 31 October 2016 that targeted workplaces with past employment standards violations is particularly illustrative. In advance of the blitz, the government announced that it was introducing a zero-tolerance policy for re-offenders. Of the 103 employers inspected as part of the blitz, ESOs found that fully 75 had re-offended. In response, ESOs issued 227 compliance orders, and employers voluntarily complied with them all. However, these were repeat offenders to whom a zero-tolerance policy supposedly applied, and thus one would have expected to see at least low-level deterrence measures routinely applied. Yet ESOs issued only fifteen NOCs and twenty-seven tickets. Assuming no employer was subject to more than one low-level deterrence measure, only 55 per cent of repeat offenders received a penalty (MOL 2017, 22 November). As such, even by the relatively permissive standards of responsive regulation, there is strong evidence of a deterrence gap.

If we apply the more deterrence-oriented strategic enforcement model, as outlined by Weil (2008b, 2010), the gap appears even larger. Unlike Ayres and Braithwaite, Weil (2010) believes that deterrence is much more central to regulatory effectiveness, in large part because he recognizes the structural pressures motivating widespread employer violations, particularly in fissured industries where employers must be fiercely competitive in order to make a profit. He argues that deterrence measures must be carefully crafted and highly publicized so that employers will know in advance that the cost of violating employment standards is likely to be higher than its benefits. For example, Weil (2010) suggests that civil monetary penalties should be routinely assessed, especially for repeat offenders.[8] He also strongly advocates imposing deterrence measures on lead firms in supply chains that have the capacity to police the activities of their subordinate entities. However, as outlined below, the MOL pays very little attention to supply chains, and the vast majority of offenders are not being penalized at all; moreover, those who are penalized tend to receive very small fines with little or no publicity other than a posting on the MOL web site. As such, despite the move towards greater use of deterrence measures in recent years, the data suggest that the MOL's approach to enforcement is still fairly distant from the prescriptions of either the responsive regulation or the strategic enforcement model.

If our interpretation of these data is correct, we need to explain *not only* the persistence of a deterrence gap, but also the observed changes in enforcement practices that have clearly taken place. We now turn to these questions, beginning with a review of how the deterrence gap has evolved historically, followed by a deeper enquiry into the daily practices of enforcement in the more recent period to better understand how a regulative compliance culture is both reproduced and altered over time.

## 2. Tracing the Evolution of the Deterrence Gap through a Political Economy Lens

As chapter 1 emphasizes, a critical political economy of employment standards enforcement understands labour regulation as a site of struggle where demands for worker protection meet the systemic pressure on governments to support profitable production and the reproduction of the relations of social class, broadly conceived, essential to it. These tensions often play out at the level of implementation, where the goal of fairness, as politically constructed, may become subordinate to the government's commitment to promote and support business interests (Dickens 2012). However, the practice of enforcement is not determined at a structural level, but rather is the outcome of historically specific conditions, including the changing political economic context and the capacity of workers' and employers' organizations to shape government policy at any given juncture. As such, we contend that specific institutional factors and enforcement dynamics are important and require an examination of how ESOs and managers come to understand their role and the use of their discretionary powers regarding the application of enforcement penalties, especially deterrence tools (Gesualdi and Vallée 2016; Phillips 2016; Snider 2009; Ugwudike 2011).

### *Historicizing the Deterrence Gap*

There is a long history of regulating terms and conditions of employment and providing employees with expeditious mechanisms to recover unpaid wages dating back to early master-and-servant statutes (Hay and Craven 2004). While those statutes made it a crime for servants to breach their contracts of service, they only offered servants civil remedies for employer breaches, so there was no scope for deterrence or a deterrence gap.[9] It was only in the context of early factory Acts where government officials were vested with an authority to enter workplaces and to take punitive enforcement actions that the possibility of deterrence arose and, in fact, it was at that moment when a deterrence gap first appeared.

Carson (1979) forcefully argues that the early enforcement of British factory legislation by inspectors produced what he characterized as "the conventionalization of early factory crime," a notion akin to the normalization of employment standards violation, evasion, and erosion touched on in chapter 1.[10] By "conventionalization" Carson refers to a state in which criminal activities are so infrequently punished that violations come to be considered as customary and rationalized as acceptable activity, rendering perpetrators largely immune from penal and other adverse sanctions, except in the most egregious circumstances. Carson sees conventionalization as a process for resolving the contradictory pressures for effective regulation and the structural and ideological imperatives of capitalist social formations in which factory owners are required to produce for profit and given a morally elevated status for their entrepreneurial accomplishments. From this early time, presaging regulatory new governance, factory inspectors developed a world view that minimized the significance of violations of the law they enforced and characterized employers as essentially "good apples" contributing to the public good, who could be gently persuaded to comply with the law, which in any event should be sensitive to the challenges employers faced. Once entrenched, this view became a material force shaping future generations of factory inspectors who accepted this "common sense" understanding of their jobs.

We can trace a similar influence in Ontario, beginning with the enforcement of its first *Factories Act*, which came into force in 1886 (Tucker 1990). In the following decades, there were hardly any prosecutions for *Factories Act* violations, even when deaths and serious injuries resulted. The labour movement saw the lack of prosecutions as evidence that the law was not being enforced: "It has been the experience of every labour man that after the fight to get an Act passed has been made and it has become law the trouble has only commenced, for you have got to keep hammering away all the time make the Government put the law in force, and if the people who are opposed to the Act have any pull with the party in power it is almost impossible to get any Act in the interest of labour enforced. This has been clearly demonstrated in the Ontario Factories Act" (Trades and Labour Council, 1899, 10–11).

Faced with criticism from the labour movement, the Ontario government inspectors defended their approach, frequently citing statements of British factory inspectors. Such views permeated annual conventions of factory inspectors, which Ontario inspectors attended. Indeed, at the 1908 convention, held in Toronto, the deputy minister in charge of Ontario's factory inspectors addressed the assembled inspectors, defending the "conventional" wisdom:

> There is a prevailing idea on the part of many people who are not familiar with this work that the office of the Factory Inspector should be that of enforcing the law.... We have not followed that course in the Province of Ontario.... I know the instructions they receive; I know that they have found it advisable ... to go into the factories and stores and apply to their business that common sense which alone can bring to a common footing the employer ... and the employees.... We shall by the adoption of this course, keep upon a common footing and bring together these two classes, which otherwise would likely be kept apart, and which being kept apart, are likely to bring disruption into the community and work harm rather than good. (Cited in Tucker 1990, 199–200)

Employers were not a class whose violations of the law harmed subordinated workers; the overriding purpose of the law was to smooth class relations that might otherwise produce undesirable conflict.

After health and safety, the next area of legislated minimum standards was minimum wages for female workers (McCallum 1986; Russell 1991). As chapter 1 illustrates, the legislation established a minimum wage board that set rates at the lowest possible level to cover a single woman's most basic costs of living, on the assumption that women's participation in the labour force would end as soon as they married and became responsible for the care of a husband and children. The legislation provided that employers who violated a wage order committed an offence punishable by a fine not exceeding $500 but not less than $50 for each employee affected.[11] Initially the law made no provision for inspections, and enforcement depended entirely on complaints. In 1921, however, legislation imposed a duty on factory inspectors to report minimum wage violations to the wage board.[12] These inspectors had no enforcement powers; it was up to the board to take whatever action it deemed necessary. In practice, the board focused almost entirely on wage recovery, ignoring evidence pointing to intentional and widespread violations. In fact, the only case prosecuted in the first five years of the law's existence was against an employer who sent the board incomplete and misleading information (McCallum 1986, 49–56). Employers who paid less than the minimum wage did not need deterrence, but those who defied the authority of the board did.

Despite the limited use of prosecutions, in 1932 the government of Ontario enacted legislation to cut the penalties for wage order violations to between $20 and $200.[13] In testimony before the Royal

Commission on Price Spreads in 1934, the chair, R.A. Stapells,[14] defended the low penalties as appropriate, given his view that most violations were committed unwittingly (Royal Commission on Price Spreads 1934, 33). He also pointed out that, in addition to relying on the factory inspectors to report violations, the board hired four "specially trained negotiators" whose role was to address the "delicate adjustment" of wage violations when dealing with "firms who are flouting the board or with firms who do not report their wage sheets" (26). However, these employers were viewed as a tiny minority, while the majority of firms were projected as cheerfully cooperating with the board. Given these assumptions, the board prosecuted only as a last resort and in the most egregious cases: "The board does not feel that it is bound to prosecute employers who, unwittingly, offend against its orders, and so long as such firms, on request from the board, bring their wage rolls into complete conformity with the law, and pay such arrears to their employees as may be found due, the board feels that it should be satisfied" (52). Since the overwhelming majority of employers fit this description, enforcement officers and managers rarely saw the need for deterrence measures.[15]

This compliance approach to the *Factories Act* and enforcement of the minimum wage for women came to be deeply embedded in the institutional culture and practice of minimum standards enforcement and was carried over into *ESA* enforcement when the law came into force in 1969. Thomas (2009, 98–107) documents the enforcement practices of that era. Consistent with findings presented in chapter 5, he finds that workplace inspections were marginal to a scheme that depended primarily on complaints and rarely prosecuted employers who violated the Act. The predominant view, still operative into the 1960s and the following decades, was that most violations were the result of employer ignorance or incompetence and, therefore, did not warrant punishment or deterrence measures. As Thomas (2009) and others note, this orientation was further reinforced between 1995 and 2003 when a new Conservative government implemented policies aimed at unburdening business from state regulations and interference (see also Keil 2002). Indeed, as the Ontario Attorney General's Office reported in the 2004, there was no meaningful deterrence of employment standards violations during this period, in part because the MOL relied almost entirely on investigating complaints from individuals against their former employers, with no meaningful proactive inspections or prosecutions. The report concluded that there was little incentive for employers to voluntarily comply (Auditor General 2004b, 239–40).

### *Deterrence in an Era of Regulatory New Governance: A (Neo-) Liberal Response*

Similar to changes occurring in Britain and elsewhere (Smith and Morton 2006), the election of a new (Liberal) government in 2003 was accompanied by a discursive shift in Ontario towards the re-regulation of employment standards and other labour regulations. Poverty, income inequality, and the protection of "vulnerable workers" became key policy objectives as the neoliberal excesses of globalization and deregulation were increasingly acknowledged in many Western contexts. While still committed to neoliberalism or globalization, proponents of a "third way" argued that an efficient competitive economy required more attention to the creation of a level playing field for both employees and employers (Thomas 2009; Smith and Morton 2006). Against this backdrop, early Liberal government statements framed "tougher enforcement" as essential to protecting vulnerable workers from exploitive employers. Consistent with this emerging deterrence discourse, the MOL added a new ticketing system (MOL 2004, 14 July) and soon after announced its intent to shift resources to targeted inspections of workplaces in industrial sectors with high rates of non-compliance (MOL 2004, 26 November). It also emphasized the importance of establishing an "immediate and effective deterrent" (MOL 2005) targeted at protecting vulnerable workers (Hall et al. 2019).

Although enforcement data for the period prior to 2012/13 are incomplete, MOL enforcement statistics indicate that the use of tickets within inspections almost doubled from 2005/06 to 2006/07 (305 to 583). However, this increase was not sustained, as tickets dropped substantially in the subsequent year (2007/08) to 371, while Part III prosecutions remained quite low throughout this period, ranging from five in 2010/11 to twenty-four in 2007/08 (MOL 2018c, 17). As outlined in chapter 1, the government also began to move away from its deterrence and enforcement messages in its public communications, placing more emphasis on the importance of increased education, self-help, self-regulation, and community partnerships – all important elements of a new governance model. While the introduction of additional legislative reforms addressing temporary agency work and live-in caregiving in 2009[16] suggests that the government was continuing to respond to political-economic pressures revolving around precarious employment, the introduction of the *Open for Business Act (OBA)* in 2010 was squarely oriented towards reducing the costs of regulation and increasing efficiency through further emphasis on self-regulation and facilitated settlements. The MOL also reversed its course on inspections by substantially reducing proactive inspections and reassigning ESOs from dedicated enforcement teams to a special task force to deal with the backlog in complaints, which had developed over the previous three years (see chapter 3).

Likely related to these changes, the number of tickets issued in inspections dropped substantially from 487 in 2008/09 to 192 in 2010/11 (MOL 2018c, 17). However, once the effects of the 2008–09 financial crisis had eased and the backlog in employment standards complaints was eliminated, the MOL re-established and expanded its teams of ESOs dedicated to focusing on proactive inspections (MOL 2012, 8 June a; 2012, 8 June b). While the number of inspections increased substantially in the 2012/13 to 2013/14 period, as noted in table 6.1, the percentage of violations detected through inspections that resulted in tickets or NOCs changed only modestly. Moreover, the government did not return to its deterrence discourse of the early 2000s, as MOL policy communications continued to place more emphasis on education and compliance (Hall et al. 2019). However, in February 2015 the government announced that it was launching an independent expert review of the *ESA* and the *Labour Relations Act*, known as the Changing Workplaces Review. Among the range of recommendations, made by experts in their 2016 report, was that the MOL move to a more consistent strategic enforcement approach, with increased targeted inspections and stronger penalties and deterrence (Mitchell and Murray 2016, 11). It is notable that even before appointing the review panel and without any public fanfare or announcement, the government increased its employment standards enforcement. This is especially evident in the increased use of NOCs and Part III prosecutions beginning in 2015, noted above. Presumably, growing public concern that the *ESA* was failing to address the growth of precarious employment and press coverage of Ontario workers' experience of wage theft contributed to the government's decision to step up enforcement, as well as its decision to launch the review (Mojtehedzadeh 2015, 10 May).

In sum, the history of the *ESA* in the first two decades of the twenty-first century suggests that the MOL has been managing contradictory demands from government, business, worker advocates, and media, which revolve principally around using employment standards to moderate labour market insecurities and the resulting social and economic consequences, while trying to avoid a political backlash and major increases in the costs of regulation. As argued in chapter 1, the MOL was encouraged by the Liberal government to move towards a regulatory new governance approach as a key managerialist strategy for negotiating these conflicting demands. The combination of self-regulation, increased education and community engagement, more targeted proactive inspections, and graduated deterrence measures for repeat offenders offered the promise of increased compliance through a more efficient use of a full range of employment standards enforcement tools and staff resources. This history suggests that political and economic pressures, whether from business or worker advocates, or from shifting economic conditions, such as the 2008 recession or increased government deficits, have influenced government policy discourse around employment standards since 2003. Sometimes those pressures led to tougher enforcement measures, and sometimes less so, while compliance, education, and self-regulation have been arguably the more consistently emphasized message throughout the Liberal government's term of office (2003–18).

To get a better understanding of how and why change happens and why it is often limited, even in the face of an apparent government or administration shift in policy, we need to look more closely at the enforcement practices on the front lines. In our view, two questions need to be explored: first, what substantial changes did management introduce in order to achieve increased enforcement? Second, how did the front-line enforcement staff respond to those changes and why? Given that our interviews with enforcement officers and managers occurred from 2014 to 2016, our focus is on developments during these years.

## 3. Inspection Culture and Dynamics: The View from Within

### *Signs of a Policy Shift*

ESOs and local and senior managers suggest that the MOL actively sought to increase the use of penalties beginning in 2012 and stretching through 2015/16. Although still confined within a responsive regulation model, which simultaneously stressed the importance of education and self-regulation as the central means of achieving compliance, several policy steps indicate a substantive attempt to increase the use of deterrence measures. This substantive effort was implemented in several ways, including new recruitment criteria for ESOs, new training programs on prosecutions, a new escalated enforcement policy, changes in ticketing procedures and technologies, and improvements in time allowances. As one ESO put it, "The new push is into prosecutions. We were not there a number of years ago. We were not prosecuting employers. The program training is trying to get officers to be confident and comfortable. In leading that way, our enforcement tools, the ticketing, they have made that easier and have come up with an electronic system where we can generate tickets right online. It takes the whole ticket book work out of it.... It has helped us be more aggressive."

Local and regional managers also concur that a different message was coming from senior MOL administrators regarding enforcement, which they see as also having an impact on ESO enforcement actions. As one manager said, "I think there has to be a balanced approach and ... there definitely needs to be more enforcement and ... the staff [ESOs] now have taken that approach 'cause they do tickets a lot more and I think ... that was the message from – from higher up." In response to this change in the senior administrators' message around moving to a stronger enforcement orientation, most managers also note that they are now actively encouraging and advising all their ESOs to use deterrence tools more frequently. As one manager asserted, "At meetings, I try to instil that to everybody, that need to escalate enforcement where it's appropriate." This escalation policy, which the MOL referred to as an "informed judgment matrix" (see below), was grounded in the principles underpinning responsive regulation, insofar as it called for ESOs to escalate their responses from education and formal compliance orders to different penalties, depending on the seriousness of the violations and the employer's record of violations (see figure 6.1).

Again, while the regulatory new governance–styled model still placed substantial weight on education and compliance, managers and ESOs argue that the main message they understood from the training, procedural changes, and policy directives delivered from the MOL was that the administration's goal was to increase prosecutions and fines using the judgment matrix, again suggesting that this was a clear effort to reduce some of the deterrence gap. This approach was supported by a shift in ESO hiring criteria, with an emphasis on enforcement background and orientation (e.g., ex–police officers, insurance investigators, forensic auditors). Many of the newer ESOs – that is, those hired between 2013 and 2017 – reported that they understood that they were being hired specifically for their enforcement background, skills, and orientation and, accordingly, were focusing their efforts on deterrence measures, such as regularly issuing tickets. According to one ESO: "We are [have been] lacking in enforcement. I know that they [the senior administration of the MOL] are changing now and they are changing that with my hiring group. My whole group is enforcement crazed. We're all the same. It is really funny, because they announced that and said we are gearing more towards enforcement and they hired my group and we're all the same type of people. We all come from an enforcement background."

Figure 6.1. Informed Judgment Matrix

The informed judgment matrix is provided as a reference for all ESO2s for use in claim investigations and inspections. An officer may refer to the matrix, which offers guidance in assessing the appropriate enforcement action, if any, when a violation (monetary or non-monetary) is found, taking into account the severity of the offence and the enforcement history of the employer. See chapter 7A (Prosecutions) of the *AMES* for details of the prosecution policy.

| | Type of Violation | | | | |
|---|---|---|---|---|---|
| COMPLIANCE HISTORY | Non-monetary violation only | Monetary violation only | Both non-monetary and monetary violation (up to four different standards)** | Both non-monetary and monetary violation (more than four different standards)** | Obstruction of officer |
| 1. Previous Part I or Part III convictions | - Part I or Part III prosecution | - Part III prosecution<br>- Order to Pay if no voluntary compliance | - Part III prosecution<br>- Order to Pay if no voluntary compliance | - Part III prosecution<br>- Order to Pay if no voluntary compliance | - Part III prosecution |
| 2. Previous violation (same standard) | - Next step in progression of compliance tools* (or higher level if appropriate) | - Next step in progression of compliance tools* (or higher level if appropriate)<br>- Order to Pay if no voluntary compliance | - Next step in progression of compliance tools* (or higher level if appropriate)<br>- Order to Pay if no voluntary compliance | - Part I or part III prosecution<br>- Order to Pay if no voluntary compliance | - Part III prosecution |
| 3. Previous violation (different standard) | - Compliance Order<br>- Part I or NOC | - Compliance Order<br>- Order to Pay if no voluntary compliance<br>- Part I or NOC | - Compliance Order<br>- Order to Pay if no voluntary compliance<br>- Part I or NOC | - Compliance Order<br>- Order to Pay if no voluntary compliance<br>- Part I or NOC | - Part III prosecution |
| 4. No history | - Compliance Order<br>- Part I or NOC | - Compliance Order<br>- Order to Pay if no voluntary compliance<br>- Part I or NOC | - Compliance Order<br>- Order to pay if no voluntary compliance<br>- Part I or NOC | - Compliance Order<br>- Order to Pay if no voluntary compliance<br>- Part I or NOC | - Part III prosecution |

** NOTE on number of violations: would not be limited to a single location if an employer has more than one under inspection or there are multiple claims against a single employer.
Source: AMES, appendix 7A.

Managers also suggested that the MOL adapted the time management system (i.e., introducing the Balanced Score Card discussed in chapter 3) for ESOs to give them the time to apply enforcement measures while getting credit for those activities. "I think one of the reasons why people ... are more willing to take the enforcement ... is because now they get credit for it. So, prior to this, it was basically 'Count the number of claims you did every year and you get credit for that.' We've now gone to a system where enforcement action is taken ... into account in terms of credits, so we have a points system now that's less focused on the number of claims that you do and more focused on the type of work that you do."

In addition, local and regional managers noted that they actively encouraged ESOs to pursue Part I and Part III prosecutions in meetings and in case consultations with ESOs. They also reported working to give ESOs more space in their caseloads when preparing or pursuing prosecutions, while also assisting ESOs in developing the skills and confidence necessary to shift to an enforcement orientation. As one manager stated, "Many of the employment standards officers are ... not comfortable, and have never been called on to go face-to-face, with someone they're gonna charge, which is what you're doing when you're serving them. They're not comfortable with that, so I go with them, do that for them or help them do it."

Taken as a whole, the interview data and the change in the use of deterrence measures suggests that beginning in 2012 the MOL made a concerted effort to shift ESOs enforcement orientation, with particular emphasis on repeat violators and reaching a greater number of violators overall. While statistics show that they had some success in increasing the use of penalties, it is nevertheless clear that the increase was not as substantial as might have been expected, given the resource and policy changes. There is also evidence, as outlined above, that the escalation of penalties for repeat or serious offenders did not happen consistently (see also Casey et al. 2018). The remainder of this chapter considers why these limitations persisted.

Part of the answer, we suggest, is captured in the sentiments of the manager cited above, that not all the ESOs were "comfortable" shifting from a compliance to an enforcement approach. However, as we shall show, the problem is not a simple matter of individual ESO comfort; rather, the lack of comfort is but one indicator of the long-standing compliance orientation, which has defined the traditional regulator habitus, dating back to *Factory Act* enforcement in the late nineteenth century and continuing in the MOL since the introduction of the *ESA*.

Following the work of Snider (2009) on Canadian securities regulation and the work of Ugwudike (2011) and others on the development of enforcement and compliance practices in the British probationary service, we argue first that the historical compliance orientation within employment standards regulation shaped an inspectorate culture, or what can be understood as a persistent compliance-oriented habitus among front-line officers that is resistant to the new demands for more enforcement (Robinson and Ugwudike 2012; Snider 2009; Ugwudike 2011). In the context of MOL steps to change this culture, including the hiring of new ESOs with stronger enforcement backgrounds and orientations, we first show that divisions and tensions regarding when and how penalties should be used emerged, modifying yet also reproducing a dominant compliance orientation. We then examine the professional adaptations of the inspectorate to the overall policy shift to regulatory new governance, arguing that the contradictory features of the model itself contribute to a reconstituted professional culture or habitus, which, while still substantially compliance-oriented, did yield a substantive increase in prosecutions.

*Compliance, Habitus, and Professional Resistance*

As noted above, in recent years, senior administrators in the MOL moved to hire new staff with stronger enforcement backgrounds, while using training and other policy tools to encourage a shift in skills and orientation among veteran ESOs, many of whom had been working exclusively in complaint investigations. However, our interviews with ESOs revealed a wide variation in their deterrence orientation and reported use of tickets and other penalties. As indicated previously, many newer ESOs enthusiastically believed that deterrence measures needed to be used more frequently, whereas others, often the ESOs with longer tenure, were less convinced. Some veteran officers and a few more recent hires admitted that they refused to use tickets or other deterrence measures, despite their training and manager encouragement to do so. These positions were usually explained using the traditional compliance thinking that education and persuasion are more effective enforcement tools because the vast majority of violations are due to employer ignorance or misunderstanding. However, some of the newer ESOs, along with some veteran ESOs, embraced the view that deterrence was necessary because many employers were violating the law intentionally as a business strategy and thereby creating pressure on others to also violate the law to remain competitive. Accordingly, these ESOs were more likely to claim that they used tickets or NOCs frequently, as prescribed by the new MOL policy on progressive enforcement.

Some of the variation in the use of tickets or NOCs also related to whether ESOs were involved principally in complaint investigations or dedicated enforcement teams. Although MOL policy, at the time of writing, called for the use of the progressive enforcement model in both complaints and inspections, many ESOs expressed the belief that complaint investigations should focus on compliance exclusively, while deterrence measures, if used, were more appropriate in inspections. According to one ESO, "I've never issued a ticket. We had training in it ... [but] because we are claim [i.e., complaint] based and we are only dealing with a claim [i.e., complaint] ... the process is that you do an event and you let the dedicated enforcement team ticket and deal with it on a broader basis."

MOL data confirm that there is a substantial difference in the rate of tickets given for ticketable offences detected in inspections compared to complaints. Yet this difference may also be linked to ESO orientation inasmuch as deterrence-oriented ESOs may have been management- or self-selected into inspections, whereas veteran ESOs with a long history investigating complaints may have preferred to stick with what they knew. Managers acknowledged that this was often the case, although there were efforts to encourage all ESOs to rotate through both complaints and inspections teams. In any case, it would be wrong to suggest that a compliance orientation existed only among ESOs involved in investigating complaints. As one dedicated enforcement team ESO acknowledged:

> Ticketing does not work, but I think there is a quota now for Part I, but ... I'm getting [the] job done without Part I or III prosecutions. They may be aiming for us to do more, but I feel my focus is education not punishment. [There was] only once where I felt prompted to do it in an inspection. Some of my colleagues think this is bad. One of my DET [dedicated enforcement team] colleagues told me that I should not be in DET because I don't issue tickets. It is a mindset that they have, identity they have, that MOL is pushing, but I'm not trying to develop it. I'm going with what feels right for me.

More recently the MOL moved to eliminate the distinction in enforcement roles, assigning all ESOs to both workplace inspections and complaints duty. Managers interviewed after this change argued that they understood that one of the goals was to allow and encourage ESOs to follow up on complaints against employers they are investigating with inspections rather than leaving it to other ESOs on the dedicated enforcement team. While also suggesting that senior management was trying to change the traditional compliance culture among many ESOs, managers expressed concerns that not only are many ESOs still resisting the use of deterrence measures, whether in inspections or complaints, but that they do not have the skills or background necessary to shift to more enforcement. While, as noted, the MOL gave ESOs training on enforcement and prosecution measures, the view of some managers was that after being compliance-oriented for their entire careers, many ESOs were simply not comfortable with or capable of using deterrence measures and would continue to avoid doing so. One manager said,

> You have to have the right people who can do this, but there are some people who are caught that don't know how to interpret legislation, aren't comfortable with enforcement, but they've been around for awhile and they're – they're caught in that middle now. So you're – you start to write policies and procedures for those people. They don't have that enforcement mind. So that hasn't helped over the years. You know, it's kind of been a – been an obstacle that ... we've seen.

Managers reported that despite the new policy on having all ESOs involved in both complaints and inspections, they tried to work around it by keeping the compliance-oriented ESOs in the complaints area. While this local management adaptation may have undermined the cultural shift sought by senior management's integration of complaints and inspections roles, other managers argued that they often tried different strategies to develop skills and confidence to use deterrence measures more frequently across the inspectorate, such as accompanying ESOs to serve tickets.

While capability and professional resistance to using deterrence measures among the compliance-oriented ESOs may explain some of the continuing deterrence gap, reluctance to use tickets and other deterrence measures was not confined to this group. Certainly the more deterrence-oriented ESOs were more likely to report frequent ticketing and one or more recent efforts to prepare a case for Part III prosecution, but some of these ESOs also reported that they did not tend to use tickets or NOCs, because they viewed the penalties as too low to have any deterrent effect. From their perspective, the legislated deterrence measures and their powers of enforcement were ineffective and, accordingly, not worth the trouble and time they involved. As one ESO complained, "People are not paying orders. Why [are] they going to pay notices of contravention? I'm a bit of a sceptic, because I think I came in new and we were all blazing. I am issuing orders to pay and nobody is paying ... why would I issue a notice of contravention?"

Whereas other ESOs still felt that their ability to give out multiple tickets for multiple offences gave them the capacity to send a deterrence message to employers, others saw the need for the kinds of penalties available in Part III prosecutions. Managers often stressed in their interviews that in response to senior administration directives and increased training in Part III prosecutions for ESOs, they were making extra efforts to encourage ESOs to prepare briefs, which includes making sure that they had the time needed to do the work. At the same time, however, many ESOs acknowledged that the challenges associated with successful Part III prosecutions, including the time required to prepare detailed crown briefs, ensured that Part IIIs would likely be used only in the most egregious cases. As one ESO explained, "One of the disincentives is that, to recommend the Part III, the officer has to prepare a Crown brief, which is a fairly labour-intensive work, and they get a very little credit for doing that towards meeting their case numbers."

While managers have a greater capacity to push for more prosecutions and support initiatives to do so, they too tend to recognize that Part III prosecutions are time consuming and, in light of competing caseload demands, can be supported only under "just the right conditions and circumstances," where successes are likely, thus limiting their frequency and, ultimately, their general value as a deterrence measure. This implies that even in the context of a seemingly substantive increase in the number of Part III prosecutions, the MOL's capacity to further increase their use to the level necessary for effective deterrence is limited, given competing resource and time demands. It is worth noting, for example, that after reaching a high of 133 Part III prosecutions in 2016/17, the following year they dropped back to 9 (MOL 2018c, 16).

The other important point to again make here is that the main focus of prosecutions is still directed at employers who fail to respond to MOL orders. This focus implies that the institutional objective of increasing the use of Part III prosecutions revolves more around restoring authority to the ESOs and their compliance orders than deterring serious and repeat violators of employee rights, although it is possible that some of those employers prosecuted for not obeying orders are repeat offenders.

Turning back to low-level penalties, some ESOs also expressed frustration that their ticketing efforts were constantly undermined by the refusal of other ESOs to use tickets or NOCs, tempering their willingness to devote the extra time to use these measures. For some, the frustration over the lack of consistency in enforcement by other ESOs was significant enough for them to suggest that unless the MOL moved to restrict ESO discretion by requiring more frequent use of tickets, they would not continue to make the extra effort. As one ESO commented,

> I think increased fines for sure in terms of the tickets would be a good place to at least start. Maybe making it mandatory in some cases – for example there might be a change to the program policy where if you find that an employer is in contravention of a certain provision or section then having it be a part of the policy that we issue a Part I, something like that. I also find that the way the program is right now issuing those type of tickets and being completely discretionary, some officers won't do it at all.

Others argued that they were experiencing more pushback from employers because of the lack of consistency in enforcement, again discouraging their continued use of tickets. Although the more enforcement-oriented ESOs insisted that they do not worry too much about employer grievances, managers, in particular, were aware that ESOs were enforcing the standards in a political and economic context of competing MOL objectives. That is, they knew that the MOL is charged with enforcing employment standards *without* undermining business success and employment, and without creating political pushback and undue media attention. Managers were especially aware of the need to strike this balance between enforcement and political fallout, which they recognized could lead to policy reversals: "I get the sense that the media drives this MOL's agenda. Our political masters are too cognizant, too afraid of setting a course and sticking with it." This reminds us that the regulative social field continues to be characterized by unequal power relations, which feed into both a conventional habitus of compliance and counter efforts by those actors within the MOL who are trying to push a stronger deterrence orientation.

However, the historical legacy of reform and counter-reform is also important. ESOs and managers also often cited past experience with MOL reforms as dampening their willingness to embrace the new policy fully. Veteran ESOs and managers talked about a "swinging pendulum" on enforcement, referring to trends and fads over their years of service. They also often insisted that there are substantial regional differences in enforcement, which indicated to them varying levels of support among the managers and regional program coordinators. As one ESO explained,

> I guess it also depends on the manager, if you have a manager who encourages and enforces this kind of work. There is a wide range of activity amongst offices. Probably ... more experienced officers have been doing

> this for fifteen, twenty, to twenty-five years; they have been through a political pendulum swing from "Leave business alone, don't you dare make a bad name for the Ministry of Labour" to "Listen, we have to get on this guy with both feet." I can see where their training and their willingness to go back and forth has been dampened.

For some ESOs, reversals and regional differences in enforcement practices encouraged scepticism, and perhaps cynicism, about the demand for more frequent use of deterrence measures by MOL officials. For others, the current inconsistencies and past reversals were, at minimum, reasons to be cautious about investing too much time or energy into more aggressive enforcement activities.

Thus far, our analysis suggests that the historical compliance orientation of many ESOs has played a role in fuelling professional resistance to the new enforcement policy directives (Uduwike 2011), which in turn weakened and undermined the efforts and commitment of the more enforcement-oriented ESOs and managers. Time constraints, procedural requirements, and weaknesses in the penalties also reinforced ESOs' reliance on longstanding compliance-oriented rationales and practices, while constraining the perceived value and practicality of the available deterrence measures for those who were more receptive to deterrence thinking. Next, we consider the role that the key elements of regulatory new governance, as implemented in Ontario, play in sustaining compliance-oriented practices and rationales within the context of this call for escalated enforcement of employment standards violations by using more deterrence measures in specified circumstances.

## 4. Adapting to the Contradictions Inherent in Regulatory New Governance

Although the responsive regulation model adopted within the context of a regulatory new governance approach recognizes the need for deterrence, the use of formal enforcement penalties is understood as the last step in a longer regulative process, which is still grounded fundamentally in compliance thinking and "bad apple" theories of employer violations. This mentality, which is consistent with a compliance habitus, still assumes that most employers can be persuaded and educated to comply with the law, and that only a small minority will need to be prosecuted or fined. Moreover, it was evident in the discourse of managers, who while talking about the need to increase the use of penalties, simultaneously emphasized the need for "balance" and "appropriate" penalties. This tension is also evident in managers' acknowledgment that, along with encouraging reluctant ESOs to use penalties, they also have to temper those ESOs who become too aggressive, while reminding them that education is still a key aspect of enforcement policy: "They [the ministry] wanted more enforcement because they realized that, you know what, we need more of those, but then you got some [ESOs] that were just too much. It was like, you still have to ease off, because there's still those smaller employers ... but it's like, 'Procedures say I have to issue a ticket and I have to do this,' and it's like okay, but, you know, you still have to have that – the educational component."

The regulatory new governance model and the theories underlying it fit quite nicely with the traditional compliance culture, which, for those ESOs groomed under the old institutional complaint investigation approach, reinforces their capacity to function essentially as before, while rejecting or paying only lip service to the call for more fines or prosecutions. "I have issued a few tickets probably because my boss said, 'What if you do your Balance Scorecard and try to get a couple of tickets.' And then I said I don't see a need. I think I have been able to educate the employer. [My manager then said], 'There has been a violation, I want you to do tickets.' So I gave one employee's employer six tickets and said, 'There you go.' Not a big fan of tickets."

Moreover, although several managers insisted that the MOL was pushing them to encourage ESOs to use tickets and/or NOCs more frequently using the judgment matrix, they acknowledged that the policy manual states only that "an officer *may* refer to the matrix, which offers guidance in assessing the appropriate enforcement action" (MOL 2016a). By seeking to preserve the principle of ESO discretion, adherence to the matrix is neither prescribed nor recommended explicitly as the standard by which all cases should be judged.

Against this backdrop, it is relatively easy for traditionally oriented ESOs to argue that they retain the discretion to focus entirely on education, especially in the context of complaints investigations, where they continue to define their traditional role as dispute resolution officers. As well, given the lack of set policy criteria for judging when escalation is warranted, there is considerable room for variation and inconsistencies in ESO interpretation, judgment, and application. Although ESOs are instructed to "weigh all the relevant factors" (MOL 2016a), the relative weight given to the different mitigating and aggravating factors is left undefined. As such, while many ESOs expressed a willingness to consider tickets based on the frequency and seriousness of an employer's previous violations, there was also variation among ESOs in judging when an employer's record warrants an escalation. For example, while some ESOs interpreted progressive enforcement to mean that a previous violation of the same standard should lead to a ticket, others set the bar much higher. As one ESO said, "If I ever find an employer where they have the same violation *over and over* again, yes I *may* want to issue that [ticket], but it is *up to my discretion* [emphasis added]." Similarly, whereas some ESOs think tickets are important to consider whenever there are numerous violations of a given standard, others, once again, require more. As another ESO stated, "Part I tickets ... are really more for ... situations where there are not only numerous violations but also numerous claims [i.e., complaints]."

Part of the variation seems to derive as well from the fact that, although the judgment matrix encourages ESOs to focus on the record and seriousness of violations, it also includes factors such as the degree to which employers are compliant. One traditional indicator of compliance is whether employers volunteer to pay the substantiated employee entitlements. Although the policy clearly states, "Voluntary compliance may be appropriate in [only] rare circumstances (where contraventions are caused by a minor oversight)" (MOL 2016a), many ESOs, especially those involved in complaints investigation, placed considerable weight on voluntary compliance in judging whether or not a ticket or any other enforcement action is needed. This tendency may partly reflect the historical value placed by the MOL on voluntary compliance as a successful outcome within the complaints process. As well, both managers and ESOs recognize voluntary compliance as a quick, clean result, which can be constructed as favourable to the complainant, the employer, and the efficient management of their complaint load. One ESO explained, "When I first contact the employer, I give them the option [to voluntarily comply] right away. My role is to get an early resolution. 'I want to fix this for you and the claimant [i.e., complainant]. I want to make everyone happy here.'... They can say, 'Oops, sorry I messed up and I'm going to voluntarily comply.'... Then I will make arrangements for the employer to pay the claimant [i.e., complainant]." To the extent that compliant employers are still assumed to be responsive to education and information, a key feature of the compliance habitus, the quick resolution of cases through settlements or voluntary compliance, is understood as a way to free up ESOs to focus their deterrence efforts on the more "at-risk" employers.

As emphasized previously, even enforcement-oriented managers recognized the continuing tension between the time needed to use deterrence measures and the time required to resolve complaints expeditiously to avoid the creation of a backlog (Phillips 2016; Ugwudike 2012). They acknowledged that within the new enforcement-oriented policies, the complaint load still must be managed "efficiently." While efficiency as a public management concern is not unique to regulatory new governance, there is, as noted, a managerialist logic (as addressed in chapter 3) often underlying regulatory new governance claims that its methods can better realize and balance multiple institutional goals (i.e., compliance and deterrence) in a more cost-effective way (Chan 1999; Ugwudike 2011; Vosko, Grundy, and Thomas 2016). However, this tension between competing priorities also gives compliance-oriented ESOs a further rationale for refusing or tempering administration demands for the increased use of deterrence measures, while also pushing enforcement-oriented ESOs and managers to manage their compliance and enforcement activities in selective ways. In practical terms, voluntary compliance and settlements (as emphasized in chapter 4) often become two ways of preserving the MOL's capacity to focus on problem employers. However, even enforcement-oriented ESOs become increasingly uncertain about where to place their emphasis, leading them be more selective in their enforcement efforts as a way of adapting to the multiple demands. As one ESO explained, "The problem I think you've probably heard from many of us is ... [that it] is very hard to distinguish what's [the] priority. Right now, I've got fifteen claims [i.e., complaints] on my caseload, I've got a Part III [prosecution] I've just started."

A related concern presented by some ESOs is that the judgment matrix requires them to collect and analyse more and better information in their investigation of complaints and inspections in order to discern which measures are required. Some of this information may be relatively straightforward, such as an employer's claims and inspections record, but ESOs can judge quite differently the point at which a record is sufficiently detailed to warrant Part I tickets and Part III prosecutions. Indeed, relatively few ESOs thought the employer's record alone is a sufficient basis for using a deterrence measure. Most ESOs also tried to judge employers' intentions, knowledge, and attitudes, which are much more problematic and challenging to assess, and therefore require more time in the field interacting with employers and employees. Ultimately, however, ESOs are making impressionistic judgments, often on limited information, and, of course, relying on their common understanding or habitus, about which characteristics signal more serious offenders. Not surprisingly, in their discussion of such judgments, ESOs often diverged on the application of criteria and standards of evidence, again reinforcing the frustrations of deterrence-oriented ESOs, who feel there is no consistency in the use of deterrence measures, thereby undermining their value. As one ESO noted, "With us, it is based on perception. Sometimes it is clear, but a lot of cases, a lot of charges are not laid. The only charge we have ever laid really to be heard in court is the failure to pay an order. I've done that a few times. But to charge somebody with failing to pay wages, you need a lot of evidence, and witness statements, etc., to take before the court. If we tried and do that, we have to put it in the hands of the legal branch and then they take forever."

While some ESOs talked about making these judgments on the basis of feelings or suspicions, which they saw as a kind of "sixth sense" (see also Snider 2009), others expressed a reluctance to use even low-level deterrence measures without full information. As another ESO stated, "Ticketable offences work quite well when it is a clear contravention, [but] again you have to have the evidence to support this." Understood in this way, the lack of sufficient evidence, or the lack of time or powers to collect the evidence, becomes an important rationale for many ESOs in explaining their reluctance to use deterrence.

Since one strategy often associated with regulatory new governance is to use limited enforcement resources to target "high-risk" employers, the criteria used to identify those employers is crucial. This strategy relies heavily on individual complaint statistics which, in this context, has led to targeting industries with a preponderance of smaller employers and franchise operations (e.g., restaurants, farms, nail and hair salons, auto repair, etc.). As Snider (2009) found in her study of securities regulation, this means essentially that the larger employers tend to be excluded from the inspections program and, ultimately, from any deterrence measures. However, there may be other reasons why violations are less visible in larger firms. One may relate to the MOL's practice of seeking voluntary and informal settlements (see chapter 5). Several managers and ESOs indicated that complaints involving larger firms are more readily settled without formal orders or charges, in part because they have the financial and legal resources to quickly settle the matter. It is also quite possible that workers in larger firms are less likely to complain, because their employment is more stable and few workers complain while they are still employed by the employer about whom they are complaining. At the same time, ESO experiences with larger firms seem to reinforce the common sense understanding that violations by larger firms are not only less numerous or serious, but also less intentional. In part because of the targeting of smaller firms, ESOs view smaller employers with vulnerable workers as being less knowledgeable about the law, having less access to human resource experts, and being less competent in running a business. As such, ESOs are more likely to view employer ignorance and misunderstanding as the likely causes of violations, which reinforces a belief in the appropriateness of a compliance orientation that focuses on education and persuasion. In a very real sense, these employers are themselves viewed as "vulnerable," which is then taken into account by ESOs in judging employers as "good" or "bad" apples. This orientation undercuts the focus of the judgment matrix on the nature of the violations and shapes decisions about which employers are high-risk and should be subject to proactive inspections (Snider 2009). As one ESO stated, "It's our own discretion to issue a ticket. I would look at if you are a company with certain size. You should have those resources to get things done in a proper way. You have your HR and your accounting, and you have your legal counsel or you are sort of big, and I look at your payroll: you do have a pretty payroll, you do have money. You are a big company, you should follow the Act, better than the others." As this comment also implies, ESOs often see small employers as having very limited financial resources and narrow profit margins (see also chapter 5). Some express concerns that these firms may not survive even the limited fines from tickets or believe that just the Order to Pay Wages or comply with other *ESA* requirements are sufficient deterrents.

## 5. Conclusion

This chapter has sought to demonstrate the application, and indeed the value, of a critical political economy analysis in understanding the persistence of weak deterrence measures in employment standards enforcement. Along with identifying the historical origins of a persistent compliance-oriented culture (Carson 1979; Snider and Bittle 2010), the empirical analysis reveals that both structural and conjunctural political and economic forces shape the context within which enforcement takes place. Structural forces shape the contradictory position of the state in late capitalism, most notably the challenges associated with regulating the margins of the labour market without undermining profit-driven growth, and without provoking political backlash from workers and employers. The shape and intensity of these pressures vary, as do their resolution, depending on the ever-shifting challenges in the accumulation regime and the balance of political and dominant ideological orientations. Contemporaneously, increasing inequality and rising precariousness in labour markets have galvanized workers and social activists to demand strong employment standards enforcement, while at the same time globalized financial capital presses governments to produce legal and regulatory regimes favourable to profit maximization. The resulting tensions help to explain much of the discursive and policy back and forth on the question of deterrence over the ten years of focus herein. Dickens and Hall's (2006) description of New Labour's approach to labour regulation in Britain is apt here. In this context, while the government in power declared commitment to both fairness and efficiency, in practice fairness was subordinate to efficiency.

But while the foregoing analysis helps to explain the origins of shifts in general government policy on deterrence, it does not explain fully the implementation of those policies at the ground level of enforcement. As the Ontario case suggests, even when senior administration introduces policy changes and makes substantive efforts to address limitations in staff skills, knowledge, and cultural orientations, the variations and differences among ESOs can undermine many of these efforts to address the deterrence gap. Some of these inconsistencies reflect the longstanding compliance culture or habitus (Snider 2009), which manifests in forms of professional resistance. Resource and time limitations, as well as competing MOL priorities, further support the cultural orientations of older ESOs, while also pushing new ESOs with different orientations towards adaptive compromises and concessions to the compliance framework (see Ugwudike 2011).

All this said, we do not intend to suggest that substantive changes to employment standards enforcement are impossible in this context. The increase in inspection activity, low-level penalties, and Part III prosecutions demonstrates that change is indeed possible. However, such changes are difficult to sustain. As we have attempted to demonstrate, the political and economic conditions of labour market regulation under global capitalism, underlined in chapter 1, generate ongoing pressure to reduce employment standards and their enforcement. Although subject to change, ideological and common-sense assumptions regarding the nature of the employment relationship, and especially the imperatives to tolerate employers' needs for "flexibility," continue to be dominant, not only within the MOL (Thomas 2009), but often among the public at large. At the same time, it is clear from the recent history of employment relations in Ontario that there are economic, political, and ideological pressures pushing government and its enforcement bureaucracy towards a substantive effort to achieve greater control at the margins of the labour market (Vosko 2010), whether in terms of better enforcement or an extension of *ESA* coverage. The Changing Workplaces Review and the government's legislative response, the *Fair Workplaces, Better Jobs Act* (2017), are cases in point. Yet responding to these forces requires a constant struggle to overcome the structural pressures on governments of all stripes to produce a business-friendly environment and, as we saw in the recent 2018 Ontario election, popular unrest may result in the election of conservative governments even more amenable to profit-maximizing logics. Moreover, challenges do not only operate at the macro-level. There are persistent micro- and meso-level obstacles to more effective enforcement. These obstacles need to be addressed through a sustained commitment from the agency leadership, with political support, to achieving structural and cultural change at the level of the inspectorate, of the order that took place at the federal level in the United States under David Weil's leadership during the Obama administration, described in chapter 11.

*Chapter Seven*

# Strengthening Participatory Approaches to Enforcement

Although the enforcement of employment standards is generally conceptualized as the responsibility of government agencies, in practice both government and non-government actors may participate in ensuring compliance with employment standards. Set in the context of an ongoing crisis of employment standards enforcement described in chapters 1 through 6 (see also Fine and Gordon 2010; Vosko, Grundy, and Thomas 2016; Weil 2014), this chapter considers the potential of forms of participatory employment standards enforcement involving non-government actors to counter the employment standards enforcement gap. We focus on forms of participation in employment standards enforcement involving community organizations, considering the capacity of these organizations to create alternatives to individualized complaint-based enforcement mechanisms that fail to counter the inherently unequal power relations in workplaces and "top-down" enforcement strategies of government agencies that accord workers a passive role in the enforcement process.

In this analysis we focus primarily on workers' centres – community-based organizations that provide advocacy, resources, and collective representation for non-unionized workers. As discussed in the chapter, these organizations are engaged in activities that relate (directly or indirectly) to employment standards enforcement. Where possible, we also provide examples from community legal clinics – non-profit clinics that employ lawyers, community legal workers, and paralegals and that provide legal services, including legal advice and representation, in an array of legal contexts. Some, though not all, community legal clinics offer services in employment law, including assistance with the employment standards complaints process.

The analysis proceeds in four parts. The chapter begins with a review of scholarly literature on models of "participatory enforcement," focusing on the participation of community organizations in employment standards enforcement, the involvement of workers' centres, and the (actual and potential) role of trade unions in supporting these processes. Next, on the basis of an analysis of data collected through individual interviews with workers, early resolution officers (EROs), employment standards officers (ESOs), representatives of community organizations, a focus group comprising representatives of ten community organizations in the province, and publicly available government documents, the chapter highlights the limits of an enforcement regime tied to reliance on individual workers compelled to play the role of the "protagonist" (Tucker 2013a) via the complaints system and EROs and ESOs who conduct inspections and investigations. Using examples from community organizations based in Sudbury, Windsor, and Toronto, the chapter then examines the ways in which – through advocacy, legal support, labour rights education, assistance in negotiating the complaints process, and community organizing – such organizations provide support for workers as they navigate the enforcement process. While not always engaged in employment standards enforcement directly, by contributing to the empowerment of workers in precarious jobs, and thereby enhancing worker agency, and by fostering a worker-centred approach to employment standards enforcement, community organizations may counter some of the weaknesses of the current approach to state-centred enforcement. In its conclusion, the chapter raises additional factors to consider in the development of participatory enforcement that can address the crisis of employment standards enforcement.

## 1. On "Participatory Enforcement"

This chapter addresses the issue of "participation" in employment standards enforcement in two ways: first, by examining how different actors participate in the enforcement process, and second, by exploring how employment standards enforcement can be made more participatory for workers, beyond simply promoting the individualized participation of workers in the employment standards regime. Before turning to a discussion of our research on participatory enforcement in Ontario, we offer a brief review of the scholarly literature on participatory enforcement, with particular attention to the role of community organizations in enforcement.

The notion of participation developed in this chapter is linked to a broader literature on democratic theory, political participation, and civic engagement, and its critique of the individualistic practices of forms of representative politics present in liberal (capitalist) democracies (see Barber 1984). A thorough review of this literature is beyond the scope of the chapter. However, key points of influence are the assertions in this literature that (1) civic engagement in political processes creates potential for a stronger democratic polity characterized by greater social equality; and (2) increased political participation can be achieved through institutional reform (Zittel 2006). While recognizing the many limitations to both political participation and institutional reform in late capitalist democracies, in the following analysis we explore the dynamics of participatory employment standards enforcement in this context and consider the potential for institutional reforms premised on enhancing participation in ways that could alleviate the crisis of employment standards enforcement. In doing so, we take care to recognize that the *form* of participation is crucial and that not all actors may be equal participants within a given institutional context. For the purpose of this chapter, this recognition requires situating our understanding of "participation" in the context of precarious employment in late capitalist labour markets, paying attention to the ways in which its persistence and/or rise affects actors' participation in employment standards enforcement and, in particular, the ways in which the voices of the precariously employed may be muted or silenced.

Participatory employment standards enforcement has connections to policy reforms influenced by the paradigm of regulatory new governance outlined in chapter 1 (Vosko, Grundy, and Thomas 2016), which often seeks to build regulation through arrangements in which authority is seemingly dispersed between the government, employers, and civil society. Strategies inspired by regulatory new governance may include the (limited and/or symbolic) involvement of non-traditional and non-governmental actors in regulation, such as community groups, professional and industry associations, and external, certified monitors. Responding to the critique that bureaucratic governmental agencies are distanced from the sites they regulate, such strategies aim to develop governance processes derived from the knowledge, experience, and expertise of those more directly engaged in activities subject to regulation. They also aim, in theory, to broaden the scope of democratic participation in society through the involvement of multiple stakeholders. In terms of employment laws and policies, a genuinely participatory approach informed principles guiding the development of occupational health and safety legislation in Canada in the 1970s (Tucker 2013b), which was premised on enhancing worker involvement in workplace monitoring and in addressing health and safety risks in the workplace.

Although they create openings for new regulatory processes, concerns have been raised about the implementation of regulatory new governance–inspired strategies, including in the employment context.

Critics have drawn attention to the potential for power imbalances to be exacerbated through processes that fail to address the structured inequalities present in the workplace, including the employer–employee relationship, as well as dynamics of race, gender, citizenship and immigration status, ability, age, etc. (Vosko, Grundy and Thomas 2016). Without attention to such power relations, individual workers may be reluctant and even unwilling to participate in employment standards enforcement in a meaningful way, as discussed in chapter 2 (see also Thomas 2009). The degree to which different stakeholders are given weight in regulatory processes is also critical; here, questions centre on the extent to which workers and their representatives are integrated on an equal footing with employers and their representatives in multi-stakeholder strategies (Fine and Gordon 2010). While multiple stakeholders might participate in enforcement, they do not have the same power or capacity to influence its outcome. Moreover, given structural imbalances, stakeholder participation should not be considered a substitute for effective hard-law mechanisms (Vosko, Grundy, and Thomas 2016). Participation in employment standards enforcement must be evaluated, therefore, in terms of the means through which, and the extent to which, the inherently unequal power relations that characterize workplaces are countered by inclusive processes.

In the realm of employment standards, a growing body of literature examines the enhanced participation of community organizations in the enforcement process (Vosko and Thomas 2014). The involvement of community organizations – specifically, a range of community-based actors including worker centres, community legal clinics, and non-governmental agencies – is set in a context of declining union density and the neoliberal reregulation of labour markets, which, together, heighten precariousness, generating the need for new strategies to address (individual and collective) workplace grievances. In Britain this literature, for example, addresses the role of the community organization Citizens Advice in assisting employment standards complainants, as well as the challenges faced by this organization as the result of inadequate resources (Holgate et al. 2012; Jones 2010; Pollert 2008). In Australia, scholars consider how the fair work ombudsman has sought to enhance regulatory collaboration with industry and community-based organizations, including through targeted campaigns, in order to improve employer compliance with employment standards (Hardy 2011; see also chapter 9). In the United States, in turn, scholarly examinations of the participation of community organizations focus on the rise of worker centres as sites for employment rights advocacy and organizing among non-unionized workers (Fine and Gordon 2010), as well as on providing in-depth knowledge of workplace practises at a local level (on the United States more broadly, see chapter 11). Furthermore, information from community partners can bring new perspectives on the networks of contracting companies. In addition to having in-depth knowledge of workplace practices at a local level, they help to give us a larger picture of the global networks of precarious employment. Scholarly researchers have also documented how the involvement of community organizations can enhance worker agency and improve the implementation of labour standards in global supply chains, including through activities such as providing labour rights education, organizing, supporting collective action, and whistle-blowing (Kaine and Josserand 2018; Lesniewski and Canon 2016). Hetland (2015) makes a case for the importance of community organizations in the struggle for protecting immigrant workers in low-wage jobs, arguing that such organizations can organize more effectively than traditional trade unions around ethnicity and geography and can offer a unique perspective on conditions of precarious low-wage work. Key to the involvement of community organizations, particularly in the absence of unions, given the decline of union density (see chapter 1), is that they must construct structures that enable meaningful participation for workers, enabling the articulation of worker voice (Vosko 2013; Vosko, Grundy, and Thomas 2016; see also chapter 11).

The context of union decline referenced above notwithstanding, examples of union participation in employment standards enforcement can also be seen in some jurisdictions (Vosko 2013; Vosko and Thomas 2014). In the United States, for example, building trades unions in Los Angeles play a role as employment standards inspectors in public works projects. As Weil notes in chapter 11, unions may have considerable knowledge of industries, employers, and workplaces, even in non-unionized settings. In Australia, under the country's *Fair Work Act (FWA)*, unions are able to support employment standards complaints through the courts. In this case, however, Hardy and Howe (2009) caution that the enforcement regime established by the *FWA* is not based on a truly collaborative, tripartite model of government-trade union partnership. It thereby constitutes a shift from the historic role accorded to Australian unions as "joint regulators" alongside government agencies, instead according unions the role of "junior partners."

In the Canadian context, the formal involvement of unions in employment standards enforcement is constrained by legislation in jurisdictions, such as Ontario, that has pushed unions out of enforcement processes (see chapter 1). Nevertheless, unions may play advocacy roles in terms of employment standards reform and, in some cases, may offer limited financial support and other resources (e.g., office space) to workers' centres. They may also provide legal support to address employment standards violations. A case involving several employment standards complaints about the right to refuse overtime hours at Toyota Motor Manufacturing Canada in Ontario in 2002 illustrates the participation of unions, as well as collaboration between labour and community groups, in the employment standards enforcement process (Thomas 2007). As Toyota was a non-unionized workplace, complaints about the violation of overtime standards were subject to the *Employment Standards Act (ESA)*. The complaints launched by individual employees were given legal support by the Canadian Auto Workers union and several community legal clinics in the Greater Toronto Area. The overall initiative was coordinated and publicized by the Employment Standards Work Group, a coalition of unions, activists, and community legal workers based in downtown Toronto.[1] Unions may also support the collective efforts of workers mobilizing around low-wage issues, as illustrated in union support for protests organized by the Fight for $15 and Fairness campaign against Tim Horton's in Ontario in the winter of 2018.

These examples of union involvement in employment standards enforcement notwithstanding, relationships between unions and low-wage worker organizations such as workers' centres often exist in an uneasy state. In terms of organizing amongst low-wage workers more generally, Fine (2007) notes that in the United States, collaboration between trade unions and workers' centres has been limited until very recent times, citing "mismatches" in structure, culture, and ideology as prominent impediments. Such "mismatches" at times prevent the formation of deeper connections between trade unions and workers' centres. Yet, in the context of both growing precariousness in employment and declining rates of unionization, Givan (2007) suggests that there is strong potential for strategic alliances between unions and community-based worker advocacy groups, particularly as the latter may be better positioned to engage with workers in the low-wage economy (see also Wills 2009).

Given the importance of a wide range of "collective labour agents" (see Coe and Jordhus-Lier 2011, 225), the potential for greater involvement of community organizations in employment standards enforcement has led to proposals for more formalized partnership-based enforcement models. Such partnerships can involve close relationships between government regulators and labour market intermediaries, with intermediaries helping to gather information and assist workers with complaints (Weil and Pyles 2006), as well as with advocacy groups playing educational roles inside and outside the workplace (Weil 2014). One such approach includes a model of "co-enforcement" based on collaboration between non-governmental actors and government regulators to "jointly produce" employment standards enforcement (Amengual and Fine 2016; Fine 2014). This model also hinges on recognizing the "non-substitutable elements of state and society" (Amengual and Fine 2016, 7), whereby each party holds unique capabilities that cannot be replicated by the other. For example, workers have the most direct and immediate knowledge of workplace violations, work processes, workplace networks, etc. Thus, they are uniquely positioned to identify violations and enhance enforcement strategies, given their first-hand experience.[2] Furthermore, through worker representatives, community organizations such as workers' centres can more directly monitor day-to-day employer practices and gather information that may be more difficult for government officials to access. They also serve a worker advocacy role that government officials cannot play and can assist in identifying the systemic roots of individualized complaints. Key to the role of worker organizations is their capacity to gain the trust of workers (Fine 2014; Fine and Lyon 2017), whereas even those regulatory strategies designed to address precarious employment (such as a special investigation team in Quebec; see chapter 10) may reinforce, rather than transcend, power imbalances that heighten workers' insecurity. Government officials, on the other hand, do hold unique capacities to conduct inspections, implement compliance and deterrence measures, undertake prosecutions, and compel employers to change non-compliant behaviour. They also have substantial investigative powers (and access to wider datasets regarding employment standards complaints). Building on the distinct capacities of each party, Amengual and Fine (2016) suggest that the model of co-enforcement offers a means to complement government-driven enforcement mechanisms. As Fine (2014) notes as well, even where formal partnerships are not established, regularized communication between parties may be an asset in enforcement.

The more formalized approach to co-enforcement can be viewed as a form of tripartism, defined by Fine (2013, 816) as "an enforcement regime that partners workers' organizations with government inspectors to patrol their industries and labour markets for unfair competition." Proposals for co-enforcement aim to leverage the unique capacities of government regulators and community organizations and to respond to the crisis of employment standards enforcement, particularly in the context of the spread of precarious employment, which traditional mechanisms of employment standards enforcement have been unable to effectively address. Fine (2013) notes that while targeted inspections are a key strategy for curtailing non-compliance in sectors where precarious employment is prevalent (see Weil 2014), without effective mechanisms for worker voice, they are limited in their capacities to detect violations at the bottom of supply chains. Community organizations, including workers' centres, can thus play a key role in supporting the work of government regulators with more formalized roles in employment standards enforcement, particularly in low-wage sectors. Specifically, community organizations may improve detection of non-compliance through, for example, specialized knowledge of industry conditions and employer practices. They may enhance complaints-based enforcement and targeted inspections by undertaking outreach to workers that could involve providing information or offering space for workers to gather and discuss problems. They may help to collect evidence of employer non-compliance and may support workers in coming forward with complaints. Finally, community organizations may facilitate strategic partnerships through, for example, industry task forces that bring together government regulators and labour and community groups (see also Vosko 2013).

In exploring the potential of tripartism, Fine and Gordon (2010) suggest that tripartism must fulfil four criteria to be effective. Relationships must be *formalized*, where parties openly negotiate expectations, commitments, and distribution of resources. Partnerships must be *sustained*, so that meaningful relationships can be built between organizations. Such partnerships must also be *vigorous*, in that the role of community organizations should be integrated into enforcement strategies in meaningful, rather than marginal or symbolic, ways. Finally, partnerships must be sufficiently *resourced* to undertake the work and to ensure that all actors are meaningful participants. With regards to formalization, Fine (2013) cautions that this is a necessary but insufficient condition: just because a partnership is formal, this does not ensure that it will be effective. The other conditions must also be in place to ensure the collaboration is meaningful. Conversely, depending on the political environment, informal partnerships may hold greater potential to pursue strategies that might be constrained through more formalized relationships. These criteria for tripartism provide a useful means through which to evaluate the potential of participatory enforcement and to identify avenues for institutional reform designed to enhance participation.

## 2. Government and Worker Involvement in Employment Standards Enforcement in Ontario

As illustrated in chapters 2 and 5, employment standards enforcement in Ontario occurs through two mechanisms: complaints and inspections. Within this system, employees can make complaints against their employers if they believe that their rights have been violated. EROs and ESOs, in turn, investigate these complaints, and ESOs also launch workplace inspections.[3] In both cases, we argue, the participation of community organizations, such as workers' centres, would enhance the efficacy of enforcement.

*Enhancing Workers' Capacities to Launch Effective Complaints through the Participation of Community Organizations*

As discussed in chapter 2, employees' engagement in the enforcement of employment standards begins when they file a complaint with the MOL that details the alleged violation(s). Given that reactive enforcement has been and continues to be a dominant strategy used in Ontario, employment standards enforcement relies heavily on the small subset of employees who come forward to claim their entitlements after having faced employment standards violations (on employees' reticence to complain and its roots, see chapter 2). In promoting reactive enforcement, employees are often constructed by the MOL as well as in the media as "empowered" actors taking action against their employers to protect their rights. Accordingly, the MOL website features a video, available orally in English only (French subtitles may be enabled in YouTube), titled *The Employment Standards Act: Know Your Rights*. An MOL official speaks against a soothing instrumental background. She calls on employees to monitor their working conditions, learn whether their employers are exempt from sections of the law by using a self-help web tool, and make calls to the MOL if they detect violations of the law.

There is, however, a stark contrast between the language of empowerment that accompanies the opportunity to file individual complaints that is used by the MOL, and the language of disempowerment used by employees, who characterize filing a complaint as a risky venture with potentially serious consequences, such as intimidation, reprisal, and dismissal (see chapter 2). Employees further note that while they may participate in employment standards enforcement by filing complaints, they not only receive limited support from the MOL, they also assume substantial risk as a result of this participation in the enforcement process. Indeed, of the thirty-six workers interviewed who filed a claim with the MOL, fourteen workers did so with the assistance of a workers' centre ($n$ = 11) or legal clinic ($n$ = 3). These workers were diverse in gender, race, immigration status, and education level. They also worked in a wide range of industries at the time of filing their claim. While some workers made direct contact with workers' centres or legal clinics themselves, others were referred from other community organizations, such as immigrant organizations.

With respect to the role of workers' centres, one employee in the construction sector stated, "[The Workers' Action Centre] does most of the job [that] the Ministry of Labour [is] supposed to do for me. I mean, they give the information ... 'Look [at] this, this, and this'.... The MOL is supposed to [give me the information] but they don't. So ... I understand they [the Workers' Action Centre] are doing most of the work which the ministry counsellor or someone has to do."

Another employee in the building cleaning and maintenance industry sought the help of Legal Aid Windsor after she was unfairly fired. Legal Aid helped her through the process and ensured she filed for all the provisions she was entitled to: "Legal Assistance looked over all the information and said, 'You have been very wrongly accused, and what he is doing. We're going to take that situation into our own hands now and we will [contact] the Ministry of Labour.'... They [Legal Aid] were asking for wrongful dismissal and the two weeks' severance pay. They were asking for vacation pay and they were asking for phone bills that should have been reimbursed.... Plus, they wanted me to be paid for all the hours of shovelling that he was invoiced for."

Both the fear of reprisal and the precarious nature of jobs lead to power asymmetries in the employment relationship, which often makes the process of complaining risky for employees, a condition further heightened for women workers and workers of colour. In this context, worker centres and legal clinics play a substantial role in assisting and empowering employees. One employee in graphic design services, for example, decided to file a complaint with the MOL after she contacted the Workers' Action Centre in Toronto: "[Workers' Action Centre] really helped me ... because they gave me the support to fight [by saying]. 'You have a right.... You can do this, you can do that. You don't have to be afraid.' If they don't advise me, maybe I can't do anything."

Overall, our interviews with employees suggest that given how the government has organized the enforcement process, including the ways in which employee complaints are structured, methods of facilitating and supporting employees who engage in the enforcement process – such as those offered by community organizations like workers' centres and legal clinics – are needed.

### *Enhancing Ministry Capacities through the Participation of Community Organizations*

MOL officials, EROs and ESOs in particular,[4] could benefit from the greater participation of these community organizations for three reasons. First, in the context of the complaint system (chapter 2), EROs and ESOs are taught to act as "neutral" adjudicators between employers and employees. This approach of "neutral adjudication" within the complaint system begins in the training that EROs and ESOs receive. They come to understand their participation in the enforcement of the law in terms of principles of "natural justice" and "impartiality." The importance of the training in fostering this understanding of neutrality is explained by one ERO:

> My role as an officer is to investigate the claims by contacting the claimant and the employer and I apply natural justice. Natural justice is huge with our ministry. They drill that into us. What we want, what natural justice is to get – to get both sides of the story and make a decision based on the available evidence. Both parties have an opportunity to explain their side and both parties have an opportunity to provide evidence as proof. So we request the evidence from both sides, and we remain impartial. I don't represent the employer, I don't represent the employee, I represent the *Employment Standards Act*, and whatever the act says, that's what I stand behind, that's the stool I'm standing on, OK. So both parties have an opportunity to explain and to provide evidence, and you give them both the same timeframes. We're guided by our ... Administrative Manual ... [of] Employment Standards.

In interviews, EROs and ESOs often mentioned that, to ensure natural justice and procedural fairness, they give employees and employers equal "opportunity to provide their version of events, their evidence in a timely manner." They thus see themselves as impartial adjudicators who evaluate and make judgments on materials presented to them. In the words of one ESO, "As ministry employees and officers, while we are investigating claims [in a complaint], we aren't on either side. We are neutral, impartial, objective adjudicators.... I think one of the most important things that we have to keep in mind throughout the investigation is that we have to be very careful of making sure that we don't bring any biases to the situation and investigation, and I think that we have to make our decision on the best available evidence."

This notion of "neutrality" goes hand-in-hand with the individualization of the employment standards enforcement regime and neglects power imbalances inherent in the employment relationship, which are amplified among employees belonging to social groups historically disadvantaged in the labour force. "Neutrality" is particularly problematic, as it overlooks the historical and institutional context of systemic discrimination.[5] By failing to acknowledge power imbalances in the workplace, the process of "neutral" adjudication by EROs and

ESOs carries the risks of reproducing the systemic inequalities in the employment standards regime. In this context, community organizations such as workers' centres and legal clinics can play a much-needed role as advocates for workers navigating the complaints process and thereby mitigate the power imbalances characterizing the workplace, which are not fully countered through the "neutrality" of the officer. Achieving this objective would also be aided by altering the training and curriculum for EROs and ESOs in ways that foster an understanding of workplace power dynamics with, for example, greater attention to the need for strategic enforcement as emphasized by the Wage and Hour Division (WHD) of the U.S. Department of Labor (see chapter 11).

Moreover, despite this stated desire to act without bias, paradoxically, interviews reveal that some EROs and ESOs hold biases that may (mis) inform their understandings of the nature of employment standards violations. These biases include ethnic stereotypes such as the assumption that immigrant-run enterprises tend to violate the law. As one ESO stated, "We also have a significant number of small businesses operated by new immigrants to Canada who have language barriers and tend to sometimes run their business the way they might have in their own culture."

Community organizations can counter such biases and stereotypes by providing deeper and more grounded insight into the causes and consequences of employment standards violations. For example, given their first-hand interaction with employees, which provides a deeper understanding of workplace problems in both small and large enterprises, combined with a broad knowledge of the structural problems of the labour market, workers' centres are well positioned to provide EROs and ESOs with specialized knowledge of employment structures and practices that are at the root of employment standards violations. Such knowledge can effectively contest assumptions regarding employment standards violations that are rooted in ethnic stereotypes. Indeed, as discussed in chapter 11, under the Obama administration, the WHD sought to adjust its selection criteria for new inspectors, including by making multiple-language capability a key criterion, and by aiming to hire inspectors that better reflect the communities of workers with whom they would interact, in order to foster an inspectorate that is better able to connect with and develop trust with workers experiencing workplace violations – measures that would be highly desirable in Ontario.

Hands-on, day-to-day, local knowledge from community organizations is also likely to enhance the capacities of ESOs to make more informed decisions on proactive inspections (Fine and Lyon 2017). Currently, the identification of which business, industry, occupational group, or form of employment to inspect involves a range of MOL officials on the basis of provincial and/or local needs (see chapter 5). More robust participation of worker advocacy groups as official advisors in the inspection process would better enable individual and collective voice amongst the precariously employed.

Finally, EROs and ESOs themselves recognize the importance of community organizations in the enforcement process. Officers we interviewed, particularly ESOs, emphasized that their work involves engaging in partnerships to facilitate effective enforcement of employment standards by enhancing knowledge and awareness about employment standards rights and obligations. To this end, they deliver presentations about employment standards to community groups and employer organizations interested in learning more about the *ESA* and how it affects them. Some of the groups and associations they partner with in that regard include "community groups that are doing the same kinds of work, the immigrant associations, the YMCA [Young Men's Christian Association], businesses, the CFIB [Canadian Federation of Independent Business], [and] business improvement associations." These presentations delivered by ESOs are part of the MOL's Education, Outreach, and Partnership strategy. Initiated in 2009, the strategy aims to create an environment where employers and employees better understand their rights and obligations under the *ESA* and to provide employers with tools to increase their awareness of responsibilities under the *ESA* and thereby to help them comply (MOL 2015). The scope of the strategy is confined to education and communication; it does not involve employee or employer engagement in enforcement. Although the word *partnership* is contained in the title of the initiative, the way partnership is conceptualized by the MOL does not denote a formalized relationship in which parties can jointly produce employment standards enforcement (see Amengual and Fine 2016; Fine 2014). The absence of this formality contrasts sharply with the meaning of partnership developed within the literature on participatory enforcement. More formalized forms of engagement between ESOs and community organizations could be enhanced through the development of MOL staff positions dedicated to outreach, as has been undertaken by the WHD in the United States (see chapter 11).

Despite the lack of an initiative based on formalized partnerships, EROs and ESOs note the important role that community organizations play in ensuring that individual employees have the support needed to come forward with complaints. As one ESO stated, "I think if you are a person with minimal means, you have to have free legal clinics, the worker centres in Toronto and other satellite offices, where you can have your case represented before the Employment Standards Branch, Employment Insurance Branch, and other such places."

Another ESO told us, "If they've [employees] gone to a legal clinic and they've gotten help from a legal clinic, very seldom there's no merit to the claims" that comprise the complaint. Under the *ESA* it is assumed that MOL officials will investigate all eligible complaints filed and will conduct a number of workplace inspections within a certain time period. However, limited resources allocated to investigations and inspections create constraints that make it difficult for ESOs to complete this work in a timely way (on the persistent problem of backlogs, see chapter 3; Mitchell and Murray 2017). In this context, the work that workers' centres and legal clinics do to properly prepare documents related to complaints, for example, is important for EROs and ESOs, as it reduces the time they spend on investigations. Time and workload constraints thereby shape the ways in which EROs and ESOs construe the role of community organizations. Hence, it is not surprising that some ESOs, who investigate complaints, note that they explicitly direct employees to community organizations: "I will say to them [employees], if they have an employer who isn't paying them properly... then they have the option to file a complaint. There's always someone that can help them to do that, whether it is with ... the workers' action centre, for example, or the YMCA, or the immigrant settlement area."

Community organizations are even more important when ESOs are investigating a complaint submitted by an employee with limited English proficiency. As an ESO stated,

> If I see parties are not able to communicate with me, I may suggest to them that they could seek out these legal clinics at one point or another who have people that could speak their language that can help them with the process.... If, for example, it is a French person, we do have people that specialize in French services. They will be in charge of the case. I will recuse myself, and the colleagues who have the French language skills will deal with those cases in that language.... I don't think we have it for anything else.

In these ways, ESOs clearly recognize the important role of community organizations in the effective enforcement of the *ESA*, even though they are rarely recognized as official participants in the enforcement process within the larger structures that govern their roles.

### 3. Community Organizations as Participants in Employment Standards Enforcement

In Ontario, community organizations including workers' centres and legal clinics play multiple roles in the employment standards enforcement process through education, advocacy, mobilization, and outreach.

Focusing on examples from Sudbury, Windsor, and Toronto, we examine the ways in which workers' centres and legal clinics participate, directly and indirectly, in employment standards enforcement by advocating both on behalf of individual workers and for policy reforms, providing labour rights education, helping employees to file complaints with the MOL, and engaging in community organizing.

*Education, Advocacy, and Community Mobilization*

Workers' centres and legal clinics support the precariously employed (as individuals and collectively), as these workers most often lack union protection (Cranford et al. 2006). While workers' centres and legal clinics often work alongside unions who share the same goal of improved working conditions for all, they are not affiliated with any particular union. As such, Cranford and colleagues (362) see workers' centres as occupying the middle of the continuum of organizing between worksite-based unions and other community groups. In the three communities – Sudbury, Toronto, and Windsor – where established workers' centres were present, these centres mainly provide labour rights education to non-unionized workers.[6] The centrality of providing labour rights education for workers' centres was articulated by a focus group in Toronto: "We have one piece that is the educational piece; we have workshops in-house that's called 'Info Session,' that is we also have workshops at different organizations around workers' rights. We also have a phone line, information line where we help workers to solve problems and try to give them [an] orientation and information." The phone line is a key part of the work done by the Toronto Workers' Action Centre. This phone line is often the first point of contact for workers. The workers' centres in Windsor and Sudbury, however, have only local numbers, not a toll-free number.

With respect to workers' rights education in Sudbury, a representative from the Sudbury Workers' Education and Advocacy Centre explains their role, which includes hosting "front-line [worker rights] workshops with [our community partners] so that when clients would go to them, if they had questions, they would have either the answer or know to refer back to the worker centre, and then we would encourage them."

Workers' rights education is but one of the ways in which community organizations participate in the enforcement process. This form of education serves the purpose of not only informing workers of their rights, but also enabling workers to assert rights in the workplace, and thereby enhancing worker participation in employment standards enforcement. As a representative from the Windsor Workers' Education

Centre explained, "If workers can organize, if workers have the knowledge ... of the Act, and what the process is, workers at times will come together and say, 'OK, let's have a meeting and let's do this as a group,' but that means that workers have to have the information as to what employment standards are ... and they have to have an understanding of the process and they have to be prepared to do that together as a group and then move forward."

These organizations also engage in individual advocacy by helping individuals to file employment standards complaints. They can address the multiple socio-economic dimensions of a complaint often in ways that are more effective than labour inspectorates, given their capacities to gain workers' trust, their ongoing relationships with workers, and often more diverse language capabilities (see Fine 2014). For example, during interviews and focus groups, workers' centre and legal clinic representatives discussed how the current claims system is not accessible to all workers, and many workers find it a challenge not only to access the claims process online, but also to find the information needed to proceed to this step. As a representative for the Sudbury Legal Clinic described the inaccessibility of the current claims process for individual workers, "Everyone thinks, 'Oh, well, telephone access is the way to go' and these things. No. For people without phones or with cell phones with a limited number of minutes, having to call a central number and being put on hold is a way of creating an insurmountable barrier to access."

In addition, these organizations are able to advocate on an individual's behalf, whereas EROs and ESOs – who, as discussed above, must maintain a level of impartiality – are not. There are also lengthy timelines for processing a complaint through the MOL, whereas community organizations may be able to address the needs of employees more quickly. A representative of the Windsor Workers' Education Centre, for example, explained the case of an employee suffering from a mental health condition who was owed several days of wages after being fired by a greenhouse owner for taking medication at work. The centre helped the employee to file the complaint. Subsequently, the Windsor Workers' Education Centre representative accompanied the employee in the follow-up meeting with the ESO, the owner of the greenhouse, and the recruiters. This support resulted in a settlement in which the employee received the money owed, despite limited official records.

The role of community organizations, particularly workers' centres, is pertinent to employment standards enforcement in industries where violations are frequent. In such cases, workers' centres are able to adapt and strengthen advocacy and education to workers, including in ways that reflect localized specificities. These interventions can be seen as "proactive strategies for enforcement" (Fine 2014, 69). A case related to the film industry in Sudbury provides an illustration: "Some workers are unionized, but then a lot of workers are not unionized – and what's happening is [that] these film industries are coming to Sudbury and then leaving right away, so then it makes it really hard for these workers if they want to get their money back. They don't know who to go to, because these employers may be from Vancouver, they may be from, you know, Halifax or down in Toronto."

Finally, beyond individual worker advocacy, community organizations also take on broader advocacy and organizing roles related to employment standards. For example, they may take a proactive approach to employment standards reform by advocating for legislative change. A representative from the Legal Assistance Windsor explained: "My role specifically is to provide some of the ongoing support and counselling and ongoing advocacy, both at an individual or direct service level as well as a systemic level, so I do a lot of work around municipal programming and policy as well, provincial policy, advocacy at times, or systemic advocacy, and then, depending on the population and the issue, it may also be a federal level as well."

Community organizations also support networking and facilitate the mobilization of workers in specific industrial contexts. A representative from the Windsor Workers' Education Centre illustrated the way the centre supports worker organizing as a collective strategy to respond to employment standards violations: "My role here as a volunteer ... was to meet with workers and understand their situation, try to do some organizing, especially if there were several workers with the same problem in the same workplace, trying to see if we could do something collectively to solve whatever the problem was.... And more broadly, organize workers – and we're talking about non-union workers, of course. That's our focus ... how can we organize non-union workers even across different sectors."

Involvement in organizing also includes contributing to broader campaigns for workplace rights. A representative from the Sudbury Workers' Education and Advocacy Centre explains that "we joined the Fight for $15 and Fairness Campaign and then eventually we started getting involved in the Living Wage Campaign."

While all these activities – advocacy, education, and mobilization – demonstrate ways in which community organizations participate – directly and indirectly – in enforcement, they ultimately also contribute towards enhancing the capacities for workers themselves to participate. A representative from the Sudbury Workers' Education and Advocacy Centre indicated that a primary goal of their organization is "trying to empower the workers to advocate for themselves, to know what their rights are, to share that with co-workers, to be comfortable to stand up for themselves in the workplace, to seek out help and to file those complaints and to tell their story."

Combining elements of community unionism with labour organizing, community organizations can thus be situated in the middle of what Cranford et al. (2006, 363) describe as the "process" continuum of organizing, with unions on one end and community groups on the other. In the current political and economic climate that is based on an individual rights regime (Fine 2013, 815), where it is extremely difficult for workers to organize and protect themselves against workplace violations, community organizations such as workers' centres and legal clinics address some of the limitations of government-based enforcement and help to ensure employment standards compliance.

*Financial Pressures and Sustainability*

Despite the advantages of community organizations to the overall employment standards enforcement process discussed above, many of these organizations, particularly workers' centres, are currently under-funded or operate on a solely volunteer basis, as government funding does not cover their activities. Though the Toronto Workers Action Centre has managed to grow through fundraising and grant-funded projects, the workers' centres in Windsor and Sudbury have struggled financially, relying primarily on volunteers to sustain their services. There are several dimensions to the problem of the search for sustainable funding, including the time-consuming task of applying for grants, the limitations of restrictive funding sources that are project based, and a lack of core funding opportunities. With limited non-government funding available, especially in smaller communities such as Sudbury and Windsor, maintaining these centres is challenging, as the lack of sustainable resources makes it increasingly difficult to maintain services and meet the needs of workers in the community. To the Sudbury Workers' Education and Advocacy Centre, the process of applying for funding itself is a challenge: "It's just roadblock after roadblock, and then you're working within the current political, with what's happening politically.... [I]t's not like they are going to start funding worker centres in Ontario to start educating people about the changes in the labour laws, but we'll have to wait and see."

Workers' centres rely on private donations, grants, or foundations for financial support and receive little public funding (on formalized public funding arrangements in Australia, see chapter 9). Much of the funding these centres receive is project-based, which does not support the daily operation of the centres. This project-based funding makes it a challenge to "keep services stable" (Sudbury Workers' Education and Advocacy Centre), which forces workers' centres to reinvent themselves each time they apply for government funding.

Compounding these financial pressures is the often uneasy relationship between workers' centres and trade unions. The union movement provides some additional financial support for workers' centres through their community or social justice programming, and occasionally unions have provided direct support through union locals. In the case of the Windsor Workers' Education Centre, the centre has received some limited financial support from local trade unions. As well, a representative from the Windsor Workers' Education Centre indicated that workers' centre involvement in community-based organizing may also support unionization drives. However, in general, trade unions are not able to offer sustainable core funding for workers' centres, and representatives from community organizations indicate that workers' centres are often isolated from the trade union movement. The Sudbury Workers' Education and Advocacy Centre has also received small amounts of financial support from the local labour movement, but it is "very little, it's not ongoing, it's little pockets of money here and there." Still, although this support is limited, it comes as unrestricted funding that can be used to support operational activities or fill financial gaps that grant funding does not cover. The financial crunch nevertheless led to the closure of the Windsor Workers' Education Centre office in downtown Windsor, leaving it with no space to conduct its operations. A representative of the Windsor Workers' Education Centre expressed this frustration: "We know the need is there and we could do more. So ... how do we sustain this worker centre model so that we get more? We're more relevant to the workers that we know could use help in the workplace."

Struggling for funding requires workers' centres to spend much of their time looking for funding. As a representative from the Toronto Workers' Action Centre noted, "Planning way in advance and trying to think through, if you have applied for a project, nine months or ten months before it's about to start and you may need to hire someone but you don't actually know if you got the money until three weeks before the project is about to start. How do you manage that?... [Figuring] out how projects connect, with other projects ... [and the] evolution to the work ... [it] takes a lot of time."

To improve the sustainability of workers' centres, a representative of the Windsor Workers' Education Centre suggested that MOL funding could be made available:

> I don't know what the Ministry of Labour might have for grants, but you know, if there is funding for the training we do, for the skills training, that sort of thing, because it is a form of adult education. So is there something there that would not constrain what we already do? I mean, the Ministry of Labour, I think they are committed to hiring more employment standards officers, but it probably would not be enough for the need that is out there, and will they fund the worker centres to do the outreach? So that is the work we need to do, but could we get some funding to do it?

To avoid compromising the autonomy of workers' centres, however, there is a need to consider how and to what degree formalized tripartite arrangements should be pursued. Workers' centres need to maintain a critical distance from government agencies, without which their capacities to both act as worker advocates *and* to continue to pressure government agencies to effectively enforce employment standards will be compromised. Thus, regulatory strategies that bolster the involvement of workers' centres and other community organizations should do so while simultaneously supporting the capacities of government agencies and representatives to better ensure employment standards compliance. In other words, any participatory model should not undermine hard-law, government-based enforcement mechanisms (see Vosko, Grundy, and Thomas 2016). As a representative from the Toronto Workers' Action Centre stated, employment standards enforcement "is the role of government, and we should ensure that there is strong regulation and there is strong funding for that."

Overall, we see community organizations such as workers' centres and legal clinics as essential to a participatory model of employment standards enforcement. While they are engaged in activities that both directly and indirectly affect enforcement, they contribute overall to a worker-centred approach to enforcement by enhancing worker agency and empowerment. First, they operate from a bottom-up approach, working at a grassroots level within a community, giving them greater awareness of conditions of employer non-compliance with employment standards, as well as the factors that may be generating non-compliance. Second, they provide in-person education and promotion of worker rights, whereas the MOL has moved to a self-help model with information made available online, or through workplace-based posters/notices. Third, they are less intimidating and more accessible to workers, as they are situated within the community, often have services available in the chosen language of the worker, and are often operated, in part, by volunteers or members who have shared experiences with the workers accessing their services. Fourth, they enable a more holistic approach to providing assistance to workers through partnership networks with other community organizations; in contrast, since the MOL is able to address only the specific workplace complaint, it cannot deal with other issues a worker may face such as loss of housing due to unpaid wages. Finally, being external to the government allows community organizations to advocate for changes to the current system based on the true needs of workers, with fewer concerns about political palatability. Whereas the MOL is constrained by existing legislation, community organizations can provide a collective voice to advocate for legislative change to meet the needs of workers within the current employment climate. The Fight for $15 and Fairness campaign, and the role of community organizations in preparing submissions to the Changing Workplaces Review are examples of key successes.

## 4. Conclusion

As demonstrated in chapters 1 through 6, a long-building crisis characterizes employment standards enforcement in Ontario, whereby traditional enforcement methods have proven unable to ensure effective workplace protections in the arena of employment standards. This crisis, while longstanding and rooted in the *ESA* since its inception, has intensified since the onset of neoliberal labour market reregulation. In a context where EROs and ESOs are trained to be and consequently see themselves as neutral adjudicators, community organizations are a necessary counterbalance to employer power in and beyond the workplace. Employers and employer associations often hold substantially greater power than individual employees to prepare documents for inspectors' review, as well as to advocate for exceptions for industry-specific reasons. Interviews with workers illustrate that prevailing enforcement processes create many barriers to effective participation. In Ontario, community organizations such as workers' centres and legal clinics are well positioned to provide much-needed forms of support to workers to counter the deficiencies of the current system. However, when considered in relation to the criteria outlined by Fine and Gordon (2010), many challenges remain to achieving such a system. Rather than being *formal* partners with *sustained* relationships, community organizations in Ontario are not formally integrated into the enforcement process, whether through the complaints procedures or through the inspections process. More often, when connections are made, they are in a consultative form, rather than in a fully integrated, *vigorous* manner. Moreover, adequate *resourcing* is a major challenge faced by many community organizations, which severely compromises their capacities to participate in employment standards enforcement. Finally, as there are only three workers' centres in Ontario, our examination of their work offers a just glimpse of what might be possible, rather than a generalizable account of advocacy work ongoing across the province.

Participation by community organizations in the forms examined above could enable greater access to information about workplace violations, identify collective and systemic dimensions of employer non-compliance, facilitate networking, help to counter the power dynamics of the employer–employee relationship, and contribute to collective worker mobilization. This potential is present in Ontario, as evidenced by the range of activities in which community organizations are engaged; yet such a system is much more promise than reality, as these forms of participation are not well integrated into the formal system of employment standards enforcement governed by the MOL. The often uneasy relationship between trade unions and community organizations, which may result from the ways in which workers' centres' may be isolated from the broader trade union movement, is another factor shaping the challenges that community organizations face in deepening their participation in employment standards enforcement.

To underscore the need for a more participatory approach to employment standards enforcement, however, we offer a concluding cautionary note: the prospect of formal partnerships between government agencies and community organizations raises questions regarding how to construct a model of participatory enforcement that does not compromise the autonomy of community organizations. Formal integration into government-regulated enforcement runs the risk of continuing to marginalize workers' voices unless workers have strong, independent organizations that are well resourced and can mitigate the power of *both* employers *and* government institutions. To effectively address the crisis of employment standards enforcement, workers require independent collective organizations that can alter the unequal power relations inherent in the employment relationship itself.

# PART TWO

# Views from Elsewhere: Contextualizing the Employment Standards Enforcement Gap in Ontario

*Chapter Eight*

# Unpaid Britain: Challenges of Enforcement and Wage Recovery

Precarious employment is prevalent in Britain, paralleling the other jurisdictions that are the focus of this book. Long-term labour force trends – such as declining unionization rates, the growth of forms of employment that deviate from the norm of the standard employment relationship characterized by security and durability, including zero hours contracts and new regulatory challenges associated with platform employment – are prompting renewed interest in ensuring a decent floor of employment standards applicable to workers[1] in Britain. This chapter explores the regulation of employment standards (focusing on wages) in Britain, and the debate between compliance and enforcement therein, comparing it with the situation in Ontario and the other employment standards systems addressed in this book. Its central argument is that an employment standards enforcement gap, fuelled by the persistent emphasis on soft-law enforcement strategies, prevails in Britain that, while sharing similarities with that documented in Ontario, entails unique features, given the country's distinct configuration of what are known in this context as "employment rights" and elsewhere labelled "employment standards."[2]

The ensuing analysis proceeds in three parts. Section 1 offers an overview of employment standards in Britain. Setting the context for the enforcement gap, section 2 surveys recent developments in the British labour market, revealing deepening insecurity among workers. Section 3 then explores the enforcement of employment standards, highlighting key actors and methods involved in the realization of these rights and entitlements; it emphasizes drivers of the enforcement gap, including impediments that workers face in initiating a complaint, low recovery of wages due to workers, and the persistent emphasis on soft-law compliance-oriented enforcement strategies. In conclusion, the chapter offers suggestions for improved enforcement in Britain.[3]

## 1. Overview of Employment Standards in Britain: Scope and Access

In Britain the basis of employment relationships is the employment contract, with the onus placed on the parties to it for its enforcement. However, since the 1980s there has been a gradual rise in the significance of individual legal rights. These legal rights differ according to the status of the worker. Employment standards for those defined as "workers" differ from those of "employees," and almost none are extended to the self-employed.[4] Unfortunately there are no clear definitions of these categories, which depend on precedents set in the courts and are under considerable debate as employers attempt to deploy misclassification to reduce labour costs (see chapter 1). If work is contracted to be performed personally, but not necessarily at times and in places determined by the employer, then the category of "worker" may apply. Most temporary agency staff, casual, and some seasonal workers will fall into this category. If the employer is obliged to provide work, which the worker is obliged to accept at times and in places determined by the employer, then "employee" status likely applies. Those who are genuinely working on their own account, and who can send someone else in their place to carry out the work at times of their own choosing, are likely considered self-employed.

According to solicitor Seery (2016, 9 September), broadly, employees are entitled to protection from unfair dismissal, redundancy rights, notice periods, and maternity leave (subject to meeting service requirements). Both workers *and* employees are entitled to the national minimum wage, paid holidays, regular breaks, and protection from deductions from wages. The only right the self-employed enjoy alongside the other two groups is protection from discrimination on the grounds of a protected characteristic (e.g., gender or race). Defining a worker as self-employed can save an employer 12 per cent of annual pay in holiday entitlement, in addition to a further 13 per cent in employers' National Insurance contributions. As of April 2017, employers are also obliged to make pension provision for workers who are aged twenty-two or over and earn more than £10,000 per annum. Pension contributions rose to 3 per cent in 2018, a development further motivating the growth of complex contracts designed to misclassify work as self-employment.

Lastly, a group of workers who have no rights is those lacking lawful contracts. This situation could emanate from a mutual understanding between workers and employers that some or all their pay is not declared for taxation and/or social security. Or it could flow from workers' social location, such as their immigration status; for example, workers could be migrants with no authorization to work for pay in the country. The idea that unlawful contracts cannot be enforced goes back into the eighteenth century and is discussed in detail by Bogg (2013) as it applies, in particular, to undocumented migrant workers.

### *Minimum Wage*

All workers[5] are entitled to be paid at least the national minimum wage for every hour they work. There are different rates, depending primarily on the worker's age. The apprentice rate is payable to apprentices under nineteen years of age, or if apprentices are older, during their first year of apprenticeship. The minimum wage for workers above twenty-five years of age was introduced under the misnomer of the "living wage" in April 2016, with the express aim of countering the growth of low wage/low income households. At the time, some commentators also suggested that the introduction of this critical social minima might transfer some of the costs of supporting older workers from the state (in the form of in-work benefits); consequently, it was accompanied by proposed cuts to benefit levels. Minimum wage rates are subject to annual review, based on a report from the Low Pay Commission. At present, the adult minimum wage is higher than that in the United States and Quebec, slightly behind Ontario, and considerably behind Australia.[6]

### *Working Time and Paid Holidays*

Working time regulations are based on the European Working Time Directive; however, Britain secured the "right" for individuals to opt out of the maximum of forty-eight hours per week. The right to breaks (of twenty minutes) after six hours' work (of eleven hours) between two working days, and (of twenty-four uninterrupted hours) weekly are included in the regulations. Regulations also provide for 5.6 weeks' paid holidays, paid at average earnings. For those with irregular hours and earnings, holiday pay is accrued at the rate of 12.1 per cent of pay.

### *Sick Pay*

All employees and agency workers who earn above the National Insurance threshold (£116 per week in 2018) are entitled to statutory sick pay for absences due to illness of more than four days. The current level of sick pay is £92.05 per week (payable for up to twenty-eight weeks).

## 2. The British Labour Market

Chapter 1 set out features indicative of precarious employment in Ontario. The extent to which such features exist in Britain is summarized below, to locate the enforcement framework more clearly in its socio-economic context.

*Low Hourly Pay*

Hourly income distributions derived from national datasets (the Labour Force Survey and the Annual Survey of Hours and Earnings) show a significant bunching around the level of the national minimum wage per hour, although the proportion of workers at or below the national minimum wage in the Labour Force Survey is higher than in Annual Survey of Hours and Earnings, perhaps reflecting the impact of hours worked but not paid.[7] Considering the Annual Survey of Hours and Earnings data for 2016, the median full-time wage was £538.6, and the median reported working week for full-time workers was 37.5 hours. Two-thirds of the median hourly rate equates to £9.58 per hour. Based on the distribution of hourly pay, about 32.5 per cent of the workforce is paid below this level. There is a strong gender difference: 26 per cent of men were paid less than this, compared to nearly 40 per cent of women.[8]

The Office for National Statistics takes a different approach to low pay, using the adult minimum wage rate as the benchmark (£6.70 per hour in April 2016). It found that there were four industries with high proportions of workers receiving less than the national minimum wage: hairdressing (7 per cent), child care (4 per cent), hospitality (3.8 per cent), and cleaning (3.7 per cent). In terms of the number of underpaid workers, however, the retail, hospitality, and social care industries were the most significant (Office for National Statistics 2016). The Low Pay Commission,[9] meanwhile, calculates the proportion of workers in each age category likely to receive the statutory minimum per hour. In 2017, 6.5 per cent for workers aged twenty-five and over were likely to receive the statutory minimum wage, rising to 10.4 per cent for those aged sixteen to seventeen years (Low Pay Commission 2017). As in Ontario, young people are more likely than their older counterparts to rely on the national minimum wage, even at the substantially lower rates set for them.

*Short Tenure*

Following a change introduced by the last government and taking effect in April 2012,[10] employees in Britain require two years' uninterrupted service to qualify for certain rights, such as protection from unfair dismissal[11] and redundancy pay. Calculations carried out on data from the 2014 Labour Force Survey by the Unpaid Britain project showed that almost a quarter (24.7 per cent) of the workforce had less than two years' service with their current employer and thus enjoyed no protection in law from summary dismissal. In food and beverage services, almost half the workforce (48.6 per cent) are excluded from protection by virtue of their service. With so little protection from termination of their contract, the difference between temporary employees and those with less than two years' service is limited in terms of statutory rights and may help to explain the relatively low level of temporary employment in Britain, as in the United States (Vosko 2010).

### *Small Employers*

Small employers are on the rise in Britain, particularly within the private sector. In 2011, 48.2 per cent of private sector employment was in small enterprises (fewer than 50 employees), 12.6 per cent in medium-sized enterprises (50–249 employees), and 41.2 per cent in large enterprises (250 or more). Figures for 2017 show a small decline in the share of large employers to 40 per cent, while small employers still accounted for 48 per cent of private sector employment. However, of the 12.8 million workers in small firms, 4.7 million were in enterprises with no workers, that is, they were effectively self-employed (Department for Business, Energy and Industrial Strategy 2017a). By contrast, in the public sector, the proportion of the workers employed by large employers is much larger. Employment in the National Health Service, for example, stood at 1.6 million in March 2017, and, while this subset of the British labour force may be shared across a number of local National Health Service Trusts, all of these trusts engage more than 250 employees. In 2017 civil service employment stood at approximately 420,000 (Office for National Statistics 2017b).

### *Types of Contracts*

Official labour force statistics fail to reveal substantial recent changes in the structure of the labour force as measured by contractual status. The proportion of the workforce in full-time employment has dropped over twenty years (from 64.4 per cent in 1998 to 62.9 per cent in 2018), largely as the result of an increase in the level of part-time self-employment (from 2.7 to 4.4 per cent). At the same time, the number of labour force participants has increased substantially, by 5.7 million, meaning that even though a smaller *proportion* of the workforce is in full-time employment, the *number* has increased by 3 million. Meanwhile the proportion (but not the number) of part-time employees is about the same now as it was twenty years ago, while both the number and proportion of those that are temporary has fallen. The only form of employment that has grown in both relative and absolute terms is part-time self-employment, but this form still accounts for just 4.4 per cent of all those engaged in paid work.

One highly insecure form of employment, which has attracted considerable media attention in Britain, is the zero hours contract in which workers are not guaranteed any minimum number of hours of work. Zero hours contracts can lead to wide fluctuations in earnings, with workers waiting to be called in to work or sent home when demand is low. The Labour Force Survey attempts to identify these workers, but not all of them are aware that this is their contractual arrangement. According to the Labour Force Survey, approximately 4 per cent of the workforce has such a contract, but they are highly concentrated in certain industries, notably the security industry and food and beverage services, where over 10 per cent of the workforce report having a zero hours contract. By contrast, many industries have no workers reporting zero hours contracts – much of manufacturing, telecommunications, or insurance, for example (Clark and Herman 2017, November).

Another notable phenomenon is false self-employment, where an employer may require workers to become self-employed to retain their jobs or will offer work only on an allegedly self-employed basis. It is difficult to measure the extent of this phenomenon, which resembles misclassification in Australia, Canada, and the United States, although Citizens Advice attempted to determine the true status of a sample of 491 clients who described themselves as self-employed and found that 1 in 10 were probably workers or employees (Citizens Advice 2015). On the basis of median self-employed earnings at the time, applying this finding would yield a loss of £1288 per year per worker in unpaid holiday pay alone. The issue has been examined in a number of high-profile cases at British Employment Tribunals, an institution distinct from the Ontario Labour Relations Board as described below. For example, in cases against Pimlico Plumbers and Uber, a plumber and a taxi driver respectively claimed (successfully) to be workers rather than self-employed contractors.[12] However, these cases do not oblige employers to change all contractual arrangements; while a case may set a precedent (if it reaches a higher court), a precedent is of use only if another worker makes a similar claim. Such cases thus neglect to disrupt the employer strategy of paying out only to workers who press their claim (usually after leaving the job).

*Unionization*

As in Ontario and elsewhere, the proportion of the labour force covered by collective agreements has been declining for decades in Britain. According to the Labour Force Survey, trade union membership in 2016 stood at 6.5 million (Department for Business, Energy and Industrial Strategy 2017d). The membership rate amongst employees was 23.3 per cent (21.1 per cent of men, and 25.9 per cent of women). Union membership was concentrated in the public sector, where 52.7 per cent of workers were unionized, compared to 13.4 per cent in the private sector. The sector with the highest density was education (at 48 per cent), whereas density in accommodation and food services was a mere 2.5 per cent. Between 1996 and 2016, collective bargaining coverage fell from 36 to 26.3 per cent (23.2 to 14.9 per cent in the private sector, 74.4 to 59 per cent in the public sector).[13] The decline in union membership and collective bargaining in the face of increasingly hostile labour legislation and economic conditions increased the significance of the statutory floor of employment standards in Britain, in much the same way as it has in Ontario.

## 3. Enforcing Employment Standards in Britain

Employment standards in Britain do not provide an effective floor of rights, partly as the result of poor state enforcement and judicial processes. As in Ontario, in Britain[14] the state gives the impression of securing basic entitlements for workers, while the evidence based on outcomes shows that such attempts are ineffective for many workers. The protections offered in Ontario exceed those in Britain, particularly in penalties, but fall short of the provisions for insolvency of employers. Both systems favour compliance over deterrence, reflected in the approaches adopted by regulators towards non-compliant employers. However, there are also specifics of the British system of employment standards and their enforcement that differentiate it from that of Ontario. It is to these specific features that we now turn.

Although there are several bodies with a remit to regulate certain aspects of employment relations in specific parts of the labour market (described below), there is no general labour inspectorate equivalent to the Ontario Ministry of Labour (MOL). Workers faced with breaches of their rights have a choice of three routes, once attempts to resolve it through employer channels have failed.

- Taking an individual claim to an Employment Tribunal or County Court, with all the intervening opportunities for pre-hearing resolution. This is the only route for matters such as unfair dismissal, discrimination, or non-payment of holiday pay.
- Going through state regulators, each of which has specific and limited remits (set out in table 8.1) and is approached mostly through the gateway of the Advisory, Conciliation and Arbitration Service (a government body) pay and work rights helpline.
- "Organic enforcement" through collective action of workers, unions, or other supporters.

### GOING TO COURT

Most employment standards can be enforced by the individual worker only through the Employment Tribunal system (for those without trade union representation in their workplace). The four most frequent

Table 8.1. Unpaid Wages as Measured by Official (or Administrative) Data

| Source | Description | Period | No. cases |
|---|---|---|---|
| Insolvency Service Freedom of Information request (FOI) | Wage arrears | 2014/15 | 38,949 |
| Insolvency Service FOI | Unpaid holiday Pay | 2014/15 | 35,547 |
| Department for Business Innovation and Skills evidence to 2016 Low Pay Commission | National Minimum Wage enforcement | 2014/15 | 26,000 |
| HMRC management information (FOI) | Statutory pay disputes received* | 2014/15 | 5,991 |
| Citizens Advice data (Advice Trends, Q3 2015-16) | Clients advised on Unauthorised deductions from wages | 2015 | 9,000 |
| Advisory, Conciliation and Arbitration Service (Annual report 2014-15) | Early Conciliation notifications received "fast track" ** | 2014/15 | 36,499 |
| HM Courts & Tribunals Service quarterly statistics main tables | Employment Tribunal claims accepted for "Unauthorised deductions" | 2014/15 | 28,701 |
| HM Courts & Tribunals Service quarterly statistics main tables | Employment Tribunal claims accepted for "Working Time Directive" | 2014/15 | 31,451 |
| Gangmasters Licensing Authority | "Direct intervention" to prevent exploitation | 2014/15 | 3,064 |

* Mostly Statutory Sick Pay and Statutory Maternity Pay and Leave cases.
** These are for "simple" cases, such as unpaid wages and holiday pay. This is the first full year for obligatory conciliation before Employment Tribunal claims.

"jurisdictions" under which claims are made are equal pay, unfair dismissal, unauthorized deductions from wages (unpaid wages, essentially), and working time (mostly relating to failure to provide paid holidays). In 2017/18 about 110,000 claims were accepted at Employment Tribunals, representing 172,000 separate jurisdictional complaints (Ministry of Justice 2018). Of these complaints, 35,000 related to equal pay, 24,000 to unpaid wages ("wages act" cases), 17,000 to unfair dismissal, and 17,000 to working time breaches.

Since 2014 all claimants must first contact the Advisory, Conciliation and Arbitration Service to attempt pre-claim conciliation. Prior to 2014, such contact was voluntary. The introduction of this requirement has resulted in a growth in the number of cases handled. In 2016/17, 37,910 "fast track" cases (simple claims, such as unpaid wages or holiday pay) were conciliated, representing 43.2 per cent of all cases, compared with 8,335 in 2011/12.

The Advisory, Conciliation, and Arbitration Service can conclude a legally binding agreement (COT3), which may or may not match the claimant's legal entitlements (including those that might be subject to contractual defaults, such as the national minimum wage). In this sense, the system may suffer from the same problems identified in chapter 4 regarding the Ontario MOL's system of ESO-facilitated settlements. In order to conclude the dispute with some chance of payment, workers may sign away some of their rights, in a legal agreement brokered by an agent of the state. Data from the 2013 Survey of Employment Tribunal Applications found that the median claim for unpaid wages in 2012 was £800, but that the median award was higher at £900; for comparative purposes with chapter 4 on Ontario, this represented 148 hours work at the then minimum wage. Settlements, however, were lower at a median of £590 (ninety-seven hours at the national minimum wage), suggesting that, just as in Ontario, there is a risk that workers are encouraged or at least enabled to sign away some of their rights, apparently with state approval.

It is only after conciliation has either been declined by either party, or attempts at conciliation have failed, that a complaint can be lodged with an Employment Tribunal. Claims must be made within three months of last occurrence of the event.

Workers can also pursue money claims, such as unpaid wages, holiday pay, or breach of contract, through the County Court system. Claims can be lodged up to six years after the event, and fees are payable related to the monetary size of the claim. Claims for less than £10,000 can be processed through the online "small claims" system.

Table 8.1, based on one originally published in *Labour Research* (Clark 2016), shows the relative numbers of cases relating to unpaid wages in 2014/15. This table reveals the relative importance of the various routes, although the categories overlap in some cases. A worker might, for example, approach a Citizens Advice Bureau first, then be referred to the Advisory, Conciliation, and Arbitration Service, and finally end up at an Employment Tribunal. Also included are some of the regulatory bodies that are discussed below.

### STATE REGULATORS

The variety of bodies that have some involvement in regulating Britain's workplaces can be confusing; therefore, it is little wonder that most offences probably go unreported.

Individual workers concerned that their rights have been breached are able to call the Work and Rights Helpline, which is run by the Advisory, Conciliation, and Arbitration Service. They can only provide advice about rights at this stage, but also act as the gateway to enforcement bodies. For example, workers who consider that they have not been paid the appropriate national minimum wage can complain via the Advisory, Conciliation, and Arbitration Service, who should then pass this on to Her Majesty's Revenue and Customs, which provides the minimum wage inspection and enforcement service.

Other agencies can be approached directly (such as the Gangmasters and Labour Abuse Authority or the Statutory Payments disputes team), as well as through the Advisory, Conciliation, and Arbitration Service helpline. The various regulators, their roles, and their location within the state, are set out in table 8.2.

For the sake of simplicity, only regulators who deal with the key issues of unpaid (or underpaid) wages and holiday pay are considered below.

The National Minimum Wage Inspectorate investigates complaints (which can come from workers or third parties[15]) and inspects workplaces to enforce compliance with the national minimum wage. The arena in which the inspectorate operates has been expanded over recent years, with the introduction of a "naming and shaming" scheme where offenders detected by Her Majesty's Revenue and Customs have their details published online in a spreadsheet. The online employer lists provide details of the sector and region as well as the number of workers affected and the sum outstanding. Since the scheme was established in 2013, 1,539 employers have been named, and according to a minister, £8 million in back pay "identified" for 58,000 workers, with 1,500 employers fined a total of £5 million (Dunstan 2018, 4 February).

Table 8.2. Rights and Regulators in Britain

| Breach of rights | Regulator/agency and remit | Branch of government | Powers of enforcement |
|---|---|---|---|
| Unpaid wages | For pay up to national minimum wage (all workers): national minimum wage inspectors | Her Majesty's Revenue and Customs (on behalf of Department for Business, Energy and Industrial Strategy) | Notice of underpayment, fines, civil recovery, "naming and shaming" |
| | For temporary agency workers in food processing & agriculture: GLAA | Home Office | Improvement notice, Withdrawal of agency's licence |
| | Other temporary agency workers: Employment Agency Standards Inspectorate | Department for Business, Energy and Industrial Strategy | Requirement to pay, debar directors from running agency |
| | Unpaid due to employer insolvency: Insolvency Service | Department for Business, Energy and Industrial Strategy | Payment up to maximum limits |
| Unpaid holiday pay | For temporary agency workers in food processing & agriculture: GLAA | Home Office | Improvement notice, Withdrawal of agency's licence |
| | Unpaid due to employer insolvency: Insolvency Service | Department for Business, Energy and Industrial Strategy | Payment up to maximum limits |
| Failure to provide breaks | Health and Safety Executive (HSE) | Department of Work and Pensions | Improvement notice, can prosecute |
| Unpaid statutory pay (e.g. sick pay) | Statutory Payments disputes team | Her Majesty's Revenue and Customs | Can issue a ruling |
| Discrimination relating to a protected characteristic | Equality and Human Rights Commission | Department of Education | Can apply for injunctions, support of joint legal proceedings |
| Charged fee for finding work | Agency workers or job seekers: Employment Agency Standards Inspectorate | Department for Business, Energy and Industrial Strategy | Debar directors |

Fines have also been introduced, and Her Majesty's Revenue and Customs can initiate civil court actions to recover unpaid minimum wages. Since 2010, 532 cases against employers have been pursued in courts; however, the government is unable to specify how much money has been recovered for workers by these means (Dunstan 2018, 4 February). Nor is it clear how many fines have actually been paid, and that is a concern, given the low rates of recovery documented in Ontario in chapter 4. The effectiveness of national minimum wage recovery nevertheless can be tested by examining one of the largest cases where the employer was named by Her Majesty's Revenue and Customs. Total Security Services Ltd was cited as owing £1.74 million to over 2,500 workers (equivalent to the majority of the security guards employed). It was two years before any workers were paid, and, even then, over £1 million of provision for this was written off in 2016 on the grounds that the workers had left the company and repayment was by then unlikely. It proved impossible to obtain any clarification on this matter from Her Majesty's Revenue and Customs, who cited confidentiality, or from the employer, who failed to respond to enquiries.

In this case, naming and shaming seemed to have little effect. This outcome supports Dickens's (2012, 223) doubts about the potential of employers' concern over reputational damage to leverage improved employer behaviour.

### *Gangmasters and Labour Abuse Authority*

The Gangmasters Licensing Authority was established in 2005, partly in response to the deaths of twenty-six Chinese cockle pickers in Morecambe Bay the previous year. It was given the task of regulating the supply of temporary employment in the agriculture, shellfish, and food processing industry. This task was to be fulfilled through a system of licensing, supported by inspection of licence applicants against a code based on existing labour, health and safety, and related legislation. Labour providers ("gangmasters") operating in these regulated sectors without a licence could be subject to criminal charge, as could labour users making use of the services of an unlicensed gangmaster. Although the Gangmasters Licensing Authority was not assigned a formal employment standards enforcement role, by threatening to revoke the licence of an offending agency, it could often secure recompense of owed wages, or the provision of documents such as contracts and payslips.

The remit of the Gangmasters Licensing Authority was expanded (by the *Immigration Act, 2016*) to include a general duty to tackle labour exploitation, and the name was changed to the Gangmasters and Labour Abuse Authority. The Gangmasters and Labour Abuse Authority has also been granted new police-style powers of search (it already had powers of arrest) and since November 2016 has had the power to apply for Labour Market Enforcement Undertakings and Orders. The first of these (an undertaking) was not imposed until April 2018. However, according to the Gangmasters and Labour Abuse Authority Annual Report (Gangmasters and Labour Abuse Authority 2018, 11 April), "Since April last year, we've arrested 97 people, identified over 1,140 workers as suffering direct abuse and recovered nearly £151,000 for workers." Budget and staffing had been increased to take account of the new responsibilities. Despite the commitment in the Gangmasters and Labour Abuse Authority's strategic plan to the "Hampton Principles" of regulation, the agency has a record of pursuing prosecutions and recovery formerly perceived to be impossible, but it remains to be seen if this best practice continues.

*Director of Labour Market Enforcement*

The newly established role of director, held by Sir David Metcalf, is to focus on the minimum wage, licensing of gangmasters, operation of recruitment agencies, and modern slavery. In effect, this means overseeing the three principal enforcement bodies: National Minimum/Living Wage Enforcement Teams in Her Majesty's Revenue and Customs; the Gangmasters and Labour Abuse Authority; and the Employment Agency Standards Inspectorate. Regarding modern slavery offences involving the exploitation of workers, the director is to indirectly monitor bodies such as the National Crime Agency and the police (Metcalf 2017). The director has published his enforcement strategy for 2018 (Metcalf 2018), which recommends changes to strengthen both compliance and deterrence, as well as to reduce gaps in the enforcement regime (e.g., regarding holiday pay).

*Insolvency Service*

Under the *Employment Rights Act, 1996*, workers whose wages or holiday pay are unpaid as a result of the insolvency of their employer can claim up to eight weeks' wages and six weeks' holiday pay from the Insolvency Service, which makes payments from the National Insurance Fund, an institution sharing similarities with the wage protection funds discussed in chapter 4. Such payments are, however, subject to an upper limit on a week's pay (currently £508). This limit means a maximum payment of £4,064 (CAD$7,200) for outstanding wages and £3048

(CAD$5,425) for holiday pay; it is thereby considerably more generous than the Ontario system (see chapter 4). Workers in insolvent companies may also present claims for statutory redundancy and notice pay.

Calculations based on data provided in response to Freedom of Information requests show that the average amount paid out over recent years was one and a half week's wages and about four days' holiday pay. Usually, but not always, workers are owed both wages and holiday pay. Any wages owed over and above the limits set out above are preferred debts but come after secured debts (such as mortgages) and fees for the insolvency practitioner. They are capped at £800. Any wages owed beyond that are unsecured debts.

*The Enforcement Gap in Britain*

Chapter 1 discussed the turn towards compliance and regulatory new governance in the Ontario enforcement regime. Clearly a similar tale can be told of Britain. The notion that non-compliance is accidental (and therefore best rectified through education) has a long history. When Bayliss wrote his book on the Wages Council System, he claimed that "ignorance and incompetence are the main reasons for failure to pay the worker his due" (Bayliss 1962, 119). However, he failed to identify any data to support his claim, and it seems likely that this was the view expressed to him by the inspectors to whom he spoke. The compliance orientation continued through the 1972 Robens Report on Health and Safety and the 2005 Hampton Report on reducing the "administrative burden" on business relating to enforcement of regulations. Both reports came down in favour of non-statutory codes, and inspections being reduced to supposed "high-risk" cases (See Nicholls 1997; Tombs and Whyte 2010).

By contrast, the Unpaid Britain project revealed a range of methods and strategies used by employers to deprive workers of their earned pay and to evade any penalty for doing so (Clark and Herman 2017, November). These methods and strategies included unpaid time, from small, regular amounts of as little as twenty minutes per shift up to all time travelled between assignments; misclassification of work or work relationships (labelling work as unpaid training, volunteering, profit share, or self-employment); withholding holiday pay, and paying it only when specifically asked; cessation of pay, which may be deliberate or inadvertent around impending insolvency, or absconding; failing to pay the last pay period when a worker leaves; deductions from pay, such as fines for lateness or for work clothes; and pretended ignorance of regulations (e.g., regarding the national minimum wage).

The underlying causes of non-payment identified included punishment (for turning up late, or for leaving the job); labour hoarding (underpaying staff so severely that they fear to leave employment, that is, outstanding sums become almost beyond recovery); reduction of costs (not paying holidays can save up to 12 per cent of the wage bill); meeting targets (local supervisors or managers may cut corners to keep to centrally set targets for wage costs); and incompetence or lack of understanding.

These are very similar to the breaches taken up by ESOs in Ontario, as described in chapters 1 and 4, and taken up in chapter 11 on the United States, suggesting that the drivers of this behaviour are more related to contracting arrangements themselves, and specifically to fissuring, than to the regulatory processes in and of themselves.

In his thorough examination of globalized industry, Smith (2016, 81) points to one of the benefits of outsourcing for larger enterprises: "Arm's-length also means 'hands clean' – the outsourcing firm externalizes not only commercial risk ... it also externalizes direct responsibility for pollution, poverty wages and suppression of trade unions." Unpaid Britain detected similar processes; however, it revealed them not only in outsourced supply chains, but within larger companies. By setting (excessively low) labour cost targets for managers, tied to bonuses, central management can set them impossible tasks, which can be resolved only through managers cutting corners on workers' pay and conditions. If detected, such cost-cutting can be dismissed by corporate managers as the result of poor local practice with limited threat of punishment for wrongdoing, an enforcement gap that Australia's new provisions for accessorial liability seeks to close (see chapter 9).

The extent of actual violations in British workplaces is hard to assess. As chapter 1 points out, administrative data can capture only the experiences of those who enter the administrative system. Similarly, the British system will record offences only at the point at which the Advisory, Conciliation and Arbitration Service pre-claim conciliation is engaged. Records prior to the pre-claim conciliation process go unmeasured (except perhaps by Citizens Advice Bureaux and law centres). Even unions gather limited data about the day-to-day activities of lay and regional full-time officers. Most (unrepresented) workers faced with unpaid wages or holidays will not immediately approach the authorities, but they may take advice from friends, family, and colleagues. The most frequent course of action is to approach a line manager, but this route to recourse is often unsuccessful. Only about 7 per cent of such cases go on to initiate any formal process to recover the money (Pollert and Charlwood 2009). As in the other jurisdictions included in this book, workers in Britain are deterred by a variety of issues. Fear of reprisal is amplified for those with tenuous residency status (examples include non–European Economic Area students, asylum seekers, and over-stayers). Workers' failure to recognize breaches of their rights due their perceptions of employment standards violations as part of the normal course of doing business was also encountered in the Unpaid Britain Project. This failure was reinforced by peer/mentor advice, from an actor's agent (not to demand all payments included in a contract), from senior chefs ("kitchen is kitchen"), or even from a trade union (to defer complaining about unpaid training).

Those who take no action may be reluctant to act for fear of damaging their career prospects, or of losing their job, or suffering other forms of retribution. They are also often poorly informed about the methods of recovery available. That said, knowing more of the poor chances and expense of securing recovery might well deter potential claimants from pursuing their cases (see also chapters 1, 2, 4, and 7). Those who take action are also under pressure to withdraw claims and settle, either because they fear the litigation process, or because they are threatened with costs orders by respondents. The use of limited liability also reduces the chance of claims against firms thought likely to wind up and "phoenix."

As discussed above, workers may face the possibility of agreeing to settle for less than they are owed through the pre-claim conciliation process. This possibility continues until the Employment Tribunal hearing. Moreover, our examination of wages cases at Employment Tribunals suggests that most claims are withdrawn before the hearing, and that this is the result of a settlement of some kind. However, nearly all pre-hearing settlements are paid, unlike cases that go to a hearing. A study in 2013 found that only 53 per cent of successful claimants received any payment whatsoever, and even then, not necessarily the entire all of the award (Department for Business, Energy and Industrial Strategy and Ministry of Justice 2018, February, para. 19). In part, such recovery outcomes flow from the additional costs incurred in attempting to enforce a judgment (via the County Court, for example, it could mean fees of over £150). Indeed, Unpaid Britain found that the majority of employers losing a case over wages were likely to wind up the company soon afterwards, thus evading payment. Consequently, there would be little sense in throwing good money after bad in a recovery process that was unlikely to succeed.

A new scheme to penalize employers not paying awards was introduced in 2016 and has had 513 notifications, of which 483 warning notices were issued. Of these, 92 resulted in awards being paid, suggesting that, even now, enforcement remains problematic. A similar picture emerges with the national minimum wage. Government announcements regarding the national minimum wage arrears say that they have been "identified." The very significant case of Total Security Services cited above shows that there may be little justification for claiming that identifying the underpayment will result in recovery of owed wages.

*Organic Enforcement*

One case examined by Unpaid Britain dealt with two high-end bar/restaurants (both called Beach Blanket, and Babylon), which had become notorious for holding back significant parts of staff's wages (Clark and Herman 2017, November). A number of workers had become so enraged that they began holding demonstrations outside one of the two establishments, attracting media interest. One by one, the demonstrators were paid off over a period of a few weeks. Others chose to take the Employment Tribunal route, and all received default judgments months later.[16] However, in subsequent interviews, it seems that the employer was adept at avoiding collection agents, such as bailiffs, who are required to return to an address only a limited number of times. Consequently, some remain unpaid.

On a larger scale, construction workers on the EDF construction project at Hinkley C stopped work after being threatened with non-payment for work that was cancelled as the result of poor weather – and also prevented workers from going home. After two days of occupying the on-site canteen, talks between the workers' union and EDF resulted in payment being made (*Bristol Post* 2018, 6 March).

The immediacy of the action, and rapidity of the outcomes, in these cases contrast starkly with the drawn-out, bureaucratic, and uncertain processes described above. While businesses continue to operate, collective action is poised to be an efficient means of obtaining redress – indeed, the outcomes of such cases go some way to strengthening the argument for participatory enforcement made in chapter 7.

Collective action of this scale is not possible in all cases, particularly in the fissured workplaces described by Weil (2014), which calls for creative approaches to staffing inspectorates of the order proposed in chapter 11. Still, unions and workers' and community organizations, more broadly, have a particular interest in restraining the race to the bottom in employment conditions and are often closer (geographically and culturally) to the workplaces involved.

RECENT DEVELOPMENTS

There has been a change in emphasis regarding the British government's approach to enforcement of employment standards. As in Ontario in early 2018, before they were withdrawn by a new provincial government later that year, penalties and resources available to the National Minimum Wage Inspectorate have increased somewhat, as have resources and powers for the Gangmasters and Labour Abuse Authority. In addition, a director for labour market enforcement has been appointed, and the government has commissioned an investigation into "modern working practices," to be overseen by former Blair advisor Matthew Taylor (now CEO of the Royal Society of Arts).

Although Taylor (2017) considered that advice and assistance to comply with employment standards are the most effective means of improving the quality of work, he made fifty-three recommendations for changes to which the government has responded (Department for Business, Energy and Industrial Strategy and Ministry of Justice 2018).

Taylor's proposal to establish a new employment category of "dependent contractor," akin to that in the Canada Labour Code and several other provincial jurisdictions in Canada, is unlikely to be adopted. Resembling certain proposals in Ontario's Changing Workplaces Review in 2016/17, the idea of offering temporary agency and other zero hours contract workers improved contracts after twelve months in the same job will be subject to further consultation (but would leave at least a third of such workers exposed by not meeting the service requirement).

Regarding enforcement, Taylor argued that holiday and sick pay should be enforced by Her Majesty's Revenue and Customs in the same way as the national minimum wage (and restricted to workers in low paid work). This recommendation has been endorsed by the director for labour market enforcement (Metcalf 2018). Both Metcalf and Taylor also endorse the "naming and shaming" of those not paying Employment Tribunal awards. But since the most likely means used to evade payment is to wind up the company, this is likely to be an empty gesture.

Taylor also criticized the lack of use of penalties (for parallels in Ontario, see chapter 6). For example, Her Majesty's Revenue and Customs' instructions were not to prosecute employers for not keeping proper payroll records (although this practice could potentially be prosecuted as a criminal offence), unless this offence was accompanied by other more egregious offences, specifically, those of employing undocumented workers and/or evading taxation. It remains to be seen whether offences against workers will be accorded the same status as those against the state.

In response, the government has made a limited number of proposals, including setting up a "naming and shaming" scheme for employers evading payment of Employment Tribunal awards; increasing the (rarely imposed) aggravated breach penalty for persistent or extreme offenders to at least £20,000; and accepting the case for state enforcement of core rights, but making no concrete proposals for implementation (such as holiday pay). The government has also made further vague commitments to take "strong action" against repeat offenders and non-payers of Employment Tribunal awards and to simplify enforcement processes. But no details or timetable have been proposed, simply a consultation process (Department for Business, Energy and Industrial Strategy and Ministry of Justice 2018).

Some attention had already been paid to Employment Tribunals. On one hand, the introduction of fees had a dramatic dampening effect on claims. Moreover, evidence from Unpaid Britain's examination of cases going to London Employment Tribunals suggests that at least as many potentially successful claims were discouraged as those less likely to succeed. Now that the introduction of Employment Tribunal fees has been ruled unlawful and reversed,[17] the number of claims is once again on the rise, but the possibility of fees being re-introduced remains. On the other hand, penalties for egregious offences were introduced in 2014 to deter employers from wilfully repeating offences. However, very few have been imposed. Twenty penalties have been imposed since 2014, with a value of £54,400, of which £17,700 has actually been paid (Department for Business, Energy and Industrial Strategy and Ministry of Justice 2018, paras 65–6).

## 4. Conclusion

By far the largest group of workers experiencing wage theft in Britain are those who do not pursue the matter (certainly beyond their immediate supervisor). Reasons for their reluctance to go forward include fear of retribution for those still employed by the offending employer, lack of faith in the system's capacity to enforce repayment, absence of advice or support, and to some extent workers' lack of information about their rights (see chapter 2). This last reason reflects the proportion of workers (15 per cent, according to the 2015 Labour Force Survey) reporting that they do not know their entitlement to paid holidays, a finding similar to a study conducted for the Department for Business, Energy and Industrial Strategy in 2008, which found that only 87 per cent of those employees surveyed were aware of the legal right to paid holidays (Fevre et al. 2009).

The British-style regulatory new governance approach to employment standards enforcement emphasizes providing information to employers and workers over hard enforcement. As both the Unpaid Britain and Ontario–based research suggest, such provision is largely symbolic, given that violations are often deliberate or wilfully negligent (see Vosko et al. 2017). Improving information to workers and employers will not lead to more effective restitution or reduce employer recidivism on its own, especially if workers understand that they are unlikely to retrieve their money. Strategies to provide soft-law information need to be accompanied by measures that are likely to lead to improved enforcement. Serial offender identification and penalty is worth pursuing, but only if there is a realistic prospect of such mechanisms being used against large as well as small employers. However, information gathering amongst unions and advice bodies might well shine a light on the worst serial offenders – if cooperation can be maintained through the sort of engagement advocated for Ontario in chapter 7. Finally, even with their reduced numbers and coverage, unions remain the bodies with the greatest potential for ensuring workers receive their entitlements. Empowering unions to take up cases on behalf of groups of workers (e.g., challenging sham self-employed contracts) would remove from individuals the risk of retribution and blacklisting, and represent an important step towards improved employment standards enforcement in Britain.

*Chapter Nine*

# Out of the Shadows and into the Spotlight: The Sweeping Evolution of Employment Standards Enforcement in Australia

For many years, the federal labour inspectorate in Australia was under-loved and overlooked. However, in 2006, this all changed. The inspectorate – now a statutory agency known as the Office of the Fair Work Ombudsman (FWO) – was unexpectedly thrust into the public spotlight in the wake of controversial legislative reforms introduced by the Howard conservative government (Hardy 2009). Notwithstanding several changes of government since this time, the federal labour inspectorate has continued to play a prominent role in workplace relations. And yet, much like the situation in Ontario, there remains a persistent "enforcement gap" (Berg and Farbenblum 2017; Bright, Fitzpatrick, and Fitzgerald 2017). Indeed, the long-held assumption that the vast majority of Australian employers were law abiding and that non-compliance may be explained "as a moral evil rather than as a consequence of structural factors" (Bennett 1994, 151) has now come unstuck. In 2015 a series of underpayment scandals rocked some of the country's best-known brands, including 7-Eleven and Domino's Pizza (Australian Broadcasting Corporation 2015, 31 August; Australian Broadcasting Corporation 2015, 4 May; Senate Education and Employment References Committee 2017). Four years on, the media continues to be awash with stories of worker exploitation, community concern about wage theft is still high, and the FWO remains under intense scrutiny (Berg and Farbenblum 2018; Clibborn and Wright 2018; Fels and Cousins 2019).

This chapter considers some of the compliance and enforcement challenges presented by employment standards regulation in Australia and the way in which the FWO has sought to respond to the problem of employer non-compliance with workplace laws. We begin by surveying the broader historical, legal, and political processes through which domestic employment regulation and enforcement has emerged and continues to evolve in Australia. As part of this overview, we touch on a number of key developments, including the recent passage of statutory reforms designed to better protect vulnerable workers (*Fair Work Amendment (Protecting Vulnerable Workers) Act 2017* (Cth)). We then turn to the internal administration of the agency, including the FWO's attempts to move away from an individualized, complaints-oriented approach towards a more "responsive" and "strategic" enforcement model.

## 1. An Overview of the Regulatory and Enforcement Framework in Australia

Historically, the federal conciliation and arbitration system in Australia allowed an independent industrial umpire to resolve collective disputes by imposing protective employment standards across industry sectors or occupational classes in the form of "awards." Trade unions were effectively charged with "policing" this system and were afforded extensive privileges and protections to perform this supervisory function, including rights of entry and legal standing to commence court proceedings (Hardy and Howe 2009; Bennett 1994). During this early period, government labour inspectorates remained in the shadows (Maconachie and Goodwin 2006, 339).

The general neglect of the federal labour inspectorate, which persisted over the course of the twentieth century, appears to have been premised on an assumption that enforcement of employment standards was "unproblematic" (Bennett 1994, 145) and more properly the role of trade unions than government (Hardy and Howe 2009). These perceptions appear to have led to a chronic lack of resources of the federal labour inspectorate (as well as the subnational state enforcement agencies). Severe resource constraints, low penalties, and judicial reluctance to impose heavy fines against employers led labour inspectors to adopt a weak, persuasive compliance approach to enforcement.

This regulatory landscape, and the entrenched role of trade unions within it, began to shift with the introduction of the *Workplace Relations Act 1996* (Cth) under the Howard coalition government. This first tranche of statutory reforms encouraged individualization strategies, restricted union rights, and curtailed the powers of the federal industrial tribunal. However, these issues dramatically escalated in 2006 with the controversial introduction of the coalition government's *Work Choices* legislation (*Workplace Relations Amendment (Work Choices) Act 2005* (Cth)). This subsequent set of radical reforms greatly expanded the federal jurisdiction over workplace relations (at the expense of state [provincial] jurisdictions) and further curtailed the role of the industrial relations tribunal. It also sought to usurp the collective, award-based framework by entrenching a core set of minimum employment standards in legislation and promoting individual statutory agreements as the industrial instrument of choice.

Replacing a collectivist system with a rights-based model elevated the role of formal enforcement mechanisms utilized by the federal labour inspectorate and overseen by the courts. This new model came at the expense of informal dispute resolution initiated by unions and administered by the federal tribunal.

In the wake of *Work Choices*, there was growing unease amongst the general public that many hard-won employment conditions had been, or would be, jeopardized by these reforms. In a bid to address these concerns and confirm that entitlements would be duly "protected by law," the Howard coalition government expressed a somewhat surprising enthusiasm for enforcement. While the *Work Choices* legislation was ostensibly designed to "deregulate" the labour market, the Conservative government provided the federal labour inspectorate with a substantial injection of much-needed funds.[1] Combined, these factors directly led to a boost in the inspectorate's workforce, a shift in enforcement strategy, and a spike in litigation (Hardy, Howe, and Cooney 2013).

The Rudd Labor government, elected in late 2007, sought to unwind some of the most extreme measures adopted by the previous government. The *Fair Work Act 2009* (Cth) (*FWA*), which mostly came into force on 1 January 2010, removed easy access to individual statutory agreements, reinstated the central place of enterprise bargaining, and restored some sense of regulatory legitimacy to unions. However, the *Work Choices* legacy lived on in a number of critical respects. For a start, the federal takeover of workplace relations was further consolidated under the *FWA*, and most businesses and employees in Australia now fall within the federal jurisdiction (rather than under state jurisdiction). Basic working conditions, including minimum rates of pay, leave entitlements, termination, and redundancy pay continue to be embedded in legislation.

The *FWA* also established the Office of the FWO – the federal agency that has been charged with primary oversight of employment standards regulation in Australia. While the enforcement framework was strengthened and a number of new powers were introduced, funding to the FWO was substantially reduced beginning around 2010 in the wake of the global financial crisis (Workplace Express 2013, 14 May). Resourcing constraints, combined with a perception that the FWO was being too aggressive at a time of significant legislative change, prompted a change to the FWO's dominant compliance and enforcement approach (Wilson 2012, 30 April). The agency – which had consciously built a reputation as a rigorous enforcer of the laws since 2006 – started to soften its stance in some respects. For example, it downplayed its use of coercive sanctions, emphasized its educational tools, and expanded its dispute resolution activities. The move towards more cooperative approaches was further entrenched following the election of a Conservative coalition government in 2013. While this shift in regulatory narrative and enforcement strategy – which was promoted as a form of "strategic compliance" – may have been more economically sustainable and politically palatable, it has proved to be problematic for the agency. One obvious drawback is that much of the day-to-day work of the FWO became less visible (Andrew 2017).

This move towards cooperative approaches may have backfired on the FWO following the explosion of media and public interest in wage theft akin to that in Ontario, documented in chapter 4. In particular, the public portrayal of the FWO as "business friendly" may have exposed the agency to heavy criticism for its part in failing to stem serious wage theft in key segments of the labour market and amongst precarious groups, including temporary migrant workers. In response, the FWO argued that their efforts had been hampered by limitations within the legal framework (FWO 2017d). Numerous public inquiries that explored these issues in the immediate aftermath tended to agree with the FWO's assessment in this respect. Accordingly, a series of far-reaching recommendations were put forward; many have since been acted upon (Senate Education and Employment References Committee 2016; Forsyth 2016; *Labour Hire Licensing Act 2017* (Qld) (commenced on 16 April 2018); Labour Hire Licensing Act 2018 (Vic) (commencing 1 November 2019)).[2]

The latest instalment in this potted history is potentially the most momentous – the introduction of *Fair Work Amendment (Protecting Vulnerable Workers) Act 2017* (Cth) (*PVWA*). As the title of the legislation suggests, the *PVWA* is designed to curb "deliberate and systematic exploitation of workers" in Australia (Minister for Employment 2016–17, ii). In the lead-up to the 2016 election, stamping out wage theft emerged as a key battleground with both parties seeking to outdo the other in this space (Liberal Party of Australia 2016; Australian Labor Party 2016). The coalition government not only promised to plug some of the most glaring statutory holes, it also committed AU$20 million in additional funding for the FWO. But ultimately, political rhetoric did not match reality. Recent budget assessments indicate that the funding received by the FWO has remained virtually frozen over the past three years (Clibborn and Wright 2018, 217).

This move is somewhat unsurprising, given that the introduction of this new set of reforms is sharply at "odds with the Coalition's employer-oriented approach to industrial relations, exemplified by its recent 'crack down' on unions" (Rawling and Schofield-Georgeson 2018; see also Forsyth 2017). While the *PVWA* is far from perfect, it has still made some regulatory headway. In particular, the amending legislation raised the maximum penalties available for "serious contraventions" to over half a million Australian dollars, extended liability beyond the direct employer to franchisors and holding companies in certain circumstances, reversed the onus of proof where there has been a failure to keep or maintain employment records, and bolstered the investigative powers of the FWO.

With a federal election looming in early 2019, calls for more far-reaching reforms became increasingly urgent. For example, as part of its "Change the Rules" campaign, the Australian Council of Trade Unions argued that the Fair Work Commission (the federal industrial tribunal) should be allowed to conciliate and arbitrate disputes regarding the non-payment of wages (McManus 2018, April), and liability for wage theft should be extended to lead firms in a range of different business formats, such as supply chains and labour hire (Workplace Express 2018, 13 March; Senate Education and Employment References Committee 2018). At the state level, there have been moves to introduce criminal sanctions for deliberate wage theft (Kennedy and Howe 2018; Education, Employment, and Small Business Committee 2018). In short, the regulatory framework and the institutional apparatus remain in a state of great flux in Australia.

## 2. The Remit, Responsibilities, and Resources of the Fair Work Ombudsman

The FWO is responsible for a number of functions under the *FWA*, including educating employers and employees about workplace rights and taking action to determine and sanction non-compliance with relevant rights and obligations arising under the *FWA*, its auspices, and other relevant instruments. While the agency is most well known for its work promoting and ensuring compliance with minimum employment standards, the remit of the FWO is fairly broad.

The FWO is responsible for overseeing civil remedy provisions for "adverse action" (which is similar to anti-retaliation provisions), anti-discrimination (a jurisdiction it shares with other state and federal bodies), and sham contracting (otherwise known as employee misclassification). Somewhat controversially, the federal agency has also been tasked with supervising union behaviour and has standing to investigate and enforce provisions for unlawful industrial action, coercion, and freedom of association (Hardy 2018).

While it has a very wide mandate, the FWO has very few inspectors. There are approximately 12 million employees and 2 million businesses in Australia (Australian Bureau of Statistics 2017). While not all of these employees fall within the federal system, the vast majority do. And yet, overseeing workplace relations compliance are around 200 Fair Work inspectors. Similar to the Ontario's Ministry of Labour (MOL), the resources allocated to the FWO are "not keeping pace with the growing number of workplaces and workers covered by employment standards" (Vosko, Grundy, and Thomas 2016, 4; see also chapters 2 and 3). This, along with a growing awareness of the limitations of conventional compliance and enforcement, has led the regulator to move away from detailed complaints investigations towards more strategic, experimental, and collaborative initiatives (see Figure 9.1). As the preceding chapters have identified, and as we will explain in greater detail below, these strategies have had mixed success.

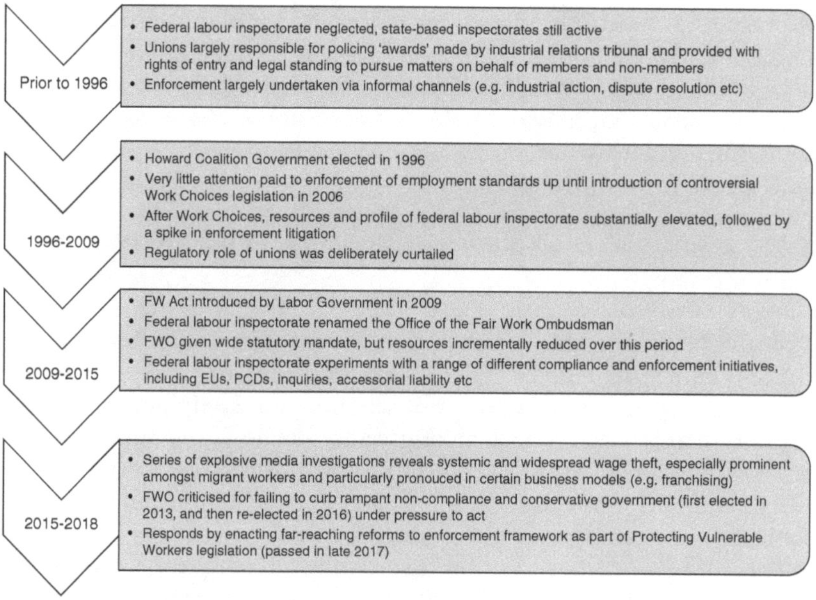


Figure 9.1. Enforcement of Employment Standards in Australia: A Historical Timeline

## 3. Recent Shifts in the FWO's Enforcement Strategy

In contrast to the adversarial premise of the conciliation and arbitration system, the *FWA* expressly provides that a key function of the FWO is "to promote harmonious, productive and cooperative workplace relations" (*FWA*, s. 682). The FWO seeks to fulfil this statutory objective by monitoring, enquiring into, investigating, and enforcing compliance with relevant workplace laws.

Officially, decisions concerning how the FWO approaches its regulatory task, prioritizes resources, and performs key functions are now guided by the Compliance and Enforcement Policy. This policy sets out "guiding principles" that shape the work of the FWO. In particular, the agency seeks to adopt an approach that is "risk-based and proportionate," "open and transparent," and "collaborative," and effects "cultural change" (FWO 2017b, 2–3).

While these principles do not expressly refer to either the theory of responsive regulation or the model of strategic enforcement, they implicitly reflect key tenets of both approaches. For example, the policy states that the FWO will "focus our compliance and enforcement efforts where there is serious non-compliance and where we can deliver the greatest benefit," which is very much in line with the principle of "prioritization" (Weil 2010). In relation to these priority industries, strategic enforcement further suggests that labour inspectorates consider simultaneously whether or not regulatory intervention is likely to be successful in changing compliance behaviour in a way that is both sustainable (limited recidivism) and systemic (has effects beyond the individual firm) (75). It is arguable that both the "sustainability" and "systemic effects" principles have shaped the FWO's thinking in this respect, in that an express aim of the agency, as set out in the Compliance and Enforcement Policy, is to "develop solutions to address structural and behavioural drivers that lead to widespread non-compliance in certain industries and sectors" (FWO 2017b, 3).

Less apparent from the FWO's policy, and arguably from the agency's public documentation more generally, is the principle of deterrence, which is absent to a similar degree in the Ontario case (see chapter 6). Indeed, the FWO's applicable key performance indicators suggest the opposite. In particular, the requirement for the FWO to privilege self-help and dispute resolution strategies over investigation and deterrence-based approaches may be driven by the stated aim to finalize "at least 90% of requests for assistance involving a workplace dispute ... through education and dispute resolution services" and "no more than 10% through compliance and enforcement tools" (FWO 2018a, 9; on the parallel situation in Ontario, see chapter 3). The FWO's apparent reticence to routinely invoke the principle of deterrence, or use coercive-based sanctions, may be driven by a desire to meet or exceed these key performance indicators.

An alternative reason for downplaying deterrence – and one flagged in earlier chapters – is the enduring legacy, and ongoing influence, of responsive regulation theory and the pyramidal model of enforcement. In line with this theory, a common mantra of the FWO is that "most employers want to do the right thing" (James 2017, 1 May, 1). However, as we discuss below, the notion of what this phrase means has rapidly evolved in response to continuing furore over migrant worker exploitation and political demands for the labour inspectorate to do more to hold lead firms to account.

We turn now to consider how these broad models and guiding principles have shaped the day-to-day operations of the FWO, including the way it detects contraventions, filters complaints, engages in dispute resolution, sanctions employers, and otherwise seeks to leverage key individuals and lead firms to positively contribute towards a culture of compliance.

### *Education and Assistance*

As noted above, the FWO continues to assume that the majority of employers are put on the path to non-compliance through a lack of information or understanding. Accordingly, the FWO devotes much time and resources to building and disseminating educational materials and self-service tools through various mediums, forums, and campaigns.

Further, since the 2015 underpayment scandal that engulfed 7-Eleven and precipitated a national enforcement crisis, the nature of the FWO's educational offering has rapidly evolved. Rather than simply informing employers of the relevant standards that apply, the FWO has shifted its attention to lead firms. In the last year or so, the FWO released guidance material on labour supply chains that was designed to help businesses monitor and manage their contract arrangements to ensure that all employees throughout the relevant business networks are lawfully engaged and paid (FWO 2018c). Similar guidance materials have been tailored to, and directed at, the franchise sector. In promoting these materials, the FWO has been keen to stress the need for firms to take a range of additional steps to protect their business against brand damage and reputational risks, as well as reduce potential liability (FWO 2018d). In light of the new extended liability provisions introduced under the *PVWA*, the direction to take such steps is less likely to be treated as an empty threat, especially in the franchise sector.

*Detection – Complaints, Campaigns, Tip-offs, and Inquiries*

For some time the FWO has publicly avowed to move away from reactive, complaint-based investigations towards more proactive regulatory techniques (Campbell 2013, May). Nevertheless, it is clear that employee complaints or "requests for assistance involving a workplace dispute" continue to direct much of its compliance and enforcement activity, including dispute resolution work. In 2017/18 the FWO received over 28,000 such requests (FWO 2018a).

While complaints remain central to the FWO's day-to-day operation, the agency is acutely aware that there is "chronic underreporting of exploitation" to the regulator (Senate Education and Employment References Committee 2016, 67), particularly amongst international students. As the former FWO herself recognized, for this group of workers, their "primary concern is often their visa status as opposed to their minimum rate of pay" (James 2017, 14 September). The FWO has implemented several initiatives that seek to tackle this particular problem.

First, in an attempt to reduce some of the barriers facing migrant workers and encourage reporting to the regulator, the FWO has developed a Multicultural Access and Equity Plan, which includes development of in-language information tools, and the introduction of a dedicated telephone enquiry line for visa holders. In addition, the FWO has further ramped up collaborations with community groups – both on the employer and employee side – in an attempt to educate key ethnic communities about workplace rights and responsibilities (FWO 2017a, 18).

In September 2017 the FWO published an open letter to international students making it clear that they have the same rights as all workers in Australia. More recently, and for the first time, the FWO has entered into, and publicized, a formal protocol with the Department of Home Affairs. The protocol provides that a workers' temporary visa will not be cancelled if they report exploitation, are actively assisting the FWO with an investigation, and commit to comply with future visa conditions.

In our view, there are three alternative activities carried out by the FWO that are better placed to capture contraventions that affect vulnerable workers, without necessarily compromising the employee's visa status or future work prospects. It is important to recognize that while these activities may enhance the FWO's ability to identify contraventions at different scales and track key trends, these detection mechanisms may not necessarily lead to improved redress for workers (Berg and Farbenblum 2017).

The first relevant initiative is the FWO's Anonymous Report tool (FWO 2018, February). Since introducing this reporting tool – which is now available in up to sixteen languages – the agency has received more than 20,000 tip-offs alleging potential contraventions of workplace laws. These reports emanate from concerned members of the community, including workers themselves, competitor businesses, and the general public. This tool is especially significant in high-risk sectors. For instance, the hospitality industry (a sector renowned for rampant non-compliance) accounts for 17 per cent of all complaints but features in more than 36 per cent of all anonymous tip-offs (FWO 2018, February). While there have been some limited instances where tip-offs have triggered a full and immediate investigation, in most instances the data captured through anonymous reporting is generally pooled with "intelligence" gathered from a range of other sources, including referrals and information obtained from community groups, industrial associations, government ministers, and the media, to map and measure risks to a relevant business, locality, industry, or network (FWO 2018b). This pooled information is then used to determine the focus and direction of other compliance and enforcement activities, including campaigns and inquiries. Indeed, the previous head of the FWO observed, "When we see vulnerable workers coming to us for help, we do look closer, because unfortunately these examples tend not to be isolated incidents or an error, but indications of a broader pattern of non-compliance. Acknowledging that in spite of our best efforts, vulnerable workers do not always come to us for help, the Fair Work Ombudsman digs deeper" (James 2017, 14 September).

While campaigns vary in scope and methodology, the FWO has suggested that targeted activities are best suited to segments of the labour market where employees are least likely to complain but are most exposed to the risk of underpayment. In 2017/18 the FWO undertook 4,572 audits of businesses and recovered around $6.1 million in unpaid wages (which represents 21 per cent of all monies recovered by the FWO in the same fiscal year). Almost half of these audited businesses were found to be non-compliant with basic workplace laws (FWO 2018a). In a previous report, the FWO had observed that the continuing poor compliance rate reflects "an improved ability to target businesses suspected of non-compliance, rather than signifying a decrease in overall workplace compliance" (FWO 2017a).

The importance of auditing is underlined by our recent survey of around 600 businesses exploring their perceptions of, and responses to, FWO's enforcement activities. This research revealed that respondents had a greater fear of detection than of sanction (Hardy and Howe 2017). In light of this finding, it is somewhat confounding that campaigns are routinely undertaken on an announced basis, as in Ontario (see chapters 5 and 6; in the United States, by contrast, inspections are not announced, see chapter 11), generally adopt a desk-based audit methodology rather than site visits (contrary to Ontario and the United States), and have a strong educational bent, as in Ontario (see chapters 2 and 5). This somewhat outdated approach appears to reflect the "flexible compliance" approach adopted more generally by the FWO in its earlier years (Workplace Express 2010, 2 June).

However, in line with the findings in Ontario, there is growing evidence that non-compliance with labour standards in Australia is not due to a lack of understanding, but "a strategy of labour cost reduction for a growing number of employers" (Vosko, Grundy, and Thomas 2016, 379). Continuing with the FWO's default format for campaigns may be more efficient from a resourcing perspective, and less hostile from an inspector's point of view, but it has exposed the FWO to heavy criticism. More generally, campaigns that emphasize education and voluntary compliance over auditing and deterrence may compromise the overall regulatory value of targeted audits.

The shortcomings of desk-based audits, and the value of site visits, is highlighted by the apparent extent of non-compliance with record-keeping requirements. In 2016/17 the FWO reported that 73 per cent of all enforcement proceedings concerned with wages and conditions also alleged pay slip and record-keeping contraventions. The FWO indicated that because there were insufficient records, it was unable to calculate all or some of the underpayments owed to employees in many of these matters. More worrying still is the fact that almost one third of the litigation initiated in the 2016/17 financial year alleged that the employer had created false or misleading workplace records in order to deliberately mask the non-compliance (FWO 2017a, 23). In 2017 the head of the FWO, Natalie James, noted, "Unless workers have meticulously kept their own records of their hours of work, it becomes very difficult to assess whether underpayments have arisen" (James 2017, 1 May, 2). These problems are potentially exacerbated by the FWO's conservative approach to litigation and investigation. Our research has revealed that the agency overemphasized the need for documentary evidence and undervalued oral testimony from workers. A consequence of this approach is that the worst offenders were often let off the hook (Howe, Hardy, and Cooney 2014; Berg and Farbenblum 2017, 326).

The current situation underlines the critical importance of the reforms to record-keeping provisions and investigative powers that were introduced under the PVWA. While these provisions are yet to be tested, it is quite possible that the reverse onus of proof, along with increased uptake of the FWO's Record My Hours app by employees (FWO 2018e), is likely to be a game changer. Addressing record-keeping issues is not only important in relation to campaigns, and not only critical in matters that reach litigation, but they may also be important in bolstering the bargaining position of employees who find themselves seeking recovery through the FWO's dispute resolution process or in the small claims court. Most importantly, it may prompt the FWO to reconsider its own biases in assessing the merits (or otherwise) of workers' claims. Improving record-keeping may have flow-on implications for how the agency assesses which regulatory response is most "appropriate." Generally speaking, mediation is viewed as suitable by the FWO where there is conflicting or limited evidence, which is perceived to make investigation and litigation more difficult. However, it is arguable that the new evidentiary presumptions introduced under the *PVWA* should effectively shift this criterion in favour of employees in many cases.

The third activity we want to highlight is a relatively new initiative of the FWO and one that differs quite substantially from campaigns: the formal, public enquiry. These in-depth inquiries – twelve of which have now been concluded – are generally prompted by allegations or concerns about systemic employer non-compliance in an industry, region, supply chain, or labour market. They normally entail the regulator undertaking a detailed examination of the drivers of compliance through site visits, interviews, and payroll audits. Specific focus is placed on the role of lead firms. At the conclusion of an enquiry, a report is made publicly available, which sets out the key findings, the regulator's recommendations, and any actions taken, including whether the regulator has initiated (or is likely to initiate) enforcement litigation against one or more persons (FWO 2015).

On the one hand, these inquiries – which require huge resources – can be justified by the fact that they have generated enormous media interest and have inflicted serious reputational damage. On the other hand, the recommendations of FWO at the conclusion of these inquiries, while embarrassing, have sometimes proved insufficient to compel the lead firm to readily submit to voluntary initiatives, particularly in the absence of credible threats of liability.

### *Dispute Resolution and Mediation*

In most instances, and much in line with the MOL's approach, the FWO encourages prospective complainants to engage in self-help by raising the relevant issues with the employer (on the Ontario case, see chapter 2). If this direct method fails to achieve the desired outcome or is deemed inappropriate, a team of experienced FWO staff then assess the matter, using a fixed set of criteria to determine the level of resources and assistance to devote to resolving the complaint. According to the FWO's Compliance and Enforcement Policy, in determining which response is most "appropriate," the assessors will consider a host of factors, including any past attempts to resolve the matter; the seriousness of the alleged conduct; the relevant characteristics of the parties; the confidentiality of the process; if and when the employment relationship ended; whether there is sufficient information and evidence to support an argument that a breach has occurred; and the public interest (whether the community expects the FWO to be involved) (FWO 2017b, 10).

Given the flood of requests for assistance that the FWO continues to receive (FWO 2017a)[3] and its small inspectorate, dispute resolution has become increasingly critical for the regulator. In the last fiscal year, over 96 per cent of requests for assistance received by the FWO were resolved through education and dispute resolution (FWO 2018a, 9). While a resolution was reached more quickly (an average of 7 days), as compared to requests that were resolved through investigation and enforcement channels (an average of 167 days), the average amounts recovered by employees were far more modest (AU$768 in the case of dispute resolution, AU$2248 following an FWO "compliance activity") (13).

While the speed or quantity of resolutions is not a firm indicator of the nature or quality of the outcome, an efficient "resolution" of a complaint is clearly perceived favourably. This is reflected by the fact that one of the FWO's key performance measures is assessed by reference to the "average number of days requests for assistance involving a workplace dispute are finalized." In 2017/18 the target was thirty days and the FWO reported that the average resolution time was fourteen days (FWO 2018a, 9). While the desire for a speedy resolution can be detrimental from a regulatory perspective, it can be especially important in a practical sense – that is, when the worker is seeking rectification of an underpayment from a business that is financially precarious. If the business fails, then most redress mechanisms are rendered relatively futile. In these circumstances, the employee may be forced to rely on the federal government's Fair Entitlements Guarantee scheme (a legislative safety net to cover unpaid employment entitlements) (*Fair Entitlements Guarantee Act 2012* (Cth); Anderson 2014).[4]

In line with these concerns, the mediation service is promoted by the FWO as a "fast, confidential and free way to help employers and employees find solutions to disputes about workplace issues"

(FWO 2018e). However, given that mediations have a time limit of two hours and are conducted by telephone, there is limited capacity for the mediators to make any legal assessment of the employee's relevant rights and entitlements. In any event, that is not the objective of the exercise. Rather, the mediator is said to take "a neutral stance" (FWO 2017a, 12) in order to "allow parties to create their own solutions to disputes, instead of having a decision made by someone else" (FWO 2018g).

As was pointed out in the chapters comprising Part One, negotiated settlements that lead employees to accept less than their legal entitlement effectively turns questions of law enforcement into matters of dispute resolution (see also Vosko, Noack, and Tucker 2016). Similarly, adopting a position of mediator neutrality not only masks inequalities of bargaining power, it potentially compounds them.

While the FWO dispute resolution model may be quick and cost-effective in solving individual complaints, the privatization of the deliberations and outcomes means that these processes may do little to develop and legitimize norms of workplace practice beyond the individual employer (Riley 2009). They not only diminish the diffusion of best practice, they also tend to "limit the exemplary power of the law; that is the extent to which justice is *seen to be done*" (Colling 2004, 573). Although mediation may provide an avenue for short-term redress for workers, it may ultimately exacerbate the overall enforcement gap; by perpetuating perceptions that there is a low probability of detection and sanction, employers may be further emboldened and workers further silenced (Hardy 2014).

Although these issues are all significant, it is also arguable that if a labour inspectorate wants to engage in strategic enforcement and more proactive and preventative measures, then engaging in dispute resolution processes may be a necessary evil. In very crude terms, by resolving complaints quickly and cheaply, the labour inspectorate is not only able to achieve some redress for workers, it is able to redirect precious resources towards more deterrence based activities. That said, triaging must be approached cautiously and conservatively to ensure that vulnerable workers are not left to advocate for their own interests. The role of traditional and alternative labour market intermediaries is absolutely crucial here (Hardy 2011, 2017b).

### *Administrative Tools and Coercive Sanctions*

Where a contravention is detected and compliance cannot be achieved or is resisted, two main options are broadly available. If the claim is not deemed "appropriate" for further investigation, the FWO may end its involvement at this point. In these circumstances, the employee is then left to take action in the small claims jurisdiction, or through the ordinary courts. Even with the assistance of a union or community legal centre, the current costs, rules, and the lack of legal aid makes this a very difficult and expensive path, and successful recovery of the underpayment (let alone penalties) is far from guaranteed (Arup and Sutherland 2009; *FWA*, s. 570).[5]

Alternatively, a formal investigation may ensue. This scenario is more likely where non-compliance is "serious," namely, there is evidence to suggest that there is exploitation of vulnerable workers; significant public interest or concern; blatant disregard for the law or a court or Fair Work Commission order; deliberate distortion of a level playing field to gain a commercial advantage; or an opportunity to provide an educative or deterrent effect (FWO 2017b). If the contraventions are substantiated, inspectors may then access a suite of regulatory tools, including letters of caution, infringement notices, compliance notices, enforceable undertakings, and proactive compliance deeds (Hardy and Howe 2013; Owens 2016). This range of sanctions is intended to provide "the FWO with another option to deal with non-compliance (by encouraging co-operative compliance) instead of pursuing court proceedings" (Minister for Employment and Workplace Relations 2008, 400).

These formal enforcement tools are not invoked as a matter of course, but rather are reserved for "cases of serious non-compliance where other options such as dispute resolution or small claims are not appropriate to resolve the matter" (FWO 2017b, 22). As table 9.1 shows, use of the most coercive tools available to the FWO – enforceable undertakings and civil remedy litigation – has dropped considerably in the last financial year. The reasons for the decline in deterrence-based mechanisms have not been explained in the annual report, or otherwise. However, it is also important to point out that these raw data do not readily reveal the relative impact of these mechanisms on employees in these workplaces, or on employers in the relevant geographical locality or industry.[6] This is a critical gap, and the FWO has recognized that

Table 9.1. FWO's Use of Enforcement Tools, 2016–2018

| Enforcement tool | 2016–17 | 2017–18 |
|---|---|---|
| Infringement notices issued | 665 | 615 |
| Compliance notices issued | 192 | 220 |
| Enforceable undertakings executed | 40 | 7 |
| Litigation proceedings commenced | 55 | 35 |
| Total | 952 | 877 |

more research is needed here. Not only would such research be useful in showing that the agency has met the fourth relevant key performance indicators – that the FWO has had "a positive impact on sectors/ regions or issues of importance to the community" (FWO 2018a, 9) – but it may also guard against the risk that the inspectorate privileges particular regulatory responses on the basis that they are more easily measurable, but ultimately less effective.

Arguably the most visible aspect of the agency's enforcement activities is civil remedy litigation. However, our research of business knowledge of the FWO's enforcement activities reveals that while firms may be broadly aware of the FWO's litigation, there is little recollection of the details. Moreover, our research suggests that the general deterrence effects of lesser-known sanctions (such as enforceable undertakings) may be restricted by general lack of recognition or understanding about the circumstances in which these tools may be used and the relevant consequences.

While the general deterrence of enforceable undertakings and proactive compliance deeds may be less than theory predicts, these instruments continue to deliver other critical regulatory benefits. Similar in some ways to the settlement agreements used by Wage and Hours Division (WHD) at the federal level in the United States, enforceable undertakings and proactive compliance deeds represent a "top-focused enforcement strategy": namely, one that strategically targets lead firms, such as franchisors, in order to build sustained compliance among the subordinate units.

By way of background, proactive compliance deeds are voluntary agreements that are generally struck between a lead firm and the FWO. Unlike enforceable undertakings, proactive compliance deeds are not made under the *FWA* and are not directly enforceable in court. While there are some differences between enforceable undertakings and proactive compliance deeds in application and enforceability, the instruments are similar to the extent that both generally require firms to make far-reaching commitments to enhance compliance with workplace laws. For example, under the terms of these instruments, firms frequently commit to engaging an independent and qualified third-party professional to undertake periodic auditing of a sample of employment records and report these findings to the FWO. It is also relatively common for firms to agree to rectify any outstanding underpayments within their firm (or in some cases, within their supply chain or franchise network); implement workplace training; set up an employee complaints hotline; and donate an agreed sum to a community group or legal centre.

In general the FWO has promoted enforceable undertakings and proactive compliance deeds as a way for franchisors, and other reputation sensitive firms, to protect their brand. While enforceable undertakings and proactive compliance deeds have allowed the FWO to preserve resources by shifting some of the enforcement burden to powerful lead businesses, there is growing unease about these "softer" mechanisms. For a start, it is increasingly uncertain to what extent (if at all) lead firms would be willing to adopt voluntary compliance mechanisms in the absence of consumer pressure, regulatory scrutiny, and/or the credible threat of liability. The former head of the FWO has observed, "Franchisors can be reluctant to proactively engage with the FWO before issues are uncovered, either by the FWO or through the media. Reputational leverage works as a 'push' factor for franchisors to act, but has had limited effect as a general deterrence measure to encourage other franchisors to take reasonable steps to detect non-compliance and support franchisees to be compliant" (FWO 2017d, 14). Indeed, even where lead firms have actively cooperated with the FWO and made formal commitments to improve compliance under the auspices of an enforceable undertaking or proactive compliance deed, it is not clear that these commitments have actually translated to substantive, rather than cosmetic, improvements in compliance (Ferguson and Christodoulou 2017).

In the last few years the regulator has acknowledged that leveraging reputational concerns is not sufficient, especially where this is not supported through a credible sanctioning regime. But ensuring that the relevant collaboration – whether through enforceable undertakings, proactive compliance deeds, or otherwise – is rigorous, independent, and accountable has also proved difficult. Indeed, the challenges summarized underline the importance of "hard" enforcement mechanisms (Vosko, Grundy, and Thomas 2016, 379).

## 4. Holding Key Persons, Advisors, and Entities to Account

### *Accessorial Liability*

Under the statutory regime in Australia, the principal mechanism by which the FWO has sought to hold parties to account has been via a threat of accessorial liability under the *FWA*. Under these provisions, persons found to be "involved in" a contravention of the *FWA* may be liable under a civil remedy provision, even where they are not the actual employer of the worker whose rights have been breached. Broadly speaking, a person will be taken to be "involved in" a contravention if the person has aided, abetted, or been in any way, by act or omission, "knowingly concerned" in the contravention (*FWA*, s. 550(2)(c)).

The FWO has been particularly active and innovative in using the accessorial liability provisions to diversify the target of its litigation beyond the direct employer. In the 2016/17 financial year, an accessory was named in over 90 per cent of all proceedings (FWO 2017a, 22). Holding key individuals and advisors, such as company directors, HR managers, lawyers, and accountants, liable for underpayment contraventions has practical advantages and regulatory benefits.

At a practical level, ascribing liability to an accessory often allows for full or part rectification of an underpayment claim, where this would not otherwise be possible as the result of liquidation or deregistration of the employer entity (*Fair Work Ombudsman v Step Ahead Securities* [2016] FCCA 1482). Further, in order to maximize the chances for full recovery of the underpayment, the FWO has been increasingly creative in relation to court-based remedies. In the recent past, the FWO has sought orders requiring accessories to pay compensation (in addition to penalties) (*Fair Work Ombudsman v WY Pty Ltd, Chong Yew Chua and Ning Yuan Fu* [2016] FCCA 343; Anderson and Howe 2012), freezing orders in relation to accessories' assets (*Fair Work Ombudsman v Trek North Tours [No 2]* [2015] FCCA 1801), and restraints in relation to potential future contraventions (*FWO v James Nelson Pty Ltd & Anor* [2016] FCCA 531).

From a regulatory perspective, threatening or attributing liability to "gatekeepers" (i.e., individuals who can monitor and control corporate conduct) provides a direct incentive for these individuals to perform their responsibilities effectively and to deter corporate wrongs (Kraakman 1986). In a landmark case, the FWO used the accessorial liability provisions to obtain penalties against an accounting and payroll firm for "knowingly helping one of its clients exploit a vulnerable worker." The trial judge acknowledged that while the relevant accessory – Ezy Accounting 123 Pty Ltd – was not directly responsible for the underpayment, "Ezy was involved in a relationship with [the employer entity] where it provided payroll services. As such it must put compliance with the law ahead of business interests. Ezy had a responsibility to ensure there was compliance with, *inter alia*, the FWA" (*Fair Work Ombudsman v Blue Impression Pty Ltd* [2017] FCCA 2797 at [105]; decision upheld on appeal: *EZY Accounting 123 v FWO* [2018] FCA 134).

The FWO has also been willing to test the boundaries of the law in fissured work arrangements, and the agency has increasingly sought to bring proceedings against non-employer firms in supply chains or other business networks (Hardy and Howe 2015; Hardy 2016). However, this has had more limited success, particularly in franchises.

The limitations of the accessorial liability provisions in this context became glaringly apparent in the 7-Eleven case. While the FWO found, as part of an in-depth enquiry, that the Australian franchisor, 7-Eleven Stores Ltd., had frequently failed to prevent or detect franchisee contraventions of workplace laws, the regulator ultimately concluded that there was insufficient probative evidence to pursue the franchisor under the accessorial liability provisions of the *FWA* (Hardy 2017a). In the absence of litigation, the franchisor ultimately entered into a "compliance partnership" with the FWO.

One of the problems identified in the 7-Eleven case is that, unlike employer contraventions of minimum employment standards, which are ordinarily ascribed on a strict liability basis, to impose liability on accessories the FWO must prove that the person had the requisite level of knowledge about the contraventions (*Fair Work Ombudsman v Devine Marine* [2015] FCA 370; *Potter v Fair Work Ombudsman* [2014] FCA 187; Ranieri 2018). The knowledge threshold has been interpreted narrowly by the courts, and this has made it more difficult, though not impossible, to pin liability on the alleged accessory in a supply chain or franchise network (see, e.g., *Fair Work Ombudsman v Yogurberry World Square Pty Ltd* [2016] FCA 1290).

*Protecting Vulnerable Workers: A Summary of Key Statutory Reforms*

The *PVWA* is designed explicitly to address the fact that some franchisors may "operate on a business model based on underpaying workers" and "have either been blind to the problem or not taken sufficient action to deal with it once it was brought to their attention" (Minister for Employment 2016–17, 6). In particular, the *PVWA* makes franchisors and parent companies responsible for underpayments by their franchisees or subsidiaries respectively where they knew or ought reasonably to have known of the contraventions and failed to take reasonable steps to prevent them (*FWA*, s. 558B). In addition, the *PVWA* has increased the maximum penalties available for "serious contraventions" of prescribed provisions of the Act by a factor of ten (*FWA*, s. 557A). This increase may allow the regulator to seek severe fines against employers who knowingly and systematically contravene prescribed employment standards.[7]

*Difficulties of Deterrence*

However, some of our more recent research of business awareness of, and responses to, deterrence raises doubt about the extent to which penalties will have the expected or predicted deterrence effects. In summary, our findings mirrored the findings of earlier research into deterrence in occupational health and safety regulation, which suggested that key individuals within firms generally displayed "a very significant degree of inattentiveness to information on penalties for non-compliance" (Purse and Dorrian 2011, 32). This finding seems to run counter to the idea that businesses are rational and calculative – if they cannot recall the target or amount of the penalty (i.e., the potential costs), then they cannot weigh this up against the costs (and benefits) associated with compliance.

Nevertheless, our findings suggest that enforcement litigation may still be having positive compliance effects. For example, our survey revealed that even though the constrained resources of the FWO mean that it can conduct audits of a small subsection of all employing businesses, and pursues litigation only in limited instances, almost half of businesses believed that it would be likely or highly likely that the FWO would detect business underpayment of workers, and almost 70 per cent felt that it was at least likely that underpayment would be penalized. These results suggest that the FWO is generally seen as much more powerful by the regulated community than may actually be the case (Hardy and Howe 2017). This is a critical finding, given that previous research has found that "the perception of deterrence itself can make a significant difference to any deterrent effect, over and above that associated with the likelihood of detection of ... offences and the imposition of sanctions" (Purse and Dorrian 2011, 24).

Finally, while our results did not confirm that deterrence-based mechanisms function in the way predicted by theory, our survey findings supported the idea that many firms – who were already motivated to comply with the law – took knowledge of the FWO's enforcement as either reassurance that competitors who were not compliant would be detected and punished, or took the knowledge as a reminder to review their internal systems to ensure that they were compliant.

## 5. Conclusion

The move away from conciliation and arbitration as the basis for employment standards regulation not only marked a new era in standard-setting, but also prompted a watershed in regulatory enforcement of minimum employment standards. Unfortunately, despite the spirited attempts of the federal labour inspectorate over the past decade or so, there remains a vast enforcement gap. As in Ontario, this gap appears to be of catastrophic proportions in certain segments of the labour market (e.g., in the Australian context, amongst international student workers and within franchise networks).

The FWO has continued to modify its approach in response to political demands and community expectations, as well as a deeper appreciation of the breadth, depth, and underlying drivers of these problems. The FWO has developed and rolled out new tools to enhance detection and support migrant workers to report exploitation. It has sought to leverage reputational concerns of big business in a bid to coerce them into using their power, authority, and resources to monitor subordinate businesses in their networks and prod them into compliance. While these initiatives are valuable, there are limits to their utility. Recent amendments to the *FWA* – extending liability to franchisors and holding companies, increasing sanctions for serious contraventions, and reversing the onus of proof in the absence of employment records – are critical for strengthening the regulatory power of the FWO.

This chapter has identified close parallels and striking differences between the FWO and its Ontario counterpart. For example, labour inspectorates in both jurisdictions have embraced self-help strategies and dispute resolution processes. While there may be a range of practical and political reasons for adopting this approach – not least of which are quantitative key performance indicators – reducing reliance on dispute resolution may create a separate set of challenges. It appears, in particular, that both regulators are struggling to strike the right balance between ensuring access to justice and providing adequate avenues for employee redress, while still preserving sufficient resources to undertake proactive and strategic activities to prevent contraventions in the first place.

*Chapter Ten*

# Enforcing Employment Standards in Quebec: One Step Forward, Two Steps Backward?

In Quebec, minimum employment standards are embedded in the *Act Respecting Labour Standards (LSA)*[1] and in its regulations. The *LSA* was adopted in 1979 in the context of a re-orientation of state labour policies. Conscious of the fact that the vast majority of employees were not unionized, the government intervened to establish universal standards applicable to unionized and non-unionized workers, as well as independent mechanisms for ensuring compliance (Vallée and Gesualdi-Fecteau 2007, 169). Thus, as of the mid-1970s, in addition to the *LSA*, various normative instruments were adopted such as the *Charter of Human Rights and Freedoms*,[2] the *Act Respecting Occupational Health and Safety (OHSA)*,[3] the *Act Respecting Industrial Accidents and Occupational Diseases*,[4] and the *Pay Equity Act*.[5]

The *LSA* addresses the limits of previous employment standards legislation. Unlike previous legislation, which dealt only with specific sectors or occupations through collective agreement decrees[6] or ordinances,[7] this Act has universal scope and applies to all employees within the meaning of the law, whether they be unionized or not. Subject to specific exceptions permitted by the law, the standards established in the *LSA* forge a set of minimum employment standards from which a contract of employment, collective agreement, or collective agreement decree may not derogate.[8] Thus, as in Ontario (see chapter 1), the *LSA* has often been characterized as the "collective agreement of non-unionized workers [trans.]" (Desîlets and Ledoux 2006, 120). In 2014 the working conditions of 54.2 per cent of employees in Quebec, some 1.89 million, were subject only to the *LSA* (Labour Standards Commission 2015, 14).

The *LSA* addresses several important dimensions of the employment relationship. It establishes minimum wage rates, which are periodically adjusted by Quebec's Ministry of Labour through decrees,[9] and provides for a regular forty-hour work week and for overtime pay rates for longer hours.[10] The *LSA* also establishes seven statutory holidays[11] and entitles employees, inter alia, to an annual leave,[12] to family or parental leaves, and absences,[13] and allows absences from work owing to sickness.[14] The *LSA* includes anti-reprisal measures for employees who exercise a right granted under the Act.[15] It also provides recourse for unjust dismissals.[16] Finally, the *LSA* stipulates that employees have a right to a work environment free from psychological harassment[17] and gives them a right to recourse.[18]

Unlike the *Employment Standards Act (ESA)*,[19] however, the *LSA* contains few provisions to strengthen employment standards for particular groups of vulnerable employees. Furthermore, the *LSA* prohibits disparities in treatment based solely on the employee's hiring date with respect to a matter covered by a labour standard[20] and prohibits the employer from paying a lower rate of wage or reducing the annual leave of an employee solely because of the employee's employment status, and in particular because the employee usually works fewer hours each week.[21] Many commentators have long believed that the *LSA* should be amended to provide adequate protection for those persons engaged in non-traditional employment (Bernier, Vallée, and Jobin 2003). In response, an Act amending the *LSA* passed on 12 June 2018. Under this new law, temporary help agencies must be licensed, and deterrence measures have been added for a client who withholds the services of an unlicensed agency (for a discussion of parallel developments in Ontario, see Vosko 2010). This Act also amended the *LSA* to provide for joint liability and equal pay for equal work and introduced specific obligations for employers hiring workers through a temporary migrant worker program.[22]

The *LSA* grants the administrative body in charge of ensuring compliance with its provisions a wide range of enforcement powers. This chapter examines the role of the labour inspectorate in Quebec, with a particular emphasis on its role in comparison to its Ontario counterpart.[23]

## 1. The Origins and Current Characteristics of the Enforcement of Employment Standards in Quebec: A Comparative Overview

To understand the specific characteristics of employment standards enforcement in Quebec, it is necessary to trace its origins as well as to analyse enforcement measures found in the *LSA*.

### *Origins*

As in Ontario, employment standards enforcement in Quebec is rooted in the first labour inspection system, established in 1888 after the adoption of the *Quebec Factories Act* (Desîlets and Ledoux 2006, 38).[24] To ensure its enforcement, the Act provided for the appointment of inspectors with extensive powers, who could enter any factory premises at any reasonable hour and require the production of documents. The inspectors had the power to initiate penal prosecutions under the Act following an inspection or upon receiving a complaint (30, 32).

It was not until 1919, in response to the increased presence of women in the labour force during the First World War, that the first minimum wage laws were passed with the *Women's Minimum Wage Act* (1919).[25] Gradually, in particular with the adoption of the *Fair Wage Act* (1937)[26] and the *Minimum Wage Act* (1940),[27] employment standards for hours of work and the minimum wage were covered by laws that applied to both women and men. These laws had in common the establishment of "commissions"[28] or "offices,"[29] which were tasked with ensuring compliance with the ordinances' contents and had the power to initiate penal prosecutions against an employer who paid too low a wage (Desîlets and Ledoux 2006, 60–1, 110–11, 153–4). Such entities also had the power, recognized in law since 1937, to levy from employers the funds needed for their activities (107–8, 133, 138).[30] However, these commissions remained under close government control, and every expenditure and administrative decision was submitted for official approval (134, 151, 204). Penal prosecutions against employers were practically non-existent between 1919 and 1931. It was only with the Great Depression that the situation began to change (Ledoux 2003, 81). Between 1919 and 1940, negotiating the reimbursement of workers in exchange for the withdrawal of prosecutions appeared to be a standard practice of successive commissions (Desîlets and Ledoux 2006, 84, 134, 270). It was only with the *Minimum Wage Act* (1940) that the commission was granted power to initiate a proceeding against an employer on behalf of an employee (32, 153).

This historical context is essential to understanding the creation of the Labour Standards Commission (LSC) with the adoption of the *LSA* in 1979. As with its predecessors, the LSC was funded mainly through employers' contributions. The LSC was considered a legal person managed by an administration board consisting of thirteen members, including at least one person from categories such as non-unionized workers, unionized workers, big business, small- and medium-sized enterprises, the cooperative sector, women, young people, families, and cultural communities.[31] The plurality of social groups represented on the board of directors ensured the LSC's expertise in employment standards. The LSC did not have the power to issue ordinances establishing minimum employment standards, unlike the Minimum Wage Commission established by the *Minimum*

*Wage Act* (1940). Rather, its mandate was to monitor the implementation and application of employment standards. The decision to claim amounts on behalf of employees lay with the LSC, without any requirement of governmental authorization (Desîlets and Ledoux 2006, 292). Its modus operandi contrasted starkly with the centralized "control" that was the hallmark of previous commissions.

In 2016 the powers formerly vested with the LSC were transferred to the Labour Standards, Equity, Occupational Health and Safety Commission (LSEOHSC). This commission is the product of the merger of three commissions: the LSC, the Pay Equity Commission, and the Occupational Health and Safety Commission. Before 2016 the Pay Equity Commission was responsible for the implementation and enforcement of the *Pay Equity Act*, and the Occupational Health and Safety Commission was responsible for occupational health and safety as well as for workers' compensation.[32] The LSEOHSC seeks to be "the single gateway to unique labour services [trans.]"[33] This one-size-fits-all model represents a significant change. As with the LSC, the LSEOHSC is considered a legal person managed by an administration board. This board comprises fifteen members, including a president and fourteen other members chosen from lists provided by the most representative unions and employers' associations.[34] The LSEOHSC is funded by employers[35] and is accountable to the minister.[36] Although possessing a degree of autonomy when determining its organizational priorities,[37] it is subject to the rules of the Quebec Treasury Board, particularly in the management of its workforce.[38]

The emergence of this merged commission reflects new public management, a paradigm introduced in chapter 3 and, specifically, its foundational assumption that all administrative criteria should be directed at the optimal use of resources (Gow and Dufour 2000; Bolduc 2014). As new public management operates in this context, managers in public administration are called upon to mobilize the principles and management techniques adopted in the private sector (Charbonneau 2012, 1). In Quebec the implementation of new public management in the public sector dates to the early 2000s; the adoption of the *Public Administration Act*[39] was a major turning point towards new public management, given its results- and "performance-based orientation" (Rouillard and Bourque 2011). The merger that led to the creation of the LSEOHSC stems from this logic, as it was essentially brought forward for cost-cutting reasons (Vallée 2017, 104–6).[40]

By contrast, in Ontario, the Ministry of Labour's (MOL) Employment Standards Branch enforces the *ESA*, an important structural difference in the enforcement of employment standards in the two jurisdictions.

### *Ensuring Compliance with the LSA: The Role of the Commission*

The intervention of the LSEOHSC is generally triggered by a complaint filed by an employee. The LSEOHSC can also process anonymous reports or undertake an investigation on its own initiative;[41] unlike in Ontario, despite proposals to proceed otherwise herein (see chapters 2 and 7), a claim can also be brought by a non-profit organization dedicated to the defence of employees' rights, enabling non-profit organizations to file complaints on behalf of an employee who consents.[42] The LSEOHSC's scope of intervention is generally limited to non-unionized workplaces; as in Ontario, if an employee is covered by a collective agreement, the employee must resort to the grievance procedure (Vosko and Thomas 2014).[43]

After a complaint or a proactive inspection is initiated, the LSEOHSC must "make an inquiry with due dispatch" to determine if the employee, or the group of employees, are owed any entitlements under the *LSA*.[44] Similar to ESOs in Ontario, the "inspector-investigator" (inspector) designated by the LSEOHSC examines the available documents and communicates directly with the employee and the employer to gather additional information. The inspector also gives each party the opportunity to present evidence in support of their case and may visit the employer's premises. Inspectors are vested with the powers and immunities granted to commissioners appointed under the *Act Respecting Public Inquiry Commissions*,[45] with the exception of the power to impose imprisonment.[46]

In Quebec the inspector decides whether or not to substantiate the claim in whole or in part, and, if applicable, determines the amount of money owed. As with early resolution officers (EROs) in Ontario, inspectors may also assess entitlements that exceed the original claims. The inspector can require documents and summon employers' representatives to appear, and the inspector can visit the employers' premises at any reasonable time.[47] Overall, the role of the inspector designated by the LSEOHSC is comparable to that fulfilled by the ERO (see chapter 1).

It is important to mention that the LSEOHSC shall not, during the enquiry, disclose the identity of an employee by or on behalf of whom a complaint has been filed, unless the employee consents to such disclosure.[48] Nevertheless, in small firms the effectiveness of this provision is dubious, especially at the judicial stage where the LSEOHSC has no choice but to reveal the identity of the employee.

If the LSEOHSC refuses to proceed with an enquiry, notice of its decision must be given to the complainant by registered mail "giving the reasons therefor and informing him of his right to apply for a review of the decision."[49] The complainant may, within thirty days, apply in writing for a review, and the LSEOHSC must render a final decision within thirty days of receiving the application.[50]

When, subsequent to an investigation, the LSEOHSC considers that money is due to an employee, two means of enforcement are available. First, the LSEOHSC can seek the recovery of the employee's wages by a summons requiring the employer to pay the sums within twenty days.[51] However, unlike an Order to Pay Wages under the *ESA*, the summons is not enforceable against the employer. Rather, if the employer fails or refuses to comply, the file is sent to the Legal Department of the LSEOHSC and a lawyer from the department is assigned to the employee (at no cost to the employee) who will initiate a civil action for the amount owing[52] before the appropriate court, depending on the amount of money sought.[53] The inspector who handled the investigation will testify on the behalf of the commission. Other witnesses, such as the employee or the group of employees involved in the claim, may also be called to testify. If the court gives judgment in favour of the employee, the lawyer appointed by the LSEOHSC will also enforce it if the employer does not pay.

Similar to Ontario, the employer and the employee may choose to settle a wage claim at any stage. While in some cases employers may agree to pay the entire amount owed to the employees, in others the employees may settle for less than the amount to which they are legally entitled. In addition, facilitated settlements can be reached through the LSEOHSC's "mediation service" in which a professional is appointed to "bring the parties together." Such facilitated mediations normally take place before an inspector determines the legal entitlement related to the claim.

The second enforcement mechanism available to inspectors is penal prosecution.[54] Penal prosecution can be instituted in response to any violation of the *LSA*.[55] It can also be used to sanction employers who prevent the LSEOHSC from carrying out its mandate.[56] LSEOHSC inspectors who wish to initiate a prosecution must send an offence report to the Department of Legal Affairs of the LSEOHSC. It is up to the department to determine whether to initiate a prosecution. Fines vary from $600 to $1,200 for an initial conviction and from $1,200 to $6,000 for any subsequent conviction. Penal prosecutions are carried out under the *Code of Penal Procedure*[57] and are heard by the Criminal and Penal Division of the Court of Quebec.[58] Since 2007 the LSEOHSC has developed a strategy to prevent repeat offences by publicizing the names of recalcitrant employers and the type of offences for which they have been convicted,[59] a measure that is aimed at strengthening the deterrent nature of the penal provisions contained in the *LSA*.

Two major differences regarding deterrence measures characterize the Quebec case vis-à-vis deterrence (see chapter 6). First, Quebec inspectors do not have the power to directly impose low-level penalties such as tickets and Notices of Contravention (NOCs). Second, although they are rarely used (chapter 6), sentences for Part III convictions under the *ESA* are far more severe than those under the *LSA*. Maximum fines for individuals are nearly ten times higher and for corporations nearly 100 times higher, and there is the possibility of a prison sentence.[60] In Quebec, imprisonment is explicitly precluded.[61]

**2. Enforcement in Action: Contemporary Dynamics**

The LSEOHSC has diverse means at its disposal to ensure that the protections arising from the *LSA* are effectively enforced. It is widely agreed that the complaint-driven approach does not make it possible to grasp, from a qualitative or quantitative perspective, the trends or changes in employment standards violations. The literature shows that sectors known for extensive violations of employment standards generate only a small number of complaints (Noack, Vosko, and Grundy 2015; Weil 2008b; Weil and Pyles 2006). Other studies demonstrate that, in most cases, complaints are filed by employees who no longer work for the employer targeted by the complaints (LSC 2012a, 18; Vosko et al. 2011, 34). Thus, to ensure that employment standards are enforced, the complaint-driven approach must be supplemented by proactive enforcement measures as well as deterrence measures.

In the following section, we illustrate how, in Quebec, the *LSA* gives legislative expression to these aspects of enforcement. In addition to analysing the nature and the scope of the powers of the LSEOHSC, we explore how that body exercises its powers. To this end, we use the administrative data provided by the LSEOHSC and its predecessor, the LSC. We also draw on the results of two empirical studies on the application of the *LSA* to different categories of workers (Gesualdi-Fecteau and Vallée 2016, 2017; Vallée and Gesualdi-Fecteau 2017, 2016; Gesualdi-Fecteau 2015a, 2016). One study examined how foreign workers hired through a temporary migrant worker program used the protections set out in the *LSA*.[62] The other study sought to better understand the extent to which *LSA* provisions on hours of work constituted a useful protection for workers subject to a considerable obligation to be available to work for their employer outside their actual working time.[63] These studies aimed first to identify the obstacles encountered by employees holding "new" forms of employment who sought to benefit from the protections provided for in the *LSA*. They also shed light on the LSC/LSEOHSC and its agents' capacity to strategically adjust to the challenges generated by the reality of this workforce.

*Enforcement via the Complaints System*

There are no recent studies demonstrating in which industries employees are more likely to file employment standards complaints in Quebec, and the data provided by the LSEOHSC do not allow for the identification of who accesses the employment standards complaints system. Nevertheless, a study carried out in 2010 reveals that 58 per cent of the people surveyed experienced at least one violation of the *LSA* (LSC 2010b). The same study showed that the most common violation concerned overtime pay. Moreover, more than two thirds of employees in the hospitality industry had experienced one or more violations of the *LSA* (LSC 2010a). These findings are consistent with those on Ontario presented in chapter 2.

Although it is impossible to provide a profile of employees who access the complaints system, it is important to point out that the LSC shifted practices from receiving complaints by mail or fax to electronic online filing of complaints in 2009; as explored in chapter 2, Ontario also shifted to online filing in 2005/06. Similarly, in Quebec this transition coincided with the decision to close down several regional offices where workers could formerly file their complaint and gather information about the process. In April 2009 the LSC centralized its complaints structure in five regional offices (LSC 2009b, 14). Until 2011, the Service Statement mentioned that the LSC provided services in fourteen regions (LSC 2011, 81). In 2012 the Service Statement was changed and provided that, in order to ensure "speedy access to its services, the LSC would concentrate on telephone or online communications [trans.]" and that only under "certain circumstances" would an investigator meet an employee in person (LSC 2012b, 89). Thus employees now have no other choice but to file complaints online or seek assistance during business hours by calling the information service of the LSEOHSC.

Given that in both Quebec and Ontario the enforcement of employment standards rests primarily on individual employees filing complaints, the move to online complaints brings the degree of computer literacy of some non-unionized categories of employees into focus. A study carried out by the Institut de la Statistique du Québec in 2012 shows that immigrants, both those who are newcomers and those who are established, overall have lower literacy, numeracy, and problem-solving skills in the use of technology than their Canadian-born counterparts (Desrosiers et al. 2015). Furthermore, in Quebec, immigrants recruited by temporary help agencies are more likely to experience three or more violations than

Canadian-born workers (LSC 2013a, 10). Although there are no statistics to capture the full extent of the problem, it is reasonable to assume that certain categories of employees have abandoned the very idea of filing a complaint (Engel 2016). In previous work we demonstrate the repercussions of language barriers on the ability of temporary migrant workers to access online complaint systems independently (Gesualdi-Fecteau 2015a). Consequently, complaints lodged by these employees are generally brought via third parties, such as workers' centres and sometimes even consular staff, who act as their representative with the LSEOHSC (Gesualdi-Fecteau 2015b). Although the administrative data available do not allow for quantifying the number of complaints lodged by third parties, unlike Ontario's *ESA* but similar to Australia's *Fair Work Act (FWA)* (chapter 9), the *LSA* enables non-profit organizations to become intermediaries between the LSEOHSC and employees, creating an environment more conducive to complaints from categories of employees traditionally reluctant to participate in employment standards enforcement.

The *LSA* also includes anti-reprisal protections on the ground that an employee has exercised one of his or her rights under the *LSA*; its anti-reprisal measures also protect employees that have given information or participated in an enquiry led by the LSEOHSC.[64] In such cases the Administrative Labour Tribunal may reinstate the dismissed employee or order the employer to cease the reprisal; the employer may also have to compensate the employee for the loss of salary or other benefits because of the reprisal.[65]

While anti-reprisal measures in the *LSA* may appear to be a useful tool for giving voice to the grievances of employees, they are not the solution to all ills: almost 90 per cent of complaints are lodged by employees who are no longer in the job about which they are complaining (Henry 2016). In part, processing times explain this trend. In 2016, for example, it took an average of 709 days to deal with a wage recovery complaint and 511 days to deal with one addressing reprisals (LSEOHSC 2017b, 172). As in Ontario (see chapter 3), processing times in Quebec remain substantial.

A significant number of complaints are, however, resolved through settlements.[66] The LSEOHSC promotes its mediation service, which it considers an "important activity of the employment standards sector [trans.]" that has "contributed greatly to the de-judicialization of the resolution of employment standards disputes [trans.]" (LSEOHSC 2017b, 28). This "alternative dispute resolution mechanism" is touted in a new section of the LSEOHSC's website on the mediation service. One of the key elements of that section is a video clip that highlights the speed and harmonious nature of mediation. In 2016 the mediation service of the LSEOHSC conducted 4,456 facilitated mediations, of which 3,090 ended in a settlement (173). The number of settlements that occur throughout the process without being facilitated by the mediation service of the LSEOHSC is unknown. Thus in 2016 the LSEOHSC processed 27,262 cases and only 4,472 required the intervention of the Department of Legal Affairs. Hence, 22,690 of all the cases processed by the commission, that is more than 83 per cent, were either denied or settled (172).[67]

The mediation service emerged in a context where important resource constraints were imposed on the LSC as part of the implementation of a new public management–styled managerial initiative. The *Act Respecting Workforce Management and Control within Government Departments, Public Sector Bodies and Networks and State-Owned Enterprises*,[68] adopted in 2014, was the last in a sequence of laws that sought to "optimize the work organization" by, for example, freezing staffing levels.[69] Because mediation allows for faster claims processing times that reduce backlogs, it was viewed by the LSC as a salient strategy to address the imposed resource constraints.

We nevertheless know very little about the true functioning of such "facilitated mediations" and "about the justice that it concretely puts in place [trans.]" (Veilleux and Trudeau 2007). Settlements are generally confidential and are limited to the particular context of the dispute between two parties; they are not publicized and are not binding in the event of future disputes between the parties (Urbani, Roux, and Legault 2014). Moreover, significant power imbalances frequently prevail; while the employer will generally benefit from the presence of a legal counsel, the LSEOHSC does not provide legal representation to employees participating in facilitated mediations (Henry 2016).

In sum, the complaint process is beset by numerous problems. Lengthy processing times are likely to create pressure to settle, which may result in situations where complainants receive less than their legal entitlement and contradicts the conception of employment standards as a floor of social minima below which nobody should fall (see chapter 1). They also reduce the efficacy of anti-reprisal measures, highlighting why, in part, complaints related to unpaid wages are lodged by employees who are no longer in the job about which they are complaining.

### *Ensuring Compliance with Employment Standards through Proactive Monitoring and Enforcement*

The *LSA* provides that one of the roles of the LSEOHSC is to "supervise the application of employment standards."[70] Thus it has the power to engage in proactive enforcement and workplace inspections.[71] Whereas in Ontario inspections are circumscribed by the emphasis on eleven inspectable employment standards, in Quebec the proactive enforcement carried out by the LSEOHSC can cover all employment standards. Workplace inspections can result from a decision of the LSEOHSC to profile a given employer and verify the full application of the employment standards in the firm; they can also target a specific economic sector such as hospitality or agriculture. This form of monitoring can lead the LSEOHSC to carry out what chapter 5 characterizes as blitz, regular, and re-inspections. Unlike in Ontario, workplace inspections can also follow from a complaint or anonymous report from a third party; in the case of the latter, they often lead to so-called expanded investigations in the language adopted in Ontario. Thus the monitoring role of the LSEOHSC ranges from reactive to proactive.

In 2002/03 the LSC conducted 3,165 workplace inspections. Employers were targeted, and the LSC conducted on-site inspections, whose purpose was "to ensure that the employer complied with the LSA [trans.]" and to have the employer, if necessary, "make the appropriate corrections in order to comply with employment standards [trans.]" (LSC 2003, 19). Thus the aim of these workplace inspections was to compel the employer to take corrective measures to comply with the *LSA* (19). In 2002/03, violations were found in 55 per cent of the cases; almost all employers complied without the need for prosecution (20).

The LSC's proactive enforcement strategy underwent a major change in 2006/07. That year the LSC's annual report introduced a distinction between "preventive activities" and "compliance activities." "Preventive activities" were to provide information about employment standards to employers with clean records with the LSC. "Compliance activities," on the other hand, could take the form of "preventative interventions" or consist of re-inspections of workplaces in which violations had previously been detected (LSC 2007, 38). In 2006/07, 780 "preventive activities" and 2,568 "compliance activities" were performed by the LSC.

The "preventative action plan" adopted by the LSC in 2009, in accordance with its strategic goals at that time (LSC 2009a), included three categories of compliance measures (12). The "primary prevention [trans.]" strand of the plan aimed at "avoiding [trans.]" the violations by, inter alia, "the development of an informational approach [trans.]" (12). The second strand, labelled "secondary prevention [trans.]," sought to avoid the harm caused by violations through "reconciliation activities [trans.]" between the employer and employees (12). Finally, the third strand, characterized as "tertiary prevention [trans.]," led the LSC to conduct dissuasive or remedial activities (13); the LSC could then introduce wage recovery proceedings in the name and in place of employees.

An initiative carried out by the LSC between 2009 and 2012 reflects this three-pronged approach. In this period, the LSC assumed that migrant agricultural workers were likely to constitute "a vulnerable workforce in terms of [employment standards] enforcement [because] of the cultural and linguistic differences these workers were faced with [when arriving in Quebec], which often made it difficult for them to exercise their rights at work [trans.]" (LSC 2008, 20). Consequently, migrant agricultural workers were designated as an "organizational priority [trans.]," and the LSC set out to explore the extent to which these workers knew their rights and whether they asserted them (20).

Between 2009 and 2012 approximately 2,805 migrant agricultural workers and 174 employers operating in the agricultural sector that used temporary migrant work programs were targeted by the LSC (LSC 2010c). The inspections involved a team of LSC inspectors who had undergone specialized training. Their investigations were carried out on site, generally in the evening, and interviews with employees and employers were conducted simultaneously but separately. Consistent with the approach adopted by the Wage and Hours Division (WHD) in the United States, as documented in chapter 11, the agent leading the meeting with the employees spoke fluent Spanish. In 2009/10 the LSC decided to conduct strictly primary and secondary prevention interventions. Consequently, in cases where a violation of the *LSA* was found, the LSC did not initiate any proceeding of any sort. Instead, an effort was made to "reconcile" the parties by urging the employer to comply. Between 2010 and 2012 the LSC conducted primary, secondary, and tertiary prevention interventions simultaneously. During that period, regular inspections and re-inspections were conducted, which could lead the LSC to initiate legal proceedings if the inspection detected violations[72] (Gesualdi-Fecteau and Vallée 2017, 18–21).

With the exception of the effort at mirror representation (i.e., the selection of an inspector with appropriate language skills), this three-pronged approach reflected the influence of regulatory new governance, a paradigm also influential in Ontario (chapter 1). The LSEO-HSC's 2017–19 strategic plan still endorses this paradigm. Under its auspices, compliance with the *LSA* is considered in terms of two axes, where the first seeks "greater awareness of the Act in the work environment [trans.]" and the second seeks to promote the enforcement of the law by "supporting [trans.]" the stakeholders. The strategic plan also emphasizes that the enforcement of employment standards is the "joint responsibility of employers and employees [trans.]" and that those two groups should be made "better equipped to ensure compliance of employment standards [trans.]" (LSEOHSC 2017a, 9). As in Ontario, the LSEOHSC's approach to compliance focuses on education by reminding employers of the content of the *LSA*, thereby raising awareness of rights and responsibilities.

The latest annual report of the LSEOHSC shows that workplaces inspections are now generally triggered by a complaint or an anonymous third-party report. At best, the LSEOHSC conducts expanded investigations, which represent the prototypically reactive type of workplace inspection (see chapter 5). In 2016 the LSEOHSC conducted 820 workplace inspections of employers, particularly in the restaurant and retail sectors, deemed likely to be in breach of the *LSA* (LSEOHSC 2017b, 172); no further details are provided in the report. We can, however, conclude that, unlike in Ontario, neither "regular random inspections" nor sectoral "blitz inspections" are carried out anymore.

The only proactive inspections planned are those of the "special investigation team" [trans.], an entity akin to the dedicated enforcement team that existed briefly in Ontario, created in 2011 to address "the problem of undeclared work in the context of temporary work agencies [trans.]." However, distinct from Ontario, the *LSC* was then called on to collaborate with the Department of Employment and Social Solidarity, Revenu Québec, and the Department of Finance (LSC 2012b, 22). Even though the sole role of the LSC/LSEOHSC is to claim on behalf of employees when their employment standards are violated, the special team's essential task is to uncover "illegal networks, to improve the supervision of the industry, and to encourage workers to rejoin the legal employment market [trans.]" (Ministère des Finances 2011, A-65). Thus, between 2011 and 2015, 1,525 businesses including temporary help agencies and businesses in the food processing sector were inspected.[73] In 2016 the team inspected 143 temporary help agencies and seventy-nine businesses in the food processing sector (LSEOHSC 2017b, 172). In its most recent annual report, the LSEOHSC expressed its desire to bolster its team to ensure its long-term survival through measures aimed at the development of staff and a recruitment plan (29).

As explored in chapter 1, given the social location of workers highly likely to find themselves in such precarious forms of employment, the simultaneous protective and punitive role of the special investigation team leads us to wonder how employees view its activities. This is a key question, given that employees' perception of the LSEOHSC most likely determines such workers' degree of willingness to enter into the formal employment standards complaints system.

*Penal Provisions and Other Deterrence*

As noted earlier, in Quebec, penal prosecutions are the sole deterrence provided for under the *LSA*, and the decision to issue a statement of offence, which instigates penal prosecutions, lies with the Department of Legal Affairs. With regard to penal prosecutions, the role of LSEO-HSC inspectors seems comparable to that of the ESOs in Ontario who can only recommend Part III prosecutions. From a Quebec perspective, however, the ESOs have more power than LSEOHSC inspectors to mobilize deterrence because they can issue NOCs for any violation of the *ESA* and tickets for prescribed offences.

In both systems, however, deterrence is rarely used. In Quebec, in 2014/15 the LSC obtained 191 convictions; approximately seven out of ten penal proceedings appeared to result in a conviction (LSC 2015, 56). While the number of convictions is greater in Quebec than the annual number of convictions in Ontario (see chapter 6), the difference could reflect the fact that inspectors in Quebec do not have the alternative of using low-level deterrence measures. However, even after taking into account the broader range of penal measures available in Ontario, it is fair to conclude that in both Quebec and Ontario penal prosecutions are little used and are confined largely to cases where employers defy the authority of the state and knowingly impede the work of ESOs or inspectors, or, in Ontario, where they violate an ESO's order and not when they violate employees' rights (Gesualdi-Fecteau and Vallée 2016, 372–3).

How can we explain this underutilization of deterrence measures in such divergent jurisdictions? The weight of internal dynamics seems to be an explanatory factor common to both provinces. In an earlier study conducted in Quebec (Gesualdi-Fecteau and Vallée 2016, 2017), we identified the importance of factors linked with the internal organization of responsibilities and resource requirements in establishing solid proof at the penal level to explain the low recourse to penal provisions under the *LSA*. However, the lack of alternative deterrence measures in the *LSA*, the small amount of the fines for the violation of the Act, the lack of prison sentences, and lack of meaningful review of the fines provided for by the *LSA* since its adoption in 1979[74] all contribute to a view that the low rate of penal prosecutions could be due, in part, to the contents of the *LSA* itself.

One factor cited in various chapters of this book to explain the underuse of deterrence measures in Ontario is the prevailing compliance-oriented culture of enforcement. Our research also indicated that, in Quebec, inspectors' work culture is marked by scepticism concerning the effectiveness of the penal provisions of the LSA (Gesualdi-Fecteau and Vallée 2016, 371). Some inspectors confessed that they very rarely initiated penal proceedings because, as one respondent said, "If you put a comma in the wrong place, the penal prosecution will be unsuccessful [trans.]" (371). These inspectors preferred other strategies and perceived penal prosecutions as a measure of "last resort" aimed at "recalcitrant" employers (371). When an employer wished to cooperate in the investigation, inspectors first transmitted an "inspection follow-up" to the employer indicating that the latter must comply with the employment standard in question. These inspectors conducted a non-coercive intervention to assist these employers on the road to compliance. In the months following the transmission of the "inspection follow-up," the employers had to establish that they were complying with the *LSA*, although some respondents mentioned that this follow-up was not conducted systematically. In sum, these compliance-oriented inspectors opted for a compromise aimed at "complying with" the requirements and motivations of the parties that other more critical inspectors characterized as a "slap on the wrist" strategy (371).

The lack of funding and resources to prepare a recommendation to prosecute is another common internal factor that might explain the low level of recourse to deterrence in Quebec as in Ontario (Gesualdi-Fecteau and Vallée 2016, 368–1; chapter 6). For example, the fact that in Quebec inspectors sparingly exercised the power recognized by law to "enter at any reasonable time any place of work or establishment of an employer"[75] could be due, at least in part, to managerial rules that did not encourage visits to businesses because travel expenses were costly. Such visits had to be authorized. As we demonstrate above, it appeared that the inspectors' visits were favoured in targeted sensitive sectors and entrusted to a special team of experienced inspectors who visited the workplaces. It was less common for inspectors to make visits for cases of violation following a complaint or a report from a third party. On this basis, as one respondent mentioned, inspectors acted more as "investigators" than "inspectors" insofar as their work involved exchanges with the various parties on the telephone or in writing in order to establish the factual circumstances giving rise to a complaint or report from a third party. This way of operating may be inadequate when instituting penal prosecutions with a genuine prospect of success, considering the proof required to demonstrate that a penal offence was committed. As explained by a respondent, it is easier to prove that the employer hindered the LSEOHSC's ability to discharge its duties, which is an offence defined in the *LSA*,[76] when the employer refuses to allow inspectors to enter the workplace, than when the employer fails to reply to a letter from an inspector. This lack of site visits may also encourage employers to bypass the legal pecuniary obligations of the *LSA*; for example, when an employer targeted by a pecuniary complaint concerning unpaid work does not provide the inspector with information on the number of hours of work per day or per week performed by the employees that should appear in its registers. In such cases, instead of exercising the power to enter at any reasonable time any place of work, inspectors may report the existence of a "minor [trans.]" penal offence, that is, the employer's refusal to provide the information requested by the LSEO-HSC (Gesualdi-Fecteau and Vallée 2016, 369–70). Because the fines are low, it is more advantageous for the employer to plead guilty and to pay a fine for an offence than it is to provide information on which a pecuniary complaint that would be assessed for a much larger sum.

The criteria used to assess the performance of inspectors also appear to account for the under-mobilization of deterrence measures in Quebec. The role of inspectors in selecting cases that, in their eyes, might also constitute a penal offence did not appear to be recognized or valued, since recommending a penal prosecution generated "more work" for them and constituted an additional burden that brought them nothing in return, since it did not figure in "their statistics" (Gesualdi-Fecteau and Vallée 2016, 368).

Another internal factor that could explain the limited use of penal prosecutions as a means to enforce compliance with the *LSA* is the evaluation of the strength of a case by the lawyers of the Department of Legal Affairs. As one respondent explained, a penal prosecution concerning the violation of a wage standard in the law, such as relating to unpaid overtime, is usually instituted only when the evidence could be established "on paper [trans.]," such as through the analysis of wage registers or pay sheets (Gesualdi-Fecteau and Vallée 2016, 372). Evidence based solely on oral testimonies is not deemed sufficient to undertake such prosecutions. Two reasons could explain the department's standpoint. First, contradictory versions may be given by the employee and the employer; without "documentary" evidence of the violation, the Department of Legal Affairs will not be able to satisfy the burden of proof required in penal matters, especially when employers are likely to raise both evidentiary and legal defences (e.g., that the employee was a self-employed worker and not covered by the *LSA*). Second, testimonial evidence in a penal prosecution is very fragile, because it is unlikely that employees will miss work in order to testify, especially in a proceeding from which they have nothing to gain. The lawyers of the Department of Legal Affairs do not use the power to compel an employee to testify, since they are aware of the consequences of such a constraint on the worker. While not a factor explored in this book, it may be that the Legal Services Branch of the MOL evaluates the strength of a case when it makes the final decision to prosecute. This last factor could, in combination with the three other factors, reinforce the compliance-oriented approach of inspectors and ESOs and cloud their view of the deterrence measures foreseen by the *LSA* and the *ESA*.

### 3. Conclusion

Although the means provided for under the *LSA* and the *ESA* to ensure enforcement of employment standards vary somewhat, two areas of common ground emerge. The first is the existence of an enforcement gap in both systems. The second is the significant impact of organizational factors within the bodies charged with the concrete implementation of employment standards – for example, the introduction of an online complaints system, which deters some complainants from filing, and the lengthy processing times that undermine the efficiency of anti-reprisal measures. The valorization of settlements also seems to be an avenue put forward in both jurisdictions to address the backlog of complaints but increases the likelihood employees will settle for less than their legal entitlement. Furthermore, the assessment of the performance of ESOs and of inspectors and the resources at their disposal provide a partial explanation for the underutilization of deterrence measures and the limited number of workplace inspections. Finally, the efficiency of targeted workplace inspections has as much to do with the allocation of resources for that purpose as the expert knowledge of the administrative body in identifying high-risk sectors.

Highlighting these factors makes it possible to anticipate the negative effects that the creation of LSEOHSC could have on employment standards enforcement in Quebec. As we have seen, the LSEOHSC was established to meet cost-cutting imperatives, which has, in turn, led to a reduction in the resources available for employment standards enforcement. Indeed, since January 2016, the employers' contribution rates under the *LSA* have decreased from 0.08 per cent to 0.07 per cent of the employers' annual payroll, and these sums are now also used to fund the activities of the LSEOHSC in respect of pay equity.[77] Prior to the merger, the actions of the Pay Equity Commission were funded entirely through the budget of the minister of labour. In this context, one might wonder if the required resources will be available to extend workplace inspection.

Furthermore, as mentioned above, the Board of Directors of the LSEOHSC, which determines its strategic orientations, is markedly different from that of the Board of Directors of LSC. It is doubtful that the expertise in employment standards achieved by the diverse social groups represented on the Board of Directors of the LSC will be preserved and find an equally coherent voice, given the broader mandate of the LSEOHSC. Where will employment standards fit in the strategic priorities of the LSEOHSC? Notably, as demonstrated above, the expertise of the body responsible for enforcement of employment standards and its autonomy in identification and execution of its enforcement priorities motivated the "blitz investigations" conducted by the LSC involving migrant agricultural workers and their employers.

Finally, the merger of the LSC, the Occupational Health and Safety Commission, and the Pay Equity Commission might occasion a shock of organizational cultures and practices within the LSEOHSC, which would add to the distinct inspectors' professional cultures within the organizations that have merged. One might wonder if there are too many irreconcilable responsibilities for one body.

This upheaval in the monitoring of employment standards comes at a very delicate moment: the spread of precarious employment and broader workplace transformations have implications for the context in which labour inspection occurs. Chapter 1, along with other Quebec-specific studies (LSC 2010b, 46–52), have shown that employees in precarious jobs and fissured workplaces are more frequently the victims of repeated breaches of the law. The bill amending the *LSA* that passed in June 2018 makes no specific provision for improving enforcement.[78] Yet any legislative reform that fails to redefine the goals and the practices, as well as increase the resources of the labour inspectorate, will struggle to bridge the employment standards enforcement gap.

Labour inspection, as an institution, is more necessary now than ever. However, its effectiveness depends on the resources at its disposal, the scope of its means of intervention, its autonomy in relation to the administrative power, and maintenance of its specialized expertise. Implementation of the protections provided for in the *LSA* necessarily entails a labour inspectorate capable of adapting its strategies of intervention that take into account contemporary workplace realities with adequate resources for that purpose.

*Chapter Eleven*

# Improving Workplace Conditions through Strategic Enforcement: The U.S. Experience[1]

Millions of low-wage workers in the United States face many of the same challenges in enforcing employment standards that confront those in Ontario laid out in this book. Business restructuring has created greater incentives for non-compliance while also making responsibility for those conditions murkier. Coinciding changes in the industries and labour markets surrounding those workplaces place further downward pressure on wages and working conditions. And the muting of workers' voices arising from the decline of unions, restrictions to traditional voice mechanisms (i.e., linked to collective bargaining), and a workforce particularly subject to fears of retaliation, have made the traditional trigger of enforcement – complaints – a problematic indicator of underlying problems.

At the same time, federal and state agencies in the United States empowered to enforce employment standards, like their Ontario and Canadian federal counterparts, have used complaint-based, workplace-focused approaches to recover back wages owed to workers. The focus on complaint-based wage recovery created a decades-long enforcement gap in the United States, particularly exacerbated by the same kind of resource constraints that have hampered Ontario. Yet, during the Obama administration, the approach to enforcement at the U.S. Department of Labor's Wage and Hours Division (WHD), the federal agency charged with the responsibility to enforce standards addressing minimum wage, overtime, and child labour under the *Fair Labor Standards Act (FLSA)* as well as related employment standards laws under a dozen other Acts fundamentally changed their approach to the enforcement gap.

The approach, referred to in the United States as "strategic enforcement," in many ways rejected the dichotomy between command-and-control regulation and regulatory new governance, instead embracing productive pieces of both but in a larger context of pursuing strategies and supportive organizational changes that sought to improve employment standards conditions by *changing the behaviour of businesses that lead to non-compliance.* By altering the strategic approach to enforcement and instituting a major organizational transformation in the process, agency leadership sought to expand enforcement capacity to ensure that the 130 million workers covered principally by federal employment standards laws would receive those vital protections.[2]

In order to provide a U.S. perspective on Ontario's efforts to deal with the enforcement gap detailed in Part One, I lay out the challenges faced by the WHD in dealing with a similar constellation of factors. I discuss the major elements of strategy that we put in place to undertake a more strategic and impactful approach to improving compliance with employment standards. I review several critical organizational innovations that were established to translate broad strategic directions into action that bear particular relevance to challenges that continue to face Ontario in its efforts to bridge the enforcement gap. I conclude with observations on the political, strategic, and organizational relevance of the U.S. experience to Ontario and other countries seeking to improve labour standards for working people.

## 1. Macro-Level Conditions Facing the WHD

Chapter 1 discussed the development of employment standards law in Ontario, with principal features driven primarily by provincial rather than federal developments. In contrast, a greater interplay between the federal government and the states shaped the core statutes underlying the employment standards system in the United States. Federal and state governments have long interacted in their efforts to improve workplace conditions. At the turn of the twentieth century, states led the way in crafting policies to reduce hours of work, improve conditions for children and women, and institute minimum wage standards for workers, particularly in the emerging railway and manufacturing industries (Commons and Andrews 1916). In the oft-quoted words of Louis Brandeis, "It is one of the happy incidents of the federal system that a single courageous State may, if its citizens choose, serve as a laboratory; and try novel social and economic experiments without risk to the rest of the country."[3]

Workplace regulatory innovation shifted to the federal level in the 1930s as the United States faced economic depression, collapsing wage structures, and social unrest with the rise of union activity in core manufacturing industries. The New Deal legislation and its institutionalization by the National War Labor Board led the federal government to be the driving force of workplace policy for decades (Lichtenstein 1982). This included passage of the *FLSA* in 1938, which made the setting of bedrock labour standards on minimum wages, overtime and hours, and child labour a national rather than state-level activity (Grossman 1978).[4] That law, which created the WHD in the Department of Labor to enforce its provisions, remains the centrepiece of employment standards. But the interplay between state and federal government continued, most strikingly in states taking the initiative to raise minimum wages when national politics thwarted efforts to increase it at the federal level. The political will to pass increases of the federal minimum wage often occurred after numerous states, impatient with congressional inaction, passed their own increases exceeding the federal level. This led to a fracturing of business coalitions that blocked federal minimum wage increases, with large, multi-state companies seeking greater consistency in minimum wage requirements through passage of federal-level increases alongside the continuing resistance of small businesses, which ultimately allowed minimum wage increases, although they emerged in a slow and episodic manner (Weil 2008a).[5]

As with Ontario, as documented in chapter 1, the labour force developments and trends affecting workplace conditions and therefore compliance with laws have changed since the passage of the *FSLA* in 1938. These changes have had major impacts on compliance and how the WHD's efforts and enforcement strategies have evolved. Three developments are particularly notable: first, the growth of the U.S. economy and expansion of employment standards coverage means that the WHD's statutes are the principal source of labour protection for roughly 7.3 million establishments and 135 million workers.[6] Under the Obama administration (and despite the ongoing opposition by the Republican-held Congress during six of the administration's eight years), the WHD increased the number of investigators to almost 1,000 from a low of 700 at the end of the Bush administration. Yet that is still a tiny number relative to the scale of workplaces the agency oversees. Thinking about how to prioritize and ensure that the agency's investigators and efforts focused on where we could have greatest impact on compliance therefore became central. Our shorthand for this approach was strategic enforcement.

Adopting this approach was also crucial as the result of a second development. Employment relationships have been transformed across a growing number of industries in what I have called the "fissured workplace" (Weil 2014). Over the last twenty-five years, major businesses facing pressure from private and public capital markets focused increasingly on core competencies (e.g., brands, logistics excellence, and product development) while passing on many of the activities required to do that work to other business organizations. Using a variety of organizational methods, including subcontracting, third-party management, and franchising, major businesses shed more and more of the work required to create products and services while maintaining tight control over outcomes. As a result, although consumers still perceive a unitary company as the provider of the product or service they purchase (e.g., a Hilton Hotel room or Amazon.com delivery), the work undertaken to provide it is now often performed through a complex web of different employers.

This fissuring of employment increases incentives for non-compliance, such as at the bottom of several levels of subcontractors or between small franchisees whose margins are typically thin and competition fierce. The fissured workplace also creates greater complexity in defining who is responsible for that compliance, given the multiple organizations with a hand in setting working conditions. Consider a modern distribution centre. Workers there will be operating under the strict technical and time requirements set by the controlling retailer, via a third-party logistics company that manages the facility, which in turn hires individual staffing companies who pay their employees, sometimes on a piece rate (i.e., truck-by-truck) basis because they consider them as independent contractors. This creates a situation unconducive to establishing clear responsibility for compliance for workers, employers, or agency investigators. Addressing the fissured workplace and its impacts became another essential element of the WHD enforcement approach.

The third critical macro-level development driving a new approach to enforcement arose from political realities. The WHD – like its sister agencies, the Occupational Safety and Health Administration and the National Labor Relations Board – sits in a political fishbowl. Because of the breadth of its mandate and scope of its jurisdiction, WHD actions are closely scrutinized by congressional members of both parties.[7] Democratic members of Congress often press the agency to perform its work at a level beyond what is possible, given the size of its inspectorate. Republican members view the agency's actions beyond a narrow band of enforcement focused on what they see as a small number of bad actors as regulatory overreach and therefore destructive to business and the economy. Beyond Congress, business interests and members of the legal community who defend employers scrutinize the regulatory and administrative actions of the agency constantly while worker advocates, unions, and the plaintiff bar demand that the agency uses its overstretched resources aggressively.[8] This political environment has limited the opportunity to address changes in the structure of work and the economy and also to address a variety of policy issues through legislation. In the United States, appropriations are also affected by the political environment – both in allocating money to agencies and the constant threat of policy riders, which place limitations on agency actions as part of the appropriated budget. As a result, the core changes in strategy and organizational structure central to strategic federal enforcement involved actions that could be taken through the administrative decision-making authority of the agency.

## 2. Meso-Level Conditions: The Established Enforcement Model in the United States

Prior to the Obama administration, the WHD operated with a strategy and drew on an organizational structure fairly typical of workplace enforcement agencies, including Ontario's Ministry of Labour (MOL) (chapter 2).[9] WHD focused on responding to worker complaints. In fact, in the decade prior to the Obama administration, more than 75 per cent of investigations were complaint driven. The 25 per cent of non-complaint investigations occurred across a wide variety of industries, with little focus and limited use of data on what drove the problems that came through our portals every day.

In addition, the agency pursued workplace-by-workplace resolution of problems and the recovery of back wages. With tens of thousands of incoming cases and a staff of only about 700 investigators by 2008, the WHD sought to recover back wages for workers as provided by the law and resolve those cases as quickly as possible and move on. Investigators were evaluated by efficiency metrics linked to the number of cases processed, and the time required to do so. Investigators were evaluated on the basis of cases processed and modest individual backlogs (analogous to the attempts by the Ontario MOL to reduce investigation backlogs discussed in chapter 3).

Despite the availability of remedies like liquidated damages and civil monetary penalties, the agency was reluctant to use many of the enforcement tools provided by the *FLSA*, even though it is the primary law enforced by the WHD. Contacts between WHD and the solicitor of labor, the office that provides legal support for all Department of Labor agencies, focused on the most egregious violators and usually commenced after administrative remedies had run their course. The WHD engaged in limited outreach to workers and worker advocates (in fact, during the George W. Bush administration, outreach to unions and advocates was all but prohibited). Its outreach to employers was driven by incoming requests, rather than a larger picture of where problems with compliance arose. And outreach was largely uncoordinated and detached from enforcement.

In short, the WHD approach – similar to that of the MOL – was reactive: responding to complaints and then bringing individual offending employers into compliance. As chapter 2 suggests, on one level, responding to incoming complaints that arise from violations is consistent with what the law requires. Yet the WHD has always faced far more incoming complaints than can be handled with the budget appropriated by Congress. The agency therefore focused on ways to respond to a huge inbox efficiently and directed its organizational incentives and attention to increasing the number of complaints it processed with the resources it had. But even an efficient system of complaint response risks leaving the forces driving non-compliance unaddressed and results in an unending game of Whack-a-Mole.

### 3. The Elements of Strategic Enforcement

Responding to the macro-level shifts surrounding the agency, the approach taken during the Obama years marked a significant departure from the past. Strategic enforcement sought to achieve the WHD's official mission to "promote and achieve compliance with labour standards to protect and enhance the welfare of the Nation's workforce" in a new manner (Department of Labor n.d.). Conceptually, strategic enforcement seeks to use the limited enforcement resources available to a regulatory agency to protect workers as proscribed by laws *by changing employer behaviour in a sustainable way*. Putting such an approach into practice relied upon a combination of changes to the way the agency set priorities, allocated investigations, used core tools of enforcement, interacted with worker advocates and the businesses and organizations it oversaw, and drew upon other non-enforcement tools available to the agency, such as media and communication strategies, outreach and educational approaches, and interactions with other federal and state agencies.

Strategic enforcement also required fundamentally reshaping the organizational structure of the WHD. This included the methods of internal governance, management, and information sharing; the coordination of the different levels of the agency; and the way that the agency interacted with key stakeholders, particularly in the worker advocacy community.

In some ways the approach parallels the discussion in this book about moving away from the command-and-control approach, in that it recognized that a narrow focus on compliance could have limited impact on the underlying problem of wage theft. It recognized that some level of non-compliance arises from employers' lack of knowledge of their obligations under the law. But it also recognized that a significant part of non-compliance arises from wilful violations of the law, efforts to subvert responsibilities via regulatory arbitrage, or using legal distinctions to attempt to shift responsibility to other parties, given fissured workplace structures.

These latter sources of non-compliance require an approach that draws on a stronger set of enforcement tools than were the focus of many of the changes instituted over time in Ontario. In particular, strategic enforcement sought to use the concept of deterrence as well as change the incentive structures for non-compliance through a combination of tools. This approach stands in contrast to many of the underlying "light touch" concepts fuelling the regulatory new governance approach as described in previous chapters. Although there are many elements of the strategic enforcement approach, I focus only on a subset of particular relevance to the Ontario experience here.[10]

*Moving to Proactive and Prioritized Investigations*

Strategic enforcement required that a far larger portion of investigations be proactive, chosen on the basis of agency priorities, and undertaken as part of a plan to improve compliance. Moving in that direction required the engagement and agreement of all levels of the agency (described below). It also required WHD offices sometimes to decide not to pursue complaints, thereby freeing investigator time to pursue proactive, directed investigations. Doing so was possible in part because, in the United States, the law allows workers to undertake back-wage claims via private rights of action (e.g., hiring an attorney for an individual or sometimes class claim).

At the same time, the agency refined methods of triaging complaints so that it actively pursued incoming complaints where significant problems seemed to be present, in situations related to broader investigation priorities, and where it was unlikely that workers would be able to pursue their claims for back wages. Procedures to handle complaints more efficiently related to singular problems, such as failure to pay last pay cheques, were also refined so that investigators' time could be used to greatest effect. Through these efforts, complaint-based investigations, as a percentage of all investigations, fell from 76 per cent in 2008 to about 50 per cent by 2016.

Proactive investigations and triaging complaint investigations require setting explicit priorities. At the WHD this process was undertaken by prioritizing specific industries and certain types of practices. Priority-setting by industries started early in the Obama administration, with analyses conducted to rank industries according to two criteria. First, we prioritized by the prevalence of labour standards violations (e.g., the number of minimum wage violations per 100 workers) and the severity of those violations (e.g., the total amount of back wages owed per worker who were paid in violation). Rather than use data from past investigations to measure these outcomes, we adapted measures from household surveys done by the Bureau of the Census to create an objective measure of violations across different regions and labour standards violations.[11] Second, we used WHD administrative data on investigations triggered by worker complaints to estimate the likelihood that workers would exercise their basic rights.[12] Putting the two criteria together allowed the WHD to establish a priority list of low-wage industries with significant underlying violation problems and where workers historically had been unlikely to step forward on their own. These industries became the focus of WHD activity throughout much of the Obama administration.[13] The original list of industries included full and limited service eating and drinking establishments; hotels and motels; janitorial services; agricultural products; and home health care.

These priority industries provided the backdrop for annual agency planning. Each of the five regions and fifty-four district offices established strategic enforcement plans built around their areas. For example, annual plans in the WHD's southeast and western regions had a higher proportion of agricultural product industries reflective of their economies. Other regions and district offices selected specific industries to experiment with new approaches or focused on particularly problematic players operating in multiple locations. For example, the agency might seek to increase compliance through a coordinated set of investigations aimed at increasing attention to a particular problematic practice in a region and, in that way, create incentives for more comprehensive compliance across multiple businesses.

*Using All Enforcement Tools*

Chapter 6 discussed a number of reasons that the larger employment standards enforcement gap arises, focusing specifically on the "deterrence gap." The combination of investigative approaches focused on resolution and recovery of wages for workers directly affected by violations, and the modest nature of penalties limits the deterrent effects of laws in Ontario.

Motivated by the basic principle that strategic enforcement seeks to change behaviour, enhancing the deterrent effect of the agency was a paramount feature of the core strategy. Given the macro-political environment facing the Obama administration described above, it was necessary to look at tools under the existing *FLSA* (in tandem with the strategic focus on a subset of industries described above). In fact, a significant amount could be done in this regard: the WHD historically did not fully utilize the tools that had been provided by the *FLSA*. For example, the *FLSA* allows the agency to collect civil monetary penalties where an employer has shown a repeated, wilful, or egregious failure to comply with the law. Yet the agency used its ability to levy civil monetary penalties in fewer than half of the cases where they were entitled to do so (Weil 2010).[14]

A second remedy established in the *FLSA* is liquidated damages, which are payments made directly to workers equal to the amount of back wages owed to workers (in contrast to fines or penalties that are paid to the government). Liquidated damages compensate workers for those losses sustained several years in the past. In both the Clinton and Bush years, the WHD barely used its ability to collect liquidated damages for workers equal to the amount of back wages, even though the statute clearly provided for that remedy. Absent the use of these remedies, as is the case in Ontario (see chapter 6), employers face limited incentives (i.e., deterrence measures are scarce) to comply with the law, given that the default remedy became payment of the back wages owed workers. If the remedy remains the recovery of those payments exclusively, employers have essentially been provided a no-interest loan by its workforce. By collecting liquidated damages, employers face an economic incentive to comply with the law in the first place, creating incentive to change future behaviour.

A different tool used sparingly but with considerable effect was the provision of the *FLSA* that allows the agency to ask contractors, manufacturers, and retailers to neither move nor accept delivery of goods where investigators had found evidence of significant violations of the *FLSA* by the producer of the goods – the "hot goods" authority. This tool was used extensively in the garment industry where investigations in 2015 and 2016 found violation rates over 85 per cent among randomly selected workplaces. Because of the importance of speed in many industries, alerting an employer that their goods will be delayed in order to rectify violations creates incentives both to resolve the matter and introduce measures that will assure future compliance. Although controversial, the use of the hot goods authority in agriculture also allowed the agency to focus attention on the significant problems for workers in that industry and bring parties in the supply chain to the table to help resolve them.

In the past, the agency shied away from the above enforcement tools in part because they require a coordinated approach and close working relationship between the WHD and the Office of the Solicitor.[15] Past organizational relationships between these two parts of the Department of Labour did not foster such cooperation. Committing to using these tools was therefore only the first step: figuring out how to change the way that the WHD and the Solicitor's Office interacted nationally and in the field was a separate, difficult, but essential part of making it happen (as discussed below).

The agency also refined other enforcement tools throughout the Obama administration. Although they had been used in particular initiatives in the past, investigative tools like stakeouts, new methods of reconstructing payrolls, interviewing workers, and digging into employer claims of financial inability to pay back wages and damages, each contributed to enhanced enforcement capacities. These steps reflected broader efforts to up the agency's game in response to the challenging practices often encountered by WHD investigators.[16]

*Creating Comprehensive Regulatory Agreements to Change Behaviour*

One final fundamental element of strategic enforcement involved changes to the agreements that the WHD created in the wake of an investigation. The chapters comprising Part One of this book suggest that employment standards approaches in Ontario motivated by regulatory new governance presume that a significant proportion of non-compliance arises from misunderstandings or lack of knowledge about requirements under the law (see especially chapters 2 and 4). Resolution of specific problems by the parties – often not involving the MOL – represents a natural outgrowth of this presumption and a narrow use of post-investigation agreements.

In contrast, as in the case of using robust enforcement tools to raise deterrent effects, the strategic enforcement approach of the WHD expanded the range of regulatory agreements used to resolve investigations. That said, for most investigations, the final step followed past practice and entailed the recovery of back wages and, if appropriate, compensatory damages. This "settlement" outcome represents the bulk of resolutions.

However, the WHD developed a broader range of compliance agreements arising from administrative investigation actions, litigation, and sometimes proactive voluntary arrangements, all of which were designed to have broader and more lasting impacts than simply reaching a settlement with the parties. The WHD negotiated Enhanced

Compliance Agreements in many cases out of investigations that required litigation by the solicitor. The Enhanced Compliance Agreements included requirements to establish new positions to oversee compliance, undertake training for specified management personnel, provide mechanisms for workers to lodge complaints internally on a confidential basis, and/or establish third-party monitoring systems to undertake ongoing compliance assessment of subcontractors, suppliers, or other business partners. In some cases, such as with large farm labour contractors in California, what began as an Enhanced Compliance Agreement grew into more cooperative arrangements between the WHD and the signatory contractors. In the best cases, these arrangements allowed for joint problem-solving, as was the case in an agreement between the WHD and CalVans, a non-profit transportation organization to transport workers to farms in California's Central Valley (Department of Labor 2016, 9 August). The agreement came in the wake of farmworker deaths from being transported to and from farms by for-profit "raterios."

The WHD also negotiated voluntary agreements (akin to proactive compliance deeds in Australia) to create a mechanism for systemic compliance outside of litigation and Enhanced Compliance Agreements. In those cases, often arising from the agency's observation of systemic patterns of violations among multiple employers, but facing limitations in the authority to assert direct responsibility, the WHD created agreements with different parties to improve compliance. For example, in the summer of 2016, the WHD concluded a voluntary agreement with the fast food giant Subway. Since that system includes some 13,000 outlets across the United States, the potential for achieving compliance at scale was significant. Growing out of an informal letter of understanding between the WHD and the chief operating officer at Subway in 2011, the Subway Agreement provides for training, sharing of data on compliance as well as the status of outlets, and problem solving to deal with persistent problems (Department of Labor 2016, 26 July).[17]

*Reaching Out to Workers and Worker Advocacy Organizations*

One of the fundamental challenges facing a workplace regulatory agency is making sure that workers exercise the rights they are provided under the law. Chapter 7 discussed options for greater interaction with community organizations in the context of closing the employment standards enforcement gap in Ontario. The WHD strategic enforcement approach wrestled with many of the same challenges, arising from many of the same considerations and tensions between government agencies, workers' centres, and labour organizations.

The *FLSA* provides individual workers with a right to complain about violations of their rights. As discussed extensively in chapter 2, in regard to the use of complaints in Ontario, workers, particularly those who are vulnerable and more likely to be subjected to violations of the law, are commonly reluctant to exercise those rights because of fear of reprisal or, in worst-case scenarios, dismissal. Likewise, in the United States, in the early 2000s, it took about 130 violations of overtime provisions to elicit a single worker complaint (Weil and Pyles 2006). A fundamental task facing worker protection agencies, therefore, is to educate workers about their rights and how to use them. Strategic enforcement used a variety of communication tools, beginning with providing materials in multiple languages, and different media to communicate basic information about rights.

Even before the Trump administration, fear of retaliation represented a significant barrier to the exercise of rights – for good reason. In a study of low-wage workers in three major U.S. cities, in 2008, 43 per cent of workers who had actually complained about a workplace issue in the previous twelve months reported some form of employer or supervisor retaliation.[18] Studies have long shown that exercise of rights significantly increase if workers have a third party present – that is, a union.[19] Although unions were seldom present in the actual workplaces to which we directed our energies, unions and other worker advocacy organizations often had significant information about the industries, employers, and sometimes specific workplaces of concern. Those organizations also often were seen as safe and trusted places for workers.

As is true in Ontario, unions in construction, restaurant, service, and hospitality industries often have deep levels of workplace knowledge at the local level. Workers' centres, community organizations, immigrant rights' groups, and other advocates play a variety of informational and educational roles, often in immigrant communities (Vosko and Thomas 2014). Some function as intermediaries in day labour markets in construction, landscaping, and agriculture. Strategic enforcement therefore requires finding ways to work with unions, worker advocacy organizations, consulates, and other community groups who could serve as trusted intermediaries.

Establishing trusting relationships between those organizations and a government agency can be complicated. Workplace agencies have legal responsibilities to protect workers by enforcing the law. Unions and worker organizations are dedicated fundamentally to building power to negotiate in the interest of workers. Though overlapping in many respects, the difference in objectives can create tension and requires the development of relationships that allow these organizations to work effectively together.

Frictions sometimes arose around issues such as the type of information a government agency needs to pursue its statutory purposes (e.g., what constitutes a legally defensible record of violation); the type of information the agency can share with worker organizations and when it can do so; the pace of the investigation; and the types of changes and outcomes that can be achieved. For example, the WHD guards the identity of a complainant carefully. That limits the type of information the agency will share with any party once an investigation has been initiated. The need for confidentiality is sometimes interpreted by the agency more broadly than might be necessary under the law, but it springs from an important desire to protect complainants from discrimination by employers. On the other hand, worker advocacy organizations, which have their own distinctive internal politics, have a need to report to their members on the progress of actions, including relationships with regulators in regard to specific investigations. Inevitable tensions ensue.

Despite these complexities, the WHD developed highly effective relationships with worker advocates over time. As in any relationship, they deepened with growing trust between individuals, greater appreciation of the respective roles each organization played, experience in working through problems, and successful outcomes. Developing a dedicated staff position to undertake the overall outreach role (by the end of the administration, outreach staff had been put in place in forty-eight of the fifty-four district offices) proved to be particularly critical in this respect.

## 4. Micro-Level Change: Structural Elements to Enable Strategic Enforcement

In *Strategy and Structure,* a classic book in business history, the economic historian Alfred Chandler (1962) examined how the modern corporation developed as an organizational system to support business strategy. Regulatory agencies must similarly create organizational structures that support the strategies that have been chosen. If they do not, the investigators, managers, and staff will not have the tools, skills, or incentives to carry out that strategy.

Chapter 6 described "regulatory habitus," structural and cultural features of the MOL resulting in an overarching preference by investigators to favour compliance-based over deterrence-focused approaches to enforcement. This orientation, present in both managers and investigators in the MOL, contributes to resistance to change towards the types of approaches central to strategic enforcement (see also Coglianese 2017).

There was resistance to change at the WHD, given that the agency had pursued a similarly reactive, complaint-based approach for decades prior to the Obama administration. In order to make the major changes in direction described above, the WHD had to develop, experiment with, and refine its organizational approaches in a number of important ways to support strategic enforcement. Those efforts took place throughout the eight years of the administration, although accelerated in the second term. Once again, there were a variety of such organizational changes made in order to institute strategic enforcement. The following discussion focuses on a subset of micro-level organizational changes that were put in place to enable the strategic enforcement approach, changes that are particularly relevant to discussions of the enforcement gap in Ontario.[20]

*Changing Decision-making Processes among Agency Leaders*

Strategic enforcement at the WHD required a level of accountability by key leaders in the organization quite different from traditional approaches to managing a regulatory agency. In particular, it demanded leaders at the district, regional, and national level to be accountable for key performance outcomes central to the new approach towards the mission. Creating greater accountability also required providing appropriate resources, information, and engagement of key decision-makers so that they have the means to achieve the new objectives.

The process of setting and negotiating the priorities described above led to important discussions that furthered the aims of strategic enforcement. A region proposing to put an industry on the priority list would need to make a case for enforcement resources to be devoted to it; what evidence suggested that either the problems were greater than shown by the data used to set national priorities or what opportunities to move the compliance needle were present that justified its inclusion. In this way, setting priorities created a platform for deeper discussions of conditions in different offices and regions as well as refinement of the overall understanding of compliance conditions.

In order to connect strategic goals with resource allocation discussions, the five regional administrators (all career officials) were afforded a greater role in the budget process, including being provided detailed information on resources available to their region as well as to the other regions in the agency. The national office budget was also made more accessible to all of the senior leaders in the agency. Enhanced transparency allowed for more informed discussion about key resource choices necessary to make strategic enforcement effective. The transition to providing more open information was neither simple nor smooth. It required building systems to provide that information monthly as well as development of trust among the key decision-makers about sharing information and plans with one another and being willing openly to debate resource-allocation decisions.

Performance outcomes were also tied explicitly to resource allocations. The planning process entailed engaging decision-makers at all levels of the agency in setting performance goals critical to strategic enforcement (e.g., the percentage of directed investigations to be undertaken in the next planning cycle; the number of investigations to be undertaken; industry targets for investigations; etc.). Strategic enforcement discussions could be about both the allocation of resources towards the achievement of objectives and what was to be achieved in any time period. One of the most important impacts of tracking performance outcomes monthly at the district office, regional, and national level were the discussions they generated. Regional administrators used the measures as bases for discussions with district office leadership on a quarterly and annual basis, as did the national office in its quarterly discussions with each region. As the agency became better at producing and using the data – eventually giving district offices the capacity to generate these and other key performance outcome reports at a local level and providing leadership with access to one another's data – the sophistication of discussions of larger enforcement strategy grew. Once again, the specific tool became a device to instil a strategic approach in the mind of agency leadership rather than as an end in and of itself.

### *Creating a Culture for Investigators Supportive of a Strategic Enforcement Approach*

At the same time that senior leaders in the organization were provided greater responsibility, accountability, and control over key decisions on strategic enforcement, the agency instituted changes that gave investigators, technicians, and staff tools they needed to successfully undertake strategic enforcement. As is the case in other parts of organizational structure, this process was iterative.

The agency devoted enormous attention to the task of training investigators in the underlying ideas of strategic enforcement. The curriculum for incoming investigators and for the follow-up training that investigators later take – both fabled pieces of WHD culture – were altered to include materials about strategic enforcement and its use. The infusion of new staff at the WHD arising from both a wave of retirements and the hiring of 300 additional investigators in the early years of the Obama administration expanded the pool of those going through training, deepening exposure to these ideas.[21]

Investigators seek to enforce the law and recover back wages for workers who have not been paid what the law assures. Many investigators articulate both moral and legal reasons to support this view of the mission, so they distrust what they perceived as obstacles to undertaking their work. For many years, the agency used efficiency measures such as the number of violations found per investigation hour completed as important performance evaluation metrics. Measures like that make sense if back wage recovery is the fundamental mission of an agency. It is also consistent with a complaint-driven approach where it becomes critical to quickly log in, assign, and then complete investigations so that investigators can quickly move to the next complaint in their ever-filling inbox.

This step was particularly critical to countering defaulting to a "regulatory habitus" antithetical to a strategic enforcement approach. First, and foremost, investigators needed to spend more time on directed, proactive investigation and less time on complaints. This triaging was a hard sell at the beginning of the Obama administration, because the typical non-complaint investigation was far less likely to find violations than a typical complaint investigation.

*Creating an Agency That Reflects the Workforce*

The increased levels of outreach to worker advocates and the need to build trust between the agency and workers required structural changes to personnel policies at the WHD. One historic obstacle arose from the fact that our agency did not look like the workforce the agency sought to protect. Equally problematic was that few of our investigators could speak directly to workers who often did not have English as their primary language. Gaining the trust necessary for effective enforcement requires developing a workforce that has those capabilities.

The primary mechanism used to address this issue was using language capability as an important selection criterion to choose new investigators and technicians. Not only did this create a critical capability in our investigation workforce, but it opened our recruiting to a pool of workers that we had not adequately tapped in the past. In addition, the WHD has a culture of promoting from within. The majority of district, regional, and national office leadership began their work as investigators. This background training can be a powerful mechanism to build capabilities and a strong organizational culture. But if the incoming level of the organization from which one recruits does not reflect the community of workers with which one is to interact, those differences are reinforced at every level of your leadership. By changing our hiring protocols, more than half of our investigators by the end of the administration spoke more than one language, giving the agency an ability to communicate in Spanish, Mandarin, Cantonese, Portuguese, Polish, Tagalog, Vietnamese, and many other languages. Because of a high level of retirements and other separations, a significant number of relatively recent investigators were able to assume leadership in the organization, further expanding the diversity of the agency leadership.

### 5. Macro, Meso, and Micro Changes: Concluding Insights from South of Ontario

How can one gauge the net impact of strategic enforcement undertaken by the WHD? One means is measuring impact by the core performance metrics drawn upon by the WHD as its core internal measures of strategic enforcement. Graph 11.1 presents three measures of performance related to investigations over the course of eight years of the Obama administration and the first year of the Trump administration. It portrays

Graph 11.1. Key Performance Metrics: Percentage of Complaint and Directed Investigations with No Violations, 2009–2017

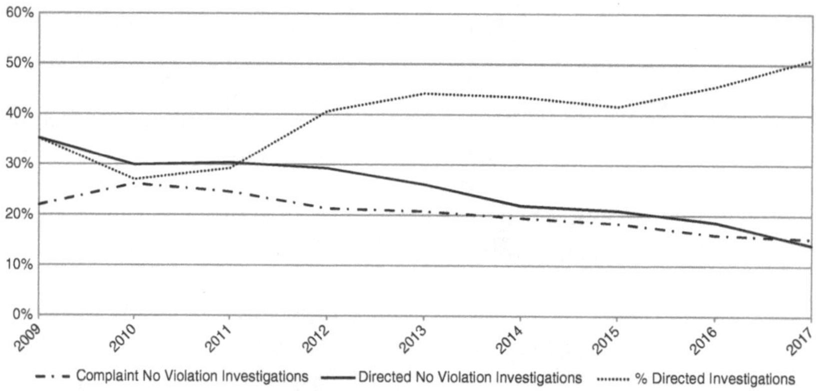


Source: U.S. Department of Labor, WHD, Enforcement Data (http://www.dol.gov/whd/data).

a steadily increasing percentage of investigations done on a proactive basis (the grey, dotted line that moves upward between 2009 and 2017). Directed (proactive) investigations as a percentage of all investigations stood at 35 per cent in 2009, fell to 27 per cent in the next year, but then began to rise steadily, going above 50 per cent by the end of 2017. Graph 11.1 also depicts the increasing improvement in targeting of both directed and complaint investigations towards workplaces with violations: this trend is depicted by the solid line depicting a downward trend in the "no violation rate" (defined as investigations where no violations were found) for directed investigations and the dash-dot line indicating reduction in that rate in complaint investigations. The pronounced narrowing of the large gap in the "no violation rate" between directed and complaint investigations in 2009 (22 per cent for complaint versus 35 per cent for directed investigations) is particularly striking. By 2017 the "no violation rates" for the two types of investigations had become almost indistinguishable from one another and significantly below where they had begun (15.4 per cent for complaint versus 14.2 per cent for directed investigations). The methods for selecting investigations across the agency's fifty-four offices had clearly changed over the eight years.

These trends indicate that the agency moved significantly in its orientation over time, undertaking a larger percentage of proactive investigations and targeting them in a manner consistent with its strategy. Other measures not presented here reinforce this story: average recovery of back wages per worker increased steadily between 2009 and 2017 in directed investigations, rising above USD$1,000 per worker in 2015. This finding is particularly striking, given that the percentage of directed investigations in *low-wage*, priority industries also rose steadily, exceeding 80 per cent of all investigations by the end of the administration (Weil 2018). These trends are not in themselves measures that the agency had changed behaviour among the universe of regulated actors in the targeted industries (representing an analysis that remains to be done). Still, they suggest that real and significant change in the fundamental model of enforcement had occurred.

The WHD experience has a number of implications for evaluating the enforcement gap in Ontario and the efforts discussed in this book. Ontario and the United States share a legacy of reactive enforcement that became particularly problematic as a result of changes in macro conditions – particularly by restructuring of work and labour markets, restive political environments, and extremely limited regulatory resources. Over the last decade, agencies in both contexts have grappled with steps to respond to these pressures, in light of a variety of legal, political, and organizational rigidities.

The changes in the United States occurred in a hostile political environment (framed particularly by a Republican-controlled Congress for six of the eight years of the Obama administration). Many of the limitations from embedded regulatory models pushing against change in Ontario were also present in the United States. Yet purposive changes were possible in this context for a number of reasons. First, the changes were supported and at some points championed by the administration, creating a supportive context for organizational innovation. Second, the strategies built on central principles (in particular the WHD mission), established albeit under-utilized enforcement tools, and core elements of the agency structure at the meso level. These features allowed a strategic enforcement approach to be built on familiar foundations, even though its elements represented a significant departure from agency practice. Finally, the efforts consciously undertook micro-level changes to the organizational structure of the WHD, particularly those elements that, if left unattended, would lead employment standards enforcement to drift back to familiar, reactive approaches. Those investments in micro-level changes were significant and comprehensive, going beyond those undertaken at the MOL. The fact that in the first year of the Trump administration, core strategic enforcement measures continued to move towards a strategic enforcement model (graph 11.1), despite rhetoric to the contrary, suggests persistence of the effort.

The experience at the WHD during the Obama administration demonstrates how far one can go in making sure that workers' lives are improved, in spite of significant limitations on the resources available and under the bright and sometimes harsh glare of political forces that seek to push against employment standards, resulting in enforcement gaps. Though the Trump administration has placed and will continue to place strains on these efforts, it appears that many of the elements of strategic enforcement remain in place for now. That perhaps can offer some solace as Ontario grapples with its own back-and-forth efforts to address the enforcement gap.

*Chapter Twelve*

# Improving Employment Standards Enforcement for People in Precarious Jobs

This book has charted gaps in employment standards and their enforcement in Ontario in comparative context. Even though employment standards reflect a collectively established normative judgment about minimally decent working conditions that must be extended to all employees, in these pages we have chronicled obstacles to their effective enforcement.

Ontario is experiencing dramatic changes in the nature of employment. These changes are also evident elsewhere, such as at the national level in Australia, the United States, and Britain, as well as in the province of Quebec. With the erosion of manufacturing and a concomitant surge in employment in weakly unionized service industries, a declining share of the province's private sector labour force is unionized. Simultaneously, many Ontario workplaces are being transformed through greater use of contracting-out, franchising, and extended supply chains.

We have argued that these changes are best approached and understood using the tools of critical and feminist political economy, which identify the foundational features of capitalism – that production is always profit-driven and that competitive pressures operate on individual employers, leading them to constantly seek some combination of technical and organizational innovation to maintain or increase profit levels – as principal drivers. Although workers continue to resist efforts by employers to extract and retain for themselves more of the value their labour produces, in recent years the balance of power has shifted in favour of employers, as reflected in lower unionization rates. Consequently, more employees depend on employment standards as the principal source of labour protection, despite the persistently subordinate status of these standards, shaped, as feminist political economists have shown, by the marginalized subjects to whom they were addressed originally.

The shift to employment standards as an increasingly important site of labour market regulation, however, does not bring about an end to conflict, merely a change in its locus. Employers have a keen interest in ensuring that minimum standards do not unduly interfere with profit-making and freedom to organize their workplaces and work-forces towards this end. Concomitantly, workers continue to be engaged in efforts to secure employment standards that protect their standard of living and provide for decent working conditions. From time to time, workers' efforts attract allies who recognize that depressing workers' purchasing power is bad for the economy and that the flexibility often demanded by employers undermines social reproduction. The result, as we have seen in the chapters that comprise Part One, is that the design and enforcement of employment standards is contested and has changed considerably since the inception of the *Employment Standards Act (ESA)* and its precursors – indeed even during the course of the research presented in this book, the pendulum swung forward, with the passage of the *Fair Workplaces, Better Jobs Act* (2017) and back again with the passage of the *Making Ontario Open for Business Act* (2018).

As a result, employment standards have not lived up to their founding promise to provide a floor of minimum terms and conditions of employment, advancing the principles of fairness and universality, as a result of deficiencies not only in their scope but also in their enforcement. Enforcement strategies are not keeping pace with workplace practices that fuel precarious employment and the related problem of fissuring. For many employees, employment standards are ephemeral, difficult to assess, or, at worst, impossible to realize in practice.

Having utilized an interdisciplinary and multi-method approach to scrutinize core aspects of Ontario's employment standards regime – the complaints system and its administration, workplace inspections, the recovery system, and deterrence tools available as well as the possibilities for participatory enforcement – we can assert with confidence that an enforcement gap of considerable depth and magnitude pervades each of its central elements. Moreover, structural barriers that prevent employees from exercising their voice, shaped by racialization and feminization as well as divisions based on citizenship and residency status and age, not only fuel but are reinforced by the enforcement gap writ large. Yet despite this bleak picture, innovative policies and practices are taking shape elsewhere, including in contexts facing similar challenges. These innovations, some of which are chronicled in the chapters that comprise Part Two, suggest that there is nothing inevitable about the employment standards enforcement gap. Leaving so many employees so poorly protected is preventable.

Of course, we do not believe that improving enforcement of prevailing employment standards is, in and of itself, sufficient to improving employment standards. Expanding coverage and, more specifically, eliminating unprincipled exemptions and special rules is, for example, also critical to this aim (Vosko, Noack, and Thomas 2016; Vosko et al 2019). Here it should be emphasized that far less exceptionalism characterizes not only Australia, Britain, and the United States but also other jurisdictions in Canada, including Quebec and the federal jurisdiction. Nor are we naive about the challenges involved in strengthening enforcement. From our critical and feminist political economy perspective, we understand that considerable employer resistance is to be expected and that the state is not a neutral institution that attends equally to employer and employee concerns. Deeply embedded institutional and social practices are not easy to change, especially when they favour and are favoured by employers. Nevertheless, through policy experimentation, motivated by workers' persistent struggles to improve employment standards, whether through workers' centres or unions – amplified by media reports that reveal workplace injustices and employment standards violations, and sometimes aided by sympathetic government officials – alternative modes of enforcement are imaginable and attainable.

Building on the lessons learned about what works and does not work in employment standards enforcement drawn from the chapters comprising parts 1 and 2 of the book, and the dialogue between theory, evidence, and practice that informs their contents, this chapter concludes by considering options for change in Ontario. It does so by reviewing central findings about the nature of gaps that characterize each aspect of Ontario's employment standards enforcement regime, the strategies of re-regulation required, and those emerging in other jurisdictions that offer promise in forging change.

## 1. Improving the Efficacy of the Complaints Regime: Augmenting Worker Voice in the Complaints Process

Our interrogation of the complaints system in the first few chapters of this book revealed the extent to which the detection and enforcement of employment standards violations in Ontario relies on individual employees reporting and pursuing claims via a complaints system, and the risks that aggrieved workers take in this time-consuming and stressful process. If they believe that a current or recent employer has violated their rights under the *ESA*, employees covered by its provisions are encouraged to file a complaint with the Ministry of Labour

(MOL). This element of the employment standards enforcement system is premised on the assumption that individual employees are the most reliable source of information about employers' practices and, further, that they have the most immediate interest in obtaining a remedy for those that are illegal. Yet qualitative interviews with employees and MOL officials, together with administrative data collected by the MOL, illustrate that the complaints system also proceeds on the basis that workers and employers are equal actors when, in an era of precarious employment, deep workplace power imbalances pervade the employment relationship. Indeed, as chapter 2 shows, these imbalances make many employees' engagement with the complaints system a risky venture. This danger is particularly acute for those still on the job, given the veritable threat of reprisal and the lengthy and uncertain processes surrounding the resolution of individual grievances. As chapter 2 also documents, such constraints mean that only a small fraction of aggrieved employees is likely to ever see their legal rights under the Act enforced.

This is the sum of the compliance orientation that underpins the complaint system in Ontario, which, as the book in its entirety contends, emanates partly from tenets of regulatory new governance that emphasize the need for de-bureaucratized and less adversarial forms of intervention. With regard to the individualized complaint system, in the period under study, the imprint and dampening effects of regulatory new governance–styled regulated self-regulation are evident, particularly in the long-lived requirement that most employees attempt to resolve their complaints with their employers before filing formally with the MOL, and the accompanying self-help and informational materials that encourage employees to enforce their own rights. Emblematic of the dulling implications of regulated self-regulation, chapter 2 charted the declining share of Ontario employees who filed a complaint in the face of the self-resolution requirement and the rising number of complaints that included a claim of reprisal in this era, among those who managed to formally enter the system.

After detailing challenges that employees face when attempting to file a complaint – and revealing that many obstacles stem from employees' labour force position, together with the organization of the complaints system itself – and thereby demonstrating how reforms influenced by regulatory new governance have exacerbated longstanding barriers to filing a complaint, the chapter developed the argument that while raising employees' awareness of their legal rights is a necessary component of any enforcement regime, more robust measures are essential. Moreover, as documented in chapter 7, having organizations like workers' centres and legal clinics assist workers in navigating the complaints process aids in moderating power imbalances between workers and employers, along with more straightforward measures, such as making complaints forms available in multiple languages and hiring inspectors whose backgrounds reflect the diversity of employment and employees in Ontario. To this end, the book's findings call for allowing for third-party and anonymous complaints and strengthening reprisal provisions. Each of these recommendations stems from the conclusion that, as it operates presently, the complaint system hinders the expression of voice, especially among employees already vulnerable on account of their social location and/or occupational and/or industrial context, such as women, recent immigrants, and young people. In the face of declining rates of unionization, particularly among such groups of employees, the findings herein also call for restoring direct access to the complaints system for unionized workers.

Were they to be adopted and adapted to the situation in Ontario, several innovations described in the chapters offering views from elsewhere show promise in rectifying these problems and pursuing several of the foregoing solutions. Foremost is the provision for third-party and anonymous complaints elsewhere, such as in Saskatchewan. Moreover, the cases of Australia, Britain, and Quebec – three jurisdictions in which third-party and anonymous tips (but not complaints) are permissible – underscore the need for greater formalization in this area since, in all contexts, government officials are not obligated to follow up on such information, leaving a gap in practice. Another innovation of relevance to Ontario is found in the legal representation offered to aggrieved employees with claims of wage theft, wrongful dismissal, and psychological harassment in Quebec. Under Australia's *Fair Work Act*, unions also have the right of entry to workplaces (albeit rarely used); securing this right in Ontario could go some way towards encouraging aggrieved employees to come forward, especially in workplaces where multiple employees face violations, as well as in preventing reprisals.

## 2. Retooling Complaints Administration: Eliminating the Backlog by Strengthening the Weakest Aspects of the Enforcement Regime

In its exploration of the long-building crisis in the administration of Ontario's employment standards complaints system, chapter 3 demonstrates that, in the province, as well as other jurisdictions following similar paths (e.g., Australia and Quebec), contemporary problems stem from the original design of the system itself: its premise was that only a modest number of uncomplicated complaints from a relatively limited population of employees would ever be filed (on the basis that most employees would be represented by unions and, accordingly, have recourse to strong collective agreements). Yet not only did this assumption prove false as early as the 1970s, when complaints administration was extremely under-resourced (Lane 1977; Thomas 2009), the magnitude of resourcing problems grew substantially in the late twentieth century with declining rates of unionization, and hence the growth of employees for whom employment standards became an exclusive source of labour protection, and the spread of precarious employment precipitating an expanded volume of complaints. This growth, as chapters 4 and 5 show, also took place in a context of limited proactivity (i.e., largely in the absence of strategically implemented workplace inspections), weak mechanisms for recovery, and limited availability of deterrence tools and weakly institutionalized processes for their utilization.

In the face of these challenges, chapter 3 shows how, in lieu of extending greater resources to complaints administration, the MOL has long sought to minimize the administrative burden inherent in complaints handling by drawing on compliance-oriented soft-law and self-regulation strategies to close claims rapidly. Such strategies, as the historical analysis in the chapter shows, reflect continuities in the MOL's efforts to minimize its administrative burden at the expense of other principles of employment standards enforcement, such as due process. Three strategies, in particular, erode effective enforcement: the reconfiguration of intake; the extension of greater support for various types of settlements; and the institutionalization of new mechanisms for evaluating employment standards officers (ESOs) that focus on performance measurement, a characteristic of the new public management administrative paradigm. While such strategies may reduce the administrative burden of complaint handling in the short run, as the empirics in the chapter show, in the long run these "quick fixes" undercut investigative integrity by, for example, turning law enforcement into dispute resolution (e.g., facilitated settlements) and engaging performance measures preoccupied with the number of cases closed rather than the quality of the outcomes. For this reason, correcting the problems that plague complaints administration requires, foremost, greater investment in the employment standards administration. Indeed, the need for greater investment promises only to grow, with removal of the requirement that aggrieved employees attempt to resolve their employment standards problems with their employers before initiating a formal complaint – a progressive change, consistent with the data analysis offered in chapter 2, that could lead to an increase in complaints that enter the system and hence greater demands in the arena of complaints administration.

Increased resources are nevertheless insufficient on their own. Instead, dispensing with the prevailing modes of performance measurement centred on quantity rather than quality and engaging instead in strategically oriented organizational change of the sort evident in the United States at the federal level is necessary. More broadly, retooling complaints administration necessitates correcting the most serious weaknesses in the regime as a whole to reduce the rate of employment standards violations that generate complaints in the first place, that is, addressing the dearth of workplace inspections, weaknesses in recovery, and lack of deterrence.

### 3. Recovery: From a Weak Link to a Foundational Element of Employment Standards Enforcement

Exacerbating systemic problems in complaints and complaints administration, recovery arguably represents a fundamental indicator of the depth of the enforcement gap in Ontario as elsewhere (e.g., in Australia, as explored in chapter 9, and in Britain, as discussed in chapter 8). Employees face persistent difficulties in collecting monies they are owed. These difficulties are apparent when ESOs investigate claims and award monetary entitlements, including those where employers incur Orders to Pay. They are evident in settlement processes, which often involve financial restitution for the complainant while foregoing the establishment of wrongdoing and the amount of monies legally owing to a complainant. And difficulties in recovering wages are also apparent when employees seek to recover wages from an insolvent or bankrupt employer under the Bankruptcy and Insolvency Act (1985).

Indeed, as chapter 4 shows, across different avenues for recovery, complainants often face barriers to restitution that hinder recovery and undermine the fundamental legal and normative underpinnings of employment standards. Such barriers are by no means inevitable, however. Numerous options for strengthening recovery, including several that operate in other jurisdictions, are available. One involves securing wages in advance through a wage protection fund, of a similar order to one that previously existed in Ontario. Optimally, such a fund would be resourced through a payroll tax, offering the potential to shift the burden of wage recovery away from employees and the general public and onto the industries where non-compliance is more prominent. It would protect employees owed money from employers that are still operating or are informally bankrupt or insolvent and place no cap on payouts or time limits restricting monies they are owed. Another option involves introducing wage bonds and other measures that make non-payment potentially very costly for employers, such as wage liens and licence debarment, similar to those available at the city and state levels in parts of the United States. Provisions introduced in the *Fair Workplaces, Better Jobs Act* (2017) – which established the MOL's capacity to impose wage liens, strengthened related employer liability for Orders to Pay, and authorized ESOs to award interest on unpaid wages – go some distance to address ineffective recovery of back wages. Still, more direct intervention is necessary, such as by revising *ESA* provisions that surround collections to allow for liquidated damages, which more accurately reflect the hardship experienced by employees facing violations, and increasing deterrence by making violations increasingly costly for employers, similar to measures widely used at the federal level in the United States. Subtler intervention is also required, such as by directing ESOs to exercise greater caution in facilitated settlements, and by expanding liability for monetary entitlements to not only address fissuring (e.g., enlarging joint and several liability) but also to make the fuller range of parties involved in violating employment standards more accountable (e.g., through measures akin to accessorial liability in Australia, which seeks to hold more responsible persons who have "aided and abetted," "counselled or procured," or "induced" a contravention, directly or indirectly).

### 4. Improving Inspections: Towards Robust Proactivity

With growing recognition that reliance on the complaints system to enforce employment standards is inadequate in the face of increasingly precarious and/or complex employment relationships and fissuring, workplace inspections offer an important means to incorporate greater proactivity. Yet chapter 5's examination of this vital aspect of the employment standards enforcement regime reveals the contradictions that underlie workplace inspections. On the one hand, in the early 2000s, in the face of mounting criticism for having underutilized workplace inspections, the MOL sought to reinvest in proactive enforcement by establishing a dedicated enforcement team and initiating targeted blitzes of industries and workplaces in which employment standards violations are endemic. The result was an increase in the number of workplace inspections undertaken by the MOL, beginning in the mid-2000s. On the other hand, three limitations persist to hamper the potential of workplace inspections to reduce the number and severity of employment standards violations. First, consistent with the emphasis on regulated self-regulation under the complaint system, the dual focus of inspections – on self-regulation and educating employers – neglects power imbalances inherent in the employment relationship and is premised on the naive assumption that most violations are unintentional. Second, when they are undertaken, inspections are narrow, both in terms of employees covered and the standards evaluated, limiting ESOs' ability to fully address non-compliance with the *ESA*. Third, inspections make very little use of deterrence measures, a practice that ultimately thwarts the goal of preventing employment standards violations in the first instance.

In response to these challenges, consistent with the 2017 promise to increase the inspectorate by 175 officers by 2021 – and despite the freeze on public sector hiring and the concomitant suspension of inspections in the summer of 2018 – chapter 5 calls for increased proactive inspections, and their quality. It also rejects the notion of delineating a subset of "inspectable" standards and reveals the profound limitations of typically evaluating just eleven employment standards in workplace inspections. Here, too, innovations that are emerging elsewhere hold promise to address the contradictions documented in chapter 5. For example, consistent with a more strategic orientation, Ontario could draw on elements of the in-depth enquiry model adopted in Australia, as documented in chapter 9, to better capture patterns of (non-)compliance by industry and hence improve efforts to target sectors where violations are well documented. The province could also draw lessons from the strategic enforcement agenda adopted by the Wage and Hour Division (WHD) of the U.S. Department of Labor to better set priorities on the basis of knowledge about particular industries or types of practices, gleaned ideally from analyses of the sort done in that context. As documented in chapter 11, this process entailed ranking industries according to two criteria: first, prioritization based on the prevalence of violations (e.g., the number of minimum wage violations per 100 workers) and the severity of those violations (e.g., the total amount of back wages owed per worker) and, second, the use of WHD data on investigations triggered by worker complaints, much like Ontario's expanded investigation type, to estimate the likelihood that workers would exercise their basic rights. In the U.S. context, putting the two criteria together allowed the WHD to establish a priority list of low wage industries characterized by substantial underlying violation problems where workers historically had been unlikely to step forward on their own. These industries then became a focus of enforcement. Simultaneously, front-line WHD inspectors also received extensive training in the principles of strategic enforcement and in the changing nature of work, with a focus on the greater prevalence of supply chains, subcontracting systems, hybrid structures involving highly complex combinations of third-party managers, subcontractors, and staffing agencies, as well as franchise systems in a variety of industries. Collectively, these strategic changes contributed to improving the WHD's understanding of patterns of violation by industry and firm-level practices. These evidence-driven, innovative approaches to strategic enforcement are worthy of consideration in Ontario (and elsewhere as well), as they promise to increase the efficacy of inspections and provide greater openings for investigating compliance with employment standards among related entities.

**5. Deterrence: Beyond Carrots and Sticks**

Increasing the frequency of proactive inspections and improving their efficacy through expanding their scope, better targeting, and limiting advance notice still leaves the problem of what happens when ESOs detect violations. As we document briefly in chapter 6 and in more detail elsewhere (Tucker et al. 2019; Casey et al. 2018), there is a serious deterrence gap in Ontario's employment standards enforcement regime. Prior to 2016/17, ESOs applied low-level deterrence measures in fewer than 5 per cent of violations detected by complaints, and only about 10 per cent of violations detected on inspections. In addition, higher-level deterrence measures are rarely used, and when they are used, it is not in response to the initial violation of the *ESA* but for the employer's defiance of the ESO's authority. As a result, an overwhelming majority of employers can expect that even if their employment standards violations are detected, the worst that will happen is that an ESO will require them to make restitution.

In chapter 6 we explored the reasons for this deterrence gap and found that it is deeply institutionalized. From the origins of labour inspection, the prevailing practice has been to gently persuade employers to comply rather than to punish them for their non-compliance. While this practice favours and is supported by employers, workers have often vociferously opposed it. Yet notwithstanding this pressure, which has resulted in governments publicly committing to and actually increasing the use of deterrence measures, a compliance orientation predominates. In order to explain this phenomenon, we introduced the idea of regulator habitus and examined influences that shape the perceptions and enforcement practices of front-line officials. The embedded institutional culture inherited from the past operates as a material force that shapes how inspectors see the world and orient themselves in it. But, we argue, history alone cannot explain the persistence of a compliance orientation among current ESOs. It is also important to take resource and time limitations into account, as well as the small size of fines, which contribute to ESO scepticism about their efficacy. Moreover, other policies that emphasize the importance of minimizing employer pushback and securing and maintaining employer trust operate at odds with a deterrence orientation and provide ESOs with mixed signals about the seriousness of a stated commitment to increased use of deterrence measures.

In order to overcome the deterrence gap, it is necessary to devise measures that are responsive to its multiple causes. First, there needs to be a clear commitment to deterrence as one of the pillars upon which the province's enforcement strategy is built. As we have seen, if the message to labour inspectors is inconsistent or ambiguous, the likelihood of a shift in their enforcement orientation will be reduced significantly. But issuing top-down directives is unlikely to succeed in the absence of a carefully thought out and well-executed plan to change the institutional culture. Weil's discussion in chapter 11 of how change was made in the WHD is particularly instructive in revealing the kinds of actions needed to achieve this kind of sustainable reform. These actions include engaging regional offices in strategic enforcement through greater accountability and information-sharing, as well as participation in decision-making processes for setting priorities and allocating resources. The recruitment and training of new enforcement officers is also crucial. This not only involves hiring officers who have an enforcement orientation, but also recruiting individuals from the communities that most heavily rely on employment standards for protection and who speak their languages.

Beyond the question of commitment and institutional change lie issues regarding the design of deterrence measures. We do not think that the Quebec model, which depends entirely on prosecutions, is desirable, since it is likely to result in less use of deterrence measures. It is sensible to have both high-level and low-level deterrence measures available, especially in light of studies that show that the fact that a penalty is imposed, not necessarily its size, generates a deterrent effect (Gray and Scholz 1993; Purse and Dorrian 2011). That said, it is important that low-level penalties are set high enough so that ESOs do not view fines as derisory and therefore not worth the time and effort it takes to impose them. The Liberal government increased penalties for Notices of Contravention (NOCs) shortly before it was defeated in the 2018 election, an action that was quickly reversed by the newly elected Conservative government. This reversal sends a clear message to ESOs that the government is no longer interested in promoting a more deterrence-oriented approach to enforcement and is likely to result in a decline in the use of deterrence measures. However, governments change and future opportunities to decrease the deterrence gap will arise. At that time, government should also reconsider whether any useful purpose is served by having two low-level deterrence measures. The Liberal government reversed course and gave priority to using NOCs, which have the advantage of being available for all employment standards violations and of greater flexibility in setting the penalty structure through regulation, including provisions for increased fines for second and subsequent offences.

Finally, there is also the question of how best to target deterrence measures. The strategic enforcement model suggests that regulators should map sectors of the economy to better understand where it can most effectively intervene to achieve systemic and sustained change, including where and how to target deterrence measures. For example, while it might be appropriate to target small employers who frequently violate the *ESA* in some sectors where they operate outside supply chains and franchise arrangements, in other sectors it would be more appropriate to focus on accessorial liability, as in the case of Australia, and thereby target leading firms that contribute to and are in a position to control employment standards violations by subordinate firms.

## 6. Participatory Enforcement: Towards Capital *S* and Small *s* Solidarity

While enforcement of employment standards is routinely seen as within the purview of government agencies, in practice, both governmental and non-governmental actors can participate in ensuring compliance with employment standards. Taking this view, chapter 7, "Strengthening Participatory Approaches to Enforcement," explores alternative modes of employment standards enforcement by considering examples that range from formalized approaches to co-enforcement, such as tripartism, to less formalized examples involving the enhanced participation of civil society organizations, including community organizations that assist workers in making complaints, and workers' centres engaged in advocacy with and on behalf of non-unionized workers. Against this backdrop, we chronicled the activities of workers' centres based in Sudbury, Windsor, and Toronto engaged in advocacy, legal assistance, labour rights education, assistance with complaints, and community organizing in support of workers navigating the employment standards enforcement process. We demonstrate the important and necessary ways in which these non-governmental actors engage in enforcement, both indirectly, by empowering workers in precarious jobs (a necessary activity, given the many obstacles workers encounter in the complaints process), and more directly by fostering a worker-centred approach to employment standards enforcement and acknowledging fundamental power imbalances in the employment relationship shaped by structural inequalities. The articulation of and attention to these power imbalances, and their link to processes such as racialization and feminization, are crucial in the face of the often top-down approach adopted by the inspectorate, where ESOs are trained to view their role as neutral arbitrators of disputes between parties that are typically cast as equal participants in employment relations.

In attempting bolster the role of non-governmental actors, as well as facilitate structures that enable workers' meaningful participation, the Australian case is noteworthy. In this context, consistent with a longstanding commitment to capital *S* Solidarity, unions have standing to participate actively in the enforcement of minimum employment standards on behalf of not only their members but non-members, regardless of the source of these standards, although they have arguably served more as "junior partners" than "joint regulators" in recent history (Hardy and Howe 2009). There are, moreover, well-rehearsed examples in the United States, such as in Los Angeles, where business representatives of building trades unions participate as employment standards inspectors in public works projects (Fine and Gordon 2010). To assist in closing the enforcement gap, unions in Ontario might wisely take their cue from these examples and lobby for greater involvement in the inspectorate – a change that could complement the foregoing call for reversing the exemption of unionized workers from recourse to the *ESA*'s standards through the MOL. Still, amplifying unions' role is but one avenue for transformation. Another is the extension of greater government support for workers' centres, as well as legal clinics, which serve non-unionized workers in precarious jobs, for whom employment standards represent the exclusive source of labour protection. Given the critical role that these organizations already play in educating the public, as well as members of the inspectorate, about developments at the local level as documented in chapter 7, these institutions need institutionalized, long-term support, though as the chapter cautions, it must be provided in a manner that enables such organizations to retain their autonomy from agencies such as governments, unions, foundations, etc. In the United States, the WHD acknowledges the centrality of non-governmental organizations in its outreach work, on the assumption that community organizations can provide in-depth knowledge of workplace practices at a local level. Moreover, the organizational changes undertaken within the WHD to train a cadre of inspectors whose life experiences and social locations closely approximate the situation of workers in precarious jobs offer one means of forging small *s* solidarity that is worth exploring in Ontario (i.e., transcending structural barriers that prevent employees from exercising their voice shaped, in particular, by processes of racialization and feminization as well as divisions based on citizenship and residency status). Teamed with greater support for legal representation of aggrieved employees of the sort available in Quebec and Australia (and perhaps "organic enforcement" of the sort advocated for in the British context in chapter 8), making such organizational changes could substantially improve protections for people in precarious jobs. Equally important, if adopted, they would contribute to rebuilding collective understanding of, and hence support for, the sentiments behind the establishment of the *ESA* and its role in ensuring minimally decent working conditions for all. To paraphrase MOL administrators of the early 1970s, what is needed is no less than a "collective agreement" for the people, one concerned, in particular, with those with limited bargaining power (MOL 1974, June).

Clearly there is much work to be done to improve employment standards enforcement, not just in Ontario but in all the jurisdictions whose experience we have examined in this book. Working within a critical and feminist political economy framework, our study has demonstrated that substantial and longstanding obstacles stand in the way of achieving systemic and sustained improvement in advanced capitalist labour markets. As evidenced by the government of Ontario's *Making Ontario Open for Business Act* (2018), which withdraws many legislative changes designed to augment employment standards and their enforcement introduced in the *Fair Workplaces, Better Jobs Act* (2017), together with subsequent measures that further erode protections offered under the *ESA*, the core historical tensions over the reform of employment standards that we identify at the outset – between the pursuit of decent work through advancing the principles of social minima, universality and fairness, and the concerns not to interfere with the operational freedom of businesses – persist. Nevertheless, sustained campaigns and organizing can help prevent employers from engaging in and promoting, and governments in tolerating, erosion, evasion, and abandonment of employment standards and may produce stronger laws and better enforcement. We hope that this book contributes in some small way to this outcome.

# Supplementary Information on Quantitative and Qualitative Methods: Ontario Component

## Research Ethics

All aspects of the project were reviewed and approved by the Ethics Review Boards at York University (certificate number: e2013-173), the University of Toronto, Ryerson University, the University of Windsor, and Memorial University. In the case of quantitative analysis, researchers analysed administrative data collected and maintained by the Ministry of Labour (MOL) as well as national statistical surveys. With regard to the former, access to these data was governed by a research protocol negotiated between the partner universities and the MOL. In the case of the qualitative interviews, research procedures provided for voluntary participation, anonymity, and confidentiality, as elaborated below. Interviews with MOL officials were also governed by a research agreement between the partner universities and the MOL.

# Appendix A: Quantitative Data

## A.1. Administrative Data

The Ontario Ministry of Labour's Employment Standards Information System (ESIS) analysed in this book is the primary administrative database (stored in a SQL database) for employment standards enforcement activities in Ontario. The ESIS was first implemented in 2007, replacing a more rudimentary database, and is used primarily as an information tracking and case management system. As such, the database stores information on employment standards complaints and workplace inspections, documenting processes from assessment to enforcement, as well as outcomes. The ESIS is also used in the management of EROs' (early resolution officers) and ESOs' (employment standards officers) workloads by routing tasks (e.g., complaints for investigations) to officers in specific regions. The data were provided to the research team by the MOL in anonymized form.

Eight main modules in ESIS link information through unique record identifiers. These modules include claim records, inspections, compliance and deterrence tools, operating locations, legal entities, appeals (Ontario Labour Relations Board [OLRB] reviews), hours of work applications, and compliance checks (self-assessments). Analyses in the book rely primarily on information from the claims records, inspections, compliance and deterrence tools, and appeals modules.

*Shortcomings of the Data*

Information is entered into the ESIS by a wide range of MOL personnel (e.g., EROs, ESOs, claims processors, registrars, payment recorders, and OLRB review recorders) and by complainants themselves through the online Claim Form. At times, MOL personnel may update or verify some of the information entered by a complainant during their investigation, which may lead to inconsistency in the information provided in the Claim Form. Moreover, since entering information into the database is secondary to EROs' and ESOs' main job functions, internal consistency and completeness of information is sometimes problematic. We approach our analysis by allowing such inconsistencies to persist, since removing cases with inconsistent information would result in a substantial loss of data, which subsequently reduces the central feature of the ESIS database as a near-complete census of Ontario's employment standards enforcement activities and their outcomes.

Since the ESIS was designed to accommodate a wide range of situations, it also contains many open-text fields, which allow complainants, EROs, and ESOs to provide narratives about the specific situation of each case. Although this format is useful for case management, open-text fields do not lend themselves well to statistical analysis; because of time and resource constraints, the analyses in this book typically do not incorporate any of the detailed information contained in these open-text fields.

Along with the open-text fields, ESIS also appears to have few required-answer or forced-choice fields (a feature that may be in place to maximize flexibility). As a result, some cases have missing information for key fields with little indication for the reason. There are several potential reasons for this missing information: for example, the information sought in the fields concerned may not be applicable to the complaint, the complainant may not know the answer to a question, or the complainant may have skipped a question in error. In the foregoing analyses, cases with missing information are retained but are excluded from reports that incorporate a field that they are missing. In cases where a large proportion of cases are missing information this situation is noted.

### *Analytic Approach*

A key feature of both ESIS and the analyses for the current study is that they are multi-level, relational, and generally organized around many-to-one relationships. For instance, one employer may be linked to multiple complaints; a single complaint may be linked to multiple claims of employment standards violations; a single inspection may be linked to multiple entitlements or incur multiple compliance or deterrence tools. This study relies primarily on three different units of analysis in this relational structure: the complaint or inspection (i.e., the case, used the most often), the claims/violations or entitlements (each complaint/inspection may have more than one claim/violation or entitlement), and the compliance or deterrence tools (such as Orders to Pay or Notices of Contravention [NOCs]), which may be linked to *either* cases (complaints/inspections) or to violations/entitlements.

To facilitate analysis, data from the main ESIS modules were imported from SQL into SPSS, the software program used for the statistical analysis. This process involved merging SQL data tables into flat files for each desired unit of analysis in order to capture the breadth of the available information. Entries that are voided, in progress, suspended, or rescinded were removed before amalgamating the data. Finally, the

SQL tables that designate field labels were used to generate syntax to label the SPSS data files.

All of the analysis in this book relies on the MOL fiscal year, which runs from 1 April to 31 March. Complaints are assigned the fiscal year corresponding to the date when the complaint was received by the MOL, regardless of when the complaint was investigated by an ESO and a decision was rendered. Workplace inspections are assigned in the fiscal year corresponding to the date when the inspection occurred. All other records associated with complaints and inspections, such as claims, deterrence tools, applications for review (appeals) and so on are also *assigned the fiscal year of the complaint or inspection that they are associated with*. As a result, the statistics presented here may not correspond with those published for each fiscal year by the MOL.

Nearly complete information about complaints, inspections, reviews, and use of compliance/deterrence tools is available only for the most recent fiscal years. The chapters in the book use different time periods for different analyses in order to make the best use of the available data. An overarching criterion for the analyses, however, is that information is reported only for fiscal years with a robust collection of data (50 per cent of cases was used as threshold). For example, data on complaints were more complete between 2008/09 and 2014/15, whereas data for workplace inspections were available from 2012/13 to 2015/16. Complaints generally take longer to investigate than inspections, meaning that more recent data on complaints cannot be used, as they are incomplete.

The descriptive outcomes produced in the book's data analyses are the result of substantial data manipulation in order to map the trajectories of each case (i.e., complaint or inspection) through the employment standards enforcement system. Since the data are cross-sectional, it is not possible to make causal inferences, and the preceding analysis should be interpreted with this caveat in mind. The challenges of using the ESIS data in the analyses offered here, as enumerated above, are typical of any research that draws on administrative data. The scope and detail captured by ESIS, however, allows for a rich analysis of employment standards enforcement in Ontario that would not otherwise be possible. We seek to fill in the silences in the administrative data and gain a fuller understanding of employment standards enforcement by using it alongside other types of data and analysis (e.g., detailed qualitative and archival analyses).

### A.2. National Surveys

Some quantitative analyses presented in this book also draw on data from Statistics Canada's Labour Force Survey. The Labour Force Survey is a mandatory, monthly panel survey collected by Statistics Canada on standard labour market indicators, such as employment status, industry, occupation, earnings, and unionization. It also captures a variety of demographic characteristics. The target population for the survey includes those aged fifteen years and over and encompasses individuals drawn from all provinces and territories of Canada. Exclusions include persons living in institutions, on reserves or other Aboriginal settlements, full-time members of the Canadian armed forces, and those in extremely remote areas (estimated to be less than 2 per cent of Canadian population; Statistics Canada 2016b).

Analyses conducted for this book were undertaken using both the public-use microdata files and the confidential data files, accessed through the Statistics Canada Research Data Centre housed at York University and the University of Toronto.

Although specific results are not presented in the book, ongoing analyses drawing on Statistics Canada's Survey of Labour and Income Dynamics (SLID) and its successor, the Canadian Income Survey (CIS), have also informed our understanding of the nature, depth, and effects of exemptions from Ontario's *Employment Standards Act (ESA).*

# Appendix B: Qualitative Data

The qualitative aspect of this project involved interviews with three key groups – workers, MOL officials, and representatives of community legal clinics and workers' centres – each with a perspective that is essential to understanding the dynamics of employment standards enforcement. At the start of each interview, participants in each group were given an informed consent form outlining the nature of the research and conditions of their participation. By signing the form, participants confirmed that they were informed about the nature of the study and agreed to participate at their own free will.

### B.1. Worker Interviews

Between December 2013 and June 2016, we conducted one-on-one semi-structured in-depth interviews with seventy-seven workers in various sectors and geographic regions across Ontario. Interviews were conducted in Sudbury, Toronto, and Windsor. Drawing upon a combination of purposeful sampling techniques to identify information-rich respondents, we screened all worker participants according to their involvement in low-wage work (earning $18/hour or less) and without access to union representation. We excluded respondents who were full-time students or who were clearly self-employed (and not misclassified employees). Additionally, we adopted a stratified form of criterion sampling to ensure that there was sufficient representation of workers who both had and had not filed official complaints. We then attempted to achieve maximum variation in industry, age, gender, migration history, and racial backgrounds.

Participants varied in age, gender, migration history, racial backgrounds, education level, and occupation. Thirty-five women, forty-one men, and one trans woman were interviewed. The research sample included a mix of racialized workers that included First Nations, new and established immigrants, as well as white workers. The results of these interviews are diverse representations of working life in a broad swathe of industries across the province including restaurant, manufacturing, construction, health sector, cleaning, and general manual labour (table B.1).

The interview guide was designed to give participants as much control over the interview process as possible. Yet it also ensured that all interviews covered the same range of questions, themes, and issues. We asked participants to reflect on their work history, experiences with employment standards violations, and responses to those violations (see

Table B.1. Description of Participant Characteristics

| | N |
|---|---|
| Location | |
| Toronto | 42 |
| Sudbury | 19 |
| Windsor | 16 |
| Gender | |
| Woman | 35 |
| Man | 41 |
| Other | 1 |
| Age* | |
| 18–24 | 4 |
| 25–34 | 17 |
| 35–44 | 21 |
| 45–54 | 20 |
| 55– 64 | 8 |
| 65+ | 1 |
| Education level | |
| Less than high school | 10 |
| Completed high school | 16 |
| Completed community college or technical school | 22 |
| Completed bachelor's degree (arts, humanities, science, engineering, etc.) | 22 |
| Completed post-graduate degree (master's, doctoral, or professional) | 1 |
| Other | 6 |
| Types of jobs | |
| Administration | 10 |
| Childcare | 2 |
| Cleaning/maintenance | 5 |
| Construction | 14 |
| Food services | 10 |
| Health care (personal support workers) | 4 |
| Research | 1 |
| Retail | 9 |
| Security | 1 |
| Telemarketing | 8 |

*(Continued)*

Table B.1. (*Continued*)

| | |
|---|---|
| Type of job (*Continued*) | |
| Transportation (taxi drivers, tow truck drivers, transportation of goods) | 5 |
| Warehousing | 8 |
| Immigration status | |
| Visitor's visa | 1 |
| Temporary work visa | 1 |
| Refugee | 2 |
| Landed immigrant/permanent resident | 11 |
| Canadian citizen | 61 |
| No answer | 1 |
| Place of birth | |
| Canada | 43 |
| Outside of Canada | 31 |
| No answer | 3 |

* Six participants did not respond to the question on age.

Worker Interview Guide below). To be able to document the exact nature of the violations that workers experienced, we integrated concept cards – a feminist method that uses visual cues to allow for respondent-driven, yet bounded discussion of employment conditions. During the course of each interview, we placed eighteen cards on the table, each capturing a violation related to the *ESA* (e.g., you were paid less than minimum wage; you were penalized for speaking up about problems at work) (see Worker Interview Concept Cards below). Serving as visual cues, concept cards allowed participants to immediately connect their experiences to our interests and position themselves as knowers without necessarily having knowledge of detailed provisions of the *ESA* (on the rationale for this strategy and its methodological underpinnings, see Mirchandani et al. 2016). Specifically, we asked participants to turn over those cards that did not apply to them and then to select the most notable challenges they faced. Rather than seeking to learn about participants' most recent jobs only, we were interested in events that respondents deemed significant or formative. As a result, we invited participants to select particular violations they wished to discuss through concept cards, and to recount their most notable work experiences, without temporal boundaries.

Participants also completed a post-interview questionnaire, consisting of a series of questions in order to gather employment, socio-economic, and demographic information (e.g., Do/did you have an agreement with your employer about working more than forty-eight hours a week? What is the highest level of education you have completed?) (see Post-Interview Job Questionnaire below).

Participants were recruited through workers' centres and legal clinics in three different cities in Ontario, each characterized by a different industrial and socio-demographic landscape. Recruitment posters in five different languages (Chinese, English, French, Spanish, and Tamil) were created and displayed as a means of recruitment. Interviews were conducted in English with seventy-six participants and in Chinese with one participant with a translator. They were held in public places (e.g., coffee shops, libraries, and malls) as well as at community centres, workers' centres, and legal clinics and lasted between one and two hours. All interviews were transcribed verbatim and analysed using Dedoose, a web-based qualitative data analysis software application, to develop codes, themes, and conceptual constructs. The interview quotes in the analysis reflect the actual transcript as closely as possible. To protect participant confidentiality, no personal identifiers are used.

### *B.1.1. Worker Interview Guide*

#### I. OPENING QUESTIONS AND PREAMBLE

We are interested in understanding what jobs are like today. We want to learn about what protections workers have in terms of basic rights at work and what happens when problems arise. Please remember that you can end the interview without penalty at any time or decline to answer any specific questions which are making you uncomfortable. We also want to assure you that everything you say to us will be kept strictly confidential. Neither your employer nor anyone else outside the research team will know about your participation, and all information that you provide will be protected, stored, and presented in ways which protect your identity.

The interview should take about 60–90 minutes. Please feel free to ask any questions as we go along. Do you have any questions before we start?

#### II. WORK/MIGRATION HISTORIES

1 Can you tell us about some of the jobs that you have had in the past few years?
   a *Probe for multiple jobs, non-standard jobs, temporary work, misclassification as independent contractor, supervisory responsibilities.*
2 How did you get into this kind of work?
   a *Probe for how background (e.g., education/migration) relates to the jobs held.*
3 Could you tell us about the problems you have faced in these jobs?

III. SPECIFIC VIOLATIONS

*Place the cards in front of the interviewee. Note: for the purposes of the audio recording, the interviewer will need to repeat orally the cards that the interviewee has removed throughout this section.*

Now we want to talk about problems you may have had at work. Please look at the following cards. I'd like you to take a few minutes and think about whether you have experienced any of these things in your work.

1 Please remove any card that you have never experienced. *Pause and give the interviewee time to consider the cards and to remove any that they have not experienced.*
2 Out of the remaining cards, which is the one you remember best?
3 Which one posed the biggest problem for you?
4 Have these also occurred in other workplaces where you have been employed?

*Talk about* each *problem displayed in each card, probing for details on the context of the violation. For example:*

1 What happened exactly and when did it happen?
2 Did others at your workplace experience this?
3 Has this happened before in other workplaces?
4 Does your employer operate at more than one location?
5 Can you describe your workplace?
6 Can you describe the make-up of your employer's workforce (age, gender, ethnicity, language)?
7 Did you talk to anyone about it? Who?
8 Did you seek advice from anyone about what you could do about the problem? Who?
   a Did your family or friends support you? How?
   b Did you go to a clinic, church, or community group? How did they help you?
9 In the end, what, if anything, did you do about it?
10 Did you know you could file a complaint for your rights at the Ministry of Labour? *(You may have to explain what filing a claim means.)*
11 Did you consider making a complaint?
   a *Ask those who considered launching a complaint*: Did you end up launching a complaint?
      i Ask those who did not launch a complaint
         – What, if anything, did you do about it?
         – Why did you do this?
         – Did you consider other actions?

- Why did you decide to proceed in the way you did?
- What factors did you consider?
- Did you feel you were taking a risk?

ii Ask those who did launch a complaint
- Can you explain the process you followed?
- Why did you do this?
- Did you consider other actions?
- Why did you decide to proceed in the way you did?
- What factors did you consider?
- Did you feel you were taking a risk?

12 What was the outcome of your actions?
13 Overall, can you explain how this experience has impacted you?
14 Overall, can you explain how this experience has impacted (a) your family, (b) your co-workers, (c) your finances, (d) your loved ones/friends, (e) your community, and (f) your relationships at work?

IV. ANALYSIS ACROSS VIOLATIONS

1 How does this job compare to your other jobs?
2 What allowed you to do something in one case but not in another?
3 Were other people also facing the same issues? What did they do? Did you/they turn to anyone for help?

V. GENERAL EXPERIENCES

1 Where do you see yourself in ten years?
2 What advice would you give to a young person just starting out as a worker (in your line of work/in general)?
3 What advice would you give to government about problems you've experienced at work? (or employers)?
4 What things should be done to make employers follow the law?
5 What things should be done to help workers when they don't get their basic rights at work?

VI. WRAPPING UP

1 Is there anything else you want to say about the issues we've been talking about?

### *B.1.2. Worker Interview Concept Cards*

Your employer owed you money.
You were working more hours than you wanted to.
You did not get your vacation days or vacation pay.

You did not get days off when you were sick.
You did not get paid while you were being trained for your job.
You were asked to pay fees to get your job.
You were not paid overtime premium pay after forty-four hours of work.
You were paid less than minimum wage.
You did not get public holiday pay.
You experienced insulting, threatening, or offensive remarks at work.
You were unfairly fired.
Your boss told you that you were self-employed or an independent contractor.
You were exposed to workplace hazards.
You did not get paid for all the hours you worked.
Money was taken off your wages for things like tools, equipment, cash shortages, or other reasons.
You did not get a record of your hours worked and deductions (like EI and CPP) with your pay.
You were penalized for speaking up about problems at work.
You have contacted or considered contacting the Ministry of Labour or any other place about your problems at work.

### *B.1.3. Post-Interview Job Questionnaire*

For this survey, we would like you to answer thinking about the job that you talked about the most during the interview today.

1 What was the main type of work you do/did in the job that you are thinking about?

______________________________________________

2 Is/was that job:
[ ] Permanent
[ ] *Not* permanent? → if so
  [ ] Seasonal job
  [ ] Temporary or contract job (non-seasonal)
  [ ] Casual job
  [ ] Work done through a temporary help agency
  [ ] Other, explain: ____________________

3 In that job, are/were you a member of a union, or covered by a union collective agreement?
[ ] Yes
[ ] No

4 About how many people are/were employed at the location where you do/did that job? __________

Does/did the employer have more than one location?

[ ] Yes – if so →

In total, about how many people are/were employed at all locations?

[ ] No

5 Which of the following statements best reflect your work in that job?

[ ] The hours change(d), depending on the season.

[ ] You only work(ed) in this job some seasons of the year and you get laid off for the rest.

[ ] You generally work(ed) the same hours all year round.

6 What was/is the start and end date of this job?

Month _________ Year_________ to Month _________ Year_________

7 Are/were you responsible for managing or supervising one or more other workers in that job?

[ ] Yes

[ ] No

8 Which of the following best describes the hours you usually work(ed) at this job?

[ ] Regular daytime schedule or shift

[ ] Regular evening shift (hours mostly before midnight)

[ ] Regular night shift (hours mostly after midnight)

[ ] Other, please explain:

9 In a typical week, how many hours do/did you usually work?

Mon Tues Wed Thurs Fri Sat Sun

Total weekly hours __________

10 How often are/were you expected to start working at your job before you are/were scheduled to begin *or* keep working after your shift is over? (*Note if the worker doesn't know*)

[ ] Most of the time

[ ] Some of the time

[ ] Only a few times

[ ] Never

[ ] Don't have a scheduled start time

On the days when this happened, how many minutes or hours extra do/did you generally have to work?__________________________

______________________________________________________

Do/did you get paid for the extra time that you worked?

[ ] Yes

[ ] No

Do/did you get extra time off because you worked extra, such as by taking longer breaks, or being able start late or leave early on another day?
[ ] Yes
[ ] No

Do/did you get something else to make up for the extra time that you worked?
[ ] Yes
[ ] No

11 Do/did you have an agreement with your employer about working more than forty-eight hours a week?
[ ] Yes – if so → Is/was your agreement
  [ ] in writing
  [ ] verbal
[ ] No
[ ] Not applicable

12 What best describes the way that you are/were paid in that job?
[ ] By the hour
[ ] By the piece
[ ] By the job or contract
[ ] On a salary
[ ] In some other way? If so, how? ______________________

13 Do/did you usually receive tips or commissions?
[ ] Yes
[ ] No

14 On average, how much do/did you usually earn in that job, including any tips/commissions (i.e., $10/hour, $400/week) ______
______________________________________________

15 In that job, are/were you ever:
[ ] *Not* paid when you expected to be paid? – if so →
  How often does/did this happen?
  [ ] Regularly
  [ ] Sometimes
  [ ] Rarely
[ ] Paid less than the full amount that you – if so →
  How often does/did this happen?
  [ ] Regularly
  [ ] Sometimes
  [ ] Rarely earned in a pay period?
[ ] Or, neither of these things ever happened

**Please tell us a bit more about yourself**

16 In what year were you born? __________

17 What is your gender?
[ ] Male
[ ] Female
[ ] Other: ____________

18 What is the highest level of education you have completed?
[ ] Less than high school
[ ] Completed high school
[ ] Completed community college or technical school
[ ] Completed Bachelor's Degree (Arts, Humanities, Science, Engineering, etc.)
[ ] Completed post-graduate degree (Masters, Doctoral, or Professional): MA, MSc, MSW, LLB, MD, PhD
[ ] Other. Please describe: ______________________________________

19 Was your highest level of education completed:
[ ] In Canada?
[ ] Outside of Canada?

20 Including yourself, how many adults sixteen years of age or older live in your household? __________________________
How many are working for pay full- or part-time? ______________

21 How many children *under* the age of sixteen live in your household?
____________

22 In the past year, did you give regular help in the form of either money or food to a person you know who was *not* living in your household?
[ ] Yes – if so →
Are any of the people who you help under the age of 16?
[ ] Yes [ ] No
Do any of the people you help live outside of Canada?
[ ] Yes [ ] No
[ ] No

23 Were you born in Canada?
[ ] Yes
[ ] No

24 What is your current immigration status in Canada?
[ ] No official status
[ ] Visitor's visa
[ ] Student visa

[ ] Temporary work visa
[ ] Refugee
[ ] Humanitarian and compassionate grounds
[ ] Landed immigrant/permanent resident
[ ] Canadian citizen
[ ] Other. Please explain: ______________________________

25 How many different jobs do you currently have? _________

26 How much employment income did you earn in the year ending December 31, 2013?
Please include income *from all sources* such as savings, pensions, rent, as well as wages.
[ ] Less than $20,000
[ ] Between $20,000 and $29,999
[ ] Between $30,000 and $39,999
[ ] Between $40,000 and $59,999
[ ] Between $60,000 and $79,999
[ ] Between $80,000 and $99,999
[ ] $100,000 or more

27 How much income did *you* and *other members* of your household earn in the year ending 31 December 2013? Please include income *from all sources*, such as savings, pensions, rent, as well as wages.
[ ] Less than $20,000
[ ] Between $20,000 and $29,999
[ ] Between $30,000 and $39,999
[ ] Between $40,000 and $59,999
[ ] Between $60,000 and $79,999
[ ] Between $80,000 and $99,999
[ ] Between $100,000 and $120,000
[ ] $120,000 or more

28 What is your postal code? ___________________________________

## B.2. MOL Interviews

We conducted eighty-one structured interviews with a range of MOL officials between 2015 and 2018. Of these interviews, we conducted fifty-two with EROs/ESOs, fifteen with employment standards regional and district managers, six with regional program coordinators, two with provincial specialists, and six with policy advisors. In conducting these interviews, we used six different sets of interview guides, one for each group of respondents. Broadly speaking, the interview guides touched on various issues, including the employment standards complaints system, workplace inspections, and central challenges facing the enforcement activities of the MOL (see MOL Interview Guides below). We developed the interview guide collaboratively with MOL officials, based on the research agreement described above. The unions representing the MOL officials (i.e., Association of Management, Administrative and Professional Crown Employees of Ontario for the Managers, Regional Program Coordinators, Provincial Specialists, and Policy Advisors, and Ontario Public Service Employees Union for the EROs/ESOs) also approved these interviews and, like the MOL, participated as institutional partners.

The interviews were conducted across the province, normally at MOL offices, and lasted between forty-five and ninety minutes. As with the worker interviews, the MOL interviews were transcribed verbatim and analysed with Dedoose web-based qualitative data analysis software to develop codes, themes, and conceptual constructs. Quotations drawn from interviews in the preceding chapters aim to be verbatim, that is, they reflect the actual transcript as closely as possible. To protect participant confidentiality, no personal identifiers are used.

### *B.2.1. Interview Guide: Employment Standards Officer I (ESO1)*[1]

Our aims:

- To learn from the expertise of ESOs about the policies, goals, and principles guiding their decision-making process.
- To understand how ESOs make decisions.

#### I. OPENING QUESTIONS AND PREAMBLE

Our research focuses on how the investigation process operates in Ontario with a view to documenting best practices. Your answers will be kept confidential and we are not asking for any identifying details, although we may ask you to use specific cases as reference points.

#### II. ESO1 WORK AND ROLE

a What is your current position?
b As an ESO1, what training did you receive initially and what training do you receive on an ongoing basis?
c As an ESO1, how would you describe the employment standards system to someone unfamiliar with employment law?
d As an ESO1, what are your main duties and responsibilities?

#### III. CLAIMS TRIAGE

a As an ESO1, what are the goals/principles that guide you during the claims [i.e., complaints][2] process?

b As an ESO1, what is the step by step process that you follow when processing a claim [i.e., complaint]?
c In your experience as an ESO1, are there any problems that you encounter more often than others when processing a claim [i.e., complaint]?
d In your experience doing claims [i.e., complaints] processing, are certain claims [in a complaint] more difficult to process than others? Are certain claims [in a complaint] easier to process than others?
e What kinds of information tend to be missing from a claim [i.e., complaint]? As an ESO1, what do you do to obtain missing information?
f As an ESO1, what is the step by step process that you follow when investigating claims [in a complaint] during the Early Resolution process?
g What is your role as an ESO1 in the settlements process?
h As an ESO1, are certain kinds of claims [in a complaint] more difficult than others to investigate? Are certain claims [in a complaint] easier?
i What makes it easier for you as an ESO1 to resolve a claim [i.e., complaint] during the Early Resolution process?
j As an ESO1, what would prompt you to escalate the claim [i.e., complaint] to an ESO2?
k In your experience as an ESO1, what are the most common challenges that you have observed employees encounter in the claims [i.e., complaint] process?
l In your experience as an ESO1, what are the most common challenges that you have observed employers encounter in the claims [i.e., complaint] process?

IV. REFLECTIONS

a As an ESO1, what improvements have you observed in the enforcement of the *ESA*?
b Are there any changes you would recommend as an ESO1 to improve compliance?
c How is your success as an ESO1 currently being measured?

*B.2.2. Interview Guide: Employment Standards Officer II (ESO2)*[3]

Our aims:

- To learn from the expertise of ESOs about the policies, goals, and principles guiding their decision-making process.
- To understand how ESOs make decisions.

I. OPENING QUESTIONS AND PREAMBLE

Our research focuses on how the investigation process operates in Ontario with a view to documenting best practices. Your answers will be kept confidential and we are not asking for any identifying details, although we may ask you to use specific cases as reference points.

II. ESO II WORK AND ROLE

a What is your current position?
b As an ESO2, what training did you receive initially and what training do you receive on an ongoing basis?
c As an ESO2, how would you describe the employment standards system to someone unfamiliar with employment law?
d As an ESO2, what are your main duties and responsibilities?

III. CLAIMS INVESTIGATION

a As an ESO2, what is the step by step process that you follow when investigating a claim [i.e., complaint]?
b To help us understand the process of claims investigation, could you please think of an investigation you did recently that is typical of most investigations. We are not looking for names or any confidential details.
  - Could you describe the basic facts of the claim [in a complaint]?
  - What type of evidence did you consider? How did you get this evidence?
  - What goals/principles guided you?
  - What is your role in the settlements process?
  - Did you use compliance orders, contravention notices, and Part I/Part III prosecutions? How did they work?
  - What was the outcome of this case [i.e., complaint]?
c What are the most common kinds of complaints you encounter? Have complaints changed over time?
d In your experience as an ESO2, what are the biggest barriers to improving compliance in workplaces?
e In your experience as an ESO2, what challenges have you observed that employees encounter in the claims [i.e., complaints] process? Do the challenges that employees face create obstacles to the resolution of claims [i.e., complaints]? If so, how do you address those obstacles?
f In your experience as an ESO2, what challenges have you observed that employers encounter in the claims [i.e., complaints] process?

Do the challenges that employers face create obstacles to the resolution of claims [i.e., complaints]? If so, how do you address those obstacles?

g As an ESO2, are certain kinds of claims [in a complaint] more difficult than others to investigate? Are certain claims [in a complaint] easier to investigate?

h In your experience as an ESO2, what is most effective at deterring employers from violating the ESA?

IV. QUESTIONS FOR ESO2s INVOLVED IN PROACTIVE INSPECTIONS

a Have you ever done a proactive inspection?
*If so, discuss questions in IV. If not, proceed to V.*

- How long have you been doing proactive inspections (or if not current, when did you do proactive inspections and how long were you doing them)?
- In your experience as an ESO2, how many inspections do (did) you do on average in a month or a year?
- What is the process for determining if an employer will be proactively inspected?
- As an ESO2, what is the step by step process that you engage in when conducting a proactive [i.e., workplace] inspection?
- As an ESO2, how do you proceed when you determine that the employer has contravened a monetary standard? How do you proceed when an employer has contravened a non-monetary standard?
- Once an inspection is completed, what are your follow-up procedures?
- In your experience doing proactive [i.e., workplace] inspections, are there contraventions that you observe more often than others? Less often?
- In your experience, what are the main challenges or difficulties that you face when conducting inspections? How do you overcome these difficulties?
- In your experience doing inspections, are certain inspections more difficult to carry out than others? How do you overcome these difficulties? Are certain inspections easier to carry out than others?
- Based on your observations, have proactive [i.e., workplace] inspections yielded sustained changes in employer knowledge, attitudes, or practices with respect to compliance with employment standards? Have there been any other compliance benefits?
- Have you observed any barriers to improving compliance through proactive [i.e., workplace] inspections in the workplace(s) visited?

- In your experience doing inspections, what is the most effective method of deterring employers from violating the *ESA*?

V. REFLECTIONS

a As an ESO2, what improvements have you observed in the enforcement of the *ESA*?
b Are there any changes you would recommend as an ESO2, to improve compliance or the effectiveness of the enforcement process?
c How is your success as an ESO2 currently being measured?

### *B.2.3. Interview Guide: Employment Standards Program/District Managers*

Our aims:

- To document what Program/District Managers do (i.e., their roles).
- To identify what policies, goals, and principles guide manager actions and roles.

I. OPENING QUESTIONS AND PREAMBLE

Our research focuses on how the complaints process and enforcement operates in Ontario with a view to documenting best practices. Your answers will be kept confidential and we are not asking for any identifying details, although we may ask you to use specific cases as reference points.

II. MANAGER WORK AND ROLE

a What is your current position? How long have you been working in your current position?
b What are the core goals and principles underlying ES administration and enforcement policy in Ontario?
c As a District/Program Manager, what are your main duties and responsibilities?

III. CLAIMS PROCESS

a In what situations do you get directly involved with claims [i.e., complaints]?
  - Why is your involvement required?
  - What is your role in the claim [i.e., complaint]?
b In what situations do you get directly involved with inspections?
  - Why is your involvement required?
  - What is your role in the inspection?
c What are the most common kinds of claims [in a complaint] you are involved in? Has this changed over time?

d In your experience as a District/Program Manager, what challenges have you observed that *employees* encounter in the claims [i.e., complaints] process?
  - Do the challenges that employees face create obstacles to the resolution of claims [i.e., complaints]?
    i If so, how are those obstacles addressed?

e In your experience as a District/Program Manager, what challenges have you observed that *employers* encounter in the claims [i.e., complaints] process?
  - Do the challenges that employers face create obstacles to the resolution of claims [i.e., complaints]?
    i If so, how are those obstacles addressed?

f In your experience as a District/Program Manager, have you experienced challenges with managing the claims [i.e., complaints] and inspection caseloads?

g In your experience as a Program/District Manager, what effect has the dedicated enforcement team had on the overall enforcement and compliance strategy?

IV. REFLECTIONS

a As a Program/District Manager, what major changes have you observed in the enforcement of the *ESA* (i.e. enforcement policies, procedures, and practices)?

b Are there any changes you would recommend as a Program/District Manager to improve compliance or the effectiveness of the enforcement process?

c In your role as a Program/District Manager, what criteria do you use to measure the success of your staff?

*B.2.4. Interview Guide: Employment Standards Regional Program Coordinator*

Our aims:

- To document what Regional Program Coordinators do (i.e., their roles and activities).
- To identify what policies, goals, and principles guide the Regional Program Coordinators' actions and roles.

I. OPENING QUESTIONS AND PREAMBLE

Our research focuses on how the complaints process and enforcement operates in Ontario with a view to documenting best practices. Your answers will be kept confidential and we are not asking for any identifying details, although we may ask you to use specific cases as reference points.

II. POSITION AND ROLE

a What is your current position? How long have you been working in your current position?
b What are the core goals and principles underlying ES administration and enforcement policy in Ontario?
c What are your main duties and responsibilities as a Regional Program Coordinator?
d What is your role in terms of enforcement policy review, implementation, and assessment?

III. ROLE WITHIN CLAIMS AND INSPECTIONS

a In what situations did you get directly involved with in a claim [i.e., complaint]?
  - Why is your involvement required?
  - What is your role in the claim [i.e., complaint]?
  - When and why is your involvement required?
  - Can you provide examples of cases or issues to illustrate your role?
b In what situations did you get directly involved with in inspection?
  - Why is your involvement required?
  - What is your role in the inspection?
c In your experience, what are the main kinds of inspections or claims [in complaints] that you encounter in this Region? Have they changed over time?
d In your experience as a Regional Program Coordinator, what type of advice or support do you provide to managers and/or ESOs?
e In your experience as a Regional Program Coordinator, what challenges have you observed that employees encounter in the claims [i.e., complaints] process?
  - Do the challenges that employees face create obstacles to the resolution of claims [i.e., complaints]?
    i If so, how are those obstacles addressed?
f In your experience as a Regional Program Coordinator, what challenges have you observed that employers encounter in the claims [i.e., complaints] process?
  - Do the challenges that employers face create obstacles to the resolution of claims [i.e., complaints]?
    i If so, how are those obstacles addressed?

g In your experience as a Regional Program Coordinator, what effect has the dedicated enforcement team had on the overall enforcement and compliance strategy?

IV. REFLECTIONS

a As a Regional Program Coordinator, what major changes have you observed in the enforcement of the *ESA* (i.e., enforcement policies, procedures, and practices)?
b Are there any changes you would recommend as a Regional Program Coordinator to improve compliance or the effectiveness of the enforcement process?

*B.2.5. Interview Guide: Policy Advisors*

Our aims:

- To document what stakeholders and researchers have identified as employment standards enforcement challenges.
- To identify what could be taken into consideration when developing advice on the legislative ES enforcement and administrative framework.

I. OPENING PREAMBLE

Our research is focused on understanding the development of past and current *ESA* enforcement objectives, policies, and practices. Your answers will be kept confidential. If specific examples or cases are requested during the interview, we remind you that we are not looking for any details which would violate Cabinet confidentiality or identify specific policies or legislation and the individuals or firms involved.

II. WORK AND ROLE

a What is your current position? How long have you worked as a policy advisor in MOL? Could you briefly describe any other related work experience that you'd wish to share?
b What are/were the main responsibilities of your role as a policy advisor in MOL?
c Have/did those responsibilities changed during the time you've been in the position, and if so, how?
d What is your role with respect to the legislative framework for ES enforcement and administration?

e In general, what steps do/did you take when developing your advice for/to government? What sources of information do you utilize to develop your advice to government?
f What are the government's current goals and objectives for employment standards enforcement in Ontario, and how have they changed over time?
g What does the government see as the main contextual challenges facing the Ministry of Labour in enforcing the *ESA* in Ontario today? In your experience, have these contextual challenges changed over time and, if so, how?
h Based on your experience as a policy advisor, what have stakeholders and researchers identified as:
  - The main challenges for workers in obtaining their *ESA* rights, particularly for vulnerable workers in precarious employment,
  - The types of challenges that employers have in complying with the *ESA* and,
  - Reforms or policies have they suggested to address these challenges?
i Based on your experience as a policy advisor, what labour market developments could be taken into consideration in relation to the development of the legislative ES enforcement and administration framework?
j How does the legislative ES enforcement and administration framework take into account regional differences such as different seasonal employment, industry differences, demographic differences, etc.? How could regional differences be considered when developing legislative ES enforcement and administration framework?
k How does the legislative ES enforcement and administration framework take into account demographic changes such as greater numbers of women, immigrants, people of colour ,and an ageing population in the labour force? How could demographic changes be considered when developing the legislative ES enforcement and administration framework?
l How are operational considerations taken into consideration when developing employment policy and legislation?

III. FUTURE DEVELOPMENTS

a With a move towards "evidence-based policy," are there any gaps in the information, research, and data available that would help you as a policy advisor? What innovative methods have you seen to consult and develop policy that could be applied to an employment standards context?

*B.2.6. Interview Guide: Provincial Specialists*

Our aims:

- To document key policy initiatives and challenges.
- To document how MOL staff assess and understand employment standards enforcement challenges.
- To identify the goals, rules, resources, and principles which guide their decisions.

I. OPENING PREAMBLE

Our research is focused on understanding the development of past and current *ESA* enforcement objectives, policies, and practices. Your answers will be kept confidential. If specific examples or cases are requested during the interview, we remind you that we are not looking for any details which would violate cabinet confidentiality or identify specific policies or legislation and the individuals or firms involved.

II. WORK AND ROLE

a What is your current position? How long have you been working in your current position? Could you briefly describe any other related work experience that you wish to share?
b What are the main responsibilities of your current position?
c In what situations did you get directly involved with an ES claim [i.e., complaint]?
  - Why is your involvement required?
  - What is your role in the claim [i.e., complaint]?
  - When and why is your involvement required?
  - Can you provide examples of cases or issues to illustrate your role?
d In what situations did you get directly involved with an ES inspection?
  - Why is your involvement required?
  - What is your role in the inspection?
e In your experience, what are the main kinds of inspections or claims [in complaints] that you encounter? Have they changed over time?
f In your experience as a provincial specialist, what type of advice or support do you provide to managers, Regional Program Coordinators, and/or ESOs?

g Have those responsibilities changed during the time you've been in the position, and if so, how?

h In general, what steps do you take when developing your operational policy? What sources of information do you utilize in developing operational policies?

i What are the government's current goals and objectives for employment standards enforcement in Ontario, and how have they changed over time?

j In your experience, what does the government see as the main contextual challenges facing the Ministry of Labour in enforcing the *ESA* in Ontario today? In your experience, have these contextual challenges changed, and if so, how?

k Based on the knowledge you have gained as a Provincial Specialist (e.g., through reading, research, stakeholder consultations, and other relevant means), what have you heard are the main challenges for workers in obtaining their employment standards rights?

l Based on the knowledge you have gained as a Provincial Specialist (e.g., through research, stakeholder consultations, and other relevant means), what are the types of challenges facing vulnerable workers in precarious employment contexts? What guidelines, educational materials, and operational policies are aimed at addressing these challenges?

m Based on the knowledge you have gained as a Provincial Specialist (e.g., through research, stakeholder consultations, and other relevant means), what are the types of challenges for employers in complying with the *ESA*? What guidelines, educational materials, and operational policies are aimed at addressing these challenges? Which reforms or policies are aimed at addressing these challenges?

n How are demographic changes (e.g., a more diverse workforce, i.e., greater numbers of women, foreign-born workers, visible minorities, and an aging population in the labour force) considered in operational reforms?

o From an operational perspective, what are the challenges with implementing targeted inspections with respect to vulnerable workers and precarious employment? With respect to vulnerable workers and precarious employment, what are the operational challenges with claims [i.e., complaints] investigation?

p What is your understanding of the enforcement tools available to officers, and when can they be employed?

q What advice do you provide to Regional Program Coordinators in the application of enforcement tools?
r What additional enforcement tools would you like to see incorporated into or removed from the *ESA*?

## B.3. Community Representative Interviews

We conducted a focus group and one-on-one semi-structured interviews with ten representatives of community organizations, including workers' centres, legal clinics, and an immigrant-serving organization. The focus group was conducted in 2013 in Toronto, and the individual interviews were conducted in Sudbury ($n$ = 4), Toronto ($n$ = 1), and Windsor ($n$ = 5) between September 2016 and September 2017. The latter involved two separate sets of interview guides: one focused on the enforcement of the *ESA*, and the other on funding available to community organizations (see Community Representatives Interview Guide I and II). The interviews were held at the respondents' workplaces and lasted between one and two hours. They were transcribed verbatim and analysed to develop codes, themes, and conceptual constructs.

The purpose of the focus group and the interviews was to have an in-depth conversation with community representatives about their experiences with workers reliant on the provisions of the *ESA*; their perspectives on the enforcement of the *ESA*; regional differences in challenges faced by workers; and the ways in which a community platform can be created that would be beneficial to the community.

### *B.3.1. Community Representatives Interview Guide – I*

#### ABOUT THE RESEARCH PROJECT

The goals of the research project, Closing the Employment Standards Enforcement Gap, are to document and understand the nature and scope of employment standards violations among low wage workers in Ontario and the associated enforcement and regulatory challenges. The purpose of the research is to develop alternative models of enforcement that may be applied in Ontario, elsewhere in Canada, and internationally. This study is being conducted by a team of researchers from several universities and community partners under the direction of Professor Leah Vosko from York University and Mary Gellatly of Parkdale Legal Services.

INTERVIEW AIMS

- To gain an understanding of the regional characteristics of workplace *ESA* violations and to explore the barriers workers encounter in their attempts to take action against these violations.
- To identify the best way that the researchers could share their findings with the range of agencies and organizations which provide support to workers in their community.

The interview is divided into four parts. First, we would like to know a little bit about you. Second, we would like to ask you some questions on your experiences with workers in Windsor/Sudbury. Third, we would like to get a sense from you, your thoughts on the current *ESA* system. Fourth, we would like your input on how we should move forward with this project in our community.

*Explain confidentiality protocols.* Please remember that you can end the interview without penalty at any time or decline to answer any specific questions that are making you feel uncomfortable. We also want to assure you that everything that you say to us will be kept strictly confidential. Neither your employer nor anyone else outside the research team will know about your participation, and all information that you provide will be protected, stored, and presented in ways which protect your privacy.

The interview should take about 60–90 minutes. Please feel free to ask any questions as we go along. Do you have any questions before we start?

PART I: ABOUT THE INTERVIEW PARTICIPANT

*Work History*

1 Can you tell us a little bit about the work that you/your organization does?
2 What is your role?
3 Can you tell us (generally) about some of the experiences you have had dealing with workers who have experienced *ESA*-related problems at work?
4 What is your role with people who experience *ESA* violations?
5 How did you get involved with this line of work?

PART II: LOCAL EXPERIENCES WITH THE *ESA*/VIOLATIONS OF THE *ESA*

Now we would like to talk in more detail about your experiences working with/helping workers who have filed ES complaints.

We would now like to explore the current level of advocacy and worker representation in the community. For these questions, think about the *ESA* system as a whole, within our community and in a broader provincial context, more than just our community.

1 Could you share a story of a worker whom you helped file a complaint?
2 In terms of the *ESA*, what are some of the issues workers face?
   a Where does the system work?
   b Where does it not work?
   c What are the problems workers face when filing complaints?
   d In what types of jobs, in your opinion, do most of these violations occur?
   e What are the most common actions people take when they face an *ESA* violation?
   f What factors hinder people from recognizing that they are experiencing an ES violation?
3 How does the setup of the complaints process affect outcomes?
4 What is the role of organizations such as yours in the complaints process?
5 What kinds of additional support do workers need most?
6 In recent years, have you seen an increase in workers going through temp agencies to find work? Explain.
   a Why do you think this is?
   b Do you see this as an issue?
   c What changes would you like to see in the *ESA* system?
7 Are you familiar with the *Open for Business Act*? What is the impact of the *Open for Business Act* on workers' ability to find decent work in the community?

PART III: REGIONAL ISSUES (Windsor/Sudbury interviews only)
We are interested in exploring the specific regional differences between Windsor/Sudbury and other cities in Ontario. We would like to you to speak about your experiences of working with workers here in Windsor/Sudbury, and to explore the specific regional context in which you are working.

1 Do you think ES complaints in Sudbury/Windsor are different from those that would occur in larger cities like Toronto? Why or why not?
2 Do you think there are adequate "good" jobs in Sudbury/Windsor?

   a What do you think about the availability of jobs in your community?
   b Is there a fair amount of choice?
3 Do you think there are many workers who are looking for work outside of the community?
   a If so, what type of work are they looking for?
   b Why do you think this is the case?
   c How does it impact on their lives at home?
4 Do you think our community has adequate and accessible public transit?
   a Yes/No, How do you think the availability of public transportation affects workers' ability to find work? To get to and from work?
   b Have workers shared their experiences with you? Can you give us an example?
5 How do the labour market conditions in Windsor/Sudbury differ from other places you may have worked in Ontario?

PART IV: ISSUES AROUND HEALTH AND SAFETY

When workers face harassment, health and safety issues in the workplace, what do you do with those and how do you deal with the claims?

1 What kinds of changes can be made in order to implement these measures?
2 How do you think health and safety issues impact low wage workers on the job? Clarify.
3 Does your office interact with the health and safety administration offices in the community? Please elaborate.

PART V: BRINGING OUR RESEARCH TO THE COMMUNITY (Windsor/Sudbury interviews only)

Finally, we would like to organize a community forum to share some of the findings from our research. We would like to hear from you about what would be most useful for the community (for community partners and/or for workers). We are interested in working with community partners (Sudbury Workers Centre and the Sudbury Legal Clinic) (Windsor Workers' Education Centre and Legal Assistance Windsor) to see how we can create a community platform that would be beneficial to the community.

1 We are thinking of holding a community forum. How do you think we could best exchange information with the community?
   a What kind of community forum would be beneficial?
   b What do you think this should look like?
   c Who would be invited?
   d Who are your community partners?

2 When should we hold it?
3 How can we best attract them to participate?
4 Do you think the forum should aim at mechanisms to streamline the employment standards complaint process (at the policy level)?
   a Would you be willing to help us organize a community forum?

*B.3.2. Community Representatives Interview Guide – II*

ABOUT THE RESEARCH PROJECT

The goals of the research project, Closing the Enforcement Gap, are to document and understand the nature and scope of employment standards violations among low wage workers in Ontario and the associated enforcement and regulatory challenges. The purpose of the research is to develop alternative models of enforcement that may be applied in Ontario, elsewhere in Canada, and internationally. This study is being conducted by a team of researchers from several universities and community partners under the direction of Professor Leah F. Vosko from York University and Mary Gellatly from Parkdale Legal Services.

INTERVIEW AIMS

- To gain an understanding of the funding sources available to community organizations.
- To identify the challenges that community organizations face when securing funding.

The interview should take about an hour. Please feel free to ask any questions as we go along. Do you have any questions before we start?

1 Can you outline the sources that are available for your organization?
2 What was the process that you went through to get back funding?
3 When you apply for project funding, how long do they usually last? What's the time frame?
4 In terms of the process for applying for these grants and how many hours it takes to work and apply for these grants, what could you say about that?
5 Would you say that there is any long-term sustainable funding?

6 Are there any restrictions or conditions to funding? Do you feel that it places restrictions on what you can do as an organization?
7 Do you have any financial support from the trade union movement?
8 Can you tell us about your organization's role in helping workers navigate the enforcement of the *ESA*?
9 Is there anything you would like to add?

# Appendix C: Archival Research

Archival research was undertaken by members of the project's Policy & Archives Working Group at the Archives of Ontario, primarily between 2014 and 2017. The majority of archival materials were government of Ontario records collected from the Archives of Ontario holdings from the Ontario Ministry/Department of Labour (Record Group 7), with additional files from the Small Business Branch and the Red Tape Review Commission (both Record Group 9) and several miscellaneous record groups. Access requests were required in order to review these government records, and access was not granted to all requested files. For those files to which the working group was given access, research agreements covering the working group members were signed with the Archives of Ontario.

Researchers reviewed files from the following record groups (RG):

**Ministry/Department of Labour, Government of Ontario**

- RG 7-1 – Minister of Labour's General Correspondence and Subject Files
- RG 7-12 – Correspondence of the Deputy Minister of Labour
- RG 7-14 – Ministry of Labour Regulations and Legislation
- RG 7-20 – Correspondence of the Executive Assistant to the Deputy Minister of Labour
- RG 7-22 – Correspondence of the Assistant Deputy Minister Regarding Labour Policy and Programs
- RG 7-53 – Correspondence of the Director of the Ontario Labour Relations Board
- RG 7-92 – Correspondence of the Director of the Women's Bureau
- RG 7-105 – Correspondence of the Ontario Manpower Commission
- RG 7-125 – Correspondence of the Director of Standards and Programs Branch
- RG 7-182 – Employment and Labour Policy Files
- RG 7-186 – Minister of Labour's Policy and Program Development Files
- RG 7-210 – Minister and Deputy Minister of Labour's Files in the Policy and Information Coordination Unit
- RG 7-227 – Ministry of Labour Central Regional Director's Files
- RG 7-228 – Ontario Government District Offices Premise and Project Occupational Health and Safety Company Files

**Small Business Branch, Government of Ontario**

- RG 9-124 – Small Business Advocacy Section Policy Development Files
- RG 9-144 – Small Business Advocacy Section Information Files

**Red Tape Review Commission, Government of Ontario**

- RG 9-207 – Original Red Tape Commission Chair's Files
- RG 9-208 – Red Tape Commission Files
- RG 9-224 – Red Tape Reduction Bills Project Files

**Miscellaneous, Government of Ontario**

- RG 3-26 – Premier John P. Robarts General Correspondence
- RG 4-37 – Registrar of Regulations Files
- RG 17-49 – Records of the Director of the Archival Operations Branch

Researchers also reviewed selected files from the Archives of Ontario holdings of the Ontario Federation of Labour fonds (F4180). Access requests were not required in order to review these records.

As outlined in the introduction to this book, researchers digitized archival records relevant to the project. A searchable catalogue of over 900 selected archival materials was prepared, with records organized according to the following themes: Exemptions and Special Rules; Enforcement; Working Time; Wages; Non-Wage Benefits; Termination and Severance; Legislative Review and Amendments – MOL Services/Operations; and Industry and Sector Profile. Individual entries in the catalogue were hyperlinked to a secured database of the digitized archival records to facilitate further research and review. As access to these records was subject to the research agreements with the Archives of Ontario, archival working group members maintained the responsibility for searching, analysing, and summarizing the archival data as needed in the preparation of this work as a whole.

# Glossary

The terms in this glossary fall into two groups: conceptual terms that are critical to understanding employment standards enforcement, and operational terms related to the enforcement of employment standards in Ontario and, where they are central to understanding the views from elsewhere, related to chapters addressing the Quebec, Britain, U.S., and Australian cases.

**Adjudication**; Employment standards claims are evaluated and resolved by adjudication. In Ontario, adjudication begins when a worker (the complainant) lodges a complaint. A claims processor will verify the information and determine if it falls under the jurisdiction of the *ESA*. If it is under the jurisdiction of the Act, the complaint is investigated by an ESO. The parties can settle at any point during the adjudication, and there are tools available to ESOs to enforce compliance if the employer does not voluntarily comply, such as Orders to Pay Wages, tickets, and NOCs.

***Administrative Manual for Employment Standards (AMES)***; The *AMES* is published by Ontario's MOL and provides a consistent set of procedures that must be followed when enforcing the *ESA*.

**Advance notice (workplace inspections)**; Advance notice is notification given to employers by the MOL that a workplace inspection is to take place. The *AMES* does not require that advance notice be given to employers, but indicates that it should be, unless there are merit-worthy reasons not to provide it. The main rationale for advance notice is that it gives the employer time to organize their records. However, it may make inspections less effective, as it allows employers to alter records and/or shape which employees are interviewed as part of the inspection (i.e., by choosing who is and is not at work on the day of the inspection). Other branches of government, such as the MOL's Health and Safety branch, do not give advance notice.

**Anonymous tips/reports**; Anonymous tips/reports refer to information provided to the government on workplace violations by anonymous individuals. Ontario does not allow anonymous reporting; all violations are identified through complaints lodged by workers or through workplace inspections. However, anonymous complaints are permitted in other jurisdictions; indeed, the FWO's Anonymous Report tool in Australia, available in sixteen languages, has identified workplace violations, particularly in high-risk sectors (e.g., hospitality).

**Audit**; An audit is a thorough investigation or evaluation. There are three different types of audits in employment standards enforcement in Ontario.

- **Test audit:** In a workplace inspection, a test audit is the initial review of an employer's records to determine if they are in compliance with the *ESA*. Advance notice of a test audit is usually given.
- **Self-audit:** A widely utilized tool, a self-audit is a self-assessment undertaken by the employer usually covering a period of six months. Typically, self-audits are conducted alongside **test audits** and find monetary contraventions of the *ESA*. Self-audits are a form of "monitored self-regulation" in which employers evaluate their compliance with the Act.
- **Full audit:** A full audit is a full investigation/examination of an employer's records. Typically, full audits are undertaken where a **self-audit** is not agreed to or is not completed; where the employer has repeated violations; or where the ESO has all the records and prefers to do a full audit. Fewer than 5 per cent of all inspections involve a full audit.

In Australia, another type of audit used:

- **Desk-based audit**: A form of audit conducted off-site rather than on the employer's premises.

**Balanced Scorecard**; The Balanced Scorecard was implemented in 2013 to evaluate the performance of employees of Ontario's MOL. For ESOs, it replaced a simple quota-based system (number of cases closed annually) with a system that assigned points to various tasks undertaken by ESOs. Its goal was to encourage rapid claims processing, while also recognizing the need for greater flexibility in performance evaluation. However, the scorecard still shaped claims processing in ways that sought to hasten processing; for example, points were allocated to closing cases within a certain period, without regard to their complexity.

**Claims processor**; In Ontario, when a worker files a complaint with the MOL, a claims processor determines if the claim is under the jurisdiction of the *ESA*. If so, the claims processor forwards the claim for further investigation, normally by an ERO.

**Collection**; Collection, in the context of Ontario's employment standards enforcement, is the process of collecting money owed by employers to workers in substantiated violations that yield entitlements. If an Order to Pay Wages is left unpaid by employers, it is usually turned over to collections. In 1996 the MOL contracted out collections to private collections agencies, but recovery rates did not improve. In 2014 collections were transferred back to the public service (the Ministry of Finance).

**Collective agreement decrees (Quebec)**; The *Collective Agreement Decrees Act* (1934) enables the provincial government to extend some provisions of a collective agreement to workers and employers in a particular location or sector who were not original parties to the agreement. Employers or workers may apply to the minister of labour for the extension of key provisions of a collective agreement to non-unionized firms in the same sector.

**Command and control regulation**; The traditional form of public regulation characterized by the imposition of standards and requirements by a public regulatory agency, backed by the threat of legal sanction.

**Community organizations**; Organizations that are formed by an independent group of individuals at the community level to address social problems and bring about desired improvements in a given area. Workers' centres, community legal clinics, and immigrant-serving organizations are examples of community organizations (see especially chapters 1 and 7).

**Complainant**; A complainant is an individual who submits a complaint to Ontario's MOL that details employer violations of the *ESA*.

**Complaints**; Made normally by aggrieved individual employees, complaints detail alleged violations of the *ESA*. Complaints may include one or more claims (i.e., enumerate one or more alleged violations of the Act).

- **Worker complaints:** Complaints submitted by individual workers.
- **Third-party complaints:** Complaints submitted by an individual or body other than the aggrieved person, such as community organizations. Such complaints are not permitted in Ontario but are allowed in other jurisdictions, such as Australia.
- **Anonymous complaints:** Complaints that are submitted anonymously. Anonymous complaints are not permitted in Ontario but are permitted in some other jurisdictions, such as Quebec.
- **Confidential complaints:** Complaints submitted by an individual or body whose identity the MOL attempts to keep unknown to the broader public.
- **Assessed complaints:** Assessed complaints have been adjudicated by Ontario's MOL with a final outcome of voluntary compliance, compliance ordered, or denial.

- **Non-assessed complaints:** Non-assessed complaints have not been adjudicated by the MOL. The final outcome is the decision of the complainant, being either withdrawal or settlement.
- **Withdrawn complaints:** Complaints that are withdrawn by the complainant, rather than kept open and resulting in a settlement or judgment. The rate of withdrawn complaints may indicate complainants' frustration at the slow process, among other factors.

**Compliance checks**; Compliance checks are self-assessments performed by employers to see if they are complying with the *ESA*.

**Compliance measures**; Compliance measures are tools available to ensure compliance within legislation.

- **Order to Pay Wages:** An Order to Pay Wages is a directive from Ontario's MOL to an employer to pay the wages that are owed a complainant. Orders to Pay Wages result from an investigation into *ESA* violations by the MOL.
- **Director's Order to Pay Wages:** An Order to Pay Wages directed at a director to pay the wages that are owed a complainant.
- **Related employer Order to Pay Wages:** An Order to Pay Wages directed to a related employer to pay the wages that are owed a complainant.

**Compliance orientation**; An enforcement orientation premised on the idea that compliance with the law can be achieved through **soft-law** mechanisms rather than **hard-law** sanctions.

**Compliance partnerships (Australia)**; In Australia, compliance partnerships are established between the FWO and businesses that want to publicly demonstrate their commitment to creating compliant workplaces. Such relationships are formalized through **Proactive Compliance Deeds**, signed by both the FWO and the business, that outline steps to be taken to ensure businesses' compliance with workplace laws.

**Dedicated enforcement team**; The dedicated enforcement team was established by Ontario's MOL in the early 2000s and was responsible primarily for conducting workplace inspections, particularly targeted blitzes of industries and workplaces in which employment standards violations are endemic. It contributed to an increase in the number of workplace inspections conducted. Other jurisdictions have similar institutions; for example, Quebec's special investigation team carries out proactive investigations, particularly among temporary help agencies.

**Deterrence effect**; In the context of employment standards enforcement, "deterrence effect" is the presumption that certain measures will prevent violations in the first instance (see **deterrence measures**).

**Deterrence measures**; Deterrence measures are tools available to punish employers for violating the law. Such punishments should be strong enough to deter employers from violating the law (or to foster compliance with the law). In Ontario, such tools include **tickets, NOCs**, and **Part III prosecutions** (see also **deterrence effect**).

- **Notices of Contravention (NOCs):** Notices of Contravention are among the deterrence measures available to ESOs in Ontario. Created in 2000, they can be applied to any violation of the *ESA*. For a first offence, as of 2019, an NOC is $350, in addition to $75 victim surcharge, a small monetary penalty for employers. Fines, however, increase for a second, third, and subsequent offence.
- **Part I tickets under the *Provincial Offences Act*:** Part I tickets – or "tickets" as used in this book – are a deterrence measure available to ESOs in Ontario. They were created in 2004 and can be issued for specific *ESA* violations (unlike NOCs, which can be applied to any violation of the *ESA*). Tickets are $295, in addition to a victim surcharge of $75, as of 2019. Tickets are used relatively rarely, limiting their deterrence effect.
- **Part III prosecutions under the *Provincial Offences Act:*** Part III prosecutions are another deterrence measure available to ESOs in Ontario. They are available for any violation of the *ESA* and, if convicted, an employer faces fines up to $50,000 (as of 2019) and the possibility of incarceration for up to twelve months. Corporations can be fined up to $100,000 for a first offence and up to $500,000 if they have prior convictions (as of 2019). Part III prosecutions have substantially more serious consequences than NOCs and tickets; however, they are very rarely used. ESOs can only recommend Part III prosecutions. A manager must approve this recommendation, after which the ESO is required to prepare a Crown brief detailing the evidentiary basis for the recommendation. The final decision to prosecute rests with the Legal Services Branch of the MOL.

**Deterrence or enforcement orientation**; Deterrence orientation is the attitude ESOs have towards deterrence. A compliance-oriented ESO is more likely to seek voluntary compliance, whereas an enforcement-oriented ESO is more likely to draw upon deterrence measures such as NOCs and tickets.

**Director of Employment Standards**; The director of Employment Standards refers to the head of the Employment Standards Branch of Ontario's MOL.

**Discretionary powers**; Discretionary powers, in the context of employment standards enforcement, refer to the ability of ESOs to make decisions they deem suitable to the situation and circumstances. While an Informed Judgment Matrix (see chapter 6) is available to guide ESOs when making decisions when confronting a series of common situations, the *AMES* states only that officers *may* refer to it, neither prescribing nor recommending the guidance offered in this matrix as the standard by which all cases should be judged. There is, therefore, considerable room for variations in interpretation and thus the application of policy.

**Employment Standards Information System (ESIS)**; The Ontario MOL's Employment Standards Information System analysed in this book is the primary administrative database for employment standards enforcement activities in Ontario. It was created in 2007 and is used primarily as an information tracking and case management system. The database stores information on employment standards complaints and workplace inspections, documenting processes from assessment to enforcement, as well as outcomes. Eight main modules link information through unique record identifiers: claim records, events/inspections, compliance tools, operating location, legal entities, appeals (OLRB reviews), hours of work applications, and compliance checks (self-assessments).

**Employment Standards policy advisors**; Policy advisors in Ontario's MOL provide policy analysis, advice, and technical expertise to senior management, the deputy minister, and the minister on a broad range of labour and employment issues, as well as consulting with key stakeholders, and negotiating and resolving conflicts to ensure that policy proposals balance competing interests. They also organize, lead, and coordinate cross-cutting project teams of staff from other divisions/branches to plan the development and implementation of policy products.

**Employment Standards program and district manager**; Program managers in Ontario's MOL plan, organize, and direct program activities for the administration and enforcement of MOL legislation and regulations, policies, and programs. They develop strategic and operational frameworks for service optimization; monitor all activities to ensure compliance with government service quality standards; participate in labour/management forums and inter-/intra-ministerial committees; and are the key district or program contact, participating on provincial and regional committees.

**Employment Standards provincial specialist**; Provincial specialists in Ontario's MOL provide interpretive advice to ministry staff and external clients on policy, regulatory practices, and enforcement; develop interpretive guidelines and materials to support the administration of the *ESA*; increase employee and employer awareness of their rights and responsibilities; and liaise with the Ontario Labour Relations Board and Legal Services Branch on applications for review under the *ESA*.

**Employment Standards regional program coordinator**; Regional program coordinators in Ontario's MOL are the primary regional resource in providing advice, guidance, and support to regional staff and stakeholders on the employment standards program and its application, and interpretation and enforcement of employment standards legislation. They also develop and manage the regional quality assurance monitoring system and perform quality program delivery audits.

**Employment standards officer – ESO1/ERO (early resolution officer, new designation in 2018) and ESO2/ESO (new designation in 2018)**; In Ontario, EROs and ESOs are the MOL employees who implement the *ESA* by investigating employment standards complaints and inspecting workplaces. Before 2018, they were called ESO1s and ESO2s. Now they are called EROs and ESOs; this book uses the latter terminology.

ESO1s/EROs carry out the first investigation of complaints after receiving them from claims processors. ESO1s/EROs assess whether or not to substantiate the complaint in whole or in part and, if applicable, determine the amount of money owed to complainants. Following this investigation, they may close the complaint by processing withdrawals, securing voluntary compliance or settlement, or issuing a denial. They also determine if further investigation by an ESO2/ESO is warranted – specifically, in cases involving reprisals, retail business establishments, temporary help agencies, and equal pay for equal work.

The investigations conducted by ESO2s/ESOs involve similar processes but are more extensive, and these officers are responsible for making the final decision. These officers may visit the employer's premises or call a meeting between the complainant and the employer. Unlike their ERO/ESO1 counterparts, ESO2s/ESOs may also conduct proactive inspections.

**Employment status**; The labour force status of a person who is either an employee or a self-employed person. Whether or not a person is an employee or self-employed is central to determining access to labour protection and social benefits (see especially chapter 1).

**Enforceable undertakings (Australia)**; A mechanism used by the FWO to formalize voluntary rectification of breaches after an investigation. An enforceable undertaking is a voluntary, statutory agreement between the FWO and an alleged violator. The violator must admit to the contravention, agree to remedy the contravention in a specific way, and identify the timeframe within which it will be remedied. If the violator fails to comply with the voluntary enforceable undertaking, the FWO may apply to the court for orders against that person. Enforceable undertakings may also contain commitments to improve future compliance, such as staff training, completion of audits, and adaptation of work systems. Furthermore, a public declaration of the contravention and remedial actions must be made.

(Note that enforceable undertakings cannot be entered into with third parties, which are not believed to have contravened, or been involved in contravening, a civil remedy provision. For example, it is difficult (although not impossible) to use enforceable undertakings to bind different companies comprising a national group, subcontractors in supply chains, or companies that make up a franchise.

**Entitlements**; Entitlements are due the complainant when an ESO finds that the *ESA* has been contravened and requires that the contraventions be rectified. They aim to ensure that the aggrieved parties receive the rights and protections to which they are due.

- **Monetary entitlements**: Monetary entitlements are monies owed to a complainant under the *ESA*. They include unpaid wages, public holiday pay, vacation pay, overtime pay, and termination pay.
- **Non-monetary entitlements:** Non-monetary entitlements are primarily entitlements that flow from administrative standards not tied exclusively or directly to remunerative issues (e.g., the absence of a poster depicting workers' rights under the *ESA* in the workplace).

***ESA Policy and Interpretation Manual (PIM)***; The Ontario MOL's *Policy and Interpretation Manual (PIM)* provides a consistent interpretation of the *ESA* (as opposed to the ***AMES***, which provides a consistent set of procedures for implementing the Act).

**Exemptions and special rules**; Shaping protective labour legislation since its inception, exemptions and special rules apply to categories of workers that are either exempted from or not fully covered by the protections of the *ESA*. They were – and are – made to accommodate demands from employers that their operations would be harmed if the general rules were to apply to them. Exemptions were often developed in response to lobbying from employer associations that emphasized the unique aspects of specific occupational groups – for example, the seasonal character of many occupations in agriculture. In 2018 the Ontario government initiated a review of the web of exemptions and special rules that limit the application of the *ESA*'s protections, which began with a review of those applicable to architects, domestic workers, homemakers, IT professionals, managerial and supervisory employees, pharmacists, residential building supervisors, janitors, and caretakers. This review was cancelled shortly after the subsequent Conservative government took power.

**Fact finding**; Fact finding is the establishment of facts during an investigation by an ESO. It principally involves ESOs reaching out to employers or complainants during the investigation process.

**Feminist political economy**; Feminist political economy is a critical, holistic, and praxis-oriented approach to the study of political economy. Its formative insight is the necessary and integral relationship between production for surplus and social reproduction (or the daily and intergenerational maintenance of people), contextualized vis-à-vis domestic and international divisions of labour in a globalized world. Historically, shaped by engagements with socialist feminism(s), feminist political economy has highlighted the gender-blindness of mainstream and critical political economic analyses and their neglect of the way in which racialized sex/gender divisions of labour are productive for capitalist accumulation and are shaped by the state in specific historical conjunctures. Capitalism as a mode of production has come to be studied though this lens as a historically, socially, and politically concrete formation shaped fundamentally by social relations of gender, sexuality, class, race, (dis)ability, and citizenship and the contradictions and tensions they reflect and engender.

**Feminization**; Feminization (of employment norms) is used in this book as a broad concept that entails the erosion of the standard employment relationship and the spread of forms of employment that exhibit qualities of precarious employment associated with "women's work" on the market (see chapter 1).

**Fissured workplace (or fissuring)**; A term coined by Weil (2014) to describe fundamental changes in the organization of employment in the twenty-first century. Fissuring entails an employment relationship that is broken into business units through mechanisms such as subcontracting, franchising, and supply chains, among others.

- **Contracting out:** A term similar to **outsourcing** denoting a practice in which an employer transfers work formerly undertaken by his or her employees to another employer, self-employed person, or intermediary (see especially chapters 1, 4, and 12).
- **Franchising:** An organizational form that combines the decentralized ownership of one or multiple units of the franchise chain at a location with centralized brand-name ownership and provision of operational know-how (see especially chapters 1, 5, 11, and 12).
- **Extended supply chains:** A multi-echelon organizational system in which the lead company integrates and coordinates the operations of different players in a production and delivery chain (see especially chapters 1, 2, 5, and 12).
- **Subcontracting:** An arrangement whereby a contractor assigns some of the obligations of the job to another party, who might be a self-employed person, an employer, or an intermediary (see chapters 2, 4, and 5).

**Form of employment**; Different categories of paid and self-employment (e.g., part-time temporary paid employment and full-time solo self-employment) (see especially chapter 1).

**Hard-law vs soft-law**; **Hard-law** encompasses legal statutes and regulations enforced by the state and backed by sanctions, whereas **soft-law** includes the promotion of norms and practices through instruments such as persuasion and information sharing that are not legally binding. As such, whereas the former are rendered and enforced by the state, the latter are shaped by the market and enforced typically through the actions of firms (see especially chapters 1, 2, 3, and 4; on soft-law in connection with regulatory new governance, see **regulatory new governance** below).

**Informed Judgment Matrix**; The Informed Judgment Matrix is an appendix of *AMES* that ESOs may use to guide claims investigations and workplace inspections. The matrix offers guidance on the enforcement tools available under the *ESA* with respect to the type of violation (e.g., monetary, non-monetary) and the compliance history of the employer (e.g., whether or not there are previous violations).

**Inspectable standards**; Inspectable standards are eleven provisions of the *ESA* investigated during workplace inspections: *ESA* poster requirement, wage statements, unauthorized deductions, record keeping, hours of work, eating periods, overtime pay, minimum wage, and public holidays. These standards are administrative or non-monetary standards, which are dissonant with the substance of the majority of complaints, which involve unpaid wages and termination pay (see also **non-monetary entitlements**).

**Inspectorate**; The inspectorate (or labour inspectorate) is the institution devoted to enforcing and implementing employment standards. In Ontario the inspectorate is the Employment Standards Branch of the MOL and all of its constituent parts.

**Inspectors**; Inspectors are the individuals within the inspectorate (see **inspectorate**) who investigate employment standards. In Ontario, inspectors in the MOL are known as **ESOs**. There are inspectors in the other jurisdictional contexts covered in this book, including Britain, Australia, the United States, and Quebec.

**Jurisdiction**; A legal term used to refer to the right and power to exercise authority over a certain territory or domain.

**Labour Standards, Equity, Occupational Health and Safety Commission (LSEOHSC) (Quebec)**; The LSEOHSC is the government body that regulates employment standards in Quebec, alongside other workplace-related laws. Seeking to be a single administrator for labour services, the LSEOHSC is the product of the merger of three former commissions. It is considered a legal person managed by an Administration Board of fifteen members, including unions and employers' associations. The LSEOHSC is funded by employers and is accountable to the minister.

**Liability**; A legal term that refers to any legal obligation, responsibility, or duty, whether created by law, contract, or tort. Traditionally, the direct employer has owed the duty to comply with the minimum standards and could be held liable for failing to do so. The fissuring of workplaces raises the question of whether or not it is adequate to impose duties on only direct employers narrowly conceived, or whether or not the definition of the employer should be expanded, or other entities be made jointly responsible for the duties imposed on the direct employer.

- **Joint and several liability:** A form of liability that extends beyond the direct employer to all related employers, such as franchisors and subcontractors, and that holds them both jointly and equally liable for violating the minimum standards (see especially chapter 4).
- **Accessorial liability:** A form of joint liability used in Australia denoting the extension of liability for violations to parties that may have a sufficient practical connection to the violations, such as human resource managers and accountants (see especially chapter 9).

**Licence debarment**; The suspension of a business licence triggered, in this instance, normally by violations of employment standards (either violations under investigation or substantiated violations yielding entitlements, depending upon the jurisdiction in which the practice operates).

**Liquidated damages**; Payments made directly to workers equal to the amount of back wages owed to them (in contrast to fines or penalties that are paid to the government), together with damages to compensate workers for those losses sustained in the past. Liquidated damages are available in the United States at the federal level.

**Litigation proceedings (Australia)**; Civil remedy litigation is a punitive sanction used by the FWO against lead firms and franchisers if serious contraventions are substantiated in non-compliance investigations. It is the most visible aspect of the FWO's enforcement activities and the most high-profile form of supply chain intervention by the FWO. More specifically, supply chain litigation and the imposition of civil penalties against lead firms are designed to act as a specific and general deterrent, which aims to encourage the original wrongdoer, as well as others in the relevant industry or geographical region, to address issues of non-compliance with employment standards regulation. Leveraging enforcement litigation against lead firms is often viewed as essential in "fissured" industries where traditional enforcement mechanisms against the putative employer are likely to have limited deterrence effects. The threat of punitive sanctions is also seen as critical to inducing lead firms and franchisors to commit to voluntary initiatives, such as **Enforceable Undertakings** and **Proactive Compliance Deeds.**

**Misclassification**; Misclassification involves incorrectly classifying workers as independent contractors or in other ways that subjects them to exemptions from employment standards. Among other terms adopted outside Canada, employee misclassification is also known as "sham contracting."

**Naming and Shaming**; Naming and shaming publicly identifies employers who violate employment standards. This publicity could involve the enforcement agency making public the names of violators on its website. Naming and shaming occurs in some American states and in Britain.

**New public management**; A public sector administrative paradigm that adopts business management approaches to govern the conduct of public policy, focusing primarily on performance, competitiveness, efficiency, accountability, and achieving results. New public management has resulted in greater use of "performance-based regulation" to evaluate the quality and operational efficiency, and to reduce administrative costs. The **Balanced Scorecard** and key performance indicators are two examples of performance measurement systems adopted in Ontario and Australia by the Ministry of Labour and the Office of the Fair Work Ombudsman, respectively, explored in this book (see especially chapters 4 and 9).

**Normative principles of Employment Standards**; Archival research conducted for this book suggests that the following normative principles underpinned the creation Ontario's *ESA* at its inception.

- **Social minima:** The notion that a minimum level of acceptable conditions of employment should be provided to Ontario workers through employment standards legislation. For example, basic protections in the areas of wages, working time, vacations and leaves, and termination and severance of employment. In this book, we consider social minima to be one of the three basic principles of the *ESA* (in addition to **universality** and **fairness**).
- **Universality:** The idea that all employers (or to the widest extent possible) should be encouraged to comply with the minimum requirements of the *ESA*, thus extending *ESA* protections to as many employees as possible. In this book, we view universality as one of the three basic principles of the *ESA* (in addition to **social minima** and **fairness**).
- **Fairness:** The imperative to address the fundamental power imbalances between employers and employees, particularly those engaged in the most precarious forms of employment. In this book, we take fairness to be one of the three basic principles of the *ESA* (in addition to **social minima** and **universality**).

**Overtime pay**; A premium or supplementary pay rate on top of the normal rate of pay for hours worked in excess of regular work hours, fixed by statute, collective agreement, or employment contract. In Ontario, all employees who are not exempt from overtime provisions under the *ESA* and who work over forty-four hours during a work week must generally be paid at a rate of at least one and one-half times (also known as time-and-a-half) the employee's established hourly wage. Under the *ESA*, hours of work may be averaged over a period of two or more weeks in order to calculate overtime pay entitlements. For example, in a two-week period, employers could schedule overtime hours without compensation at time-and-a-half, provided the total for the period does not exceed eighty-eight hours, even if hours in one week exceeded forty-four. Overtime averaging arrangements must be confirmed through written agreement with the employee (or union representative) and approved by the director of Employment Standards.

**Permit system (excess hours)**; In addition to the exemptions from and special rules under the *ESA*'s working time standards, a system of special permits was developed to enable employers to schedule hours in excess of legislated maximum hours of work. The special permit system was introduced in order to account for occupational and industrial variation in work hours, so that universal standards do not inhibit the operation of certain sectors where long hours are prevalent or where seasonal variation in production requires some flexibility in scheduling. In Ontario, excess hours permits require written consent from affected employees (or union representative) and approval of the director of Employment Standards, and allow employers to schedule weekly hours of work beyond the general limit of forty-eight.

**Personal emergency leave**; Paid time off for employee emergencies (e.g., medical appointments, care of dependents, family issues). As with other *ESA* provisions, some exceptions and special rules apply.

**Precarious employment**; Work for remuneration characterized by dimensions of labour market insecurity such as uncertainty, low income, lack of control over the labour process and limited access to regulatory protection, and shaped by form of employment (see above), social context (e.g., occupation and industry) and social location (e.g., gender, race, ethnicity, immigration status, [dis]ability, age) (see chapter 1).

**Preventive Action Plan (Quebec)**; The Preventive Action Plan was adopted by the LSC in Quebec in 2009. The plan was built on the "preventive activities" side of Quebec's enforcement strategy, which aimed to provide information about employment standards to employers with no records of violations in order to prevent employment standards violations from occurring. The preventive action plan included a three-step approach. *Primary prevention* was focused on distributing information. *Secondary prevention* was focused on reconciliation activities between the employer and employees (e.g., bringing employers and employees together to discuss and settle the issue without a formal enquiry). Finally, *tertiary prevention* included remedial activities (e.g., wage recovery proceedings) on behalf of employees.

**Proactive Compliance Deeds (Australia)**; Voluntary agreements, made publicly available through the FWO's website, that set out promises or commitments to rectify past contraventions, encourage future compliance, and shift some of the monitoring and enforcement burden to powerful corporate entities in their capacity as lead franchisors, parent companies of corporate groups, principal contractors, or recruitment agents. Advanced under the common law rather than the *FWA* and therefore neither constrained nor enabled by statutory provisions, this non-punitive co-operative enforcement tool seeks to encourage firms to make far-reaching commitments to enhance compliance with workplace laws. Such commitments could include engaging an independent and qualified third-party professional to periodically audit a sample of employment records and report these findings to the FWO, implementing workplace training, or donating an agreed sum to a community group or legal centre. The Australian FWO promotes proactive compliance deeds as a way for franchisors, and other reputation-sensitive firms, to protect their brand.

**Proactive enforcement**; A form of enforcement that allocates resources in accordance with established priorities, often involving the identification of particular sectors or groups/types of particular employers where the inspectorate has reasonable grounds to believe that violations are more prevalent and/or that workers are more reluctant to raise complaints (see especially chapters 5 and 10).

**Public holiday pay**; The remuneration employees receive for public or statutory holidays on which they do not work, and/or the premium pay employees may receive that is in addition to their basic rate of earnings if they do work on the public holiday.

**Racialization**; Classification, representation, and signification based on socially constructed racial differences (Mirchandani and Chan 2007; Bonacich, Alimahomed, and Wilson 2008). The focus on racialization moves attention away from conceptualizations based on individual traits to an emphasis on how people are socially *produced* as different. The term also helps demonstrate how racial categories change in different historical periods and under different socio-economic conditions and that they interact with other axes of differentiation (such as [dis]ability, gender, age, class, etc.) to separate people from one another.

**Reactive enforcement**; A form of enforcement that is complaint-driven, in which inspectors respond to complaints as they are received. It is the most dominant approach to employment standards enforcement in Ontario (see especially chapters 1 and 2).

**Regulatory degradation**; A term developed by Tombs and Whyte (2010) to argue that models of enforcement that emphasize compliance over deterrence are unlikely to effectively prevent or remedy employment standards violations and are bound to be shaped by market forces rather than the process of law enforcement as a form of regulatory control (see chapters 1 and 5).

**Regulatory new governance**; A model of regulation emphasizing the need for de-bureaucratized and less adversarial forms of regulation, such as self-regulation and light-touch enforcement, that are sensitive to the competitive realities facing businesses. Regulatory new governance advocates the dispersion of regulatory responsibility among a broader range of actors, including the government, firms, professional associations, and civil society groups, among others.

- **Soft-law:** A form of law founded on free market principles and aimed at reducing the regulatory burden on firms and implementing more flexible and less adversarial modes of regulation and enforcement in an attempt to enhance compliance (see especially chapters 1, 2, and 3; see also **hard-law vs soft-law**).
- **Self-regulation**: A form of regulation that leaves it to private parties to determine their practices, with or without the participation of civil society groups, often based on market signals (see especially chapters 1, 2, and 3).
- **Regulated self-regulation:** A middle ground between two other regulatory approaches: **command and control** regulation and **self-regulation**. Under a model of regulated self-regulation, the government has certain instruments at its disposal to regulate a self-regulatory process when necessary (see chapter 2).
- **Monitored self-regulation:** A term developed by Estlund (2005) to outline a form of **regulated self-regulation** premised on the contention that public authority should be limited to overseeing self-enforcement devised by firms themselves (see chapter 5).
- **Light touch regulation:** A concept, consistent with the key principles of regulatory new governance and new public management, that embraces a shift away from **hard-law** towards **soft-law** mechanisms (see especially chapters 1, 2, 5, and 6).

**Repeat violator**; An employer who has violated/contravened employment standards on one or more occasion.

**Reprisal (adverse action in Australia)**; Retaliation by an employer or person(s) acting on behalf of an employer against an employee who has filed or is in a position to file an employment standards complaint against them. A reprisal may include receiving undesirable assignments and schedules, being subject to harassment from management or co-workers, or being terminated. Vulnerability to reprisal is a central factor in discouraging employees from initiating employment standards complaints. The risk of reprisal is amplified among employees historically disadvantaged in the labour force, such as women and people with temporary or otherwise tenuous citizenship/residency status. Reprisal is known as adverse action in Australia.

**Responsibilization**; A strategy through which the state shifts some of its responsibilities onto individuals, families, communities, and other non-governmental organizations (see chapters 1 and 2).

**Responsive regulation**; A model of regulation developed by Ayres and Braithwaite (1992) that advocates starting with various forms of persuasion and compliance measures to gain compliance, escalating to more coercive and deterrent measures if persuasion fails. The most distinctive characteristic of responsive regulation is its "enforcement pyramid," with compliance at the bottom and deterrence at the apex. Responsive regulation is premised on the assumptions that compliance will be effective most of the time, because non-compliance is primarily exceptional and deterrence measures will be required only in limited circumstances to deal with the minority of "bad apples" (see chapters 1, 6, and 9).

**Right to refuse (overtime work)**; Under the *ESA*, an employee may refuse to work additional hours beyond a regular shift, unless they agreed in writing with the employer to work longer hours. This agreement can be cancelled in writing and is terminated two weeks after the employee gives written notice to the employer.

**Self-help**; An approach to employment standards enforcement that de-emphasizes the role of government in ensuring that employers uphold minimum working conditions and standards and that individualizes the problem of non-compliance with employment standards. A central aspect of regulatory new governance, it emphasizes self-regulation and education as appropriate measures for upholding employment standards and includes strategies such as shifting practices from receiving complaints by mail or fax to electronic online filing of complaints, closing down intake offices where workers formerly obtained their claim form and information about how to fill in these forms, as well as posting self-help kits for employees' self-education on information about employment standards.

**Settlements (facilitated, non-facilitated)**; In employment standards enforcement, settlements refer to a potential result of an employment standards investigation whereby the parties (normally the employee and the employer) come to an agreement that will resolve a complaint. Settlements are one avenue for complainants to receive monies from the employer during the complaints process. In Ontario, settlements that are facilitated by an ESO can be reached only before the ESO has made a decision on the basis of an investigation. Non-facilitated settlements can be reached at any time during the course of the complaint or an appeal. In the course of a complaint, after a settlement is reached, the complaint is considered withdrawn without an admission of wrongdoing. (Settlements are referred to as mediations in Quebec and Australia.)

- **Facilitated settlement**: Settlements that involve the ESO mediating between the employer and employee. Facilitated settlements were introduced in 2010 and may be appropriate where there are credibility issues, unclear facts, uncertainty about the application of the law, or each party's strengths and weaknesses are equal.
- **Non-facilitated settlements**: Settlements that are reached between the employer and employee without the involvement of an ESO.

**Severance pay**; Compensation that is paid to a qualified employee who has employment terminated. Severance pay compensates for losses (such as loss of seniority) that occur when long-term employees lose their jobs. It is not the same as **termination pay**, which is given in place of the required notice of termination of employment.

**Standard employment relationship**; A normative model of employment or the basis upon which most labour protections and social benefits were organized for much of the twentieth century and to the present (see especially chapter 1). The standard employment relationship is associated with a full-time continuous employment relationship where the worker has one employer, works on the employer's premises, normally under the employer's direct supervision, and has access to social benefits and entitlements that complete the social wage.

**Strategic enforcement**; A model of regulation developed by Weil (2008) concerned with the context in which employers operate and the systemic pressures that might lead them to cut corners and violate laws in order to make a profit. As such, it calls for inspectorates to develop a sophisticated understanding of business environments that may be conducive to labour standards violations, and to practise a kind of "regulatory jujitsu," which uses compliance and deterrence in strategic combinations that are responsive to the context (see especially chapters 1, 5, 6, 9, and 11).

**Temporary help agency**; As defined under the *Temporary Help Amendment Act of the ESA* (2009), a temporary help agency is an employer who employs persons in order to assign them to perform work on a temporary basis for clients of the employer.

**Termination pay**; Pay given to an employee in lieu of the notice of termination of employment required under the *ESA*. Termination pay is a lump sum payment equal to the regular wages for a regular work week to which an employee would otherwise have been entitled during the written notice period. An employee earns vacation pay on his or her termination pay. Employers must also continue to make the required contributions to maintain the benefits to which the employee would have been entitled had the employee continued to be employed during the notice period.

**Tripartism (in enforcement)**; A model of enforcement defined as "a strategy of enforcement that involves giving workers' organizations equal standing with government and employers" (Fine and Gordon 2010, 553) (see chapter 7).

**Trustee in bankruptcy or monitor**; A trustee in bankruptcy or monitor is a lawyer, accountant, or other disinterested professional appointed by the court as a neutral third party responsible for administering the affairs of the bankrupt firm. In the event of a formal firm bankruptcy, based on the assessment of an ESO, the MOL has the option of filing a Proof of Claim with the trustee in bankruptcy or the monitor. Once a Proof of Claim is filed with the trustee or monitor, the payment of the claim is no longer under the jurisdiction of the *ESA*. Instead, it falls under the jurisdiction of the federal *Bankruptcy and Insolvency Act*, which establishes the priority among different kinds of creditors.

**Unjust/wrongful dismissal**; The act of being dismissed, terminated, laid off, or restructured out of a job without notice and under circumstances that justify termination without notice.

**Vacation pay**; The percentage of wages that an employer must pay an employee while on vacation as mandated by a government or other agency.

**Voluntary agreements**; In employment standards enforcement systems, voluntary agreements generally are mechanisms that encourage compliance outside of the legal system; they are utilized typically when enforcement agencies observe systemic patterns of violations among multiple employers but hold limited authority to attribute responsibility. In the United States, for example, the WHD has created voluntary agreements with companies, such as Subway, to improve compliance on a large scale (the Subway Agreement of 2016 provides for training, sharing of data on compliance, as well as the status of outlets, and problem-solving to deal with persistent problems). In Australia, **Proactive Compliance Deeds** are a form of voluntary agreement whereby the FWO comes to agreements with lead firms (such as franchisors) to encourage compliance.

**Voluntary compliance**; The act of obeying a law, regulation, rule, or standard free from coercion. Under a compliance orientation to employment standards, when violations are detected and assessed by an ESO, if a complaint is not settled or withdrawn, voluntary compliance is encouraged through the use of strategies such as facilitating settlements or issuing orders that require the violator, or the employer, to do what should have been done in the first place. Strategies for voluntary compliance emphasize encouraging adherence to the law or achieving adherence after the fact, rather than pursuing deterrence and/or proactively detecting and punishing wrongdoing before it is revealed.

**Voluntary payment**; Payment made without coercion by an employer for wages owed to a complainant. It is one means by which wages are recovered after an investigation by an ESO determines that wages are owed to a complainant.

**Wage bond**; A form of liability insurance that secures wages in advance. Wage bonds are underwritten by a third party, the surety issuing the bond, which provides a financial guarantee of the business's ability to pay wages owed to employees. Such measures have a long history in industries such as construction and agriculture, but they are increasingly being proposed as a mechanism to combat wage violations in other sectors.

**Wage liens**; The right to keep possession of property belonging to another person until a debt owed by that person is discharged. The *Fair Workplaces, Better Jobs Act* (2017) permitted the MOL or its authorized collector to place wage liens on the real and personal property of employers and hold security to enforce recovery of wages.

- **Pre-judgment wage lien**: A lien issued before a judgement is made.
- **Post-judgment wage lien**: A lien made after a judgment is issued.

As it is introduced before a judgement is made, a pre-judgment wage lien is a more powerful mechanism to reduce the non-payment of **Orders to Pay Wages**. As they are issued post facto, post-judgment liens are less effective tools, especially when an employer has hidden assets during the investigation, when an employer's assets are not easily identified, or in bankruptcy.

**Wage protection fund**; A wage protection fund provides money to employees when an employer does not pay wages owed to an employee. Employees are paid the wages they are owed out of the fund. Such funds may be supported through general revenues, a payroll tax, or other means. There was a wage protection fund in Ontario from 1991 to 1995. Although wage protection funds are not necessarily restricted to bankruptcy, in Canada, at the federal level, the WEPP enables employees who worked for a formally bankrupt or insolvent employer to receive up to nearly $4,000 in unpaid wages earned six months prior to the date of the employer bankruptcy or receivership. In Britain, the National Insurance Fund similarly provides money to employees owed back wages due to employer insolvency.

**Wage recovery**; The collection of an employee's unpaid wages. Most commonly, an ESO investigates claims and determines whether or not wages are owed. In this case, recovery can occur through voluntary payment by the employer, or the employer can incur an **Order to Pay Wages**, issued to an employer or, in some circumstances, to corporate directors or a related employer. Another way in which wages are recovered is by **settlements**.

Finally, when a complainant seeks to recover wages from an insolvent or bankrupt employer, ESOs may investigate to determine how much money is owed to the complainant, and then provide assistance with the paperwork that must be submitted to the bankruptcy trustee in order for the complainant to be entitled to payment under the provisions of the *Bankruptcy and Insolvency Act* (1985).

**Wage theft**; The phenomenon of employees not being paid the wages and other monetary benefits to which they are legally entitled (see chapters 4, 6, 8, and 11).

**Workplace inspections (proactive inspections)**; Inspections of workplaces by ESOs. Workplace inspections are a **proactive enforcement** strategy (in comparison to a reactive system, which relies on complaints filed by employees) (see **proactive enforcement, strategic enforcement**). There are several different types of workplace inspections, characterized by different degrees of proactivity.

- **Expanded investigations:** A reactive type workplace inspection triggered by an individual complaint (or, in some instances, multiple complaints) formally submitted to the MOL by an employee. In the period under study, a workplace is chosen for an expanded investigation if an ESO detects a violation of one of the eleven employment standards **inspectable standards** and has reason to believe that other employees in a workplace are affected.
- **Inspections of previous violators/re-inspections:** Workplace inspections of previous violators to ensure continuing compliance with the *ESA*. They generally occur at least six, but no later than twelve, months following the initial inspection. The purpose of re-inspections is to deter future violations and impose greater sanctions on those who are still in violation. Employers may be re-inspected for adherence to all eleven inspectable standards, or only for those standards they were found to have contravened previously. ESOs have discretion in determining which employers to re-inspect; however, in an attempt to ensure immediate and future compliance, employers who are issued Orders to Pay Wages or those with more than one monetary employment standards contravention are strongly recommended for re-inspection.
- **Targeted inspections:** Proactive workplace inspections that investigate employers drawn from a sector identified by the MOL's Employment Practices Branch through an operational plan or other program initiatives.
- **Blitz inspections:** Proactive workplace inspections directed typically at certain industries, occupations, or forms of employment. They are

generally associated with substantial publicity, since they aim to both educate and alert employers in specific sectors about the importance of complying with employment standards.

- **Regular inspections:** Regular inspections are determined by ESOs or regional/district offices in a process distinct from targeted and blitz inspections. They tend not to be initiated by external sources; they can be random or may also emerge from "events" that occur when the MOL receives anonymous tips about certain businesses.

# Notes

## Chapter 1

1 The Ontario *Employment Standards Act, 2000* applies to most employees and employers in Ontario. However, in addition to exemptions and special rules for certain groups of employees (see Vosko, Noack, and Thomas 2016), many workers, such as those who are misclassified as "independent contractors," are not covered by the *ESA*, even though the character of the work in which they engage matches the employment relationship in key ways, a tendency exacerbated by workplace "fissuring" (Weil 2014). In this book we aim to navigate the politics of this terminology by using the term *employee* when referring to official enforcement processes and the term *worker* when discussing the broader issues and problems associated with these processes and addressing questions of agency.

2 The partner organizations included Cavalluzzo Hayes Shilton McIntyre and Cornish LLP; Community Advocacy and Legal Centre; Human Rights Legal Support Centre; Laurentian University; Law Commission of Ontario; Legal Assistance of Windsor; Memorial University of Newfoundland; Ontario Ministry of Labour; Ontario Public Service Employees Union; Parkdale Community Legal Services Inc.; Ryerson University; Sudbury Community Legal Clinic; Toronto Workers' Health and Safety Legal Clinic; University of Ottawa; University of Toronto; University of Windsor; Windsor Workers' Action Centre; Workers' Action Centre; and York University.

3 In this book, we use *racialization* to refer to classification, representation, and signification based on socially constructed racial differences (Mirchandani and Chan 2007; Bonacich, Alimohomed, and Wilson 2008). The focus on racialization shifts attention away from conceptualizations based

on individual traits to an emphasis on how people are socially *produced* as different. The term also helps demonstrate how racial categories change in different historical periods and under different socio-economic conditions and that they interact with other axes of differentiation (such as [dis]ability, gender, age, class, etc.) to separate people from one another.

4 In this book, we use the term *feminization* (of employment norms) to refer broadly to the erosion of the standard employment relationship and the spread of forms of employment that exhibit qualities of precarious employment associated with "women's work" on the market, a process that it is intimately intertwined with racialization (Vosko 2000).

5 On the gender contract underpinning early protective legislation in industrializing countries, see Kessler-Harris (1982); Kessler-Harris, Lewis, and Wikander (1995); and, in the international labour code, see Vosko (2010), chapters 1–2.

6 The Royal Commission on Price Spreads further articulated a prescient critique of exemptions:

> Minimum wage laws do not attempt to fix wages but only to set levels below which wages may not fall. Nevertheless, the difficulties of practical administration are very real.... When, as in one order, provision is made for different rates in six classes of communities and for six classes of workers; when the hours for which these rates are payable vary according to both the size of the community and also the regular hours normally worked by the firm; when the minimum wage may be averaged over four weeks; when the minimum wage is payable only to eighty percent of the workers; when the major instrument of investigation and enforcement consists of the employers' own reports of wage payments for sample weeks then the law and its administration begin to develop technicalities which defeat its purpose. Whether the A.B.C. firm violated the law by paying Miss Smith 15 cents an hour during a particular week is not now an easily answerable question. It has become a question of law, custom, history, geography, accounting and arithmetic. Probably the A.B.C. firm does not itself know. Certainly Miss Smith will never know. Only the most expert and unhurried inspector could ever find out." (1935, 131)

For discussion of the royal commission's enquiry into minimum wage enforcement, see Tucker (2017).

7 We are not arguing here that employment standards should not be a matter of criminal law. Rather, the fact that they are not leads violations of employment standards to be viewed as less significant than violations of laws recognized as being properly criminal. For a discussion of Canada's brief experience with the criminalization of employment standards, see Tucker (2017).

8 Termination notice requirements were added in 1971 requiring one week of notice for those employed for at least three months but less than two years; two weeks of notice for those employed between two to five

years; four weeks of notice for those employed between five to ten years, and eight weeks of notice for those employed ten years or more. In 1972 a pregnancy leave provision was added that gave employees with at least one year of seniority in workplaces of twenty-five employees or more up to twelve weeks (six and six) of pre- and post-natal leave, and entitlement to their former or a comparable position. In 1975 the overtime pay (time-and-a-half) threshold was reduced from forty-eight hours to forty-four, and pregnancy leave provisions were expanded to cover up to seventeen weeks of leave. In 1976 the province introduced a differential (lower) minimum wage rate for servers in the hospitality industry. Additionally, severance pay provisions were introduced in 1981. Workers with five years of employment became eligible for severance pay at a rate of one week's pay for each year worked up to a maximum of twenty-six weeks, but only in cases of mass layoffs involving fifty or more employees in a period of six months. Under amendments to the *ESA* made in 1987, severance pay coverage expanded beyond situations of mass lay-offs to cover employees with five years of employment at a business with an annual payroll of at least $2.5 million. Additionally, the amendments expanded the termination notice requirements for employees. Employers were required to provide termination notices one week in advance for any employee employed longer than three months, with an additional week's notice for each year of employment, up to a maximum of eight weeks. Further, in the case of mass layoffs, the legislation required that employers provide the MOL with an explanation of the economic circumstances surrounding the termination, a summary of consultations with employees and the affected community, any proposed measures to help those laid off, and a statistical profile of the affected worker.

9 During the period in which we undertook field research for this book, there were two job groups of then labelled "ESOs": ESO1s and ESO2s. At the time, ESO1s carried out the first investigation of complaints after receiving them from claims processors, assessed whether or not to substantiate the complaint in whole or in part, and, if applicable, determined the amount of money owed to complainants. Following this investigation, ESO1s could close the complaint by processing withdrawals, securing voluntary compliance or settlement, or issuing a denial. They also determined if further investigation by an ESO2 was warranted – specifically, in cases involving reprisals, retail business establishments, temporary help agencies, and equal pay for equal work. ESO2s, in turn, conducted more extensive investigations, including inspections, involving similar processes, and these officers were responsible for making the final decision.

ESO2s could also visit the employers' premises or call meetings between complainants and employers.

Shortly after our field research was complete, although their roles remained the same, ESO1s were renamed early resolution officers (EROs) and ESO2s where renamed employment standards officers (ESOs). To reflect the new names assigned to these enforcement officials, rather than retaining the designations we used in dividing interviewees by employee group, throughout this book we name all ESO1s we interviewed EROs and use the designation ESO for the remaining group.

10 In 2018, 23 per cent of women, compared to 12 per cent of men, were part-time employees.

11 General Social Survey 1989, for employees in Ontario.

12 This measure reflects the approach of the Organization for Economic Co-operation and Development (OECD), which defines low-wage work as that where remuneration is less than two thirds of the median wage for full-time employees. The OECD measure is typically calculated using annual income; given the absence of this information in the Labour Force Survey, hourly wages are used instead.

13 Other employees include both those who are Canadian-born and those who immigrated more than five years ago. This grouping is not meant to imply that the labour force trajectory of immigrants converges with that of people born in Canada. Some immigrants, particularly those who are racialized, continue to experience labour market trajectories that are substantially different from those of people born in Canada, especially once levels of education are accounted for (see below for a more detailed discussion).

14 Agricultural employees are excluded from the *Labour Relations Act*. The *Agricultural Employees Protection Act*, 2002, establishes a distinct labour relations system for agricultural workers that does not permit collective bargaining of the order of that permitted for other employees in Ontario.

15 As Fraser (2018) suggests, such processes were accompanied by the racialized subjugation of expropriated populations that marked them as less worthy and less equal. One outcome was the creation a pool of expropriated and racialized workers from the periphery seeking employment in Canada and other "core" Global North countries, characterized by terms and conditions that even exploited workers in those countries are loath to accept (Vosko, Tucker, and Casey 2019). For further analysis of the "layers of vulnerability" that confront migrant agricultural workers in Canada, see also Sargeant and Tucker 2009.

16 Specifically, it gave the MOL the ability to set multiple rates of interest for any amounts owing under different provisions of the *ESA* 2000 and its regulations, as well as money held in trust by the director.

17 The employment standards complaint form allows complainants to enter their preferred salutation. However, despite our best efforts to use this information, the information was of insufficient quality to discern the complainants' gender.

18 We recognized, as Jones (1985, 46) has noted, that "in order to understand other persons' constructions of reality, we would do well to ask them ... and to ask them in such a way that they can tell us in their terms (rather than those imposed rigidly and a priori by ourselves) and in a depth which addresses the rich context that is the substance of the meanings."

19 As one ESO noted, we "have a significant number of small businesses operated by new immigrants to Canada who have the language barriers and tend to sometimes run their business the way they might have in their own culture and don't take the time to learn what is required here or don't necessarily even believe that some of the laws are correct and don't want to comply for that reason." (For further analysis, see chapter 5).

20 Contemporary scholarship critiquing multiculturalism, especially studies attributing associated practices with nationalism (on Canada, see especially Kernerman 2005; on Australia, see Yue and Wyatt 2014), give credence to the notion that what some scholars (see, for example, Di Angelo 2011) term racism can include acts of tolerance as well as exclusion (Hage 1998).

**Chapter 2**

1 While it applies to unionized employees, as collective agreements must provide for, at least, the minimum standards established under the *ESA*, the avenue for addressing *ESA* violations for unionized employees is through the grievance process. For a sober assessment of the potential for union involvement in employment standards enforcement, see Vosko and Thomas (2014).

2 In the analyses in this book, the service industries that are conceptualized as primarily private include management, administrative and other support services; finance, insurance, and real estate; and professional, scientific, and technical services. The service industries that are conceptualized as primarily public include health care and social assistance; education; information, culture, and recreation; and public administration.

3 Unions may also exercise their rights of entry. However, since the centralization of industrial relations at the federal level, they rarely exercise these rights.

**Chapter 3**

1 However, time extensions may be permitted by the OLRB (s. 116(4)(5)).

2 Simultaneously, workplace inspections were greatly reduced to channel

the MOL's limited resources into complaints processing, which fostered the development of a complaints-handling system increasingly isolated from the actual violations confronting employees (for a discussion of workplace inspections, see chapter 5).

3 The auditor general was also critical of the MOL's virtual abandonment of workplace inspections (then called routine inspections), noting that while in fiscal year 1989 there were 18,312 complaint file completions, there were only eighty-five routine inspections; in 1990, 19,027 complaint file completions but only fifty-one routine inspections; and in 1991, 18,582 complaint file completions and forty routine inspections (Auditor General of Ontario 1991, 148).

4 Labour Force Survey 1998 (2006 census annual weight used) and 2018 (2011 census annual weight used).

5 Assessed complaints are those that have been adjudicated by an ERO or ESO and have a final outcome of voluntary compliance, compliance ordered, or denial. Settled and withdrawn complaints are excluded.

6 Notably, whereas in 2007/08 reprisal claims were included in only 6 per cent of all complaints, the proportion of complaints that have a reprisal claim grew steadily subsequently, increasing to 8 per cent in 2010/11 and 10 per cent in 2014/15. Put differently, the share of complaints that include a claim of reprisal almost doubled between 2007/08 and 2014/15. In this period, reprisal claims are also more common among complainants still working for their employer at the time they initiate a complaint.

7 The documents that complainants are encouraged to submit are: employer business cards, letterhead or job ads; pay stubs; pay cheques; a "Record of Employment" (ROE) form; a written contract of employment; records of the hours worked; T4 slips; documents related to a leave of absence (i.e. medical certificate); written notice of termination; and any other documents that could help with the investigation.

8 Unlike assessed complaints, non-assessed complaints have not been adjudicated by the MOL and the final outcome is the decision of the complainant, that is, they are either withdrawn by the complainant or settled with the employer.

**Chapter 4**

1 In this context, wage recovery refers to all monetary entitlements to unpaid wages, but also to unpaid vacation pay, public holiday pay, overtime pay, termination pay, and other wage-related entitlements under the *ESA*. We include money provided to complainants as part of a settlement in this definition.

2 This analysis of recovery focuses exclusively on that undertaken by Ontario's MOL, as its activities represent the primary means through which

workers who experience employment standards violations, including those related to wages, recover monies owed. However, there are two other paths for pursing employment standards entitlements. First, unionized workers are prevented from using the MOL to enforce their employment standards entitlements. Rather, they are limited to using the grievance system under the collective agreement (*ESA*, s 99-1; for further discussion on unions and employment standards enforcement, see Vosko and Thomas 2014). Grievance arbitrators have the power to issue Orders to Pay Wages. Although data on recovery in unionized contexts are unavailable, it is reasonable to assume that recovery is normally achieved in such situations, except in the case of bankruptcies and insolvency. The other alternative path to recovery is through a civil action in court (*Boland v. APV Canada Inc.*, 2005 CanLII 3384 ON SCDC). In some circumstances, groups of workers who have experienced a common violation, such as a denial of overtime, may be able to pursue a class action (Fulawka v. Bank of Nova Scotia, 2012 ONCA 443).

3 As of 1 January 2019.

4 Only complaints that include a monetary employment standard violation are considered in this analysis. Commonly referred to as wage theft, these include violations related to unpaid wages, overtime pay, vacation time/pay, public holiday pay, deductions from wages, minimum wage, termination pay, and severance pay (Vosko et al. 2017).

5 ESOs are directed to issue Orders to Pay Wages even if the employer is out of business but not formally bankrupt.

6 The remainder of complaints were either withdrawn or denied after being assessed by an ERO/ESO.

7 Among small and medium-size businesses in Canada, only 62 per cent survived for three years and 51 per cent survived for five years; survival rates are even lower among micro-enterprises (Industry Canada 2012, 2016).

8 A smaller portion of employers owing wages are not issued Orders to Pay Wages, often because their operational status cannot be ascertained or they cannot be located (Vosko, Noack, and Tucker 2016, 48).

9 As Thomas (2003, 337) notes, informal insolvencies have long generated a large share of employment standards complaints. In 1990 the MOL estimated that such insolvencies accounted for 75 per cent of employment standards wage claims.

10 At the provincial level, the government of Ontario has recognized that six months is an inadequate amount of time for many employees to come forward to file a complaint. Legislative changes under the *Stronger Workplaces for a Stronger Economy Act* (2014) increased the period during which employees can file complaints from six months to two years.

11 For example, changes to the *California Labor Code* that took effect in January 2016 allow the California labour commissioner to place a lien on an employer's property, including bank accounts or accounts receivable, if a final judgment against an employer is not paid (California Senate Bill No. 588 2015).

**Chapter 5**

1 Particularly relevant to the analysis undertaken in this chapter, in December 2018 the government eliminated the requirement that employers display posters on *ESA* rights and responsibilities in the workplace – one of the eleven inspectable standards in a workplace inspection. It also altered standards for hours of work as described in chapter 1. But, while it is important to note these developments, the data analysed in this chapter do not cover the period when these changes were in effect.

2 While all standards are within the scope of an inspection, the MOL's *AMES* (MOL 2017a, chap. 4, s. 4.1) indicates that "the scope of an inspection (for determining compliance with the *ESA*) is limited to ... eleven standards." It also notes that "a Proactive inspection and an Expanded Investigation inspection can either be a full inspection (of all inspectable standards) *or* a limited inspection (of one or more inspectable standards, but less than all inspectable standards)" and gives the ESO discretion over whether to conduct a full or partial inspection except in cases of provincial blitzes which are typically focused/limited and include full audits (s. 4.1).

3 Calculated from the number of inspections in the ESIS data (2015/16) and the total number of businesses with employees in Ontario in December 2016. It is not possible to identify the number of businesses with only unionized employees, which are not subject to employment standards inspections by the MOL.

4 The data reveal the presence of this "hybrid" group of inspections that appear to be situated between the reactive (complaints-based) and proactive (inspections-focused) dimensions of the employment standards enforcement regime. The inspections in this group (labelled "expanded targeted/blitz") are linked to individual complaints submitted to the MOL (and at times, identified as expanded investigations), but are also identified as being a part of the targeted/blitz group. Although it is unclear why some inspections are classified as both expanded and targeted/blitz, we presume that in such cases ESOs use complaints to identify sectors or industries comprise vulnerable workers, and the employers identified in the complaints are subsequently selected for a targeted/blitz inspection. These inspections differ from those in the previous groups in that the complaints themselves may not have triggered expanded

investigations; however, they were used to inform (or in the context of) targeted/blitz inspections.

5 The ESIS includes several classifications of workplace inspections, including the overall "Inspection Type," the "Inspection Subtype," indicating whether or not the inspection is associated with a specific blitz or targeted campaign, and the "Notification Source," which identifies who or what initiated the inspection. These three variables can, however, provide inconsistent information. Additionally, some inspections are linked to individual complaints, even though they are not necessarily classified as expanded inspections. In the current analysis, we resolve these inconsistencies by adopting the following approach to coding inspection types:

*Regular* inspections encompass those classified as regular in the inspection type variable, which are not associated with a blitz in the inspection subtype variable.

*Targeted/blitz* inspections are those classified as targeted or blitzes in either the inspection type, inspection subtype, or notification source variables.

*Expanded investigations* include inspections classified as expanded investigations in inspection type and/or notification source variables, which are linked to complaints and are not associated with a blitz. If no complaint is linked to the inspection, but the inspection type is expanded and the notification source is either undefined, a worker, anonymous, public, or expanded, we also classify the inspection as an expanded investigation.

*Expanded and targeted/blitz* inspections are taken as a "hybrid" group that includes inspections classified as expanded investigations with regard to inspection type, inspection subtype, or notification source variables, but also associated with a blitz. In a few instances, inspections are classified as an expanded investigation, and the notification source is listed as an MOL officer, manager, or Ontario Health and Safety inspector, but is not linked to a complaint or associated with a blitz; these inspections are also placed in this group.

*Re-inspections* are classified as re-inspections or previous violations under the inspection type, inspection subtype, or notification source variables.

6 As detailed in the *AMES* (MOL 2017a, chap. 4 s. 1), expanded investigation inspections can emerge from an ESO's own claim *or* "Events (tagged as an Expanded Investigation in the ESIS) created by an Early Resolution Officer (ERO) from contravention(s) found during a claim investigation or an ESO who was not able to conduct an inspection themselves."

7 Targeted and/or blitz inspections are grouped together in this analysis, since they are conceptually congruent with one another and because it is

difficult to definitively identify inspections of each type in the administrative data.

8 In recent years, however, the MOL has adopted a policy permitting random inspections in only rare situations.

9 The MOL typically distinguishes between monetary and non-monetary employment standards violations. Monetary employment standards violations capture situations where money is owed to employees, which can be in the form of public holiday pay, overtime pay, vacation pay, minimum wage, and unpaid wages. Non-monetary employment standards violations in turn capture those violations that are not linked with some sort of financial compensation such as providing eating periods, displaying posters (before 2019), and record keeping.

10 The Compliance Check pilot program, introduced in 2013, tested the use of an online self-assessment tool designed to be completed by employers (without the intervention of an ESO) in order to assess compliance with seven employment standards that are not related to pay/compensation.

11 Reasons can include if ESOs have reasonable grounds to believe that employers may remove or alter records (MOL 2017a, chap. 4, s. 4.7.2).

12 Advance notice is also not to be given if the ESO believes it "will hinder efforts to conduct an audit (for example, the officer has reasonable grounds to believe that records will be removed or altered)" (MOL 2017a, chap. 4, s. 4.7.2).

13 ESOs are directed to ensure that they interview an appropriate number and cross-section of employees (across different positions/ departments) during workplace inspections (MOL 2017a, chap. 4, s. 4.7.3).

14 Indeed, some studies of corporate compliance find that under-reporting of violations may occur during self-audits (or self-reports, in studies on tax filers) when compared to audits conducted by the overseeing agency (Kleven et al. 2011; Telle 2013).

15 Ticketable offences are any violations of the eleven standards that are inspected. These statistics include only inspections where employment standards violations were detected.

16 Even fewer employers with violations received NOCs, with less than 0.6 per cent of all offences resulting in NOCs.

17 Training in conducting workplace inspections for staff who had yet to receive it was also deferred until further notice.

18 *California Labor Code* s. 226.8(1). In addition, the Act allows for fines to be levied against any third-party advisors such as an accountant or human resource professional (but not attorneys) who "knowingly advises an employer to misclassify an individual as an independent contractor to avoid employee status" (*California Labor Code* s. 2753).

**Chapter 6**

1 Following Bourdieu (1990), "habitus" refers to deeply rooted ways of thinking and understandings that guide and generate the practices of social actors and inform their interpretations of and reactions to others within a given social field. In this regulative context, "social field" refers to the networks and the formal positions of power connecting the different actors associated with employment standards enforcement, including front-line enforcement officers, managers, senior administrators, employees, and employers (Ugwudike 2017).
2 Note that, as it is used henceforth, the term "managers" refers to managers who oversee regional and district offices and regional program coordinators who are responsible for reviewing and advising ESOs on the regional implementation of MOL policy.
3 In response to the Changing Workplaces Review, the former Liberal government modestly increased the penalties for NOCs, so that the penalty for a first offence was $350, but these were reversed by the current Conservative government in the fall of 2018 and are back down to their old level.
4 The data for 2012–17 are derived from the MOL's Employment Standards Information System (ESIS). Data for 2017/18 are from a MOL statistical summary publication, the Quick Reference Guide. The guide provides statistics on the use of Part I (Tickets) and Part III Prosecutions only.
5 The frequency of ticketing on inspections increased from about 6 to 9 per cent during this period after a targeted inspection program was reintroduced in 2012.
6 Data come from the Legal Services Branch of the MOL.
7 Data for 2017/18 are not included in this assessment, since complaint data for this year are not yet available, as it takes longer to determine the outcome of complaints than inspections.
8 U.S. law permits only civil monetary penalties for repeat offenders.
9 *An Act to regulate the Labour of Children and Young Persons in the Mills and Factories of the United Kingdom*, 3 and 4 Wm IV, c. 103 (Carson 1974).
10 Bartrip and Fenn (1980) disagreed with the conventionalization hypothesis, arguing instead that the lack of prosecution was an efficient use of scarce enforcement resources, a proposition that Carson (1980) rebutted, pointing to their denial of class interest in the calculation of efficiency.
11 *Minimum Wage Act*, S.O. 1920, c. 87.
12 S.O. 1921, c. 76.
13 S.O. 1932, c. 36.
14 Prior to his appointment to the Minimum Wage Board in 1920, Stapells was the treasurer of the Board of Trade, president of a garment

manufacturing company, and a former executive member of the Canadian Manufacturers' Association (McCallum 1986).

15 Stapells reported that in the past eighteen months 340 firms were found in violation but the board had prosecuted only 20, resulting in about $600 in fines, or about $30 per prosecution (Royal Commission on Price Spreads 1934, 39–41).

16 *Employment Standards Amendment Act* (Temporary Help Agencies), S.O. 2009, c. 9; *Employment Protection for Foreign Nationals Act*, S.O. 2009, c. 32.

**Chapter 7**

1 See Thomas (2007) for the details of the case.

2 However, as noted in chapter 1, despite having first-hand experience, workers face challenges and barriers in accessing the complaints system.

3 These actors are not equal participants in this process. The government defines and regulates the enforcement process, and thus the actions and decisions of government officials condition the participation of other actors and mediate the power dynamics that structure the employment relationship (see Coe and Jordhus-Lier 2011). Moreover, since the mid-1990s, the enforcement activities of the MOL have been shaped by neoliberalism, which has contributed to a reorientation of employment standards enforcement in ways that expose workers to market forces more deeply (Gellatly et al. 2011).

4 Although interviews with MOL officials at varying levels comprise part of the analyses in previous chapters, this chapter's analysis is confined to EROs and ESOs, as they are the main point of contact for employees and employers in matters relating to the investigation of complaints and workplace inspections.

5 Sheppard (2010) has elaborated on the contextual approach to inclusive equality that incorporates multiple layers of contextualism at the micro, meso, and macro levels.

6 We note that there are many regional discrepancies in servicing the precariously employed across the province, as many other urban centres in Ontario do not have worker centres or similarly oriented community organizations.

**Chapter 8**

1 This chapter adopts the term *worker* to encompass both workers and employees, two terms defined uniquely in Britain, as explained below, except in instances in which the narrative refers specifically to employment standards that do not extend to the broader category of workers, in which case the term *employees* is used.

2 For the sake of consistency with the foregoing chapters that address employment standards in Ontario and the subsequent chapters that address them in

Australia, Quebec, and the United States, this chapter adopts the terminology of employment standards in referring to British "employment rights."

3 Some of the findings reported here draw on research carried out at Middlesex University by the Unpaid Britain project (2015–17). Co-funded by the Trust for London and Middlesex University Business School, this project sought to identify the ways in which non-payment of wages occurs, through understanding the processes and attitudes (including employer motivation) that surround its incidence and resolution, to identify improved means of both its restitution and its prevention.

Mixed methods were used. Data from the government's Labour Force and Family Resource Surveys was analysed for evidence of abuse of workers' rights (including non-payment of holidays or overtime). Data from Her Majesty's Courts and Tribunals Service; Advisory, Conciliation and Arbitration Service; Citizens Advice employment advice service; and the Insolvency Service were also examined, together with the National Minimum Wage offenders' lists published by Department for Business, Energy and Industrial Strategy and the 2013 Survey of Employment Tribunal Applicants. These helped researchers to understand the profile of complaints and the progress that they might typically make.

In addition, over 700 judgments from Employment Tribunals involving workers in London who claimed that wages were owed were analysed, and the Companies House records for over 400 of those employers examined. This was supported by a search of academic and grey literature and a series of forty-four semi-structured interviews with key informants, workers, employers, and third parties who have been involved in cases of unpaid wages. Case studies based on the interviews examined other relevant documents including media reports, court records, and insolvency practitioners' reports.

The methodological approach was similar to that adopted by the authors of Part I of this book and described in chapter 1, and in general we have covered similar ground, but on a much smaller scale, and without access to government administrative data.

4 These distinct levels of coverage in Britain resemble the regime of exemptions and special rules under Ontario's *ESA*.

5 Apart from those defined as "family workers" – which may include live-in domestic workers – and au pairs, those on government work programs, prison inmates, and the self-employed.

6 The rates as at April 2018 are set out below. These are subject to an annual review, based on a report from the Low Pay Commission.

| Age | per hour |
|---|---|
| 25 and over | £7.83 (CAD$13.94) |
| 21 to 24 | £7.38 (CAD$13.14) |
| 18 to 20 | £5.90 (CAD$10.50) |

| | |
|---|---|
| Under 18 | £4.20 (CAD$7.48) |
| Apprentice | £3.70 (CAD$6.59) |

7 Annual Survey of Hours and Earnings data come from a sample of employer payroll records, whereas Labour Force Survey data are based on a household survey.

8 Author's calculations from Annual Survey of Hours and Earnings 2016 data.

9 The body charged with making recommendations for the revision of the national minimum wage.

10 The Unfair Dismissal and Statement of Reasons for Dismissal (Variation of Qualifying Period) Order 2012 amended the *Employment Rights Act, 1996*.

11 Certain dismissals remain unfair with no service requirement: dismissal for a protected characteristic (such as gender, race, age, disability, religion, or trade union membership), or dismissal for "asserting a statutory right."

12 *Aslam & others v Uber BV & others*, case no. 2202550/2015; *Pimlico Plumbers v Gary Smith* [2017] EWCA Civ 51.

13 In 1979, when more than half the workforce was in a trade union, collective bargaining was the norm, and in certain industries where there was little worker or employer organization, statutory Wages Councils set pay rates (including overtime) and working time arrangements including paid holidays, broadly based on what was achieved in the bargained sectors. It was estimated in the 1960s that these arrangements covered 3.5 million workers, plus a further 750,000 covered by the similar Agricultural Wages Boards. It was further estimated that as a result of their focus on retail, hospitality, and formerly "sweated" trades, almost one in two female workers was within the scope of the councils (Bayliss 1962). The last twenty-six Wages Councils were abolished under the Thatcher government in 1993, and the Agricultural Wages Board in England went the same way in 2013 (although boards survive in Wales and Scotland).

14 There is no federal/provincial split in the scope of regulation, apart from some slight differences in Employment Tribunal arrangements in Northern Ireland and Scotland, and the survival of Agricultural Wages Boards in Scotland and Wales.

15 "Third-parties will include employment agencies and/or their clients, training providers party to apprenticeship arrangements, and umbrella and managed service companies. Further third parties who may be a source of relevant information include accountants, payroll companies, trade unions, the Citizens Advice Bureau and other worker representatives, parents and friends of workers" (Her Majesty's Revenue and Customs 2016).

16 The employer, an individual barred from holding directorships, did not enter a defence.

17 *Unison v Lord Chancellor* [2017] UKSC 51, judgment given 26 July 2017.

**Chapter 9**

1 Annual funding for labour inspection more than doubled between 2005 and 2007, from AU$21 million to around AU$50 million.

2 Regulation of labour hire or temporary agency arrangements has been a focus at the state level. Legislative reforms in this area are now underway in a number of states.

3 In 2017/18 the FWO resolved 28,275 requests for assistance involving a workplace dispute (up 5 per cent from the previous fiscal year).

4 This scheme is not comprehensive in that it excludes certain entitlements (such as superannuation), caps the maximum compensation amount, and does not cover temporary migrant workers.

5 Legal costs are not generally recoverable by the successful party in enforcement claims brought under this legislation.

6 See, e.g., Proactive Compliance Deed between the Office of the FWO and Paul Sadler Swimland Pty Ltd. (FWO 2018f).

7 For most civil remedy provisions, the maximum penalty available per contravention is AU$12,600 for an individual and AU$63,000 for a body corporate. Where the contravention is deemed "serious," higher maximum penalties apply (i.e., AU$126,000 per contravention for an individual and AU$630,000 per contravention for companies).

**Chapter 10**

1 Compilation of Quebec Laws and Regulations (CQLR) c. N-1.1.

2 CQLR c. C-12.

3 CQLR c. S-2.1.

4 CQLR c. A-3.001.

5 CQLR c. E-12.001.

6 The European-inspired *Act Respecting the Extension of Labour Collective Agreements,* adopted in 1934, allowed for the juridical extension of the provisions of a collection agreement on salary rates and hours of work to include employees, male or female, unionized or non-unionized, in a given "industry" or "trade" in a stated region [SQ 1934 (24 Geo. V) c. 56]. In 1964 that Act became the *Act Respecting Collective Agreement Decrees* [RSQ 1964 c. 163] and is still in force: RLRQ c. D-2 [*CADA*].

7 The *Minimum Wage Act* (1940) [SQ 1940 (4 Geo. VI) c. 39, hereafter *MWA,* 1940], which was replaced by the *LSA,* provided for the creation of

employment standards for hours of work and minimum wages in ordinances covering specific industry sectors, occupations, or geographical areas and set minimum wage scales rather than uniform minimum wages.

8 *LSA*, ss 93–4.

9 *LSA*, ss 40ff. *Regulation respecting Labour Standards*, CQLR c. N-1.1, r. 3 [LSR].

10 *LSA*,ss 52ff.

11 *LSA*, ss 60ff.

12 *LSA*, ss66ff.

13 *LSA*, ss 79.6.1ff.

14 *LSA*, ss79.1ff.

15 *LSA*, ss 122ff.

16 *LSA*,ss 124ff.

17 *LSA*, ss 81.18ff.

18 *LSA*, ss 123.6ff.

19 SO 2000 c. 41.

20 *LSA*, ss87.1ff.

21 *LSA*, ss41.1 and 74.1. Before January 2019, these sections prohibited employers from paying a lower rate of wage or reducing the annual leave of employees because they usually work less hours each week, unless the employee was paid more than twice the rate of the minimum wage.

22 *An Act to Amend the Act Respecting Labour Standards and Other Legislative Provisions Mainly to Facilitate Family-Work Balance*, Bill 176, passage 12 June 2018. Part of the changes brought forward by this bill concerning personnel placement agencies or recruitment agencies for temporary foreign workers will enter into force on the date of coming into force of the first regulation made under section 92.7 of the *Act Respecting Labour Standards*.

23 Our chapter builds, in part, on our article first published in the *Comparative Labor Law & Policy Journal*: Gesualdi-Fecteau and Vallée (2016).

24 SQ 1885 (48 Vict.) c. 32.

25 SQ 1919 (9 Geo. V) c. 11.

26 SQ 1937 (1 Geo. VI) c. 50.

27 See note 7.

28 The Women's Minimum Wage Commission was established by the *Women's Minimum Wage Act* (1919), and the Minimum Wage Commission was established by the *Minimum Wage Act* (1940).

29 The Fair Wage Office was established by the *Fair Wage Act*, 1937.

30 Monitoring of the enforcement of collective agreement decrees under the *Act Respecting the Extension of Labour Collective Agreements* adopted in 1934 (see note 6) was entrusted to joint union-management committees funded by a contribution payable by both employees and employers. This means

of financing the monitoring of decrees may have influenced some aspects of the way in which contributions were charged to finance the work of the Fair Wage Office (Desîlets and Ledoux 2006, 89, 139).

31 *LSA*, ss 6 and 8, now repealed.

32 *Act to Group the Commission de l'équité salariale, the Commission des normes du travail and the Commission de la santé et de la sécurité du travail and to Establish the Administrative Labour Tribunal*, SQ 2015 c. 15, s. 278 (LSEOHSC). The LSEOHSC has since been established by the Occupational Health and Safety Commission, ss 137ff.

33 See the website of the LSEOHSC for the chronology of events: https://www.cnesst.gouv.qc.ca/a-propos-de-la-CNESST/structure_organisation/Pages/historique.aspx.

34 *Occupational Health and Safety Act*, ss 138, 141.

35 *LSA*, ss 39.0.1ff; *Occupational Health and Safety Act*, s. 247; *Act Respecting Industrial Accidents and Occupational Diseases*, s. 281.

36 *Occupational Health and Safety Act*, ss 163ff.

37 *Occupational Health and Safety Act*, ss 161.3–161.5.

38 *Act Respecting Workforce Management and Control within Government Departments, Public Sector Bodies and Networks and State-Owned Enterprises*, CQLR c. G-1.011. The secretary and the other officers of the LSEOHSC shall be appointed in accordance with the *Public Service Act*, CQLR c. F-3.1.1: *Occupational Health and Safety Act*, s. 157.

39 *Public Administration Act*, CQLR c. A-6.01, as mentioned in the *Occupational Health and Safety Act*, s. 157.

40 The announcement of the merger was made in the 2015–16 Budget Speech and was presented as one of the cost-saving measures to address "structural fiscal imbalance [trans.]" of the Quebec state: *Discours sur le budget 2015–2016*, delivered at the Assemblée nationale by Mr. Carlos Leitão, minister of finance, 26 March 2015, at pp. 29 and 32.

41 *LSA*, s. 105.

42 *LSA*, ss 102–5.

43 In 2010 the Supreme Court of Canada confirmed that an arbitrator considering a grievance has the power to determine, in light of the modifications to the collective agreement that flow from the public order status of the *LSA*, the legal entitlements conferred by the Act: *Syndicat de la fonction publique du Québec v. Quebec (Attorney General)*, 2010 SCC 28.

44 *LSA*, s. 104.

45 CQLR, c. C-37.

46 *LSA*, s. 108.

47 *LSA*, s. 109.

48 *LSA*, s. 103.

49 *LSA*, s. 107.
50 *LSA*, s. 107.1.
51 *LSA*, s. 111.
52 *LSA*, s. 113.
53 The Civil Division of the Court of Québec or the Superior Court: *Code of Civil Procedure*, CQLR c. 25.01, ss 33, 35.
54 *LSA*, s. 145.1.
55 *LSA*, s. 140.
56 *LSA*, ss 139–40.
57 CQLR c. 25.1.
58 *CPP*, s. 3.
59 In 2017 the list included 151 employers sentenced for 158 offences. See List of Employers Contravening the LSA (Liste des employeurs contrevenant à la LNT) online: https://www.cnt.gouv.qc.ca/publications/liste-des-employeurs-contrevenant-a-la-lnt/liste-des-employeurs-contrevenant-a-la-lnt/index.html?no_cache=1.
60 *ESA*, s. 132(a).
61 Section 231 of the *Code of Penal Procedure* provides that "except as otherwise prescribed in this Code and except in the case of contempt of court, imprisonment cannot be prescribed for offences under the statutes of Québec. Any provision inconsistent with this article is without effect unless it states that it is applicable notwithstanding this article."
62 For the purposes of this study, between September 2012 and February 2013 we consulted 149 files processed by the LSC. These files stemmed from complaints initiated by workers or associations defending their rights – files stemming from prevention and supervision interventions carried out by the LSC with this workforce and penal recourses initiated by the LSC. We also conducted thirty-six semi-structured interviews with forty-nine respondents, including five with LSC agents. See Gesualdi-Fecteau (2015b).
63 For the purposes of this study, we analysed twenty-six complaint files between February and March 2014. We also conducted seven interviews, bringing together fourteen LSC staff members between November 2014 and February 2015. This research was supported by a SSHRC Standard Research Grant "*L'obligation de disponibilité de l'employé: une nouvelle source de précarité ou de flexibilité?*"
64 *LSA*, s. 122.
65 *LSA*, s. 123.4 (2). This section refers to s. 15 of the *Labour Code*, CQLR c. C-27.
66 The situation is comparable with the Ontario context (see chapter 4).
67 In 2016 the LSEOHSC processed 14,382 recourses to recover wages, and only 2,369 required the intervention of the Department of Legal Affairs.

Hence, 12,023 of all the files processed by the commission (more than 83 per cent) were either settled or deemed inadmissible.

68 See note 38.

69 *Act to Implement Certain Provisions of the Budget Speech of 30 March 2010, Reduce the Debt and Return to a Balanced Budget in 2013–2014*, SQ 2010 c. 20.

70 *LSA*, s. 5 (2).

71 *LSA*, ss 5 and 39.

72 *LSA*, s. 105. This provision stipulates that the LSC/LSEOHSC can make an inquiry of its own initiative.

73 These figures come from an addition of the data contained in the LSC's annual management reports of 2011 to 2015.

74 When the *LSA* was adopted in 1979, fines varied from $200 to $500 and, for any subsequent conviction in the following two years, from $500 to $3,000 (SQ 1979 c. 45, ss 139–40). There was a slight increase in the level of fines in 1986, 1991, and 1997 (SQ 1986 c. 58, ss 65–6; SQ 1991 c. 33, ss 87–8; SQ 1997 c. 85, ss 367–8). Since 1997, fines vary from $600 to $1,200 and, for any subsequent conviction, from $1,200 to $6,000. The fines foreseen in the *LSA* are very low, especially when compared to the significant increase in the level of fines provided for by the *Act to Modify the Occupational Health and Safety Regime, Particularly in Order to Increase Certain Death Benefits and Fines and Simplify the Payment of the Employer Assessment*, SQ 2009 c. 19, s. 21. This Act established also the revalorization of the amount of the fines allowed under ss 236–7 of the Occupational Health and Safety Commission on 1 January each year, using the method described in the ss 119 to 123 of the *Act Respecting Industrial Accidents and Occupational Diseases* (*Occupational Health and Safety Act*, s. 237.1).

75 *LSA*, s. 109.

76 *LSA*, s. 140 para. 1.

77 LSEOHSC, ss 235 and 166.

78 *An Act to Amend the Act Respecting Labour Standards and Other Legislative Provisions Mainly to Facilitate Family-Work Balance*. The sole exception concerns temporary foreign workers; the Act stipulates that if, following an enquiry, the LSEOHSC has grounds to believe that one of the rights of a temporary foreign worker under the *LSA* or a regulation has been violated, the LSEOHSC may, even if no complaint is filed and if no settlement is reached, exercise any recourse on behalf of the worker: s. 92.10.

**Chapter 11**

1 Parts of this chapter are adapted from David Weil, "Creating a strategic enforcement approach to address wage theft: One academic's journey

in organizational change," *Journal of Industrial Relations* Vol. 60, Issue 3 (June 2018), pp. 437–460. Copyright 2018 (Sage Publishing), DOI: 10.1177/002218765551 and appear here by permission of the publisher.

2 This account is based in some ways (and perhaps biased) by my role as the head of the Wage and Hour Division from 2014 until the end of the Obama administration in January 2017. Many of the changes described here were guided by more than a decade of my academic research as well as that of other scholars, including some contributing to this book. My experience in "sitting in the seat" and being responsible for making decisions was sobering and humbling, given the implications of my decisions. It also involved the most intense tutorial of my career on the practical matter of taking ideas and translating them into organizational actions, often requiring the development of consensus and occasionally the navigating of deep divides between political and career staff. In that work I had the good fortune to be taught in the breach by talented and dedicated fellow political appointees and experienced and wise career public servants. Much of what is discussed in this chapter arose from the collective work of political and career staff inside WHD, and colleagues in the wider U.S. Department of Labor with whom we worked closely.

3 *New State Ice Co. v. Liebmann*, 285 U.S. 262 (1932).

4 The *FLSA*, pushed by President Franklin D. Roosevelt (and in particular by his secretary of labor, Frances Perkins) required significant concessions to assure passage in Congress. In particular, securing support from Southern Democrats who were a key part of Roosevelt's political coalition required exempting large groups of people, including agriculture workers, domestic workers, and other workers who were predominately African American (Katznelson 2013).

5 The difference in the federal-state dynamic in the United States relative to Ontario and Canada is explained in part by the fact that Canadian laws create separate industry coverage, while in the United States, state and federal governments both set employment standards across industry groups.

6 U.S. Department of Labor, Wage and Hour Division: Resources for Workers, http://www.dol.gov/whd/workers.htm.

7 It is no accident that I was the first confirmed Wage and Hour administrator in a decade. From 2004 to 2014, there were a series of acting Wage and Hour administrators. Neither President Bush nor President Obama was able to move nominated administrators through confirmation until my nomination in 2013.

8 I believe the active agenda of WHD during the Obama administration intensified this level of scrutiny significantly from all sides.

9 Our efforts began with a deep dive into understanding how the long-standing system operated, and how it fit into the modern workplace. The result was a six-chapter report released in 2010, *Improving Workplace Conditions through Strategic Enforcement* (Weil 2010), which became the blueprint for many of the changes undertaken by the agency over the subsequent six years. The "Green Book" (so named because of its cover) was both a fact base documenting how the agency had traditionally operated and a detailed discussion of how it could change going forward.

10 For example, we addressed the real problem of lack of employer knowledge of responsibilities under the law through a variety of methods of employer outreach, including issuing extensive regulatory guidance. For a comprehensive discussion of the elements composing strategic enforcement at WHD, see Weil (2018).

11 Specifically, we looked at the incidence of wages reported in the Current Populations Survey conducted by the Census Department that were below either the federal or state minimum wage for workers covered by the *FLSA*, to calculate the incidence of minimum wage violations. We used a combination of household survey answers related to reported weekly hours, combined with reported payment for overtime hours during the reporting week, to calculate overtime violation incidence. We used comparable data to estimate the potential back wages owed for those workers. Although there were a number of assumptions we needed to make to use these estimates, we were concerned primarily about the relative ranking of industries using these measures rather than the absolute levels that made the approach useful for setting priorities. Limitations in data from Statistics Canada described in previous chapters make development of comparable measures of the incidence and severity of minimum wage and overtime violations difficult for Ontario's MOL.

12 Here we divided the total number of complaints per industry by the estimated number of workers covered by the law in those industries to generate an estimate of the likelihood of complaint. Once again, our primary interest was the relative complaint rates across industries, rather than the absolute levels arising from this approach.

13 The basic list was laid out in the "Green Book" (Weil 2010, 2) and refined over time. Regions were allowed to add industries not on the list as part of their annual plan but had to justify such additions. For example, several regions added fracking, given the presence of fissured workplace structures and systemic problems across companies in that industry, even though relative wages in the industry were somewhat higher than the priority industries.

14 One of the more internally controversial findings of my 2010 analysis of past agency practice was that between 1998 and 2008, the WHD assessed

civil monetary penalties in only about 43 per cent of re-investigations with repeat *FLSA* violations – even though the agency had the clear authority to levy them in all of those instances.

15 Unlike other departments of the federal government, the Department of Labor relies on the Office of the Solicitor to provide legal service to all agencies. Although the department will also work with the Department of Justice on cases involving criminal activities under laws not directly administered by Labor, or where court decisions are appealed, it provides legal assistance in most instances involving litigation.

16 For example, the WHD trained investigators on how to undertake time studies in the garment and agriculture industries in order to test the veracity of payroll records (often falsified). These studies were particularly important, since workers in those sectors are often paid on a piece rate (that is, on the basis of output rather than hourly rates), but employer records are often incomplete or in some cases nonexistent.

17 Voluntary Agreement between the U.S. Department of Labor's Wage and Hour Division and Subway, 26 July 2016, https://www.dol.gov/WHD/flsa/SubwayAgreement.pdf.

18 Reported forms of retaliation varied from reduction in hours or pay or being given a less desirable work assignment to threats of being fired or reported to immigration authorities, to actually being fired or suspended (Bernhardt et al. 2009).

19 The role of unions and other workplace advocates was an early area of my research interest, beginning with my dissertation that analysed the impact of unions on enforcement under the Occupational Safety and Health Act and the Mine Health and Safety Act. See, for example, Weil (1991, 1992, 1999, 2005) for early studies, and Weil (2012) for a summary of evidence. Janice Fine has undertaken more recent research in this area (e.g., Fine and Gordon 2010; Fine 2017).

20 For a more comprehensive discussion of these organizational features, see Weil 2018.

21 The last trip I made before the end of the administration was to attend the graduation of about seventy-five new investigators who had received their first training in strategic enforcement. It was exhilarating to see a new generation of investigators with a grounding in the approach.

**Appendix B: Qualitative Interviews**

1 As explained in this book's introduction, by the time of publication, ESO1s came to be called early resolution officers (EROs). However, we have chosen to leave ESO1 in the interview questions, as this is the terminology that was used with the interviewees. Elsewhere in the book, we use ERO.

2 In an attempt to account for the inconsistencies in the use of claims and complaints, as in the preceding chapters, in the interview guides to follow, whose terminology was agreed to by MOL management, we enclose proper terms in brackets.
3 As explained in this book's introduction, by the time of publication, ESO2s came to be called Employment Standards Officers (ESOs). However, we have chosen to leave ESO2 in the interview questions as this is the terminology that was used with the interviewees. Elsewhere in the book, we use ESO.

# Bibliography

## Secondary Sources


Adams, R. (1987). Employment standards in Ontario: An industrial relations systems analysis. *Industrial Relations / Relations Industrielles, 42*(4), 46–64. https://doi.org/10.7202/050284ar

Akkaymak, G. (2017). A Bourdieuian analysis of job search experiences of immigrants in Canada. *International Migration and Integration, 18*(2), 657–674. https://doi.org/10.1007/s12134-016-0490-0

Amengual, M., & Fine, J. (2016). Co-enforcing labor standards: The unique contributions of state and worker organizations in Argentina and the United States. *Regulation and Governance, 11*(2), 129–142. https://doi.org/10.1111/rego.12122

Anderson, H. (2014). *The protection of employee entitlements in insolvency: An Australian perspective*. Melbourne: University of Melbourne Press.

Anderson, H., & Howe, J. (2012). Making sense of the compensation remedy in cases of accessorial liability under the Fair Work Act. *Melbourne University Law Review, 36*(2), 335–368.

Appelbaum, E., Bernhardt, A., & Murnane, R.J. (Eds.). (2003). *Low-wage America: How employers are reshaping opportunity in the workplace*. New York: Russell Sage Foundation.

Armstrong, P. (1996). The feminization of the labour force: Harmonizing down in a global economy. In I. Bakker (Ed.), *Rethinking restructuring: Gender and change in Canada* (pp. 29–54). Toronto: University of Toronto Press.

Armstrong P., & Armstrong, H. (1983). Beyond sexless class and classless sex: Towards feminist Marxism. *Studies in Political Economy, 10*(1), 7–43. https://doi.org/10.1080/19187033.1983.11675670

Arup, C., & Sutherland, C. (2009). The recovery of wages: Legal services and access to justice. *Monash University Law Review, 35*(1), 96–117.

Australian Broadcasting Corporation. (Producer). (2015, 31 August). 7-Eleven: The price of convenience [Video file]. Retrieved from http://www.abc.net.au/4corners/7-eleven-promo/6729716

Australian Broadcasting Corporation. (2015, 4 May). Slaving away: The dirty secrets behind Australia's fresh food [Video file]. Retrieved from http://www.abc.net.au/4corners/slaving-away-promo/6437876

Ayres, I., & Braithwaite, J. (1992). *Responsive regulation: Transcending the debate*. Oxford: Oxford University Press.

Bales, K., Bogg, A., & Novitz, T. (2018). "Voice" and "choice" in modern working practices: Problems with the Taylor Review. *Industrial Law Journal, 47*(1), 46–75. https://doi.org/10.1093/indlaw/dwx028

Banerjee, R. (2009). Income growth of new immigrants in Canada: Evidence from the survey of labour and income dynamics. *Relations industrielles / Industrial Relations*, *64*(3), 466–88. https://doi.org/10.7202/038552ar

Barber, B. (1984). *Strong democracy: Participatory politics for a new age*. Berkeley: University of California Press.

Barnes, L. (2016). Remedies for breach and for wrongful dismissal. In M. Freeland (Ed.), *The contract of employment* (pp. 599–620). Oxford: Oxford University Press. https://doi.org/10.1093/acprof:oso/9780198783169.003.0028

Bartrip, P.W.J., & Fenn, P.T. (1980). The conventionalization of factory crime: A re-assessment. *International Journal for the Sociology of Law*, *8*, 175–186.

Bayliss, F. (1962). *British wages councils*. Oxford: Basil Blackwell.

Bennett, L. (1994). *Making labour law in Australia: Industrial relations, politics and law*. Sydney: Law Book Co.

Berg, L., & Farbenblum B. (2017). *Wage theft in Australia: Findings of the national temporary migrant worker survey*. Retrieved from http://apo.org.au/system/files/120406/apo-nid120406-483146.pdf, https://doi.org/10.2139/ssrn.3140071

– (2018). Remedies for migrant worker exploitation in Australia: Lessons from the 7-Eleven wage repayment program. *Melbourne University Law Review*, *41*(3), 1–50.

Bernhardt, A. (2014). *Labor standards and the reorganization of work: Gaps in data and research* (IRLE Working Paper no. 100-14). Retrieved from http://irle.berkeley.edu/files/2014/Labor-Standards-and-the-Reorganization-of-Work.pdf

Bernhardt, A., Boushey, H., Dresser, L., & Tilly, C. (Eds.). (2008). *The gloves-off economy: Workplace standards at the bottom of America's labor market*. Ithaca, NY: Cornell University Press.

Bernhardt, A., Milkman, R., Theodore, N., Heckathorn, D., Auer, M., DeFilippis, J., ... Spille, M. (2009). *Broken laws, unprotected workers: Violations of employment and labor laws in America's cities*. Chicago: Center for Urban Economic Development, the National Employment Law Project, and the UCLA Institute for Research on Labor and Employment. Retrieved from https://www.nelp.org/wp-content/uploads/2015/03/BrokenLawsReport2009.pdf.

Bernhardt, A., Spiller, M.W., & Polson, D. (2013). All work and no pay: Violations of employment and labor laws in Chicago, Los Angeles and New York City. *Social Forces, 91*(3), 725–46. https://doi.org/10.1093/sf/sos193

Bernstein, S., Tucker, E., Lippel, K., & Vosko, L.F. (2006). Precarious employment and the law's flaws: Identifying regulatory failure and securing effective protection for workers. In L. Vosko (Ed.), *Precarious employment: Understanding labour market insecurity in Canada* (pp. 203–220). Montreal and Kingston: McGill-Queen's University Press.

Bittle, S. (2012). *Still dying for a living: Corporate criminal liability after the Westray Mine Disaster*. Vancouver: University of British Columbia Press.

Block, S., & Galabuzi, G. (2011). *Canada's colour-coded labour market: The gap for racialized workers*. Toronto: Wellesley Institute and Canadian Centre for Policy Alternatives. Retrieved from https://www.wellesleyinstitute.com/wp-content/uploads/2011/03/Colour_Coded_Labour_MarketFINAL.pdf

Bogg, A. (2013). The doctrine of illegality. In R. Bernard (Ed.), *Labour migration in hard times: Reforming labour market regulation?* (pp. 119–142). Liverpool: Institute of Employment Rights.

Bolduc, F. (2014). L'évolution de la représentation qu'ont les gestionnaires de santé de leur travail: les impacts de la réforme québécoise de 2003. *Gestion et Management Public, 2*(4), 5–20. https://doi.org/10.3917/gmp.024.0005

Bonacich, E., Alimohomed, S., & Wilson, J.B. (2008). The racialization of global labor. *American Behavioral Scientist, 52*(3), 342–355. https://doi.org/10.1177/0002764208323510

Bosch, G. (2009). Low-wage work in five European countries and the United States. *International Labour Review, 148*(4), 337–356. https://doi.org/10.1111/j.1564-913X.2009.00067.x

Bourdieu, P. (1990). *The logic of practice*. Cambridge: Polity Press.

Braithwaite, J., & Ayres, I. (1992). *Responsive regulation*. New York: Oxford University Press.

Bright S., Fitzpatrick K., & Fitzgerald A. (2017). *Young workers snapshot: The great wage rip-off*. Melbourne: Young Workers Centre.

*Bristol Post*. Hundreds of angry Hinkley Point C staff occupy nuclear power station in protest over wages. (2018, March 6). Retrieved from https://www.bristolpost.co.uk/news/bristol-news/hundreds-angry-hinkley-point-c-1305229

Burgess, J., & Campbell, I. (1998). Casual employment in Australia: Growth, characteristics, a bridge or a trap? *Economic and Labour Relations Review, 9*(1), 31–54. https://doi.org/10.1177/103530469800900102

Burns, E.M. (1926). [Review of the book *Wages and the state*, by P.H. Douglas]. *Economica, 16*, 105–106. https://doi.org/10.2307/2548557

Buzdugan, R., & Halli, S.S. (2009). Labor market experiences of Canadian immigrants with focus on foreign education and experience. *International Migration Review, 43*(2), 366–386. https://doi.org/10.1111/j.1747-7379.2009.00768.x

Campbell, M. (2013, May). The FWO's approach to compliance and enforcement. Speech to National PIR Group Conference, Canberra, ACT.

Carré, F. (2015). *(In)dependent contractor misclassification*. Washington, DC: Economic Policy Institute. Retrieved from http://www.epi.org/files/pdf/87595.pdf

Carson, W.G. (1974). Symbolic and instrumental dimensions of early factory legislation: A case study in the social origins of criminal law. In R. Hood (Ed.), *Crime, criminology and public policy* (pp. 107–137). London: Heinemann.

– (1979). The conventionalization of early factory crime. *International Journal for the Sociology of Law, 7*, 37–60.

– (1980). Early factory inspectors and the viable class society: A rejoinder. *International Journal for the Sociology of Law, 8*, 187–191.

Casey, R., Tucker, E., Vosko, L.F., & Noack, A.M. (2018). Using tickets in employment standards inspections: Deterrence as effective enforcement in Ontario, Canada? *Economic and Industrial Relations Review, 29*(2), 228–249. https://doi.org/10.1177/1035304618769772

Chan, J.B.L. (1999). Governing police practice: Limits of the new accountability. *British Journal of Sociology, 50*(2), 251–270.

Chandler, A. (1962). *Strategy and structure: Chapters in the history of the American industrial enterprise*. Cambridge: MIT Press.

Charbonneau, M. (2012). Nouveau management public. In L. Côté & J. Savard (Eds.), *Le Dictionnaire encyclopédique de l'administration publique*. Retrieved from http://www.dictionnaire.enap.ca/Dictionnaire/18/Index_par_auteur.enap?by=aut&id=50.

Chartered Institute of Personnel and Development (CIPD). (2017). *Employment regulation in the UK: Burden or benefit?* London: Chartered Institute of Personnel and Development.

Cho, E.H., Koonse, T., and Mischel, A. (2013). *Hollow victories: The crisis in collecting unpaid wages for California complainants*. Los Angeles: UCLA Labour Center and National Employment Law Project. Retrieved from https://www.labor.ucla.edu/publication/hollow-victories-the-crisis-in-collecting-unpaid-wages-for-californias-workers/

Choudry, A., & Smith, A.A. (2016). "Introduction: Struggling against unfree labour." In A. Choudry and A.A. Smith, *Unfree labour?* (pp. 1–19). Oakland, CA: PM Press.

Cingano, F. (2014). *Trends in income inequality and its impact on economic growth.* OECD Social, Employment and Migration Working Papers, no. 163. Paris: OECD Publishing. http://dx.doi.org/10.1787/5jxrjncwxv6j-en.

Citizens Advice. (2015). *Neither one thing nor the other: How reducing bogus self-employment could benefit workers, business and the Exchequer.* London: National Association of Citizens Advice Bureaux.

– (2017, February 26). Employers tricking people out of sick pay, says Citizens Advice. Retrieved from https://www.citizensadvice.org.uk/about-us/how-citizens-advice-works/media/press-releases/employers-tricking-people-out-of-sick-pay-says-citizens-advice/

Clark, N. (2016). When the boss won't cough up. *Labour Research, 105* (10), 16–18.

Clark, N., & Herman, E. (2017, November). *Unpaid Britain: Wage default in the British labour market.* London: Trust for London & Middlesex University. Retrieved from https://www.mdx.ac.uk/__data/assets/pdf_file/0017/440531/Final-Unpaid-Britain-report.pdf?bustCache=35242825

Clarke, J., & Newman J. (1997). *The managerial state: Power, politics and ideology in the remaking of social welfare.* Thousand Oaks, CA: Sage.

Clibborn, S., & Wright, C. (2018). Employer theft of temporary migrant workers' wages in Australia: Why has the state failed to act? *Economic and Labour Relations Review, 29*(2), 207–227. https://doi.org/10.1177/1035304618765906

Coe, N.M., & Jordhus-Lier, D.C. (2011). Constrained agency? Re-evaluating the geographies of labour. *Progress in Human Geography, 35*(2), 211–33. https://doi.org/10.1177/0309132510366746

Coglianese, C. (2017). The challenge of regulatory excellence. In C. Coglianese (Ed.), *Achieving regulatory excellence* (pp. 1–19). Washington, DC: Brookings Institution Press.

Colling, T. (2004). No claim, no pain? The privatisation of dispute resolution in Britain. *Economic and Industrial Democracy, 25*(4), 555–579. https://doi.org/10.1177/0143831X04047159

Colodny, D., Halejua, A., Lotto L., Pelaez, J., Pfitsch, H., Ricardo, C., & Tai, A. (2015). *Empty judgements: The wage collection crisis in New York.* New York: Urban Justice Centre, Legal Aid Society & National Centre for Law and Economic Justice. Retrieved from http://nclej.org/wp-content/uploads/2015/11/Empty-Judgments-The-Wage-Collection-Crisis-in-New-York.pdf

Commons, J.R., & Andrews, J.B. (1916). *Principles of labor legislation.* New York: Augustus Kelley.

Coulter, K. (2014). *Revolutionizing retail: Workers, political action, and social change.* USwitzerland: Springer Link. https://doi.org/10.1057/9781137361165

Cranford, C.J., Das Gupta, T., Ladd, D., & Vosko, L.F. (2006). Thinking through community unionism. In L. Vosko (Ed.), *Precarious employment: Understanding labour market insecurity in Canada* (pp. 353–378). Montreal and Kingston: McGill-Queen's University Press.

Cranford, C.J., Fudge, J., Tucker, E., & Vosko, L.F. (2005). *Self-employed workers organize: Law, policy and unions.* Montreal and Kingston: McGill-Queen's University Press.

Davidov, G. (2010). The enforcement crisis in labour law and the fallacy of voluntarist solutions. *International Journal of Comparative Labour Law and Industrial Relations, 26*(1), 61–82.

Deakin, S., & Wilkinson, F. (2005). *The law of the labour market.* Oxford: Oxford University Press.

de Tonnancour, V., & Vallée, G. (2009). Les relations de travail tripartites et l'application des norms minimales du travail au Québec. *Relations industrielles, 64*(3), 399–441. https://doi.org/10.7202/038550ar

de Wolff, A. (2000). *Breaking the myth of flexible work: Contingent work in Toronto.* Toronto: Workers' Action Centre.

Di Angelo, R. (2011). *What does it mean to be white? Developing white racial literacy*. Bern: Peter Lang.

Dickens, L. (Ed). (2012). *Making employment rights effective.* Oxford: Hart Publishing.

Dickens, L., & Hall, M. (2006). Fairness – up to a point: Assessing the impact of New Labour's employment legislation. *Human Resources Management Journal, 16*(4), 338–356. https://doi.org/10.1111/j.1748-8583.2006.00024.x

Diefenbach, T. (2009). New public management in public sector organizations: The dark sides of managerialistic "enlightenment." *Public Administration, 87*(4), 892–909. https://doi.org/10.1111/j.1467-9299.2009.01766.x

Donahue, L.H., Lamare, J., & Kotler, F. (2007). *The cost of worker misclassification in New York State* [Electronic version]. Ithaca, NY: Cornell University, School of Industrial and Labor Relations. Retrieved from http://digitalcommons.ilr.cornell.edu/reports/9/

Dunstan, R. (2018, 4 February). Honey, I shrunk the NMW arrears [Blog post]. Retrieved from https://labourpainsblog.com/2018/02/04/honey-i-shrunk-the-nmw-arrears/

Emmenegger, P., Häusermann, S., & Seeleib-Kaiser, M. (Eds.). (2012). *The age of dualization: The changing face of inequality in deindustrializing societies.* Oxford: Oxford University Press. https://doi.org/10.1093/acprof:oso/9780199797899.001.0001

Employment Standards Working Group. (1996). *Bad boss stories: Workers whose bosses break the law.* Toronto: Employment Standards Working Group.

Engel, D.M. (2016.) *The myth of the litigious society: Why we don't sue.* Chicago: Chicago University Press. https://doi.org/10.7208/chicago/9780226305189.001.0001

Estlund, C. (2005). Rebuilding the law of the workplace in an era of self-regulation. *Columbia Law Review, 105*(2), 319–404.
– (2012). A return to governance in the law of the workplace. In D. Levi-Faur (Ed.), *The Oxford handbook of governance* (pp. 540–553). Oxford: Oxford University Press. https://doi.org/10.1093/oxfordhb/9780199560530.013.0038
Fairey, D. (2005). *Eroding worker protections: British Columbia's new "flexible" employment standards.* Vancouver: Canadian Centre for Policy Alternatives, BC Office. Retrieved from http://www.policyalternatives.ca/sites/default/files/uploads/publications/BC_Office_Pubs/bc_2005/employment_standards.pdf
Fairey, D., & McCallum, S. (2007). Negotiating without a floor: Unionized worker exclusion from BC employment standard. Vancouver: Centre for Policy Alternatives, BC Office. Retrieved from https://www.policyalternatives.ca/publications/reports/negotiating-without-floor
Faraday, F. (2014). *Profiting from the precarious: How recruitment practices exploit migrant workers.* Toronto: Metcalf Foundation. Retrieved from https://metcalffoundation.com/stories/publications/profiting-from-the-precarious-how-recruitment-practices-exploit-migrant-workers/
Farbenblum, B., & Berg. L. (2017). Migrant workers' access to remedy for exploitation in Australia: The role of the national Fair Work ombudsman. *Australian Journal of Human Rights, 23*(3), 319–331. https://doi.org/10.1080/1323238X.2017.1392478
Ferguson, A., & Christodoulou, M. (2017). The Domino's effect: How Australia's biggest pizza chain has squeezed franchisees. *Sydney Morning Herald*. Retrieved from https://www.smh.com.au/interactive/2017/the-dominos-effect/
Fine, J.R. (2006). *Worker centers: Organizing communities at the edge of the dream.* Ithaca, NY: Cornell University Press.
– (2007). A marriage made in heaven? Mismatches and misunderstandings between worker centres and unions. *British Journal of Industrial Relations, 45*(2), 335–360. https://doi.org/10.1111/j.1467-8543.2007.00617.x
– (2011). New forms to settle old scores: Updating the worker centre story in the United States. *Industrial Relations, 66*(4), 604–630. https://doi.org/10.7202/1007636ar
– (2013). Solving the problem from hell: Tripartism as a strategy for addressing labour standards non-compliance in the United States. *Osgoode Hall Law Journal, 50*(4), 813–843.
– (2014). Strengthening labor standards compliance through co-production of enforcement. *New Labor Forum, 23*(2), 76–83. https://doi.org/10.1177/1095796014527260
– (2017). Enforcing labor standards in partnership with civil society: Can co-enforcement succeed where the state alone has failed? *Politics and Society, 45*(3), 359–388. https://doi.org/10.1177/0032329217702603

Fine, J.R., & Gordon, J. (2010). Strengthening labour standards enforcement through partnerships with complainants' organizations. *Politics and Society, 38*(4), 552–585. https://doi.org/10.1177/0032329210381240

Fine, J.R., & Lyon, G. (2017). Segmentation and the role of labor standards enforcement in immigration reform. *Journal on Migration and Human Security, 5*(2): 431–451. https://doi.org/10.1177/233150241700500211

Forsyth, A. (2017). Law, politics and ideology: The regulatory response to trade union corruption in Australia. *UNSW Law Journal, 40*(4), 1336–1365. https://doi.org/10.2139/ssrn.3357469

Fraser, N. (2018). Roepke Lecture in Economic Geography – From exploitation to expropriation: Historic geographies of racialized capitalism. *Economic Geography, 94*(1), 1–17. https://doi.org/10.1080/00130095.2017.1398045

Fudge, J. (1988). Labour, the new constitution and old style liberalism. *Queen's Law Journal, 13*(1), 61–111.

– (1991a). *Labour law's little sister: The Employment Standards Act and the feminization of labour*. Ottawa: Canadian Centre for Policy Alternatives.

– (1991b). Reconceiving employment standards legislation: Labour law's little sister and the feminization of labour. *Journal of Law and Social Policy, 7*, 73–89.

Fudge, J., McCrystal, S., & Sankaran, K. (Eds.). (2012). *Challenging the legal boundaries of work regulation*. Oxford: Hart Publishing Ltd.

Fudge, J., & McDermott, P. (Eds.). (1992). *Just wages: A feminist assessment of pay equity*. Toronto: University of Toronto Press.

Fudge, J., & Tucker, E. (2000). Pluralism or fragmentation? The twentieth-century employment law regime in Canada. [Special issue]. *Labour / Le Travail, 46*, 251–306. https://doi.org/10.2307/25149101

– (2001). *Labour before the law: The regulation of workers' collective action in Canada, 1900–1948*. Don Mills, ON: Oxford University Press.

Fudge, J., & Vosko, L.F. (2001). Gender and segmentation: The standard employment relationship in Canadian labour law, legislation and policy. *Economic and Industrial Democracy, 22*(2), 271–310. https://doi.org/10.1177/0143831X01222005

– (2003). Gendered paradoxes and the rise of contingent work: Towards a transformative feminist political economy of the labour market. In C. Wallace & L.F. Vosko (Eds.), *Changing Canada: Political economy as transformation* (pp. 183–213). Montreal and Kingston: McGill-Queen's University Press.

Gautié, J., & Schmitt, J. (2010). *Low-wage work in the wealthy world*. New York: Russell Sage Foundation.

Gellatly, M. (2007). *Working on the edge*. Toronto: Workers' Action Centre.

– (2015). *Still working on the edge*. Toronto: Workers' Action Centre.

Gellatly, M., Grundy, J., Mirchandani, M., Perry, A., Thomas, M.P., & Vosko, L.F. (2011). "Modernizing" employment standards? Administrative efficiency and the production of the illegitimate claimant in Ontario, Canada. *Economic and Labour Relations Review*, *22*(2), 81–106. https://doi.org/10.1177/103530461102200205

Gesualdi-Fecteau, D. (2015a). Le droit comme rempart utile? L'usage par les travailleurs étrangers temporaires des ressources proposées par le droit du travail. *Revue générale de droit*, *45*(2), 531–578. https://doi.org/10.7202/1035300ar

– (2015b). *Les travailleurs étrangers temporaires peu spécialisés: une étude de l'effectivité du droit du travail* (Unpublished doctoral dissertation). Montreal: Université de Montréal.

– (2016). Le système d'emploi des travailleurs agricoles saisonniers: portrait d'un rapport salarial multipartite. *Relations industrielles / Industrial Relations*, *71*(4), 611–638. https://doi.org/10.7202/1038525ar

Gesualdi-Fecteau, D., & Vallée, G. (2016). Labour inspection and labour standards enforcement in Quebec: Contingencies and intervention strategies. *Comparative Labor Law and Policy Journal*, *37*(2), 339–376.

– (2017). La mise en œuvre de la *Loi sur les normes du travail*: étude empirique d'un modèle singulier d'inspection du travail. *REMEST: Revue multidisciplinaire sur l'emploi, le syndicalisme et le travail*, *11*(1), 4–31. https://doi.org/10.7202/1043836ar

Givan, R.K. (2007). Side by side we battle onward? Representing workers in contemporary America. *British Journal of Industrial Relations*, *45*(4), 829–855.

Gleeson, S. (2012). *Conflicting commitments: The politics of enforcing immigrant worker rights in San Jose and Houston*. Ithaca, NY: Cornell University Press. https://doi.org/10.7591/cornell/9780801451218.001.0001

Gorrie, P. (2003, May 30). Focus falls on Rogers over ethics: Haven't been paid their work service workers say. *Toronto Star*, p. B03.

– (2004, May 29). Immigrants take a stand for money they earned: 63,000 owed $214 million, group says; Changes coming labour minister vows. *Toronto Star*, p. C15.

Gow, J.I., & Dufour, C. (2000). Is the new public management a paradigm? Is it important? *International Review of Administrative Sciences*, *66*(4), 679–707. https://doi.org/10.1177/0020852300664002

Graefe, P. (2007). Political economy and Canadian public policy. In M. Orsini & M. Smith (Eds.), *Critical policy studies* (pp. 19–40). Vancouver: UBC Press.

Gray, G.C. (2006). The regulation of corporate violations: Punishment, compliance and the blurring of responsibility. *British Journal of Criminology*, *46*(5), 875–892. https://doi.org/10.1093/bjc/azl005

Gray, W.B., & Scholz, J.T. (1993). Does regulatory enforcement work? A panel analysis of OSHA enforcement. *Law & Society Review, 27*(1), 177–213. https://doi.org/10.2307/3053754

Griffith, A., & Smith, E.D. (Eds.). (2014). *Under new public management: Institutional ethnographies of changing front-line work.* Toronto: University of Toronto Press. https://doi.org/10.3138/9781442619463

Grossman, J. (1978). *Fair Labor Standards Act* of 1938: Maximum struggle for a minimum wage. *Monthly Labor Review, 101*(6), 22–30.

Grundy, J., Noack, A.M., Vosko, L.F., Casey, R., & Hii, R. (2017). Enforcement of Ontario's *Employment Standards Act*: The impact of reforms. *Canadian Public Policy / Analyse de Politiques, 43*(3), 190–201. https://doi.org/10.3138/CPP.2016-064

Gunningham, N. (2016). Regulation: From traditional to cooperative. In S.R. Van Slykes, M.L. Benson, & F.T. Cullen (Eds.), *The Oxford handbook of white-collar crime* (pp. 503–520). Oxford: Oxford University Press.

Hage, G. (1998). *White nation: Fantasies of white supremacy in a multicultural society.* Sydney: Pluto Press.

Hall, A., Forrest, A., Sears, A., & Carlan, N. (2006). Making a difference: Knowledge activism and the workplace politics of occupational health. *Relations industrielles / Industrial Relations, 61*(3), 408–436. https://doi.org/10.7202/014184ar

Hall, A., Grundy, J., Vosko. L.F., Siemiatyki, E., & Hall, R. (2019). *Vulnerable workers and (dis)empowered claimants: Shifting subjects of regulation in Ontario's employment standards regime.* Manuscript in preparation.

Hardy, T. (2009). A changing of the guard: Enforcement of workplace relations laws since work choices and beyond. In A. Forsyth & A. Stewart (Eds.), *Fair work: The new workplace laws and the work choices legacy* (pp. 75–98). Annadale, AUS: Federation Press.

– (2011). Enrolling non-state actors to improve compliance with minimum employment standards. *Economic and Labour Relations Review, 22*(3), 117–140. https://doi.org/10.1177/103530461102200308

– (2014). "It's oh so quiet?" Employee voice and the enforcement of employment standards regulation in Australia. In A. Bogg & T. Novitz (Eds.), *Voices at work: Continuity and change in the common law world* (pp. 249–273). Oxford: Oxford University Press. https://doi.org/10.1093/acprof:oso/9780199683130.003.0012

– (2016). Who should be held liable for workplace contraventions and on what basis? *Australian Journal of Labour Law, 29*(1), 78–109.

– (2017a). Good call: Extending liability for employment contraventions beyond the direct employer. In R. Levy, M. O'Brien, S. Rice, P. Ridge, & M. Thornton (Eds.), *New directions for law in Australia: Essays in contemporary law reform* (pp. 71–82). Acton: ANU Press. https://doi.org/10.22459/NDLA.09.2017.05

– (2017b). Watch this space: Mapping the actors involved in the implementation of labour standards regulation in Australia. In J. Howe, A. Chapman, & I. Landau (Eds.), *The evolving project of labour law: Foundations, development and future research directions* (pp. 145–160). Annadale: Federation Press.
– (2018). The state strikes back: Supervision and sanctioning of unlawful industrial activity by federal government agencies in Australia. In S. McCrystal, B. Creighton, & A. Forsyth (Eds.), *Collective bargaining under the Fair Work Act* (pp. 182–205). Alexandria: Federation Press, 2018.
Hardy, T., & Howe, J. (2009). Partners in enforcement? The new balance between government and trade union enforcement of employment standards in Australia. *Australian Journal of Labour Law, 23*(3), 306–336.
– (2013). Too soft or too severe? Enforceable undertakings and the regulatory dilemma facing the fair work ombudsman. *Federal Law Review, 41*(1), 1–34. https://doi.org/10.22145/flr.41.1.1
– (2015). Chain reaction: A strategic approach to addressing employment non-compliance in complex supply chains. *Journal of Industrial Relations, 57*(4), 563–584. https://doi.org/10.1177/0022185615582240
– (2017). Creating ripples, making waves? Assessing the general deterrence effects of enforcement activities of the fair work ombudsman. *Sydney Law Review, 39*(4), 471–500.
Hardy, T., Howe, J., & Cooney, S. (2013). Less energetic but more enlightened? Exploring the fair work ombudsman's use of litigation in regulatory enforcement. *Sydney Law Review, 35*(3), 565–597.
– (2014). *The transformation of enforcement of minimum employment standards in Australia: A review of the FWO's activities from 2006–2012*. Melbourne: Centre for Employment and Labour Relations Law.
Harvey, D. (2004). The "new" imperialism: Accumulation by dispossession. *Socialist Register, 40*, 63–87.
Hay, D., & Craven, P. (2004). *Masters, servants, and magistrates in Britain and the Empire, 1562–1955*. Chapel Hill: University of North Carolina Press.
Henry, C. (2016). Le droit du travail en médiation. In D. Gesualdi-Fecteau & L. Lamarche (Eds.), *La multiplication des normes et des recours en droit du travail: quelles conséquences pour la mobilisation* (pp. 47–58). Cowansville, QC: Éditions Yvon Blais.
Hepple, B. (2013). Back to the future: Employment law under the coalition government. *Industrial Law Journal, 42*(3): 203–223. https://doi.org/10.1093/indlaw/dwt009
Hesse-Biber, S. (Ed.). (2012). *Handbook of feminist research: Theory and praxis* (2nd ed.). Thousand Oaks, CA: Sage Publications. https://doi.org/10.4135/9781483384740
Hetland, G. (2015). The labour of learning: Overcoming the obstacles facing union-worker centre collaborations. *Work, Employment and Society, 29*(6), 932–949. https://doi.org/10.1177/0950017015577898

Heyes, A. (2000). Implementing environmental regulation: Enforcement and compliance. *Journal of Regulatory Economics, 17*(2), 107–129. https://doi.org/10.1023/A:1008157410380

Holgate, J., Pollert, A., Keles, J., & Kumarappan L. (2012). De-collectivization and employment problems: The experiences of minority ethnic workers seeking help through Citizens Advice. *Work, Employment and Society, 26*(5), 772–788. https://doi.org/10.1177/0950017012451641

Holley, S. (2014). The monitoring and enforcement of labour standards when services are contracted out. *Journal of Industrial Relations, 56*(5), 672–690. https://doi.org/10.1177/0022185614523277

Hyde, A. (2012). Legal responsibility for labour conditions down the production chain. In J. Fudge, S. McCrystal, & K. Sankaran (Eds.), *Challenging the legal boundaries of work regulation* (pp. 83–100). Oxford: Hart Publishing.

International Ladies' Garment Workers Union & INTERCEDE. (1993). *Meeting the needs of vulnerable workers: Proposals for improved employment legislation and access to collective bargaining for domestic workers and industrial homeworkers.* Toronto: International Ladies' Garment Workers Union & INTERCEDE.

James, C. (2012). Students "at risk": Stereotypes and the schooling of Black boys. *Urban Education, 47*(2), 464–494. https://doi.org/10.1177/0042085911429084

James, N. (2017, 10 March). It takes more than wanting to do the right thing – The fair work ombudsman's approach to accessorial liability. Speech to Lander and Rogers, Melbourne, VIC.

– (2017, 1 May). Current issues in the regulation of Australian workplaces. Speech delivered to the Australian Industry Group 2017 Annual National Policy Influence Reform Conference, Canberra, ACT.

– (2017, 14 September). Industry led compliance is the best way forward. Speech delivered to the Asia Pacific Fuel Industry Forum, Melbourne, VIC.

Janesick. V.J. (1994). The dance of qualitative research design: Metaphor, methodolatry and meaning. In N.K. Denzin & Y.S. Lincoln (Eds.), *Handbook of qualitative research* (pp. 209–219). Thousand Oaks, CA: Sage Publications.

Jones, R. (2010). Learning beyond the state: The pedagogical spaces of the CAB service. *Citizenship Studies, 14*(6), 725–38. https://doi.org/10.1080/13621025.2010.522361

Jones, S. (1985). Depth interviewing. In R. Walker (Ed.), *Applied qualitative research* (pp. 45–55). Aldershot, UK: Gower.

Judson, T., & Francisco-McGuire, C. (2012). Where wage theft is legal: Mapping wage theft laws in the 50 states. Progressive States Network. Retrieved from https://www.researchgate.net/publication/326678129_Where_Theft_is_Legal_Mapping_Wage_Theft_Laws_in_the_50_States

Kaine, S.J., & Josserand, E. (2018). Mind the gap: Grass roots "brokering" to improve labour standards in global supply chains. *Human Relations*, 7(4), 584–609. https://doi.org/10.1177/0018726717727046

Kalleberg, A. (2011). *Good jobs, bad jobs: The rise of polarized and precarious employment systems in the United States.* New York: Russell Sage Foundation.

Katznelson, I. (2013). *Fear itself: The New Deal and the origins of our time.* New York: Liveright Publishing Corporation.

Kazemipur, A., & Halli, S. (2001). Immigrants and "new poverty": The case of Canada. *International Migration Review*, *35*(4), 1129–1156. https://doi.org/10.1111/j.1747-7379.2001.tb00055.x

Keil, R. (2002). "Common-sense" neoliberalism: Progressive conservative urbanism in Toronto, Canada. *Antipode*, *34*(3), 578–601. https://doi.org/10.1111/1467-8330.00255

Kennedy M., & Howe, J. (2018). The criminalisation of wage theft as a compliance strategy. Paper presented at the Australian Labour Law Association Conference, Gold Coast, 9–10 November.

Kernerman, G. (2005). *Multicultural nationalism: Civilizing difference, constituting community*. Vancouver: UBC Press.

Kessler-Harris, A. (1982). *Out to work: A history of wage-earning women in the United States.* New York: Oxford University Press.

Kessler-Harris, A., Lewis, J.E., & Wikander, U. (Eds.). (1995). Introduction. In U. Wikander, A. Kessler-Harris, & J.E. Lewis (Eds.), *Protecting women: Labor legislation in Europe, the United States, and Australia, 1890–1920* (pp. 1–28). Urbana, IL: University of Illinois Press.

Kirk, E. (2017). The "problem" with the Employment Tribunal System: Reform, rhetoric and realities for the clients of Citizens' Advice Bureau. *Work, Employment and Society*, *32*(6), 975–991. https://doi.org/10.1177/0950017017701077

Kleven, H., Knudsen, M., Kreiner, C., Pedersen, S., & Saez, E. (2011). Unwilling or unable to cheat? Evidence from a tax audit experiment in Denmark. *Econometrica: Journal of the Econometric Society*, *79*(3), 651–692. https://doi.org/10.3982/ECTA9113

Klijn, E.H. (2012). New Public Management and governance: A comparison. In D. Levi-Faur (Ed.), *The Oxford handbook of governance* (pp. 201–214). Oxford: Oxford University Press. https://doi.org/10.1093/oxfordhb/9780199560530.013.0014

Kolins Givan, R. (2007). Side by side we battle onward? Representing workers in contemporary America. *British Journal of Industrial Relations*, *45*(4), 829–855. https://doi.org/10.1111/j.1467-8543.2007.00663.x

Kraakman, Reinier H. (1986). Gatekeepers: The anatomy of a third party enforcement strategy. *Journal of Law, Economics and Organisation*, *2*(1), 53–104.

Lane, Marion E. (1977). *Administration in action: An institutional analysis of the Ontario Employment Standards Branch*. Paper submitted in partial fulfillment of the requirements for the LLM degree, University of California at Berkeley.

Law Commission of Ontario. (2010). *Vulnerable workers and precarious work: Background paper*. Toronto: Law Commission of Ontario. Retrieved from https://www.lco-cdo.org/wp-content/uploads/2011/02/VulnerableWorkersBackgroundPaper-December2010.pdf

– (2012). *Vulnerable workers and precarious employment: Final report*. Toronto: Law Commission of Ontario. Retrieved from https://www.lco-cdo.org/wp-content/uploads/2013/03/vulnerable-workers-final-report.pdf

Ledoux, É. (2003). Un moindre mal pour les travailleuses? La Commission du salaire minimum des femmes, 1925–1937. *Labour / Le Travail, 51*, 81–114. https://doi.org/10.2307/25149333

Lesniewski, J., & Canon, R. (2016). Worker centres, cities and grassroots regulation of the labour market. *Community Development Journal, 51*(1), 114–131. https://doi.org/10.1093/cdj/bsv059

Lichtenstein, N. (1982). *Labor's war at home: The CIO in World War II*. Philadelphia: Temple University Press.

Lipsky, M. (1980). *Street level bureaucracy: Dilemmas of the individual in public services*. New York: Russell Sage Foundation.

Lobel, O. (2004). The renew deal: The fall of regulation and the rise of governance in contemporary legal thought. *Minnesota Law Review, 89*, 7–27.

– (2005). Interlocking regulatory and industrial relations: The governance of workplace safety. *Administrative Law Review, 57*(4), 1071–1152.

– (2012). New governance as regulatory governance. In D. Levi-Faur (Ed.), *The Oxford handbook of governance* (pp. 65–82). Oxford: Oxford University Press. https://doi.org/10.1093/oxfordhb/9780199560530.013.0005

Lewchuk, W., Clark, M., & de Wolff, A. (2011). *Working without commitments: The health effects of precarious employment*. Montreal and Kingston: McGill-Queen's University Press.

Lewchuk, W., Lafleche, M., Goldring, L., Meisner, A., Porocyk, S., Rosen, D., ... & Vrankulj, S. (2013). *It's more than poverty: Employment precarity and household well-being*. Toronto: Poverty and Employment Precarity in Southern Ontario Research Group.

Luce, S. (2014). *Labor movements: Global perspectives*. Cambridge: Polity Press.

MacDonald, M. (1991). Post-fordism and the flexibility debate. *Studies in Political Economy, 36*(1), 177–201. https://doi.org/10.1080/19187033.1991.11675447

Maconachie, G., & Goodwin, M. (2006). Recouping wage underpayment: Increasingly less likely? *Australian Journal of Social Issues, 41*(3), 327–342. https://doi.org/10.1002/j.1839-4655.2006.tb00019.x

Matulewicz, K. (2015). Law and the construction of institutionalized sexual harassment in restaurants. *Canadian Journal of Law and Society / Revue Canadienne Droit et Société, 30*(3), 401–419. https://doi.org/10.1017/cls.2015.12

Maynes, M.J., Pierce, J.L., & Laslett, B. (2008). *Telling stories: The use of personal narratives in the social sciences and history.* Ithaca, NY: Cornell University Press.

McBride, S. (1992). *Not working: State unemployment and neo-conservatism in Canada.* Toronto: University of Toronto Press.

McCallum, M. (1986). Keeping women in their place: The minimum wage in Canada, 1910–25. *Labour / Le Travail, 17*, 29–56. https://doi.org/10.2307/25142592

McManus, S. (2018, April). Arbitration is fundamental to a fair industrial system. Speech to Per Capita Reform Agenda Series, Melbourne.

McNally, D. (2011). *Global slump: The economics and politics of crisis and resistance.* Winnipeg: Fernwood.

Milkman, R., González, A.L., & Ikeler, P. (2012). Wage and hour violations in urban labour markets: A comparison of Los Angeles, New York and Chicago. *Journal of Industrial Relations, 43*(5), 378–398. https://doi.org/10.1111/j.1468-2338.2012.00694.x

Mirchandani, K., & Chan, W. (2007). *Criminalizing race, criminalizing poverty: Welfare fraud enforcement in Canada.* Halifax: Fernwood.

Mirchandani, K., Vosko, L.F., Soni-Sinha, U., Perry, A.J., Noack, A.M., Hall, R.J., & Gellatly, M. (2016). Methodological k/nots: Designing research on the enforcement of labor standards. *Journal of Mixed Methods Research, 12*(2), 133–147. https://doi.org/10.1177/1558689816651793

Mojtehedzadeh, S. (2015, 10 May). Ontario cashing in on temporary workers. *Toronto Star.* Retrieved from https://www.thestar.com/news/gta/2015/05/10/ontario-employers-cashing-in-on-temporary-workers.html

– (2018, 29 June). Ontario government hiring freeze ices plan to strengthen workplace inspections. *Toronto Star.* Retrieved from https://www.thestar.com/news/gta/2018/06/29/ontario-government-hiring-freeze-ices-plan-to-strengthen-workplace-inspections.html

– (2018, 28 October). Ministry of Labour puts hold on proactive inspections, internal memo says. *Toronto Star.* Retrieved from https://www.thestar.com/news/queenspark/2018/10/25/ministry-of-labour-puts-hold-on-proactive-workplace-inspections-internal-memo-says.html

Morantz, A. (2014). Putting data to work for complainants: The role of information technology in U.S. worker protection agencies [Supplement]. *ILR Review, 67*(3), 675–701. https://doi.org/10.1177/00197939140670S309

National Employment Law Project. (2011). *Winning wage justice: An advocate's guide to state and city policies to fight wage theft.* New York: National

Employment Law Project. Retrieved from https://www.nelp.org/wp-content/uploads/2015/03/WinningWageJustice2011.pdf

Nicholls, T. (1997). *The sociology of industrial injury*. London: Mansell Publishing.

Noack, A.M., & Vosko, L.F. (2011). *Precarious jobs in Ontario: Mapping dimensions of labour market insecurity by workers' social location and context*. Toronto: Law Commission of Ontario. Retrieved from https://www.lco-cdo.org/wp-content/uploads/2012/01/vulnerable-workers-call-for-papers-noack-vosko.pdf

Noack, A.M., Vosko, L.F., & Grundy, J. (2015). Measuring employment standards violations, evasion and erosion: Using a telephone survey. *Relations industrielles / Industrial Relations*, *70*(1), 86–109. https://doi.org/10.7202/1029281ar

Owens, R. (2016). Temporary labour migration and workplace rights in Australia: Is effective enforcement possible? In J. Howe & R. Owens (Eds.), *Temporary labour migration in the global era: The regulatory challenges* (pp. 393–412). Oxford: Hart.

Palameta, B. (2004). Low income among immigrants and visible minorities. *Perspectives*, *5*(4), 12–17. Statistics Canada catalogue no. 75-001-XIE. Retrieved from http://citeseerx.ist.psu.edu/viewdoc/download?doi=10.1.1.583.8843&rep=rep1&type=pdf

Panitch, L., & Swartz, D. (2003). *From consent to coercion: The assault on trade union freedoms* (3rd ed.). Toronto: Garamond.

Patton, M. (1990). *Qualitative evaluation and research methods* (2nd ed.). Beverly Hills, CA: Sage.

Peck, J. (1996). *Work-place: The social regulation of labor markets*. New York: Guilford Press.

– (2001). *Workfare states*. New York: Guilford Press.

Peck, J., & Theodore, N. (2000). Beyond "employability." *Cambridge Journal of Economics*, *24*(6), 729–749. https://doi.org/10.1093/cje/24.6.729

Pendakur, K., & Pendakur, R. (2016). Which child immigrants face earnings disparity? Age-at-immigration, ethnic minority status and labour market attainment in Canada. *International Migration*, *54*(5), 43–58. https://doi.org/10.1111/imig.12256

Perry, A. (2003, 3 February). Salesman cut out by contracting out; wants Rogers to pay commission cable giant blames ex-subcontractor. *Toronto Star*, p. B01.

Phillips, J. (2016). Myopia and misrecognition: The impact of managerialism on the management of compliance. *Criminology and Criminal Justice*, *16*(1), 40–59. https://doi.org/10.1177/1748895815594664

Pierre, J. (2012). Governance and institutional flexibility. In D. Levi-Faur (Ed.), The Oxford handbook of governance (pp. 187–200).

Oxford: Oxford University Press. https://doi.org/10.1093/oxfordhb/9780199560530.013.0013

Pollert, A. (2008). Under-funded, overstretched and overwhelmed: The experience of Citizens Advice Bureaux and Law Centre advisers in supporting vulnerable workers. *Centre for Employment Studies Research Review*, 1–7.

– (2009). *Varieties of collectivism among Britain's low-paid unorganised workers with problems at work.* Working Paper 13. Bristol: University of the West of England, Bristol. Retrieved from http://eprints.uwe.ac.uk/7489

Pollert, A., & Charlwood, A. (2009). The vulnerable worker in Britain and problems at work. *Work, Employment and Society*, *23*(2), 343–362. https://doi.org/10.1177/0950017009106771

Porter, A. (2003). *Gendered states: Women, unemployment insurance, and the political economy of the welfare state in Canada, 1945–1997.* Toronto: University of Toronto Press. https://doi.org/10.3138/9781442675216

Prudham, S. (2004). Poisoning the well: Neoliberalism and the contamination of municipal water in Walkerton, Ontario. *Geoforum*, *35*(3), 343–359. https://doi.org/10.1016/j.geoforum.2003.08.010

Purse, K., & Dorrian, J. (2011). Deterrence and enforcement of occupational health & safety law. *International Journal of Comparative Labour Law & Industrial Relations*, *27*(1), 23–40.

Ranieri, S. (2018). Accessories and the *Fair Work Act* – Section 550 and an individual's "involvement" in a contravention: Is reform needed? *Australian Journal of Labour Law*, *31*, 181–208.

Rawling, M., & Schofield-Georgeson, E. (2018). Industrial legislation in 2017. *Journal of Industrial Relations*, *60*(3), 378–396. https://doi.org/10.1177/0022185618760088

Rawling, Michael J. (2006). A generic model of regulating supply chain outsourcing. In Christopher Arnup (Ed.), *Labour law and labour market regulation: Essays on the construction, constitution and regulation of labour markets and work relationships* (pp. 520–541). Sydney: Federation Press.

Reitz, J.G. (2001). Immigrant skill utilization in the Canadian labour market: Implications of human capital research. *Journal of International Migration and Integration*, *2*(3), 347–378. https://doi.org/10.1007/s12134-001-1004-1

Riley, J. (2009). Workplace dispute resolution under the Fair Work Act: Is there a role for private alternative dispute resolution providers? *Alternative Dispute Resolution Journal*, *20*(4), 236–243.

Robinson, G., & Ugwudike, P. (2012). Investing in "toughness": Probation, enforcement and legitimacy. *Howard Journal of Criminal Justice*, *51*(3), 300–316. https://doi.org/10.1111/j.1468-2311.2012.00707.x

Rouillard, C., & Bourque, M. (2011). Gouvernance, managérialisme et mesure de la performance: la réforme du secteur de la santé et des services sociaux au Québec. In C. Rouillard & N. Burlone (Eds.), *L'État et la société civile sous le joug de la gouvernance* (pp. 27–50). Québec: Les Presses de l'Université Laval.

Russell, B. (1991). A fair or a minimum wage? Women workers, the state and the origins of wage regulation in Western Canada. *Labour / Le Travail, 28*, 59–88. https://doi.org/10.2307/25143507

Sangster, J. (1989). *Dreams of equality: Women on the Canadian left, 1920–1950.* Toronto: University of Toronto Press. https://doi.org/10.3138/9781442623491

Sargeant, M., & Tucker, E. (2009). Layers of vulnerability in occupational safety and health for migrant workers: Case studies from Canada and the UK. *Policy and Practice in Health and Safety, 7*(2), 51–73. https://doi.org/10.1080/14774003.2009.11667734

Satzewich, V. (1991). *Racism and the incorporation of foreign labour: Farm labour migration to Canada since 1945.* New York: Routledge.

Seery, J. (2016, 9 September). Worker's status. *Unpaid Britain.* Retrieved from https://unpaidbritain.org/author/joseery/

Seidman, G.W. (2009). Labouring under an illusion? Lesotho's "sweat-free" label. *Third World Quarterly, 30*(3), 581–598. https://doi.org/10.1080/01436590902742347

Sheppard, C. (2010). *Inclusive equality: The relational dimensions of systemic discrimination in Canada.* Montreal and Kingston: McGill-Queen's University Press.

Smith, J. (2016). *Imperialism in the 21st century: Globalization, super-exploitation, and capitalism's final crisis.* New York: Monthly Review Press.

Smith, P., & Morton, G. (2006). Nine years of new labour: Neoliberalism and workers' rights. *British Journal of Industrial Relations, 44*(3), 401–420. https://doi.org/10.1111/j.1467-8543.2006.00506.x

Smith, R., & Leberstein, S. (2015). *Rights on demand: Ensuring workplace standards and worker security in the on-demand economy.* New York: National Employment Law Project. Retrieved from https://www.nelp.org/publication/rights-on-demand/

Snider, L. (2009). Accommodating power: The "common sense" of regulators. *Social and Legal Studies, 18*(2), 180–197. https://doi.org/10.1177/0964663909103634

Snider, L., & Bittle, S. (2010). The challenges of regulating powerful economic actors. In J. Gobert & A. Pascal (Eds.), *European developments in corporate criminal liability* (pp. 53–69). London: Routledge.

Stiglitz, J.E. (2016). Inequality and economic growth [Supplement]. *Political Quarterly, 86*, 134–155. https://doi.org/10.1111/1467-923X.12237

Strauss, K. (2009). *Challenging hegemonic deregulation? The UK gangmaster licensing authority as a model for the regulation of casual work.* Working paper in Employment, Work and Finance. Glasgow: University of Glasgow. Retrieved from http://citeseerx.ist.psu.edu/viewdoc/download?doi=10.1.1.539.7248&rep=rep1&type=pdf

Sweetman, D., Badiee, M., & Creswell, J.W. (2010). Use of the transformative framework in mixed methods studies. *Qualitative Inquiry, 16*(6), 441–454. https://doi.org/10.1177/1077800410364610

Tashakkori, A., & Teddlie, C. (2006). Introduction to mixed method and mixed model studies in the behavioral sciences. In A. Bryman (Ed.), *Mixed methods* (2nd vol., pp. 75–95). Thousand Oaks, CA: Sage.

TD Economics. (2015). *Precarious employment in Canada: Does the evidence square with the anecdotes?* Toronto: TD Bank.

Telle, K. (2013). Monitoring and enforcement of environmental regulations: Lessons from a natural field experiment in Norway. *Journal of Public Economics, 99*, 24–34. https://doi.org/10.1016/j.jpubeco.2013.01.001

Thomas, M.P. (2003). *Regulating flexibility: The Ontario Employment Standards Act and the politics of flexible production* (Doctoral thesis, York University, Toronto).

– (2004). Setting the minimum: Ontario's employment standards in the postwar years, 1944–1968. *Labour / Le Travail, 54*, 49–82.

– (2007). Toyotaism meets the 60-hour work week: Coercion, consent and the regulation of working time. *Studies in Political Economy, 80*(1), 105–128. https://doi.org/10.1080/19187033.2007.11675086

– (2009). *Regulating flexibility: The political economy of employment standards.* Montreal and Kingston: McGill-Queen's University Press.

– (2016). Producing and contesting "unfree labour" through the Seasonal Agricultural Worker Program. In A. Choudry & A.A. Smith (Eds.), *Unfree labour?* (pp. 21–36). Oakland, CA: PM Press.

Tombs, S., & Whyte, D. (2010). *Regulatory surrender: Death, injury and the non-enforcement of law.* Liverpool: Institute of Employment Rights.

– (2013). Transcending the deregulation debate? Regulation, risk, and the enforcement of health and safety Law in the UK. *Regulation and Governance, 7*(1), 61–79. https://doi.org/10.1111/j.1748-5991.2012.01164.x

Tucker, E. (1988). Making the workplace "safe" in capitalism: The enforcement of factory legislation in nineteenth-century Ontario. *Labour / Le Travail, 21*, 45–85. https://doi.org/10.2307/25142939

– (1990). *Administering danger in the workplace: The law and politics of occupational health and safety*. Toronto: University of Toronto Press.

– (2006). Will the vicious circle of precariousness be unbroken? The exclusion of Ontario farm complainants from the Occupational Health and Safety Act. In L.F. Vosko (Ed.), *Precarious employment: Understanding labour market insecurity in Canada* (pp. 256–276). Montreal and Kingston: McGill-Queen's University Press.

– (2013a). Giving voice to the precariously employed? Mapping and exploring channels of worker voice in occupational health and safety regulation. In M. Sargeant & M. Ori (Eds.), *Vulnerable workers and precarious working* (pp. 33–70). Newcastle upon Tyne, UK: Cambridge Scholars Publishing.

– (2013b). Old lessons for new governance: Safety or profit and the new conventional wisdom. In T. Nichols & D. Walters (Eds.), *Safety or profit? International studies in governance change and the work environment* (pp. 71–96). New York: Baywood Press. https://doi.org/10.2190/SOPC4

– (2017). When wage theft was a crime in Canada, 1935–1955: The challenge of using the master's tools against the master. *Osgoode Hall Law Journal, 54*(3), 933–958.

Tucker, E., Hall, A., Vosko, L.F., Hall, R., & Siemiatycki, E. (2016). Making or administering law and policy? Discretion and judgment in employment standards enforcement in Ontario. *Canadian Journal of Law and Society / Revue Canadienne Droit et Société, 31*(1), 65–86. https://doi.org/10.1017/cls.2015.34

Tucker, E., Vosko, L.F., Casey, R., Thomas, M., Grundy, J., & Noack A.M. (2019). Carrying little sticks: Is there a "deterrence gap" in Employment Standards enforcement in Ontario, Canada? *International Journal of Comparative Labour Law, 35*(1), 1–30. https://doi.org/10.2139/ssrn.3165580

Tufts, S. (2006). Renewal from different directions: The case of Unite-Here Local 75. In P. Kumar & C. Schenk (Eds.), *Paths to union renewal: Canadian experiences* (pp. 201–220). Peterborough, ON: Broadview Press.

Ugwudike, P. (2011). Mapping the interface between contemporary risk-focused policy and front-line enforcement practice. *Criminology and Criminal Justice, 11*(3), 242–258. https://doi.org/10.1177/1748895811401975

– (2017). Understanding compliance dynamics in community justice settings: The relevance of Bourdieu's habitus, field and capital. *International Criminal Justice Review, 27*(1), 40–59. https://doi.org/10.1177/1057567716679231

Urbani, E., Roux, D., & Legault, M. (2014). Effects of institutionalized culture of out-of-court settlement of labour disputes in Quebec on access to justice and effectiveness of labour law. *Revue de Droit comparé du Travail et de la Sécurité sociale, 3*, 74–83.

Ursel, J. (1992). *Private lives, public policy: 100 years of state intervention in the family*. Toronto: Women's Press.

Vallée, G. (2017). Lois du travail (objet, effets, mécanismes d'application) et droit commun. In JurisClasseur Québec, coll. Droit du travail, *Rapports individuels et collectifs du travail* (vol. 1, fasc. 2). Montréal: LexisNexis Canada.

Vallée, G., & Gesualdi-Fecteau, D. (2007). La constitutionnalisation du droit du travail: une menace ou une opportunité pour les rapports collectifs de travail? *Les Cahiers de droit, 48*(1-2), 153–187. https://doi.org/10.7202/043927ar

– (2016). Setting the temporal boundaries of work: An empirical study of the nature and scope of labour law protections. *International Journal of Comparative Labour Law and Industrial Relations, 32*(3), 344–378.

– (2017). Le travail à la demande et l'obligation de disponibilité des personnes salariées: portée des balises fixées par la *Loi sur les normes du travail.*" In Service de la formation continue, Barreau du Québec (Ed.), *Développements récents en droit du travail* (vol. 429, pp. 257–297). Montréal: Éditions Yvon Blais.

Van Erp, J. (2008). Reputational sanctions in private and public regulation. *Erasmus Law Review, 1*, 145–161.

– (2011). Naming and shaming in regulatory enforcement. In C. Parker & V.L. Nielsen (Eds.), *Explaining compliance: Business responses to regulation* (pp. 322–342). Cheltenham, UK: Edward Elgar Publishing Limited.

Veilleux, D., & Trudeau, G. (2007). La médiation des différends du travail au Québec: de la tradition vers de nouvelles directions. In F. Petit (Ed.), *Le règlement amiable des différends sociaux* (pp. 61–94). Paris: L'Harmattan.

Vosko, L.F. (1996). Irregular workers, new involuntary social exiles: Women and UI reform. In J. Pulkingham & G. Ternowetsky (Eds.), *Remaking Canadian social policy: Social security in the late 1990s* (pp. 265–272). Toronto: Fernwood Press.

– (2000). *Temporary work: The gendered rise of a precarious employment relationship.* Toronto: University of Toronto Press. https://doi.org/10.3138/9781442680432

– (2002). The pasts (and futures) of feminist political economy in Canada: Reviving the debate. *Studies in Political Economy, 68*(1), 55–83. https://doi.org/10.1080/19187033.2002.11675191

– (Ed.). (2006). *Precarious employment: Understanding labour market insecurity in Canada.* Montreal and Kingston: McGill-Queen's University Press.

– (2007). Precarious part-time work in Australia and in transnational labour regulation: The gendered limits of SER-centrism. *Labour & Industry: A Journal of the Social and Economic Relations of Work, 17*(3), 45–70. https://doi.org/10.1080/10301763.2007.10669351

– (2010). *Managing the margins: Gender, citizenship, and the international regulation of precarious employment.* New York: Oxford University Press.

– (2011). *The challenge of expanding EI coverage: Charting exclusions and partial exclusions on the bases of gender, immigration status, age, and place of residence and exploring avenues for inclusive policy redesign.* Toronto: Mowat Centre for Public Policy.

– (2013)."Rights without remedies": Enforcing employment standards in Ontario by maximizing voice among workers in precarious jobs. *Osgoode Hall Law Journal, 50*(4), 845–874.

– (2016). Blacklisting as a modality of deportability: Mexico's response to circular migrant agricultural workers' pursuit of collective bargaining rights

in British Columbia, Canada. *Journal of Ethnic and Migration Studies, 42*(8): 1371–1387.
– (2018). Legal but deportable: Institutionalized deportability and the limits of collective bargaining among participants in Canada's Seasonal Agricultural Workers Program. The impact of immigrant legalization initiatives: International perspectives [Special issue]. *ILR Review, 71*(4), 882–907.
– (2019). Feminist political economy and everyday research on work and employment: The case of employment standards enforcement gap. In M.P. Thomas, L.F. Vosko, C. Fannelli, & O. Lyubchenko (Eds.), *Change and continuity: Rethinking the New Canadian Political Economy*. Montreal and Kingston: McGill-Queen's University Press.
Vosko, L.F., Grundy, J., Casey, R., & Noack, A.M. (2019). A tattered quilt: Exemptions and special rules under Ontario's Employment Standards Act (2000). *Canadian Employment and Labour Law Journal.*
Vosko, L.F., Grundy, J., & Thomas, M.P. (2016). Challenging new governance: Evaluating new approaches to employment standards enforcement in common law jurisdictions. *Economic and Industrial Democracy, 37*(2), 373–398. https://doi.org/10.1177/0143831X14546237
Vosko, L.F., Grundy, J., Tucker, E., Noack, A.M., Casey, R., Gellatly, M., & Mussell, J. (2017). The compliance model of employment standards enforcement: An evidence-based assessment of its efficacy in instances of wage theft. *Industrial Relations Journal, 48*(3), 256–273. https://doi.org/10.1111/irj.12178
Vosko, L.F., Noack, A.M., Casey, R., Hall, A., & Tucker, E. (2017, July). Deterring employment standards violations? The use of certificates of offence (tickets) in workplace. Paper presented at CPSA and CAWLS, Ryerson University, Toronto, ON.
Vosko, L.F., Noack, A.M., & Thomas, M.P. (2016). *How far does the Employment Standards Act, 2000, extend and what are the gaps in coverage? An empirical analysis of archival and statistical data.* Prepared for the Ontario Ministry of Labour to support the Changing Workplace Review of 2015. Retrieved from https://cirhr.library.utoronto.ca/sites/cirhr.library.utoronto.ca/files/research-projects/Vosko%20Noack%20Thomas-5-%20ESA%20Exemptions.pdf
Vosko, L.F., Noack, A.M., & Tucker, E. (2016). *Employment standards enforcement: A scan of employment standards complaints and workplace inspections and their resolution under the Employment Standards Act, 2000.* Prepared for the Ontario Ministry of Labour to support the Changing Workplace Review of 2015. Retrieved from https://cirhr.library.utoronto.ca/sites/cirhr.library.utoronto.ca/files/research-projects/Vosko%20Noack%20Tucker-%206A%20-ESA%20Enforcement.pdf
Vosko, L.F. & Thomas, M.P. (2014). Confronting the employment standards enforcement gap: Exploring the potential for union engagement with

employment law in Ontario, Canada. *Journal of Industrial Relations*, *56*(5), 631–652. https://doi.org/10.1177/0022185613511562

Vosko, L.F., Tucker E., & Casey, R. (2019). Enforcing employment standards for temporary migrant agricultural workers in Ontario, Canada: Exposing underexplored layers of vulnerability. *Queen's Law Journal*.

Vosko, L.F., Tucker, E., Thomas, M.P., & Gellatly, M. (2011). *New approaches to enforcement and compliance with labour regulatory standards: The case of Ontario, Canada*. Toronto: Law Commission of Ontario. Retrieved from Osgoode Digital Commons http://digitalcommons.osgoode.yorku.ca/cgi/viewcontent.cgi?article=1069&context=clpe, https://doi.org/10.2139/ssrn.1975867

Walter, V., & Haines, T. (1988). Workers' use and knowledge of the "Internal Responsibility System": Limits to participation in occupational health and safety. *Canadian Public Policy Analyse de Politiques*, *14*(4), 411–423. https://doi.org/10.2307/3550413

Weil, D. (1991). Enforcing OSHA: The role of labor unions. *Industrial Relations*, *30*(1), 20–36.

– (1992). Building safety: The role of construction unions in the enforcement of the OSHA. *Journal of Labor Research*, *13*(1), 121–132.

– (1999). Are mandated health and safety committees substitutes for or supplements to labor unions? *Industrial and Labor Relations Review*, *52*(3), 339–360.

– (2005). Individual rights and collective agents: The role of new workplace institutions in the regulation of labor markets. In R. Freeman, L. Mishel, & J. Hersch (Eds.), *Emerging labor market institutions for the 21st Century* (pp. 13–44). Chicago: University of Chicago Press.

– (2008a). Mighty monolith or fractured federation? Business opposition and the enactment of workplace legislation. In A. Bernhardt, H. Boushey, L. Dresser, & C. Tilly (Eds.), *The gloves off economy: Problems and possibilities at the bottom of the labor market* (pp. 287–314). Champaign: Labor and Employment Relations Association.

– (2008b). A strategic approach to labour inspection. *International Labour Review*, *147*(4), 349–375. https://doi.org/10.1111/j.1564-913X.2008.00040.x

– (2009). Rethinking the regulation of vulnerable work in the USA: A sector-based approach. *Journal of Industrial Relations*, *51*(3), 411–430. https://doi.org/10.1177/0022185609104842

– (2012). "Broken windows," vulnerable workers, and the future of worker representation. *Forum: Labour in American Politics*, *10*(1), 1–21. https://doi.org/10.1515/1540-8884.1493

– (2014). *The fissured workplace: Why work became so bad for so many and what can be done to improve it*. Cambridge, MA: Harvard University Press. https://doi.org/10.4159/9780674726123

– (2015, 12 February). Strategic enforcement in the fissured workplace. Keynote speech presented at the John T. Dunlop Memorial Forum, Harvard Law School, Cambridge, MA.
– (2018). Creating a strategic enforcement approach to address wage theft: One academic's journey in organizational change. *Journal of Industrial Relations, 60*(3), 437–460. https://doi.org/10.1177/0022185618765551
Weil, D., & Pyles, A. (2006). Why complain? Complaints, compliance, and the problem of enforcement in the U.S. workplace. *Comparative Labor Law and Policy Journal, 27*(1), 59–92.
Wills, J. (2009). Subcontracted employment and its challenge to labor. *Labor Studies Journal, 34*(4), 441–60. https://doi.org/10.1177/0160449X08324740
Wilson, N. (2012, 30 April). Update from the fair work ombudsman. Speech to AiGroup and National Personnel Industrial Relations Conference, Canberra.
Workers' Action Centre and Parkdale Community Legal Services. (2016). *Building decent work from the ground up: Responding to the changing workplaces review*. Toronto: Workers' Action Centre and Parkdale Community Legal Services. Retrieved from http://workersactioncentre.org/wp-content/uploads/2017/12/Building-Decent-Jobs-from-the-Ground-Up_eng.pdf
Workplace Express. (2010, 2 June). FWO welcomes union/employer variation bids. Retrieved from https://www.workplaceexpress.com.au
– (2013, 14 May). Budget 2013: More dollars for FWC, less for FWBC. Retrieved from https://www.workplaceexpress.com.au
– (2018, 13 March). McManus set to outline ACTU change agenda. Retrieved from https://www.workplaceexpress.com.au
Yue, A., & D. Wyatt. (2014). Introduction: New communities, new racisms: A critical introduction. *Journal of Intercultural Studies*, 35(3), 223–231. https://doi.org/10.1080/07256868.2014.899947
Zittel, T. (2006). Participatory democracy and political participation. In T. Zittel & D. Fuchs (Eds.), *Participatory democracy and political participation* (pp. 9–28). London: Routledge. https://doi.org/10.4324/9780203969311

## Primary Sources

### *Government Documents*

Andrew, M. (2017). *Final report*. Melbourne: Treasury, Black Economy Task Force. Retrieved from https://static.treasury.gov.au/uploads/sites/1/2018/05/Black-Economy-Taskforce_Final-Report.pdf
Auditor General of Ontario. (1991). *1991 annual report of the Office of the Provincial Auditor General*. Toronto: Auditor General of Ontario.
– (2004a). *Annual report of the Office of the Provincial Auditor of Ontario*. Toronto: Auditor General of Ontario.

– (2004b). *Annual report of the provincial auditor of Ontario: Employment Rights and Responsibilities Program*. VFM Section 3.09. Toronto: Auditor General of Ontario. Retrieved from http://www.auditor.on.ca/en/content/annualreports/arreports/en04/309en04.pdf

Australian Labor Party. (2016). Rights at work. Retrieved from https://www.alp.org.au

*Bankruptcy and Insolvency Act*. (1985, c. B-3). Retrieved from http://lawslois.justice.gc.ca/eng/acts/B-3/FullText.html

Bernier, J. (2006). *Social protection for non-traditional workers outside the employment relationship*. Québec: Federal Labour Standards Review Commission.

Bernier, J., Vallée, G., & Jobin, C. (2003). Les besoins de protection sociale des personnes en situation de travail non traditionnelle. Final report of the Committee of Experts. Quebec: Committee of Experts examining the needs for social protection among people in non-traditional work situations. Retrieved from http://collections.banq.qc.ca/ark:/52327/bs52142.

*Boland v. APV Canada Inc.*, [2005] CanLII 3384 ON SCDC

*California Labor Code.* (1937). Retrieved from https://leginfo.legislature.ca.gov/faces/codes_displayText.xhtml?lawCode=LAB&division=&title=&part=&chapter=&article=

*California Senate Bill No. 588. Employment: Nonpayment of wages*. Retrieved from https://leginfo.legislature.ca.gov/faces/billTextClient.xhtml?bill_id=201520160SB588

Department for Business, Energy and Industrial Strategy. (2017a). *Business population estimates 2017*. London: Department for Business, Energy and Industrial Strategy.

– (2017b). *National minimum wage law: Enforcement*. London: Department for Business, Energy and Industrial Strategy.

– (2017c). *NLW and NMW: Government evidence to the Low Pay Commission.* London: Department for Business, Energy and Industrial Strategy.

– (2017d). *Trade union membership 2016 statistical bulletin*. London: Department for Business, Energy & Industrial Strategy.

– (2018). *Good work: A response to the Taylor Review of Modern Working Practices*. London: Department for Business, Energy, and Industrial Strategy and Ministry of Justice.

Department of Business, Innovation and Skills. (2013). *Payment of tribunal awards 2013 Study*. London: Department of Business, Innovation and Skills.

Department of Justice. (2002). *Government response to the fifteenth report of the Standing Committee on Justice and Human Rights: Corporate liability*. Ottawa: Department of Justice. Retrieved from http://www.justice.gc.ca/eng/rp-pr/other-autre/jhr-jdp/bkgr-cont.html

Department of Labor. (2001). *1999–2000 report on initiatives*. Washington DC: Department of Labor, Wage and Hours Division. Retrieved from https://catalog.hathitrust.org/Record/003826001

– (2012). US Labor Department's Wage and Hour Division launches initiative to strengthen labor law compliance in Southern California's landscaping industry [News release]. Retrieved from https://www.dol.gov/

Department of Labor. (2016, 26 July). Voluntary agreement between the U.S. Department of Labor's Wage and Hour Division and Subway. Retreived from https://www.dol.gov/WHD/flsa/SubwayAgreement.pdf

– (2016, 9 August). US Department of Labor, CalVans to Partner to Expand Safe Farmworker Transportation Plan at Fresno Event. Retrieved from https://www.dol.gov/newsroom/releases/whd/whd20160808.

– (n.d.). Wage and hour mission statement. Retrieved from http://www.dol.gov/whd/about/mission/whdmiss.htm

Desîlets, C., & Ledoux, D. (2006). *Histoire des normes du travail au Québec: de l'Acte des manufactures à la Loi sur les normes du travail*. Quebec: Les Publications du Québec.

Desrosiers, H., Nanhou, V., Ducharme, A., Cloutier-Villeneuve, L., Gauthier, M. et al. (2015). *Les compétences en littératie, en numératie et en résolution de problèmes dans des environnements technologiques: des clefs pour relever les défis du XXIe siècle*. Rapport québécois du Programme pour l'évaluation internationale des compétences des adultes (PEICA). Quebec: Institut de la statistique du Québec. Retrieved from http://www.stat.gouv.qc.ca/statistiques/education/alphabetisation-litteratie/peica.pdf

Dewees, D.N. (1987). *Special treatment under Ontario Hours of Work and Overtime Legislation: General issues. A Report prepared for the Ontario Task Force on Hours of Work and Overtime.* Toronto: Ontario Task Force on Hours of Work and Overtime.

Education, Employment and Small Business Committee. (2018). *A fair day's pay for a fair day's work? Exposing the true cost of wage theft in Queensland*. Brisbane: Queensland Parliamentary Committee.

Employment and Social Development Canada. (2015). Five-year statuatory review of the *Wage Earner Protection Program Act*: Helping Canadian workers during bankruptcy and receivership. Ottawa: Employment and Social Development Canada. Retrieved from http://publications.gc.ca/collections/collection_2015/edsc-esdc/Em8-11-2015-eng.pdf

*Employment Standards Act* (2000 S.O. 2000, c. 41). Retrieved from https://www.ontario.ca/laws/statute/00e41

*Employment Standards Amendment Act* (Employee Wage Protection Program) (1991 S.O. 1991, c. 16). Retrieved from http://digitalcommons.osgoode.yorku.ca/ontario_statutes/vol1991/iss1/18/

*Employment Standards Amendment Act* (2009 S.O. 2009, c 9 - Bill 139). Retrieved from https://www.ontario.ca/laws/statute/S09009

*EZY Accounting 123 v FWO* [2018] FCA 134.

*Fair Entitlements Guarantee Act 2012* (Cth) (Austl.). Retrieved from https://www.legislation.gov.au/Series/C2012A00159

*Fair Labor Standards Act of 1938*, as amended 29 U.S.C. 201. United States Department of Labour. Retrieved from https://www.dol.gov/whd/regs/statutes/FairLaborStandAct.pdf

*Fair Work Act (No. 28, 2009), An act relating to workplace relations, and for related purposes.* (Australia). Retrived from http://www.ilo.org/dyn/travail/docs/219/Fair%20Work%20Act%202009%20-%20current%20as%20at%20140211.pdf

*Fair Work Amendment (Protecting Vulnerable Workers) Act 2017* (Cth) (Austl.). Retrieved from https://www.legislation.gov.au/Details/C2017A00101

Fair Work Ombudsman (FWO). (2015). *Annual report 2014/15*. Melbourne: Fair Work Ombudsman

– (2017a). *Annual report 2016/17*. Melbourne: Fair Work Ombudsman.

– (2017b). *Compliance and enforcement policy*. Melbourne: Fair Work Ombudsman.

– (2017c). *Proactive compliance deed between the Office of the Fair Work Ombudsman and Woolworths (11 October 2017)*. Melbourne: Fair Work Ombudsman.

– (2017d). *Submission to the Parliamentary Inquiry into the Fair Work Amendment (Protecting Vulnerable Workers) Bill 2017 (Cth) (Austl.)*. Melbourne: Fair Work Ombudsman.

– (2018, February). *20,000 tip-offs shine a light on dodgy workplaces*. Retrieved from https://www.fairwork.gov.au/about-us/news-and-media-releases/2018-media-releases/february-2018/20180223-anonymous-report-milstone-mr

– (2018a). *Annual report 2017/18*. Melbourne: Fair Work Ombudsman.

– (2018b). Campaigns. Retrieved from https://www.fairwork.gov.au/how-we-will-help/helping-the-community/campaigns

– (2018c). Contracting labour and supply chains: Why should I manage my labour contracting. Retrieved from https://www.fairwork.gov.au/find-help-for/contracting-labour-and-supply-chains#why-should-i-manage-my-labour-contracting

– (2018d). Franchisors. Retrieved from https://www.fairwork.gov.au/find-help-for/franchises/franchisors

– (2018e). How we will help: Record my hours app. Retrieved from https://www.fairwork.gov.au/how-we-will-help/how-we-help-you/record-my-hours-app

– (2018f). *Proactive compliance deed between the Office of the Fair Work Ombudsman and Paul Sadler Swimland Pty Ltd (22 March 2018)*. Melbourne: Fair Work Ombudsman.
– (2018g). What is mediation? Retrieved from https://www.fairwork.gov.au/how-we-will-help/how-we-help-you/help-resolving-workplace-issues/working-with-you-to-resolve-workplace-issues
*Fair Work Ombudsman v Blue Impression Pty Ltd* [2017] FCCA 2797.
*Fair Work Ombudsman v Devine Marine* [2015] FCA 370.
*Fair Work Ombudsman v James Nelson Pty Ltd & Anor* [2016] FCCA 531.
*Fair Work Ombudsman v Step Ahead Securities* [2016] FCCA 1482.
*Fair Work Ombudsman v Trek North Tours [No 2]* [2015] FCCA 1801.
*Fair Work Ombudsman v WY Pty Ltd , Chong Yew Chua and Ning Yuan Fu* [2016] FCCA 343.
*Fair Work Ombudsman v Yogurberry World Square Pty Ltd* [2016] FCA 1290.
*Fair Workplaces, Better Jobs Act*: Bill 148 (2017 S.O. 2017 C.22). Retrieved from http://www.ontla.on.ca/web/bills/bills_detail.do?locale=en&BillID=4963
Fels, A., & Cousins D. (2019). *Report of the migrant workers' taskforce*. Melbourne: Migrant Workers' Taskforce. Retrieved from https://docs.jobs.gov.au/system/files/doc/other/mwt_final_report.pdf
Fevre, R., Nichols, T., Prior, G., & Rutherford, I. (2009). *The fair treatment at work report: Findings from the 2008 survey*. Employment Relations Research Series No. 103. London: Department for Business, Innovation, and Skills. https://assets.publishing.service.gov.uk/government/uploads/system/uploads/attachment_data/file/192191/09-P85-fair-treatment-at-work-report-2008-survey-errs-103.pdf
Forsyth, A. (2016). *Final report*. Victoria: Victorian Inquiry into the Labour Hire Industry and Insecure Work. Retrieved from https://s3.ap-southeast-2.amazonaws.com/hdp.au.prod.app.vic-engage.files/3615/5685/9019/IRV-Inquiry-Final-Report-.pdf
*Fulawka v Bank of Nova Scotia* [2012] ONCA 443.
Gangmasters' Labour and Abuse Authority. (2018, 11 April). GLAA Regional Seminars. Retrieved from http://www.gla.gov.uk/whats-new/latest-press-releases/110418-glaa-regional-seminars-2018/
Government Accountability Office. (2009). *Wage and Hour Division needs improved investigative processes and ability to suspend Statute of Limitations to better protect workers against wage theft*. Report to the Committee on Education and Labor, House of Representatives. Washington DC: Government Accountability Office. Retrieved from https://www.gao.gov/assets/300/291496.pdf
Government of Saskatchewan. (2017). Make a formal employment standards complaint. Retrieved from https://www.saskatchewan.ca/business/employment-standards/complaints-investigations-enforcement-and-fines/

file-an-employment-standards-complaint/make-a-formal-employment-standards-complaint

Guttman, B., & Roback, E. (1995). *An introduction to computer security: The NIST handbook. National Institute of Standards and Technology.* Washington DC: Department of Commerce. Retrieved from https://www.nist.gov/publications/introduction-computer-security-nist-handbook, https://doi.org/10.6028/NIST.SP.800-12

Hampton, P. (2005). *Reducing administrative burdens: Effective inspection and enforcement.* London: UK Treasury.

Her Majesty's Revenue and Customs. (2016). *National minimum wage manual.* (Updated 29 June 2018). London: Her Majesty's Revenue and Customs. Retrieved from https://www.gov.uk/hmrc-internal-manuals/national-minimum-wage-manual

Human Resources Development Canada. (1997). *Evaluation of federal labour standards (Phase I). Final Report.* Ottawa: Human Resources and Development Canada.

Kinley, John. (1987). *Farm workers and worktime provisions of Ontario's Employment Standards Act: A report prepared for the Ontario Task Force on Hours of Work and Overtime.* Toronto: Ontario Task Force on Hours of Work and Overtime.

*Labour Hire Licensing Act 2017* (Qld) (Austl.). Retrieved from https://www.legislation.qld.gov.au/view/html/asmade/act-2017-033.

*Labour Hire Licensing Act 2017* (SA) (Austl.). Retrieved from https://www.legislation.sa.gov.au/LZ/C/A/LABOUR%20HIRE%20LICENSING%20ACT%202017.aspx

Labour Hire Licensing Act 2018 (Vic) (commencing 1 November 2019). Retrieved from http://www.legislation.vic.gov.au/Domino/Web_Notes/LDMS/PubStatbook.nsf/f932b66241ecf1b7ca256e92000e23be/E9DCA3B5C32047A6CA2582B800122F53/$FILE/18-025aa%20authorised.pdf

*Labour Hire Licensing Bill 2017* (Vic) (Austl).

Liberal Party of Australia. (2016). The Coalition's policy to protect vulnerable workers. Retrieved from https://www.liberal.org.au

Legislative Assembly of Ontario. (2010, 2 June). *Official report of debates (Hansard), 39th Parliament, Second Session. No. 39.* Toronto: Legislative Assembly of Ontario. Retrieved from http://hansardindex.ontla.on.ca/hansardeissue/39-2/l039.htm

– (2010, 3 August). *Official report of debates (Hansard), 39th Parliament, Second Session. F-6.* Standing Committee on Finance and Economic Affairs. Toronto: Legislative Assembly of Ontario. Retrieved from: http://www.ontla.on.ca/web/committee-proceedings/committee_transcripts_details.do?Date=2010-08-03&ParlCommID=8858&BillID=2358&Business=&locale=en&DocumentID=25147

Labour Standards Commission/Commission des normes du travail (LSC). (2003). *Rapport annuel de gestion 2002–2003 [Annual management report 2002–2003].* Quebec: Labour Standards Commission/Commission des normes du travail.

– (2004). *Rapport annuel de gestion 2003–2004 [Annual management report 2003–2004].* Quebec: Labour Standards Commission/Commission des normes du travail.

– (2007). *Rapport annuel de gestion 2006–2007 [Annual management report 2006–2007].* Quebec: Labour Standards Commission/Commission des normes du travail

– (2008). *Plan stratégique 2008-2012 [Strategic plan 2008-2012].* Quebec: Labour Standards Commission/Commission des normes du travail.

– (2009a). *Programme de prévention [Prevention program*]. Quebec: Labour Standards Commission/Commission des normes du travail.

– (2009b). *Rapport annuel de gestion 2008–2009 [Annual management report 2008–2009].* Quebec: Labour Standards Commission/Commission des normes du travail.

– (2010a). *Enquête sur les conditions de travail dans les restaurants et les bars.* Quebec: Labour Standards Commission/Commission des normes du travail.

– (2010b). *Enquête sur le taux de respect.* Quebec: Labour Standards Commission/Commission des normes du travail.

– (2010c). *Projet d'intervention auprès des travailleurs agricoles étrangers: bilan d'une première expérience.* Quebec: Labour Standards Commission/Commission des normes du travail.

– (2011). *Rapport annuel de gestion 2010–2011 [Annual management report 2010–2011].* Quebec: Labour Standards Commission/Commission des normes du travail.

– (2012a). *Plan stratégique 2012–2016 [Strategic plan 2012–2016].* Quebec: Labour Standards Commission/Commission des normes du travail.

– (2012b). *Rapport annuel de gestion 2011–2012 [Annual management report 2011–2012].* Quebec: Labour Standards Commission/Commission des normes du travail.

– (2013a). *Agences de placement de personnel: profil de leurs salariés les plus à risque d'infractions à la Loi sur les normes du travail.* Quebec: Labour Standards Commission/Commission des normes du travail.

– (2013b). *Rapport annuel de gestion 2012–2013 [Annual management report 2012–2013].* Quebec: Labour Standards Commission/Commission des normes du travail.

– (2014). *Rapport annuel de gestion 2013–2014 [Annual management report 2013–2014].* Quebec: Labour Standards Commission/Commission des normes du travail.

– (2015). *Rapport annuel de gestion 2014–2015 [Annual management report 2014–2015]*. Quebec: Labour Standards Commission/Commission des normes du travail.

Labour Standards, Equity, Occupational Health and Safety Commission/Commission des normes, de l'équité, de la santé et de la sécurité du travail (LSEOHSC). (2017a). *Plan stratégique 2017–2019 [Strategic plan 2017–2019]*. Quebec: Labour Standards, Equity, Occupational Health and Safety Commission/Commission des normes, de l'équité, de la santé et de la sécurité du travail.

– (2017b). *Rapport annuel de gestion 2016 [Annual management report 2016]*. Quebec: Labour Standards, Equity, Occupational Health and Safety Commission/Commission des normes, de l'équité, de la santé et de la sécurité du travail.

Low Pay Commission. (2017). *National minimum wage*. London: Department of Business, Energy and Industrial Strategy, Low Pay Commission.

*Machtinger v. HOJ Industries Ltd.*, [1992] 1 SCR 986.

*Making Ontario Open for Business Act* (S.O. 2018, c 14). Retreived from https://www.ontario.ca/laws/statute/S18014

Medical Officer of Health. (2014). *Staff report: Onsite posting of inspection results for all fixed food premises*. Toronto: City of Toronto. Retrieved from https://www.toronto.ca/legdocs/mmis/2015/hl/bgrd/backgroundfile-78979.pdf

Metcalf, D. (2017). *United Kingdom labour market enforcement strategy: Introductory report*. London: Labour Market Enforcement.

– (2018). *United Kingdom labour market enforcement strategy 2018/19*. London: Labour Market Enforcement.

Ministère des Finances. (2011). *Plan budgétaire*. Quebec: Ministère des Finances.

– (2015, 26 March). Discours sur le budget 2015–2016, delivered at the Assemblée nationale by Carlos Leitão, Ministère des Finances (Québec).

Ministère des Finances et de l'Économie. (2014). *Plan budgétaire*, February 2014. Quebec: Ministère des Finances et de l'Économie.

Minister for Employment. (2016–17). *Fair Work Amendment (Protecting Vulnerable Workers) Bill 2017: Explanatory memorandum* (Cth) (Austl.). Melbourne: Department of Employment. Retrieved from https://parlinfo.aph.gov.au/parlInfo/download/legislation/ems/r5826_ems_e0207b3c-41de-45b8-9631-4d08f9f88e23/upload_pdf/622141.pdf;fileType=application%2Fpdf

Minister for Employment and Workplace Relations. (2008). *Fair Work Bill 2008: Explanatory memorandum*. Melbourne: Employment and Workplace Relations. Retrieved from https://www.legislation.gov.au/Details/C2008B00262/Explanatory%20Memorandum/Text

Ministry of Labour (MOL). [Department of Labour]. (1967, September). Minimum standards legislation and economic policy. *Labour Gazette*, 67.

– (1969, January). News briefs: Ontario ups minimum wage, passes new standards act. *Labour Gazette, 67.*
– (1971). *Ontario Department of Labour annual report 1970–1971.* Toronto: Ontario Department of Labour.
– (1972). *Ministry of Labour annual report 1971–1972.* Toronto: Ontario Ministry of Labour.
– (1978). *Ministry of Labour annual report 1977–1978.* Toronto: Ontario Ministry of Labour.
– (2004, 26 April). McGuinty government acts to protect workers [News release]. Retrieved from https://news.ontario.ca/archive/en/2004/04/26/McGuinty-government-acts-to-protect-workers.html
– (2004, 14 July). McGuinty government steps up employment standards enforcement [News release]. Retrieved from https://news.ontario.ca/archive/en/2004/07/14/McGuinty-government-steps-up-employment-standards-enforcement.html
– (2004, 26 November). McGuinty government makes it easier for Ontario workers to understand their rights [News release]. Retrieved from https://news.ontario.ca/archive/en/2004/11/26/McGuinty-government-makes-it-easier-for-Ontario-workers-to-understand-their-righ.html
– (2004, 10 December). New employment standards law means increased protections for workers [News release]. Retrieved fromhttps://news.ontario.ca/archive/en/2004/12/10/New-Employment-Standards-Law-means-increased-protection-for-workers.html
– (2005, 27 May). Government recovers more money owed to vulnerable workers [News release]. Retrieved from https://news.ontario.ca/archive/en/2005/05/27/Government-recovers-more-money-owed-to-vulnerable-workers.html
– (2007, 22 November). Ontario passes legislation to create fair workplaces, better jobs [News release]. Retrieved from https://news.ontario.ca/mol/en/2017/11/ontario-passes-legislation-to-create-fair-workplaces-better-jobs.html
– (2009). *Results-based plan 2009–10: Briefing book.* Toronto: Ontario Ministry of Labour. Retrieved from http://www.ontla.on.ca/library/repository/ser/266594/2009-2010.pdf
– (2009, 4 May). Fairness for temporary help agencies [News release]. Retrieved from https://news.ontario.ca/mol/en/2009/05/fairness-for-temporary-help-agency-employees-1.html
– (2010a). *Expert advisory panel on occupational health and safety: Report and recommendations to the Minister of Labour.* Toronto: Ontario Ministry of Labour. Retrieved from https://www.labour.gov.on.ca/english/hs/prevention/report/index.php

- (2010b). *Focus group on improvements to the employment standards claim form and guide, employee & advisor's focus group, 10 May 2010*. Toronto: Ontario Ministry of Labour.
- (2010, March). FAQs: Employment Protection for Foreign Nationals Act, 2009. Retrieved from https://www.labour.gov.on.ca/english/es/faqs/epfna.php
- (2010, 21 October). Open for Business Act passes: McGuinty government supporting businesses [News release]. Retrieved from https://news.ontario.ca/medg/en/2010/10/open-for-business-act-passes.html
- (2010, 25 October). New legislation modernizes Ontario's employment standards [News release]. Retrieved from https://www.labour.gov.on.ca/english/news/
- (2011, 19 January a). Know your employment rights and responsibilities [News bulletin]. Retrieved from https://webstation.hroptions.com/synchronized/2011-02.pdf
- (2011, 19 January b). Ontario promotes workplace fairness [Backgrounder]. Retrieved from https://www.labour.gov.on.ca/english/news/
- (2011, 29 July a). Employment standards: Education and enforcement [Backgrounder]. Retrieved from https://www.labour.gov.on.ca/english/news/
- (2011, 29 July b). Employment standards: Ministry successes [News bulletin]. Retrieved from https://www.labour.gov.on.ca/english/news
- (2012, 8 June a). Ensuring temporary workers' rights: McGuinty government committed to protecting employment standards [News release]. Retrieved from https://news.ontario.ca/mol/en/2012/06/ensuring-temporary-workers-rights.html
- (2012, 8 June b). Protecting vulnerable workers: Temporary help agencies [News release]. Retrieved from https://news.ontario.ca/mol/en/2012/06/protecting-vulnerable-workers.html
- (2012, 17 September). Ontario enhancing enforcement to protect workers: Ministry of Labour increases proactive employment standards protections [News release]. Retrieved from https://news.ontario.ca/mol/en/2018/01/ontario-enhancing-enforcement-to-ensure-worker-rights-are-protected.html
- (2012, 25 October). Proactive employment standards inspections [News release]. Retrieved from http://www.labour.gov.on.ca/english/news
- (2013). *Annual report 2012–2013*. Toronto: Ontario Ministry of Labour.
- (2013, 28 January). Occupational health and safety inspections. Retrieved from https://www.labour.gov.on.ca/english/hs/pubs/ohs_inspections.php
- (2013, 14 February). Temporary help agency blitz results. Retrieved from http://www.labour.gov.on.ca/english/es/inspections/blitzresults_tha.php

– (2013, 3 April). Inspection blitzes and initiatives [News release]. Retrieved from http://www.labour.gov.on.ca/english/news
– (2013, May). Role of the Ministry of Labour [News release]. Retrieved from http://www.labour.gov.on.ca/english/news
– (2013, 29 August). Notice: The compliance check pilot [News release]. http://www.labour.gov.on.ca/english/news
– (2013, 16 October). Protecting retail workers' rights [News bulletin]. Retrieved from https://www.labour.gov.on.ca/english/news/
– (2013, 4 December). Protecting Ontario's vulnerable workers: Province introducing stronger rules and enforcement measures for increased fairness [News release]. Retrieved from https://news.ontario.ca/mol/en/2013/12/protecting-ontarios-vulnerable-workers.html
– (2014, 16 January). Blitz results: Vulnerable workers. Retrieved from https://www.labour.gov.on.ca/english/es/inspections/blitzresults_vw.php
– (2014, 11 July). Blitz results: Retail services. Retrieved from https://www.labour.gov.on.ca/english/es/inspections/blitzresults_rs.php
– (2014, 16 July). Supporting Ontario's vulnerable workers: Province strengthening worker protections, making minimum wage more predictable [News release]. Retrieved from https://news.ontario.ca/mol/en/2014/07/supporting-ontarios-vulnerable-workers.html
– (2014, 20 August a). Employment standards blitz focuses on vulnerable workers [News bulletin]. Retrieved from http://www.labour.gov.on.ca/english/news
– (2014, 20 August b). Protecting vulnerable workers [Backgrounder]. Retrieved from https://www.labour.gov.on.ca/english/news
– (2015, 20 February). Role of the Ministry of Labour. Retrieved from https://www.ontario.ca/document/your-guide-employment-standards-act/role-ministry-labour
– (2015, 1 April). Blitz results: Vulnerable and temporary foreign workers. Retrieved from https://www.labour.gov.on.ca/english/es/inspections/blitzresults_vtfw.php
– (2005, 27 May). Government recovers more money owed to vulnerable workers [News release]. Retrieved from https://news.ontario.ca/archive/en/2005/05/27/Government-recovers-more-money-owed-to-vulnerable-workers.html
– (2015). Education, outreach and partnership. Retrieved from https://www.labour.gov.on.ca/english/es/eop/index.php
– (2016a). *Administrative Manual for Employment Standards: Appendix 7A.* Toronto: Ontario Ministry of Labour.
– (2016b). Terms of reference: Changing Workplaces Review. Retrieved from https://www.labour.gov.on.ca/english/about/workplace/terms.php

– (2017, 22 November). Modernizing Ontario's labour laws to create fairness and opportunity: The Fair Workplaces, Better Jobs Act, 2017 [Backgrounder]. Retrieved from https://news.ontario.ca/mol/en/2017/11/modernizing-ontarios-labour-laws-to-create-fairness-and-opportunity-the-fair-workplaces-better-jobs.html
– (2017a). *Administrative Manual for Employment Standards: Chapter 4 – Inspections*. Toronto: Ontario Ministry of Labour.
– (2017b). *Administrative Manual for Employment Standards: Chapter 5 – Claims Investigations*. Toronto: Ontario Ministry of Labour.
– (2017c). *Employment Standards Act, 2000 Policy and Interpretation Manual*. Toronto: Ontario Ministry of Labour.
– (2017d). *Published plans and annual reports 2016–2017: Ministry of Labour*. Retrieved from https://www.ontario.ca/page/published-plan-and-annual-report-2016-2017-ministry-labour#foot-3
– (2017e). Reprisals. Retrieved from https://www.ontario.ca/document/your-guide-employment-standards-act/reprisals
– (2018a). Employment Standards Special Rules Tool, Queen's Printer for Ontario. Retrieved from https://www.ontario.ca/document/industries-and-jobs-exemptions-or-special-rules?_ga=2.208978002.1768694572.1565286502-893411734.1565286502
– (2018b). *Published plans and annual reports 2017–2018: Ministry of Labour*. Retrieved from https://www.ontario.ca/page/published-plans-and-annual-reports-2017-2018-ministry-labour
– (2018c). *Quick Reference Guide (QRG), First Quarter (Year-to-Date): (Q1) 2018/2019 (April 1, 2018 to June 30, 2018)*. Toronto: Ontario Ministry of Labour.
– (n.d.). *Fiscal year reports*. Toronto: Employment Practices Branch/Employment Standards Branch, Ontario Ministry of Labour (1983/84-2015/16).
Mitchell, C.M., & Murray, J.C. (2016). *Changing workplaces review: Special advisors interim report*. Toronto: Ontario Ministry of Labour, Changing Work Places Review. Retrieved from https://www.labour.gov.on.ca/english/about/pdf/cwr_interim.pdf
– (2017). *Changing workplaces review: An agenda for workplace rights, final report*. Toronto: Ontario Ministry of Labour, Changing Work Places Review. Retrieved from https://files.ontario.ca/books/mol_changing_workplace_report_eng_2_0.pdf
New York State Department of Labor. (2011). Wage Theft Prevention Act fact sheet. Retrieved from https://www.labor.ny.gov/formsdocs/wp/P715.pdf
Ontario Labour Relations Board (OLRB). (2018). Information Bulletin No. 24. Retrieved from http://www.olrb.gov.on.ca/english/infob/infbul24.pdf
*Open for Business Act*. (2010 S.O. 2010, c. 16 – Bill 68). Retrieved from https://www.ontario.ca/laws/statute/S10016

*Potter v Fair Work Ombudsman* [2014] FCA 187.

Royal Commission on Price Spreads. (1934). *Proceedings and Evidence*. Ottawa: J.O. Patenaude.

Senate Education and Employment References Committee. (2016). *A national disgrace: The exploitation of temporary work visa holders*. Melbourne: Parliament of Australia. Retrieved from https://www.google.com/url?sa=t&rct=j&q=&esrc=s&source=web&cd=4&ved=0ahUKEwjf2aCzl-LbAhWoiaYKHXGrCq8QFgg7MAM&url=https%3A%2F%2Fwww.aph.gov.au%2FParliamentary_Business%2FCommittees%2FSenate%2FEducation_and_Employment%2Ftemporary_work_visa%2F~%2Fmedia%2FCommittees%2Feet_ctte%2Ftemporary_work_visa%2Freport%2Freport.pdf&usg=AOvVaw3KcFGafxUUwhNGWSqGHNt0

– (2017). *Corporate avoidance of the Fair Work Act*. Melbourne: Parliament of Australia. Retrieved from https://www.aph.gov.au/Parliamentary_Business/Committees/Senate/Education_and_Employment/AvoidanceofFairWork

– (2018). *Wage theft? What wage theft?! The exploitation of general and specialist cleaners working in retail chains for contracting or subcontracting cleaning companies*. Melbourne: Parliament of Australia. Retrieved from https://parlinfo.aph.gov.au/parlInfo/download/committees/reportsen/024233/toc_pdf/WagetheftWhatwagetheft!.pdf;fileType=application%2Fpdf

Smith, M. (2002). *Protecting employee wages in bankruptcy*. Ottawa: Parliamentary Research Branch. Retrieved from http://publications.gc.ca/Collection-R/LoPBdP/BP/prb0134-e.htm

Taylor, M. (2017). *Good work: The Taylor review of modern working practices. Consultation on enforcement of employment rights recommendations*. London: Department for Business, Energy and Industrial Strategy & Ministry of Justice. Retrieved from https://assets.publishing.service.gov.uk/government/uploads/system/uploads/attachment_data/file/627671/good-work-taylor-review-modern-working-practices-rg.pdf

Vézina, M., Cloutier, E., Stock, S., Lippel, K., Fortin, É., & Delisle, A. (2011). *Québec Survey on Working and Employment Conditions and Occupational Health and Safety (Summary report RR-707)*. Quebec: Institut de recherche Robert-Sauvé en santé et sécurité du travail. Retrieved from https://www.inspq.qc.ca/pdf/publications/1356_EnqQuebCondTravailEmpSanteSecTravail_VA.pdf

Weil, D. (2010). *Improving workplace conditions through strategic enforcement: A report to the Wage and Hour Division*. Washington DC: US Department of Labor, Wage and Hours Division. Retrieved from https://www.dol.gov/whd/resources/strategicEnforcement.pdf

*Workplace Relations Act* 1996 (Cth). Retrieved from https://www.legislation.gov.au/Details/C2006C00104

*Workplace Relations Amendment* (Work Choices) Act 2005 (Cth) (Austl.). Retrieved from https://www.legislation.gov.au/Series/C2005A00153

*Statistics*

Australian Bureau of Statistics. (2017). Labour Force Survey, Australia. Retrieved from https://www.abs.gov.au/AUSSTATS/abs@.nsf/second+level+view?ReadForm&prodno=6202.0&viewtitle=Labour%20Force,%20Australia~Jun%202019~Latest~18/07/2019&&tabname=Past%20Future%20Issues&prodno=6202.0&issue=Jun%202019&num=&view=&

Department of Labor. (n.d). Wage and Hour Division Enforcement Data. Accessed May 5, 2018. Retrieved from: https://www.dol.gov/whd/data/

Industry Canada. (2012). *Key Small Business Statistics*. Retrieved from https://www.ic.gc.ca/eic/site/061.nsf/vwapj/KSBS-PSRPE_July-Juillet2012_eng.pdf/$FILE/KSBS-PSRPE_July-Juillet2012_eng.pdf

– (2016). *Key Small Business Statistics*. Retrieved from http://www.ic.gc.ca/eic/site/061.nsf/eng/h_02689.html

Ministry of Justice. (2018). *Tribunals and gender recognitions certificates statistics quarterly: January to March 2018 Main Tables*. London: Ministry of Justice.

Office for National Statistics. (2016). *Low pay in the UK: Apr 2016*. Retrieved from https://www.ons.gov.uk/releases/lowpayintheukapr2016

– (2017a). *Earnings and low pay: Distributions and estimates from the Labour Force Survey*. Office for National Statistics. Retrieved from https://www.ons.gov.uk/releases/earningsandlowpaydistributionsandestimatefromthelabourforcesurvey

– (2017b). *Public sector employment, UK: Mar 2017*. Retrieved from https://www.ons.gov.uk/releases/publicsectoremploymentukmar2017.

Statistics Canada. (1997–2016). *Labour Force Survey (LFS)*, 1997–2016 (master files). Ottawa, ON: Statistics Canada (producer). Using University of Toronto/York University Research Data Centre (distributor), http://sites.utoronto.ca/rdc/

– (2011). *National Household Survey (NHS)*, 2011 (public-use microdata file). Ottawa, ON: Statistics Canada (producer). Using University of Toronto, Faculty of Arts & Sciences Data Centre (CHASS) (distributor), http://sda.chass.utoronto.ca/

– (2015a). *Employees in Ontario. The General Social Survey, 1989–2014*. Retrieved from http://www.statcan.gc.ca/pub/89f0115x/89f0115x2013001-eng.htm

– (2015b). *Labour Force Survey (LFS)*, 2015 (public-use microdata file). Ottawa, ON: Statistics Canada (producer). Using University of Toronto, Faculty

of Arts & Sciences Data Centre (CHASS) (distributor), http://sda.chass.utoronto.ca/
– (2016a). *Canadian Business Counts, 2015–2018* [beyond 20/20] (Identification Number cbc-61F0040XCB-E-2007). Using Ontario Data Documentation, Extraction Service and Infrastructure (ODESI/Scholar's Portal) (distributor). http://odesi1.scholarsportal.info.ezproxy.lib.ryerson.ca/documentation/CBC/cbc-en.html
– (2016b). *Guide to the Labour Force Survey*. Catalogue no. 71-543-G. Ottawa: Statistics Canada. Retrieved from https://www150.statcan.gc.ca/n1/en/catalogue/71-543-G2016001
– (2016c). *Labour Force Survey (LFS)*, 2016 (master file). Ottawa, ON: Statistics Canada (producer). Using University of Toronto/York University Research Data Centre (distributor), http://sites.utoronto.ca/rdc/
– (2016d). *Labour Force Survey (LFS)*, 2016 (public-use microdata file). Ottawa: Statistics Canada (producer). Using University of Toronto, Faculty of Arts & Sciences Data Centre (CHASS) (distributor), http://sda.chass.utoronto.ca/
– (2017). *Canadian Business Counts, with employees, semi-annual*. Table: 33-10-0037-01 (formerly CANSIM 552-0007). Retrieved from https://www150.statcan.gc.ca/t1/tbl1/en/tv.action?pid=3310003701

## *Archival Sources*

Canadian Federation of Independent Business. (1996). Canadian Federation of Independent Business – Bill 49 (RG9-207_B418062_1996.09.10). Archives of Ontario (AO), North York, Ontario.
Ministry of Labour (MOL). (1965, 22 November). Labour Standards and Poverty in Ontario. Ministry of Labour, Minister's correspondence (RG7-1-0-1178, box 37, p. 5). AO, North York, Ontario.
– (1967, 16 May). Further Presentation of the Ontario Hotel and Motel Association to the Industry and Labour Board for Ontario. Ministry of Labour, Employment Standards Branch, director's correspondence (RG7-78). AO, North York, Ontario.
– (1968, 31 May). Notes for an address by the Hon. Dalton Bales, Q.C., minister of labour for Ontario, during 2 reading of: The Employment Standards Act, 1968. Ministry of Labour, minister's correspondence (RG7-1-0-1407.2, box 47). AO, North York, Ontario.
– (1969). Notice to employers and employees. Ministry of Labour, minister's correspondence. (RG7-1-0-1532.1, box 54). AO, North York, Ontario.
– (1969, 8 January). Memorandum, re: Ontario Milk Distributors Association. Ministry of Labour, Employment Standards Branch, director's correspondence (RG7-78). AO, North York, Ontario.
– (1970). Ontario Department of Labour Annual Report 1969–1970. Toronto: Ontario Department of Labour.

- (1970, 21 October). Memorandum, re: request for chronological summary of Ontario's Employment Standards Programme. Ministry of Labour, correspondence of the deputy minister of labour files. (RG7-12, box 388603). AO, North York, Ontario.
- (1972, 12 October). Employment Standards Branch: Secured wages. Ministry of Labour, correspondence of the deputy minister of labour files (RG7-12, box 398297). AO, North York, Ontario.
- (1973, 2 October a). Enforcement: Limit of monetary collection. Ministry of Labour, legislation and regulation files (RG7-14, box 355525). AO, North York, Ontario.
- (1973, 2 October b). Enforcement: Non-payment of wages. Ministry of Labour, legislation and regulation files (RG7-14, box 355525). AO, North York, Ontario.
- (1974, June). The nature and level of employment standards services and techniques for achieving compliance. Paper presented to the Canadian Association of Administrators of Labour Legislation. Research Studies – Policy and Legislation (RG7-130). AO, North York, Ontario.
- (1974, 22 October). Letter, from Ready Mixed Concrete Association of Ontario. Ministry of Labour, Employment Standards Branch, director's correspondence (RG7-78). AO, North York, Ontario.
- (1975, 20 June). Memorandum, Ontario Swimming Pool Association. Ministry of Labour, Employment Standards Branch, director's correspondence (RG7-78). AO, North York, Ontario.
- (1976, 6 April). Memorandum, Re: Ontario Federation of Labour. Ministry of Labour, Employment Standards Branch, director's correspondence (RG7-78). AO, North York, Ontario.
- (1976, 15 December). Some questions concerning the purpose of employment standards legislation and government activities intended to improve work conditions. Research Branch. Ministry of Labour, Employment Standards Branch, director's correspondence (RG7-78. pp. 4–5). AO, North York, Ontario.
- (1977, March). Pregnancy leave in Ontario: A policy discussion. Women's Bureau. Ministry of Labour, Employment Standards Branch, director's correspondence (RG7-78). AO, North York, Ontario.
- (1978, 12 July). Initial submission, Management by Results and Estimates, 1979/80. Ministry of Labour, Employment Standards Branch, director's correspondence (RG7-78, p. 6). AO, North York, Ontario.
- (1979, 29 November). Memorandum, Re: Wage protection: Appendix I. Ministry of Labour, Legislation and Regulation files (RG7-14, p. 1). AO, North York, Ontario.
- (1982, 5 March). Minister's briefing: employment Standards. Ministry of Labour, Legislation and Regulation files. (RG7-14, p. 3). AO, North York, Ontario.

– (1982a). Employment standards: Comments on program indicators, Ministry of Labour, Employment Standards Branch, director's correspondence (RG7-78). AO, North York, Ontario
– (1982b). Program, statistics, and current legislation. Ministry of Labour, Employment Standards Branch, director's correspondence (RG7-78). AO, North York, Ontario.
– (1983). Employment Standards Branch: Future Outlook, 1982–83. Ministry of Labour, Employment Standards Branch, director's correspondence (RG7-78), AO, North York, Ontario.
– (1985). Termination pay (pay in lieu of notice). Ministry of Labour, Policy Subject files (RG 7-168). AO, North York, Ontario.
– (1989, 13 March). Wage protection: Background for meeting with minister. Ministry of Labour, Legislation and Regulation files (RG7-14, box 162784). AO, North York, Ontario.

Royal Commission on Price Spreads. (1935). Proposed remedies (RG 33, series 18, vol. 166). Library and Archives Canada.

Trades and Labour Congress (1899). Proceedings, Report of the Ontario Executive Committee.

# Index

Note: Page numbers followed by letters *f*, *g*, and *t* refer to figures, graphs, and tables, respectively.

**Studies in Comparative Political Economy and Public Policy**

1 *The Search for Political Space: Globalization, Social Movements, and the Urban Political Experience* / Warren Magnusson
2 *Oil, the State, and Federalism: The Rise and Demise of Petro-Canada as a Statist Impulse* / John Erik Fossum
3 *Defying Conventional Wisdom: Political Movements and Popular Contention against North American Free Trade* / Jeffrey M. Ayres
4 *Community, State, and Market on the North Atlantic Rim: Challenges to Modernity in the Fisheries* / Richard Apostle, Gene Barrett, Peter Holm, Svein Jentoft, Leigh Mazany, Bonnie McCay, Knut H. Mikalsen
5 *More with Less: Work Reorganization in the Canadian Mining Industry* / Bob Russell
6 *Visions for Privacy: Policy Approaches for the Digital Age* / Edited by Colin J. Bennett and Rebecca Grant
7 *New Democracies: Economic and Social Reform in Brazil, Chile, and Mexico* / Michel Duquette
8 *Poverty, Social Assistance, and the Employability of Mothers: Restructuring Welfare States* / Maureen Baker and David Tippin
9 *The Left's Dirty Job: The Politics of Industrial Restructuring in France and Spain* / W. Rand Smith
10 *Risky Business: Canada's Changing Science-Based Policy and Regulatory Regime* / Edited by G. Bruce Doern and Ted Reed
11 *Temporary Work: The Gendered Rise of a Precarious Employment Relationship* / Leah Vosko
12 *Who Cares?: Women's Work, Childcare, and Welfare State Redesign* / Jane Jenson and Mariette Sineau with Franca Bimbi, Anne-Marie Daune-Richard, Vincent Della Sala, Rianne Mahon, Bérengèr Marques-Pereira, Olivier Paye, and George Ross
13 *Canadian Forest Policy: Adapting to Change* / Edited by Michael Howlett
14 *Knowledge and Economic Conduct: The Social Foundations of the Modern Economy* / Nico Stehr
15 *Contingent Work, Disrupted Lives: Labour and Community in the New Rural Economy* / Anthony Winson and Belinda Leach
16 *The Economic Implications of Social Cohesion* / Edited by Lars Osberg
17 *Gendered States: Women, Unemployment Insurance, and the Political Economy of the Welfare State in Canada, 1945–1997* / Ann Porter
18 *Educational Regimes and Anglo-American Democracy* / Ronald Manzer
19 *Money in Their Own Name: The Feminist Voice in Poverty Debate in Canada, 1970–1995* / Wendy McKeen

20 *Collective Action and Radicalism in Brazil: Women, Urban Housing, and Rural Movements* / Michel Duquette, Maurilio Galdino, Charmain Levy, Bérengère Marques-Pereira, and Florence Raes
21 *Continentalizing Canada: The Politics and Legacy of the Macdonald Royal Commission*/Gregory J. Inwood
22 *Globalization Unplugged: Sovereignty and the Canadian State in the Twenty-first Century* / Peter Urmetzer
23 *New Institutionalism: Theory and Analysis*/Edited by André Lecours
24 *Mothers of the Nation: Women, Family, and Nationalism in Twentieth-Century Europe* / Patrizia Albanese
25 *Partisanship, Globalization, and Canadian Labour Market Policy: Four Provinces in Comparative Perspective*/Rodney Haddow and Thomas Klassen
26 *Rules, Rules, Rules, Rules: Multi-Level Regulatory Governance*/Edited by G. Bruce Doern and Robert Johnson
27 *The Illusive Tradeoff: Intellectual Property Rights, Innovation Systems, and Egypt's Pharmaceutical Industry* / Basma Abdelgafar
28 *Fair Trade Coffee: The Prospects and Pitfalls of Market-Driven Social Justice*/Gavin Fridell
29 *Deliberative Democracy for the Future: The Case of Nuclear Waste Management in Canada* / Genevieve Fuji Johnson
30 *Internationalization and Canadian Agriculture: Policy and Governing Paradigms*/Grace Skogstad
31 *Military Workfare: The Soldier and Social Citizenship in Canada*/Deborah Cowen
32 *Public Policy for Women: The State, Income Security, and Labour*/Edited by Marjorie Griffin Cohen and Jane Pulkingham
33 *Smiling Down the Line: Info-Service Work in the Global Economy*/Bob Russell
34 *Municipalities and Multiculturalism: The Politics of Immigration in Toronto and Vancouver* / Kristin R. Good
35 *Policy Paradigms, Transnationalism, and Domestic Politics* / Edited by Grace Skogstad
36 *Three Bio-Realms: Biotechnology and the Governance of Food, Health, and Life in Canada*/G. Bruce Doern and Michael J. Prince
37 *North America in Question: Regional Integration in an Era of Economic Turbulence*/Edited by Jeffrey Ayres and Laura Macdonald
38 *Comparative Public Policy in Latin America*/Edited by Jordi Díez and Susan Franceschet
39 *Wrestling with Democracy: Voting Systems as Politics in the Twentieth-Century West*/Dennis Pilon
40 *The Politics of Energy Dependency: Ukraine, Belarus, and Lithuania between Domestic Oligarchs and Russian Pressure* / Margarita M. Balmaceda

41 *Environmental Policy Change in Emerging Market Democracies: Central and Eastern Europe and Latin America Compared*/Jale Tosun
42 *Globalization and Food Sovereignty: Global and Local Change in the New Politics of Food*/Edited by Peter Andrée, Jeffrey Ayres, Michael J. Bosia, and Marie-Josée Massicotte
43 *Land, Stewardship, and Legitimacy: Endangered Species Policy in Canada and the United States*/Andrea Olive
44 *Copyfight: The Global Politics of Digital Copyright Reform*/Blayne Haggart
45 *Learning to School: Federalism and Public Schooling in Canada*/Jennifer Wallner
46 *Transforming Provincial Politics: The Political Economy of Canada's Provinces and Territories in the Neoliberal Era*/Edited by Bryan M. Evans and Charles W. Smith
47 *Comparing Quebec and Ontario: Political Economy and Public Policy at the Turn of the Millennium*/Rodney Haddow
48 *Ideas and the Pace of Change: National Pharmaceutical Insurance in Canada, Australia, and the United Kingdom*/Katherine Boothe
49 *Democratic Illusion: Deliberative Democracy in Canadian Public Policy*/Genevieve Fuji Johnson
50 *Purchase for Profit: Public-Private Partnerships and Canada's Public Health-Care System*/Heather Whiteside
51 *Beyond the Welfare State: Postwar Social Settlement and Public Pension Policy in Canada and Australia*/Sirvan Karimi
52 *Constructing Policy Change: Early Childhood Education and Care in Liberal Welfare States*/Linda A. White
53 *Combatting Poverty: Quebec's Pursuit of a Distinctive Welfare State*/Axel van den Berg, Charles Plante, Hicham Raïq, Christine Proulx, and Samuel Faustmann
54 *Remaking Policy: Scale, Pace, and Political Strategy in Health Care Reform*/Carolyn Hughes Tuohy
55 *Immigration and the Politics of Welfare Exclusion: Selective Solidarity in Western Democracies*/Edward Koning
56 *Bureaucratic Manoeuvres: The Contested Administration of the Unemployed*/John Grundy
57 *Small Nations, High Ambitions: Economic Nationalism and Venture Capital in Quebec and Scotland*/X. Hubert Rioux
58 *Closing the Enforcement Gap: Improving Employment Standards Protections for People in Precarious Jobs*/Leah F. Vosko and the Closing the Enforcement Gap Research Group

FSC
www.fsc.org
MIX
Papier | Fördert gute Waldnutzung
FSC® C083411

Kolibri 360 GmbH
Ferdinand-Jühlke-Straße 7
99095 Erfurt, Deutschland
produktsicherheit@kolibri360.de